SO-AWE-741

Richard A. Bloom

About the Author

BURT SOLOMON is a contributing editor for *National Journal,* where he has covered the White House and many other aspects of Washington life. In 1991 he won the Gerald R. Ford Prize for Distinguished Reporting on the Presidency. He is also the author of the acclaimed *Where They Ain't,* a history of baseball in the 1890s. He lives with his wife and children inside the Beltway.

ALSO BY BURT SOLOMON

*Where They Ain't: The Fabled Life and
Untimely Death of the Original Baltimore Orioles,
the Team That Gave Birth to Modern Baseball*

Burt Solomon

HARPER  PERENNIAL

NEW YORK • LONDON • TORONTO • SYDNEY

THE

Three Families and the

WASHINGTON

Shaping of the Nation's Capital

CENTURY

HARPER ● PERENNIAL

A hardcover edition of this book was published in 2004 by William Morrow, an imprint of HarperCollins Publishers.

THE WASHINGTON CENTURY. Copyright © 2004 by Burt Solomon. All rights reserved. Printed in the United States of America. No part of this book may be used or reproduced in any manner whatsoever without written permission except in the case of brief quotations embodied in critical articles and reviews. For information address HarperCollins Publishers, 10 East 53rd Street, New York, NY 10022.

HarperCollins books may be purchased for educational, business, or sales promotional use. For information please write: Special Markets Department, HarperCollins Publishers, 10 East 53rd Street, New York, NY 10022.

FIRST HARPER PERENNIAL EDITION PUBLISHED 2005.

Designed by Jennifer Ann Daddio

The Library of Congress has catalogued the hardcover edition as follows:

Solomon, Burt.
    The Washington century : three families and the shaping of the Nation's Capital / Burt Solomon.—1st ed.
        p.   cm.
    Includes bibliographical references (p.).
    ISBN 0-06-621372-X (acid-free paper)
    1. Washington (D.C.)—Biography.   2. Boggs, Hale, 1914–1972—Family.   3. Cafritz, Morris, 1886?–1964—Family.   4. Hobson, Julius W.—Family.   5. Washington (D.C.)—Social life and customs—20th century.   6. Washington (D.C.)—Politics and government—20th century.   7. Political culture—Washington (D.C.)—History—20th century.   8. Political culture—United States—History—20th century.   9. United States—Politics and government—20th century.   I. Title

    F193.S65   2004
    328.73'092'2—dc22
    [B]
                                        2004048112

ISBN-10: 0-06-093785-8 (pbk.)
ISBN-13: 978-0-06-093785-0 (pbk.)

05 06 07 08 09 ❖/RRD 10 9 8 7 6 5 4 3 2 1

TO MY PARENTS

Contents

THE WASHINGTON CENTURY

One

THEODORE ROOSEVELT
TO HOOVER

Before first light, young Morris Kafitz hitched up the horse and wagon and set out along the lanes of Georgetown. The gas lamps were still lit, and the reflections flickered off the cobblestones. As he rode south along Twenty-seventh Street, beneath a canopy of trees, the clopping echoed between the facing rows of houses.

Morris was accustomed to the early hour. He had a sturdy build and a strong and stolid face, with dark hair and somber blue eyes that kept their own counsel. As the eldest of the three sons, he woke each morning at four thirty and made his way across the sleepy, shuffling city of Washington, in the District of Columbia, to buy fresh produce at the Center Market and sometimes to shop for fish down at the wharf. Only after hauling these provisions back to his father's grocery store, at Twenty-seventh and O Streets, in the city's northwestern quadrant, would he rush the three and a half blocks to the Corcoran School, with its redbrick Romanesque tower.

Soon his schooling would end, after the 1901–2 school year, once he had finished the seventh grade at age fourteen. What Morris wanted for himself in this land of liberty was not found in books.

Surely there was no shame in living in unfashionable Georgetown, even in its shabbier eastern end. This was paradise compared to Lithuania. His family had fled the pogroms when he was eleven and by 1898 had wound up in Washington, where some cousins had settled. The seven of them, Nussen, Anna, and the five children, lived first in a shack twenty-some blocks north of the Capitol building, and then in an alleyway a dozen blocks closer.

Pierre L'Enfant's grandiose design for the nation's capital, with its broad avenues and elongated blocks, had created a web of alleys, out of sight, where freed slaves lived after the Civil War. The Kafitzes were among the few white residents on Glick Alley, a dirty, overcrowded lane that stretched from S Street NW to Rhode Island Avenue, between Sixth and Seventh Streets. They occupied a two-story, four-room tin-roofed brick house, all of fourteen feet wide, dark and damp, without a basement. A spigot and a privy stood in the back.

Nussen was known as Nelson or Nathan in his new country. He was a small dapper man with a round fragile face and a trimmed beard. He had a sparkle—into his eighties he would chase his second wife around a table—and a sense of humor and no desire to speak or write in English. He opened a grocery on Glick Alley, in one of the ground-floor rooms. This was the most common business for the city's immigrant Jews, because it required little money or know-how.

Within a year the Kafitzes had left the alley and moved to Georgetown. They could afford to live away from the grocery, though the row house at 2706 N Street was even narrower than the house on Glick Alley and also lacked indoor plumbing, a hardship for the children on winter nights. Most of their neighbors were colored—teamsters, servants, a porter, a deliveryman, a dressmaker, a day laborer, a washerwoman, an ash man, a laborer for the federal Bureau of Engraving and Printing. Georgetown was a quilt of black and white, of the poor and the poorer.

Forty-nine years older than the city of Washington, Georgetown had been named not for *that* George (though he had slept there many a night, a half-day's ride from Mount Vernon) but rather for Britain's King George II, whose governor of the Virginia colony had dispatched *that* George as a young colonel out to Ohio, an excursion that touched off the French and Indian War. The village, near the head of the navigable Potomac River, had originally been a thriving port for Maryland tobacco and then a point of departure for trade with the Ohio River Valley. Even after the capital was founded, in 1800, the handsome brick town houses and bustling streets of Georgetown outshined the drab and sparsely settled city next door, as a residence for foreign diplomats and the more adventurous members of Congress. Georgetown had ceased being a separate municipality within D.C. in 1871, and its social standing had withered. A port once a forest of masts had become an industrial suburb for a city lacking much industry of its own. The riverbank now harbored iron foundries, lime kilns, a sheet metal works, a bottling company, a coal yard, an electric powerhouse, and—worst of all, to the residents—an animal rendering plant, with its reek of decay. Only people who had few choices lived nearby.

Morris rode ahead toward M Street. On his left, past a prim Baptist church, an open field gave way to the ravine, dense with trees, that cradled Rock Creek. He turned left onto M Street, still known to many as Bridge Street for the iron-laced bridge that crossed the creek. He trotted above the mouth of the wide, rushing stream and into what had been properly known until recently as Washington City. Two quick turns put him on Pennsylvania Avenue, as broad a boulevard as any in the capital.

The scattered buildings stood low in the lightening sky. It was quiet here, and spacious. The paving of asphalt and coal tar climbed steadily before him, a godsend for the ever-more-popular safety bicycles. His horse sidestepped the slots for the streetcars. Morris liked to race the electrified streetcars, though once while doing so he had spilled a wagonful of groceries—oranges and everything—all over the road.

Washington was an unhurried city of barely a quarter-million inhabitants, ranked fifteenth in the nation, just behind Milwaukee. "When they say noon in New York it generally means a little before; when they say noon in Washington it always means from one to four hours later," a longtime Washingtonian explained. It was a southern city, of azaleas and magnolias, where people used proper manners and spoke softly ("reckon . . . you-all") in Tidewater accents. Most of the newcomers had moved there from Virginia or the Carolinas, accounting for the grits that people served with breakfast. The city moved at a leisurely pace. Men moved languorously on the streets, wearing broad-brimmed felt hats and Prince Albert coats. The vines, luxuriant in the steamy summertime, climbed any available wall. Washington was a green city, and a clean one, because of the sparse industry and the paucity of smoke.

Poplars lined Pennsylvania Avenue, as if guarding the clusters of row houses with elegantly rounded corners or elaborate cornices or half-moon windows and exuberantly pointed roofs that were only for show. Morris glimpsed a corner of the rambling red buildings belonging to the Columbia Hospital for Women and then passed Saint Ann's Infant Asylum. Ahead was Washington Circle, where Pennsylvania Avenue crossed K and Twenty-third Streets. Inside the circle, gas lamps and benches on curving paths surrounded a statue of General Washington on horseback, triumphant at the Battle of Princeton.

The streets grew busier as Morris approached the capital's monumental core. At Twenty-second Street he passed the Six Buildings, century-old town houses in the unadorned Federal style where James Madison and later Sam Houston had lived, and three blocks farther, the Seven Buildings, the capital's original Diplomatic Row—not that Morris knew or cared. Three- or four-story row houses lined both sides of the avenue, many with shops on the ground floor. At Eighteenth Street, a coal yard stood across the avenue from a hardware store, a dairy, a steam laundry, and a bicycle repair shop.

At Seventeenth Street, to the right, rose the city's most fantastical building, housing the government's gravest responsibilities. Nine hundred columns, flamboyant chimneys, and mansard roofs of dramatic proportions lent the State, War, and Navy Building an unembarrassed ostentation, revered by many and reviled by more. (Its architect committed suicide two years after it was finished.) Just beyond it, set back from the avenue, behind an expanse of lawn, stood its antithesis, a marvel of unforced dignity. Only recently had the brash young Teddy Roosevelt, in one of his earliest acts after President William McKinley's assassination in Buffalo, officially named it the White House. There was talk of adding east and west wings to the Executive Mansion, so he might escape his six rambunctious children while attending to affairs of state, though he was thinking he would rather keep living at the White House but move his offices someplace else. As it was, an ordinary citizen could stroll unhindered through the open gates and leave a calling card on a silver tray for the president, who was no longer merely the leader of a provincial democracy but of an emerging world power.

Morris was not a citizen yet, and he was too familiar with this stretch of avenue to be awed. He was also here every afternoon, to hawk newspapers at Fifteenth Street, by the Treasury Building's unassailable bulk. But he understood what a free country made possible—and what it took. With hard work and some daring, in this promised land, a man could make something of himself.

It was too early for the flower vendors or the organ grinders as Morris turned right onto Fifteenth Street. The government clerks would not be scurrying to their offices until just before nine. Morris turned left, to continue on Pennsylvania Avenue.

Fifteen blocks ahead, the Capitol dome loomed in a ghostly outline against a dawning sun.

Pennsylvania Avenue was the nation's main street and also Washington's primary commercial thoroughfare, though the larger stores had been trickling a few blocks north, to F Street. Its extraordinary width made keeping both sides in view at once difficult. It was 160 feet across and had remained almost undisturbed by overhead wires; the streetcars drew their power from cables underground.

To Morris's right, along the southern side of the avenue, past the livery stable, were two towers. The nearer one was rounded and graceful, the Grand Army of the Republic Building. The square granite tower of the Post Office Building rose even higher two blocks along. These concealed the jumble of warehouses and garages, brothels and saloons, lumberyards and smokestacks, the distant edge of a ramshackle Chinatown, in the triangle formed by Pennsylvania Avenue and Fifteenth and B Streets.

The northern side was busier. Beyond the drugstore, the New Willard Hotel was under construction, in place of the old, grand Willard, where Charles Dickens and several presidents-elect (including Lincoln) had stayed. Across Fourteenth Street lay a succession of small buildings known as Newspaper Row, housing the out-of-town correspondents who liked the proximity to the Treasury and the Executive Mansion and the streetcar line to Capitol Hill. Around the corner, along Pennsylvania, a narrow six-story building with an intricately ornamented stone façade housed the city's leading morning newspaper, a crime-and-scandal sheet, *The Washington Post*. Two doors down, nearly to Thirteenth Street, stood Shoomaker's saloon, which also served the city's authoritative newspaper, *The Evening Star*, less than three blocks beyond.

Morris's destination was the Center Market, past Ninth Street. He passed the dairy on Tenth Street with the windmill on the roof, to haul water up from the basement. The Center Market looked almost as unworldly. It resembled a stage set for Gilbert and Sullivan, with sand-castle towers and arched windows set off by white stripes, an immense red fortress two blocks long. A market had stood here since 1801, when the Tiber Creek flowed past, on its way from the Capitol out to the Potomac. George Washington himself had chosen the site, two days before leaving the presidency. William Henry Harrison had often been seen at the Center Market during his thirty-one days as president.

The original market had burned down thirty years earlier and this fancier one had been built. But little had changed. It was patronized by Cabinet officers and congressmen, justices and diplomats, and also workingmen's wives and boardinghouse proprietors and "mammies" and maids, shoppers of all races, everyone carrying a basket. Its vendors no longer peddled the wild geese of George Washington's day, but the more than six hundred stalls on the ground floor sold nearly anything else a Washingtonian might savor—turkeys and lamb chops, rabbits and oysters, turtles and sausages, pig's feet and peanut butter, cabbages and pickles, celery and butter, live chickens and cherry pies. Another two hundred farmers from Maryland and Virginia sold vegetables and fresh-laid eggs from their wagons behind the market, along B Street, where the creek and then the green-scummed Washington Canal had flowed, until the stench overcame the convenience. Surely the most useful change was the latest—the mechanical refrigeration, newly installed, which placed the Center Market among the most modern in the country, as well as one of the largest.

Morris loaded up his wagon and went on.

At Seventh Street he turned south, to cross the national Mall, toward the Potomac. L'Enfant had hoped to turn a swampy wilderness into an Eden, but at midcentury, at President Millard Fillmore's behest, a cow pasture had been remade into a park, a paragon of natural landscaping. Groves of evergreens and tangled shrubbery, aimless gravel paths, and sinuous carriageways—the Mall was best dared in daylight. Over the years it had grown disordered and cluttered. Railroad tracks sliced along Sixth Street, from the Baltimore and Potomac station, located on the Mall itself, in which a deranged office seeker had assassinated President James Garfield. Only recently had the Senate-led McMillan Commission recommended that the railroad station be razed, the trees chopped down, and L'Enfant's clean vista restored.

Leaving the Mall, Morris passed between the United States Fish Commission, in a square formal building with something like spout holes along the top, and the stately building that housed the Army Medical Museum. He had entered Southwest. It was the smallest of the city's quadrants, which merged at the Capitol, and the poorest. (Virginia had demanded back its third of D.C.'s original diamond in 1846, partly out of a well-founded fear that Congress might abolish the capital's slave trade.) Southwest was crowded with flimsy frame houses and the dingiest of alleyway dwellings, some of them in sight of the Capitol dome. They were occupied primarily by colored people and the recently arrived Eastern European Jews. Dignified elms lined the dusty streets of paving stone or brick.

Morris could smell the fish market blocks away. He pressed ahead to Water Street, with its wharves and its rickety wooden markets with covered porches. Inside he could buy fish from the Atlantic or from Chesapeake Bay, or sturgeon, shad, bass, or canvasback duck from the Potomac, before hurrying back to Georgetown.

The wharves, however, no longer looked out on the Potomac itself. The capital had been founded to face the river. But the dredging of mud flats a few years before had created the sluggish Washington Channel next to shore, and an artificial island called Potomac Park that concealed its namesake. Even an unsophisticated boy could tell that whatever happened on the river mattered far less to life in the capital than the intrigues that adults conducted on dry land.

Washington, D.C., had been founded on an awkward political compromise. Ever since that dangerous day in 1783 in the temporary capital of Philadelphia, Congress had wanted a home of its own, a jurisdiction under its thumb. Drunken veterans of the Revolutionary War who insisted on their back pay had pointed muskets at the first-floor windows where the lawmakers worked. When the local militia refused to intervene, Congress was forced to flee to Princeton. The Constitution was written four years later and gave Congress "exclusive" legislative power over a "District (not exceeding ten Miles square) as may, by Cession of particular States, and the acceptance of Congress, become the Seat of the Government of the United States."

The location of this District was left unspecified. Northerners wanted it toward the North, southerners toward the South. At least a dozen communities, large and small, most near the center of a long narrow nation, offered to deliver all or part of themselves into federal jurisdiction, including Williamsburg, Annapolis, Baltimore, Havre de Grace, Wilmington, Lancaster, Germantown, Trenton, Philadelphia, and of course New York, the nomadic capital's latest home. To sidestep these competing self-interests, it was decided that a capital be constructed out of wilderness, something the world had never seen. The choices soon centered on three rivers—the Delaware and the Susquehanna, both toward the north, and the Potomac, farther to the south.

The Potomac's greatest proponent was a man who had spent most of his life by its shores. George Washington had surveyed the river's course as a boy, explored its headwaters, founded the Potowmack Company to foster its navigation, long resided on its banks, and believed in its potential as a route into the country's interior, where the young nation's future lay. For southerners, siting the capital on the Potomac—the nation's true center, they said—could foil the political domination by the North, and locating the capital on land donated by Maryland and Virginia, both slaveholding states, would suggest an acquiescence to the South's peculiar institution.

It was Alexander Hamilton, President Washington's first Treasury secretary, who saw a way out of the impasse. Hamilton stopped Thomas Jefferson one morning on Broadway, in New York. For a half-hour he warned that the North might secede unless the national government assumed the various states' war debts. Most of the war had been fought in the North.

The next evening they dined over punch and Madeira and struck the deal. A month later, Congress passed the Compromise of 1790, and the president signed it. The capital would return to Philadelphia for ten years and then move permanently to someplace on the Potomac, along a stretch of more than a hundred miles from the Eastern Branch to past Harper's Ferry. The president himself would pick the site, within the boundaries that Congress had set. He situated the southern tip of the District four miles south of the legislated confines, to include the port of Alexandria, Virginia, so close to his home. This added twelve hundred acres of woodland that the president owned and the estate of Arlington, which belonged to Martha's grandson. Critics of a Potomac capital quickly accused the president of inflating the value of his family's holdings, including Mount Vernon, seven or eight miles south of Alexandria. He would not be the last president to stand accused of self-dealing.

The ten-mile-square District was to contain three cities—Alexandria, Virginia; Georgetown, Maryland; and the capital itself. The president raised no objection when the three commissioners he had appointed to supervise the District's affairs, all of them investors in the Potowmack Company, struck another artful compromise, in naming the District after Christopher Columbus and the capital city after the father of his country.

To design the new capital, the president hired a talented though imperious Frenchman who had served with him at Valley Forge and then handsomely remodeled Federal Hall, in New York, where Congress met. Pierre L'Enfant, the son of a painter in the court of Louis XV, had acquired his taste for grandeur honestly through spending much of his boyhood in Paris or at Versailles.

Jefferson envisioned the capital as an intimate village, in modular form, to be replicated as the capital needed to expand. L'Enfant wrote to the president that he preferred such a scale "as to leave room for that aggrandisement & embellishment which the increase of the wealth of the Nation will permit it to pursue at any period however remote."

The decision was the president's. He chose grandeur.

L'Enfant rode through the viny woods in the rain, through the marshes, the thickets, the open wastelands, the occasional settlements. He selected the highest hill between the Potomac and the Eastern Branch (renamed the Anacostia) as the site for Congress House—or as Jefferson called it, the Capitol, imagining it as brick. The President's Palace was to be built a mile away, by the bank of Tiber Creek, facing south toward Mount Vernon, placed in relation to the Capitol as the Grand Trianon is to the palace at Versailles. The distance was to preserve the decorum of the respective branches and to satisfy the Cabinet officers who complained of frequent visits from members of Congress. The thickets and moors that separated them required a circuitous route, so circuitous that Jefferson, as president, ceased delivering the State of the Union message to Congress in person.

Jefferson wanted to restrict the height of buildings, as Paris did, to keep the streets airy, fires more manageable, and the land values low. He also proposed to divide the city into quadrants—"here will be no waste in the square sheet of paper," he wrote—and he and James Madison prevailed on the commissioners to name the north–south streets by number, east–west by letter.

On this grid of streets L'Enfant superimposed a sun-splash of radiating avenues, recalling the long vistas of Versailles, for quicker travel from place to place. Where the avenues crossed, the Frenchman put circular plazas, as places for cannons and garrisons of troops in defending the capital, as hindrances to mobs in erecting barricades. Each avenue would carry the name of a state, roughly reflecting its location in the country. The grandest was named for Pennsylvania, not only from the luck of geography but also as a consolation for losing the capital. Its length, from the edge of Georgetown to the District's southeastern boundary, inspired the capital's early moniker "the City of Magnificent Distances," which Dickens later mocked as "the City of Magnificent Intentions."

After George Washington died, less than a year before the government moved to the city that bore his name, his widow agreed that he be entombed beneath the Capitol Rotunda, so that the capital might never be moved. But partisan quarrels over how grand a monument should be, or whether a mausoleum might prove more suitable, and how grand *that* would be—all reflecting the rivalry between the spirits of monarchy and democracy—stranded the great man's bones at Mount Vernon.

Even after Carrie Nation swooped through Washington in 1907, a man could drink his way along Pennsylvania Avenue, from the Capitol to the Treasury Building, in any of forty-seven places. There were fewer saloons near the Navy Yard, in Southeast, to serve the machinists, the metalworkers, and of course the sailors in pursuit of a beer. In 1911, Morris Cafritz—he now pronounced it *Kay*-fritz, having inserted an *r* to make it sound more German, and thus more sophisticated, with a tinge of the Ritz—bought a saloon two blocks from the Navy Yard, on Eighth Street, four doors north of K. At the Old-Timers Bar, he remade the bow windows, installed two new doors, and hung a large tin sign—WHOLESALE LIQUORS—out over the sidewalk on Sailors' Row.

Twenty-four-years-old Morris was entering his fifth line of work. At nineteen he ran his own grocery on P Street, at the eastern edge of Georgetown, while he took courses at National Law University, on I Street. He tried law school but disliked it and pursued business instead. He borrowed fourteen hundred dollars from his father and bought the Star Coal & Coke Company at 315 Q Street NW. He also set out chairs in a vacant lot and showed silent films.

Decades later, one of his sons said, "My father liked to start things, get them going, and then move on."

Morris still owned the coal company when he bought the saloon.

He lived over the saloon in the two-story brick building and slept with a gun under his pillow. The rough neighborhood did not scare him. Only five foot seven but burly and fit, he once vaulted over the bar and hustled a semipro ballplayer out to the street. He hired buses to take patrons, free of charge, to watch the Washington Nationals play baseball at the newly rebuilt ballpark out along Seventh Street NW, knowing that they would be thirsty after the game.

He had a knack for seeing a need that was unmet, even unrecognized, and had a keen talent for timing. Prohibition entered D.C. in 1917, fourteen and a half months earlier than the rest of the nation, because Congress had not needed to wait for the states to ratify a constitutional amendment. Two years earlier, Morris had sold his saloon and embraced yet another business.

Three blocks north of his saloon, an Irishman owned a small bowling alley where business was booming, and Morris became co-proprietor. Bowling was fast becoming the leading indoor sport in D.C., especially duckpin bowling, using "the little maples," which were harder to knock down than tenpins. It was touted as an exertion of mind *and* muscle, an aid to digestion and blood flow, an inducement to self-control. Morris rolled the small ball so hard that it struck the leather sheet that hung behind the pins and popped it out of place. Employers of all sorts sponsored teams, which created more and more leagues that used more lanes. The Nats' first baseman owned alleys that seated three hundred spectators for a match against a Baltimore team. "There is something satisfying about the game that you can't get in other pastimes," exulted the bowling columnist in the *Post*, "in that it is purely the individual effort that counts."

One evening Morris received a telephone call from the local representative of the Brunswick bowling company, with the news that a bowling alley downtown had failed to pay for the equipment and was up for sale.

"I know it would be a big deal for you to swing. . . ."

"I'll take it," Morris said.

At the old National Rifles Armory, a turreted building on G Street NW, between Ninth and Tenth, the target range for the local militia had turned into bowling lanes. This was no sedate business to run. When Morris picked up his pin setters at the designated street corner, most of them were drunk and spoiling to fight him. But he noticed something. When he greeted the wives and girlfriends of bowlers and suggested that they try it, too, invariably they were shy. Why not a facility for the ladies, to teach them to bowl? In 1914 he incorporated the National Capital Bowling Academy. Soon he launched leagues for women. In a single building, he operated alleys on four floors.

Morris also understood the importance of location. In 1915 he found a prized spot, one he knew well. He opened bowling lanes in the Center Market, upstairs in the Seventh Street wing. He hung a huge glittery sign—BOWLING—out from a corner tower of the market. A side wall advertised the immodest name, GRAND CENTRAL PALACE.

In the belief that competition was the heart of any sport, Morris organized weekly tournaments for bowling and for billiards, too. But he also made sure to set aside five of the eleven lanes for customers who happened by. He built a ladies' dressing room and awarded a box of candy to any woman who scored ninety-five or higher.

Soon he owned four bowling establishments, and the money began to roll in. A sportswriter dubbed him the Bowling King of Washington. One day the bowling columnist for *The Evening Star* wandered into Morris's alleys on G Street and found him daydreaming.

"What's on your mind?" the *Star*'s man asked. "Another bowling plant?"

Morris Cafritz grinned.

"No," he replied. "I want to get into something where the sky's the limit."

Friends had so often solicited Morris's advice on whether to buy particular pieces of property that he wondered why he was not advising himself. In a city without industrial wealth, its size limited by the Constitution, no business looked more promising than real estate.

A first cousin had already given him a taste. Samuel Shapiro, four years older than Morris, had been building row houses near Seventh Street that extended several blocks beyond the original boundary of the City of Washington. (Boundary Street had become Florida Avenue in 1890, after Washington City, Georgetown, and Washington County, north of Boundary Street, became a single jurisdiction.) At this distance from downtown, in a city without dirtied air, the azaleas and the dogwoods evoked the countryside.

When Samuel Shapiro invited Morris and a younger cousin, J. B. Shapiro, to join him in building and selling row houses, they immediately said yes. Morris used money he had made from bowling.

Park Place looked east onto the wooded grounds of the old Soldiers' Home, where Lincoln had spent much of the war. The neighborhood of rolling hills, west toward Rock Creek Park, was known as Whitney Close. The two-story, six-room row houses that Morris and his older cousin put up were solidly built of brick, each with a watertight foundation, an attic with dormer windows, a deep porch with decorative brick pillars, and a toddler-sized yard. They built a dozen in 1915 and almost twice as many in 1916. The houses carried affordable mortgages of $2,250 to $2,700.

Morris's timing was fortuitous. The capital had always thrived on national tragedy. Within six months of the nation's 1917 entry into the world war, eighty thousand people flocked to Washington. Dollar-a-year men, pencil pushers in war agencies, hordes of young women hired as government clerks—they brought D.C.'s population to more than a half-million. War workers squeezed into "tempos" along the Mall, beyond the Washington Monument, and scrambled to find places to live. The streetcars were jammed; the telephone service was chaotic. Crowds gathered in front of *The Evening Star*'s office to read the latest dispatches from overseas. In the summer, people swam in the Potomac and gathered for band concerts in Dupont Circle.

"Washington is, as it has never been before, the nation's real interest incarnate, the real center, the real beating heart of us," was the report in *Harper's Monthly Magazine*. "The phrase on everybody's lips is that 'America has a real capital at last.'"

A real capital needed real estate where people could live and work. After the war, when building materials became available again,

Morris started putting up houses on his own, along the northern boundary of the old Soldiers' Home, in the 100 block of Rock Creek Church Road—"which was the end of Washington," according to someone who moved in. "The woods remained behind us and on the north of us." Morris used his cousin's design, with a difference: a mansard roof. The houses looked just a little nicer than they needed to. B. F. Saul, a dignified-looking, charity-minded Catholic banker, provided Morris his first financing, and then all of it, until he grew too big.

In a spurting real estate market, Morris tried his hand at other enterprises. He bought two lots on Connecticut Avenue and another one downtown at Twelfth and H, all from Harry Wardman. The Englishman was emerging as Washington's leading developer, known for the Wardman Park Hotel out Connecticut Avenue—there was no finer one except downtown—and the seven apartment houses along R Street with names whose initial letters spelled W-A-R-D-M-A-N.

Morris's epiphany occurred in 1922. The narrow, ten-story International Building, at 1319 F Street, near the western edge of downtown, was fancy at the ground and at the roofline but mundane in between—nowhere near as grand as its name. He was talked into buying it, and within days he sold it, at a forty-thousand-dollar profit. Before another month passed, he bought back the building, and then he resold it, at a profit again.

And thus Morris fell in love with the business of real estate. He incorporated the Cafritz Construction Company, in the corporate haven of Delaware.

Real estate was exciting. Tangible things were at stake—land, bricks, shelter, money, success. Morris wore shoes with elevated heels. But he had a build like a boxer's, a slim waist and a muscular chest. He had always loved to compete—as a boy in sandlot baseball, as an adult who threw the medicine ball, swam, lifted weights, and boxed—and he had always been good at it. He believed in working hard, and he hated to lose. He believed that it was important to make something of himself.

Later that year, with money no longer tight and the labor market loose, Morris went for broke.

From late in the last century, Petworth had been a middle-class suburb, just to the north of the old Soldiers' Home, a streetcar ride away from the workplaces and stores downtown. Many of the new houses were detached, but the available land was limited by the presence of a golf course to the north. The Columbia Golf Club had already moved out to Chevy Chase (renaming itself as a country club) and hosted the U.S. Open in 1921. The old course, with its brooks and woods and undulating meadows, was for sale.

Morris bought most of it. The idea of pushing out a little farther, using land efficiently by putting up row houses while providing plenty of greenery, was appealing.

The newspapers later said that he put thirty-five thousand dollars down to purchase 160 of the club's 186 acres. Presumably the down payment was from the sale of his bowling alleys, and he borrowed the rest of the $700,000. Now he owned the equivalent of ninety city blocks in "Petworth Addition," as described in the land deeds.

Early one morning, after an all-night party, he took a sportswriter up to the deep porch of the rambling clubhouse, soon to be razed.

"Out there," Morris announced, with a sweep of his hand, "I'm going to build a thousand houses."

He started on fifty-three brick row houses in the late summer of 1922. The tint of fanciness was gone—no mansard roofs—but the cellars would stay dry for the rest of the century. Most of them featured six rooms and a bath, with a front porch, a breakfast porch, and a sleeping porch.

In addition to being well built, they were well marketed. "Cafritz Lifetime Homes," he called them. Morris wrote the ads himself. For a dollar down and seventy-five dollars a month, who could resist?

He bought three coal-fired steam shovels, like those that had dug the Panama Canal, and his own fleet of dump trucks. He hired a staff of architects, carpenters—everything—and a huge sales force. He sold the houses as fast as he could build them. Before he was finished in Petworth, he had put up more than three thousand homes.

Their $8,950 price tag was not outlandish for Washington, where single-family houses cost more than just about anywhere else in the country, certainly beyond a government clerk's easy reach. This explained the popularity of apartments in the capital, more than anyplace but New York or Chicago. Modest or luxurious, apartment houses were springing up everywhere. Before decade's end, the federal commissioner of labor statistics—with a wryness unusual in a government official—described the capital as a "city of cliff dwellers."

Morris joined in. He started on seven apartment houses side by side, a million-dollar venture, three-story walk-ups in a pleasing red brick, a brisk walk west of Petworth, near Rock Creek Park. He called the first one the Cromwell and the last one the Zellwood, to spell out C-A-F-R-I-T-Z. Yet he did not confine himself to one part of town. In 1925 he built the Corcoran Apartments, 166 units with Murphy beds at Twenty-third and D Streets, up the hill from the Lincoln Memorial, which had been completed on reclaimed swampland only three years before. A few months later he sold them to Harry Wardman, at a profit approaching 90 percent.

Morris was a man of extraordinary energy who worked from dawn until late at night, often with a round of golf in the afternoon. The same year he began building apartments, he opened a mortgage firm, acquired the last sizable tract of undeveloped land west of Fourteenth Street, and made another deal, which no one really noticed.

A three-story stucco house, more than a half-century old, stood on the southwestern corner of Fourteenth and K Streets, just west of downtown. Town houses and mansions were common along K Street, a boulevard wide with carriageways and a double row of elms, the graceful residential street that L'Enfant had envisioned. Morris bought the house and used it as the Cafritz Company's office. But he had something more ambitious in mind.

Sixteenth Street was known as the Avenue of the Presidents, because the White House was visible for two miles from the north. This bold, well-shaded roadway was originally to have had an even grander stature, as the new nation's prime meridian, its line between east and west.

Instead, Sixteenth Street was destined to become a dividing line of another sort, between the haves and the have-nots, and a prestigious address of its own. As wide as Pennsylvania Avenue, from building line to building line, it beckoned to the capital's Jews, who were so eager to be seen as true Americans. When they went looking for a suitable site to build a Jewish Community Center in 1925, what more conspicuous a location could they choose? They needed to make a statement that they had arrived, that they were becoming Americans at last.

Washington attracted fewer Jews than cities to the north, and they all knew one another, or seemed to. It was an intimate community of fourteen thousand, and more all the time, who had settled in pockets—along Four-and-a-half Street in Southwest, H Street in Northeast, Seventh Street in Northwest, in Georgetown. After the war, Jews started to move uptown, into neighborhoods such as Petworth.

They had outgrown the Y, the Young Men's Hebrew Association, which was located in the small, squat building at Eleventh and Pennsylvania. The point of moving, however, was only partly practical. At Sixteenth and Q Streets, the Jewish community would build a Greek-pillared temple to culture, to civic works, to recreation and athletics—above all, to a second generation of American Jews.

Morris Cafritz, one of the four charter members of the Y, was chosen unanimously without his knowledge to head the $250,000 fund-raising campaign. Unlike his father, he was not a religious man, but he was proud to be a Jew, and an American. He had been naturalized as a citizen through his father, before he was eighteen, and had lost all but a few traces of his accent. His friends at the Y took him out to a summer lodge across the Maryland line and prevailed on him to accept.

He donated $5,000 as part of the first $50,000 and showed some imagination in raising the rest. The Y sold seats in its Pennsylvania Avenue windows for the inaugural parades—President Harding's in 1921, President Coolidge's in 1925—and even for the Holy Name Society's parade of Catholics. When Walter Johnson, "the Big Train," pitched the Nats to their first pennant in 1924, and then another in 1925, the Y's windows on Eleventh Street offered a perfect view of the scoreboard with the automatic base runners that was on *The Evening Star*'s pearly façade across the road. Morris organized his fund raisers into three men's teams and three ladies' teams, each with a general, captains, lieutenants, and privates.

By the spring of 1925 they had raised enough to lay a cornerstone. It was not unprecedented for a president to attend. In the previous century, President Ulysses S. Grant had spoken at the dedication of a synagogue in Washington, and McKinley had helped lay a cornerstone for another. Silent Cal did not make speeches unnecessarily, but this time he had something to say.

Mrs. Coolidge and the attorney general joined the president and five hundred dignitaries on a warm Sunday afternoon. They sat in rows, behind bunting, on the corner where the building would rise. First Morris mumbled a few remarks. Then a Jewish leader from New York argued that counter to the calumny a Princeton professor had recently advanced, American Jews were indeed willing to assimilate. Then Rabbi Abram Simon of Washington Hebrew Congregation, the city's leading Reform synagogue, poured consecrated oil on the cornerstone as it was lowered into place. The Marine Corps Band played.

Yet it was the president, a New Englander of rectitude and uncomplicated principle, whom the nearly five thousand spectators in the roped-off streets had come to see. As he enunciated into a microphone, his dry, brisk delivery went out by radio to a nationwide audience.

He made no direct reference to the Ku Klux Klan, which was planning a march along Pennsylvania Avenue three months later. Most of the president's message recounted the role of the Jews in building a nation. The Old Testament references in half of the statutes in the New Haven code of 1655, the fourteen Jewish merchants who signed the nonimportation resolution of 1765, the financiers of the Revolution, the Continental Army's four Jewish lieutenant-colonels—he offered evidence in place of platitudes. Twice he quoted a historian's observation: "Hebraic mortar cemented the foundations of American democracy." In spirit, the Jews *were* Americans. "It requires no great stretch of logical processes," the president said, "to demonstrate that the children of Israel, making bricks without straw in Egypt, had their modern counterpart in the people of the colonies, enduring the imposition of taxation without representation!"

His larger point was unmistakable. "If our experiment in free institutions has proved anything," he declared, "it is that the greatest privilege that can be conferred upon people in the mass is to free them from the demoralizing influence of privilege enjoyed by the few. This is proved by the experience here, not alone of the Jews, but of all the other racial and national elements that have entered into the making of this nation."

Morris looked younger than his age and often lied about it, by a half-dozen years. Still unmarried at forty-one, he shared a redbrick town house at 1422 Massachusetts Avenue with Ivy Pelzman, a friend since childhood, who was a urological surgeon and a recent widower. When Ivy had a medical fellowship to train on cadavers in Europe, he found his way to Budapest. He visited a girl he had known in high school in D.C., Lillian Coblenzer, who had married an accomplished Hungarian physician. After Ivy laid eyes on their nineteen-year-old daughter, he went home and told Morris, "I met the girl for you."

Gwendolyn Detre de Surany had ivory skin and ebony hair, with high cheekbones in a startlingly oval face. In repose, she was far from beautiful; her nose was blunt and her mouth too large. But Gwen was rarely at rest, and when she moved, she was unforgettable. She had a sleek figure, a leonine grace. Her dark lynx eyes, their sultry lids, her playfulness, only underlined her intelligence. She had gone to schools in Rome, Paris, and Los Angeles, as well as Hungary, and was fluent in five languages. She had studied art at the Sorbonne (she would grab a breakfast roll and run off to paint before school) and earned a degree in the history of art from the University of Budapest; her thesis was on Fra Angelico, the friar and early Renaissance painter who portrayed his piety in brilliant colors. Her husky voice and languid accent and self-assured carriage lent her an exotic air.

And best of all, Gwen was moving with her family to Washington.

For years Lillian had wanted to go home. Hungary had grown uncomfortable for Jews, as scapegoat for the federation's humiliation and dismemberment in the Great War. Jewish students bloodied in Budapest, anti-Semitic bombings that went unpunished—Gwen remembered a lawless city, with machine gun nests on the streetcorners. The family belonged to the Hungarian Reformed Church, in hopes of acceptance. Lillian arrived first in Washington with both daughters and lived with her mother, until her husband could find a suitable position.

Dr. Laszlo Detre de Surany was an interesting-looking though far from handsome man, with an aquiline nose and a brush mustache. He was internationally known among immunologists for having coined the term *antigen* and having codiscovered what became known as the Wassermann test. August von Wassermann, working in Germany, at the center of the medical world, published his work on a diagnostic test for syphilis in apes just two weeks before Dr. Detre reported his findings on humans—which, a medical textbook concluded, "failed to gain the recognition it deserves." He was a kind man (and an expert bridge player) of serious demeanor and a quiet courage: He had often been known to experiment on himself.

He stayed behind in Budapest. In Washington, Morris met Gwen at an apartment on Columbia Road, just off Sixteenth Street. It belonged to a stiff but pleasant man still known as Judge Strasburger, though he had left the D.C. municipal bench to resume private practice eleven years earlier. He was Morris's lawyer and also, in this intertwined community, Gwen's uncle.

Though linked by family and business, Morris and Gwen were strikingly different—in education, in cultural refinement, in age. In her heels and high hair, she was taller than he was. They did not fall in love at first sight. "I fell first in love with the grandmother and then with the mother," Morris said later, "before I fell in love with the daughter." Bertha Coblenzer liked to give parties and Lillian did, too. Lillian in particular drew Morris's attention, and no wonder. Tall and rangy, with chestnut hair, she combined a warm and inquisitive smile with a European sophistication. (She played the piano, and her husband, the violin.) Lillian charmed people she liked and made them feel important; she struck others as phony.

According to the family's stories, Lillian refused to divorce her absent husband and marry Morris, but she did offer her elder daughter instead. "He was thrilled," one of their sons said later, but "I think Mother, if she'd had her choice, would have rather selected her own husband. . . . Mother needed a little bit more time for growing."

Dr. Detre took a job at Johns Hopkins in Baltimore, maybe earlier than he had intended. Only later did he land a post in Washington, as an immunologist at the U.S. Public Health Service and a visiting professor at Georgetown University's medical school.

Morris's first date with Gwen was three hours on horseback. As they courted, Morris stopped by the Wardman Park Hotel, out Connecticut Avenue, at five-thirty or six in the morning to awaken Gwen and drive her down to the stables on the Potomac, near the water gate in Foggy Bottom. They rode through Rock Creek Park or along the Mall, past its tempos, smokestacks, and trees, down to the Capitol. Morris liked to gallop and Gwen could keep up. Slender and athletic, she also swam, played tennis, and took fencing lessons—and loved it.

Despite the gap of twenty-three years in their ages and the obvious disparity between a willowy woman of sophistication and a burly, self-made man, they made a suitable match. They were affectionate together, and tender; and each offered what the other lacked. She could polish his rough edges and lend an aura of success that was more than financial. His wealth would enable her to live the life she had dreamed, in a country where people were free to make of themselves whatever they wished.

Six months after they met, on a refreshingly cool night in July 1929, Morris and Gwen were married at the four-year-old Mayflower Hotel, just above K Street along gracious Connecticut Avenue. The Fifth Avenue of Washington, it was called, with its smart shops and embassies and tony apartment houses, long known for its Easter promenades and its Sunday constitutionals by presidents and diplomats. The Mayflower was meant to mimic the grand hotels of Europe—carriage lights and terra-cotta trim, marble statues and Oriental carpets, a ballroom ornamented with more gold leaf than any building in Washington other than the Library of Congress. Into this secular temple walked Rabbi Simon, with his prim features and rimless spectacles. He wanted Jews to be more like their Christian neighbors by moving the Sabbath services to Sunday and ending the custom of kissing the Torah as it was carried around the synagogue. Rabbi Simon declared them man and wife.

For five weeks they honeymooned in Hungary and across Europe, then sailed home on the S.S. *Ile de France*. Upon returning home Gwen formally filed a petition for citizenship ("My occupation is *Housewife*. . . . My race is *Hebrew*").

After a stint at the Wardman Park, they moved into Morris's latest success, the Ambassador Hotel, at the southwestern corner of Fourteenth and K. The twelve-story hotel was made of burnt-orange pressed brick and was flat and functional in design. The Ambassador was meant as a moderate-scale hotel, priced for the traveling business-man, though not without instances of luxury. Each room had a radio, with a choice of two programs, relayed by the radio control station on the roof, and in the basement Morris built the first indoor swimming pool in a D.C. hotel. The newlyweds took a spacious apartment on the top floor and furnished it with stunning blond wood pieces in the Art Moderne style so popular in Europe but little known in America.

For Gwen, this was a step down from the Wardman Park, and far short of what she considered necessary to entertain properly. The Ambassador was never intended as their permanent home.

Morris had recently built massive apartment houses at Nineteenth and F Streets, then at Twenty-first and Pennsylvania. In mid-October 1929 he announced plans to build the Miramar Apartment Hotel at Fifteenth and Rhode Island.

But he had noticed something already: The sales at Petworth had slowed. Whether it was intuition or judgment, Morris sensed a loss of confidence ahead. He had laid off most of his sales force at Petworth and ceased most construction, sold property on three corners of the intersection at Eleventh and E, unloaded the Park Lane at Twenty-first and Pennsylvania within a year of building it, hurried to finish his projects, and put the construction company into hibernation.

When the stock market crashed, and then the national economy, Morris was spared.

Gwen fared less well, in a more literal crash, the following January. On a cold wet morning, she mounted her horse at the Potomac

Riding Club at Twelfth Street and Ohio Avenue, between Pennsylvania Avenue and the Mall, and set out for the bridle path and her customary ride in Potomac Park.

At Thirteenth and B Streets, crossing into the Mall, her horse lost its footing on the slippery cobblestones. Gwen pitched headlong over the mane and onto the pavement and was knocked unconscious. A passing motorist drove her to the nearest hospital.

She was unconscious for hours while the doctors wondered whether she would live. When she eventually recovered, some of her friends thought that her personality had changed. She had been a sweet and lovely girl with a Continental accent, who had sailed for America in her blooming time. Now she became impatient with people, not all the time, but more than those around her would have liked. She held herself a little bit apart. There seemed to be something remote and unknowable at her core, and a willfulness that would not be denied.

Two

ROOSEVELT

Carol Joy Andrews accompanied her mother into Woodward & Lothrop, the stately department store on F Street, on a spring afternoon in 1937. They were looking for a dress for Carol to wear to her graduation from Shaw Junior High, and they had tried Hecht's, Kann's, Lansburgh's—almost every store downtown. But nothing hung just right on her gangly frame.

Woodie's occupied the block from Eleventh Street almost to Tenth. Carol and her mother passed beneath its awnings, through the heavy doors, along the pillared walkway past the gleaming cases of jewelry, through the crosscurrents of perfume. Light-skinned colored women operated the elevators, and they asked Negro shoppers where they were going, because they could not try on anything above the first floor.

Carol's mother asked for the business office, on the top floor.

They got off at Junior Misses, on the fourth floor.

They saw a dress that both of them liked. It was navy blue, of moire taffeta, with a big white collar and an organdy rose. "It matched my skinny frame," Carol long remembered.

But Carol's mother would not buy the dress unless her daughter could try it on. She was a stylish, light-skinned, self-possessed, devoutly Christian woman. Her ex-husband had owned a successful grocery store in downtown Houston, before he became the pastor at one of the largest colored churches in Dallas, and the better stores always took clothes to their house. After her divorce, she had packed everything into a second-hand Oldsmobile and moved to Washington with Carol, the youngest of her six children, worried about Richard, the eldest, who was already there.

Carol was born on Christmas Eve in 1923. Richard, who was eleven years old then, had chosen Carol's name—as the word that follows *Christmas*—and he suggested *Joy* as her middle name. She grew up to think of her handsome brother as her rock. He had graduated from Fisk University and was now the manager of the Lincoln Theatre, on boisterous U Street—the colored Connecticut Avenue, it was called, the black Broadway. Beneath the bright lights, men strolled in jackets and ties, the women in high style, as they paraded in front of the theaters or waited in a line blocks long for the doors to open. Eleanor Roosevelt or Joe Louis might happen by, to hear Cab Calloway or Billie Holiday or Duke Ellington playing in the clubs and cabarets. The Duke, whose family lived a block away, at Twelfth and T Streets, had performed at the Lincoln Theatre's opening in 1921. The theater had terrazzo floors and fluted Corinthian columns and plaster bas-reliefs of the Great Emancipator. There was also a pipe organ that was almost as beautiful to the ear as Radio City's. The Lincoln sometimes showcased black theater, vaudeville, and beauty pageants, but mainly it screened movies—silent ones, then talkies.

Richard wore a white shirt and tie but earned a paltry $17.95 for a seven-day week. His mother and sister lodged with Mrs. Lyons, the theater's cashier, and in 1939 he married the organist.

Carol liked a lot of things about Washington. The summer heat was no worse than in Texas, and here she could sleep on a blanket out in Rock Creek Park, her purse at her side, and nobody would steal it. The signs she had seen on segregated water fountains and public bathrooms in the South were nowhere to be found. Here she could ride in the front of the trolley or sit in the grandstand at Griffith Stadium. At the National Theatre, colored people were permitted to perform but not to watch; at Constitution Hall, they could watch but not perform.

From its beginning, the capital had had a large proportion of dark-skinned residents, most of them slaves but many of them free. After the Civil War, the Radical Republicans had sought to make the capital a light unto the nation. Black celebrants waltzed at President Grant's second Inaugural; Frederick Douglass served as a federal marshal for D.C. and the recorder of deeds; all ordinances were amended to end the distinction between colored and white, and that meant that refusing to serve a customer for reason of race could draw a fine. For four glorious years, even colored men could vote for mayor and city council, before the prominent white citizens prevailed on Congress to supplant the city's elected self-rule with an appointed territorial government. For a half-century longer, the capital was home to more colored people—ninety thousand—than any other American city.

But the small privileges and the absence of WHITE ONLY signs were misleading, even dangerous. The police expected everyone to know, without the benefit of signs, which parks were for white people—the better ones in D.C.'s jurisdiction—and which were open to all. Jim Crow, then Woodrow Wilson, had restored segregation to the government and, by example, to D.C. (The Virginia-born president's wife was horrified to see colored men sharing quarters with white women at the Post Office Department.) The distinguished colored guests at the 1922 dedication of the Lincoln Memorial, extending the Mall to the river, had been separated from the whites. Swimming pools and playgrounds were segregated, as were the downtown movie houses and the soda fountains at Peoples drugstores. Between the Capitol and the White House, no restaurant would serve colored patrons except behind a screen. The stores along F Street sold their wares to anyone but hired only whites as salesclerks. Colored mothers who shopped downtown left their small children at home, because there were no available toilets.

In the schools, separate was far from equal, but not all of the colored schools were awful. At Dunbar High School, staffed by teachers with Ph.D.s who were barred from better jobs, most of the graduates continued on to college. But other schools were hand-me-downs. "Shameful Shaw," as the students called it, a sprawling brick building at Seventh and Rhode Island, had been a white school until it started to run down. The cellar flooded; students scared one another with stories about swimming rats.

The school routinely held students back a year if they had moved there from the South.

But Carol's mother would not hear of this. "Not my daughter," she said.

The principal agreed to test Carol, and she was allowed to advance to the seventh grade.

Then she learned that there was color prejudice within her all-colored school. The upper class in colored Washington were mainly mulattoes. This included the principal at Shaw, who favored light-colored teachers, who in turn favored light-colored students. In Carol's classroom, seats were assigned by the grades the students earned (the ones who, say, scored eighty or better in math sat together), and within each group the students were arranged by color. The fairer the students, the closer they sat to the front. The paper bag test, as it was called, comparing skin color to the light brown of a grocery sack, judged Carol a shade or two too dark.

She had never experienced anything like this before. "I came from a community where everybody looked up to the Andrewses," she recalled. "To come to a community where people only looked up to you based on your income and your complexion was horrifying." Kindness shined on students whose parents were professionals or owned a house "up the hill," near Howard University. Carol and her mother lived on Girard Street, several blocks west of Howard, in a stately row house with a generous front porch, but everyone knew they rented. When Carol's father visited from Texas, her homeroom teacher asked how such a big handsome man could have an ugly, nappy-haired child who would surely not amount to much.

Every evening, Carol sat at the bottom of the stairs in the front yard and cried.

Perhaps her unhappiness at school had inspired her mother to buy her a pretty dress for graduation. Woodie's was the city's oldest department store, founded by two New England dry goods merchants in 1880. Seven years later they were the first to move the two long blocks from Pennsylvania Avenue north to F Street; by the 1920s the city's center of commerce had followed. Society ladies gathered for tea in the department store's seventh-floor restaurant, when they had tired of Peacock Alley at the Willard Hotel.

The salesclerk in Junior Misses refused to allow Carol to try on the dress. Carol and her mother ascended to the business office, where they seated themselves in the anteroom and waited. When somebody inquired what they wanted, Carol's mother replied, "My daughter is graduating from junior high, and I want her to have a very pretty dress, but I'm not going to buy it if she can't try it on."

Everyone ignored them, but for an occasional glare.

They sat for two hours or more.

At closing time, the business manager emerged, and he and Carol's mother had words. They kept their tempers, but Carol's mother was determined. They made their points, then made them again.

The business manager asked her whether they had picked out the dress.

"Yes."

He phoned down to the fourth floor. All the other customers had gone.

They went down, and Carol tried on the dress with the rose and took it home.

Months later, Carol's parents remarried. "I was so glad," she said, "to get out of this town."

Morris Cafritz treated the Depression as a business opportunity. Property was cheap, and more often than not, he was in a position to buy. Harry Wardman, the showman, had overextended himself, with his six luxury hotels and his baronial apartment houses, as well as his own mansion out Connecticut Avenue. But by 1930 he had lost it all. Morris took receivership of the Corcoran Courts apartment house, bought it back, and then sold it again—again, at a provocative profit—to the government for use as a State Department annex.

Whenever the rest of the country collapsed, the capital thrived. As the Depression threw a quarter of the nation's workers out of a job, "the very air of Washington crackled," by Frederick Lewis Allen's account. "Suddenly this city had become unquestionably the economic as well as the political capital." In President Franklin D. Roosevelt's first Hundred Days, he struck a New Deal, and agencies sprang into being, with the government scrambling to house them. Chinatown was demolished (and moved to two blocks along H Street, hemmed in by white merchants who acquired the property nearby to prevent it from expanding), and the long stretches of warehouses and whorehouses gave way to the Federal Triangle. The grim and glorious National Archives rose where the Center Market had stood. The Department of Commerce, the world's largest office building, went up first, and then the ponderous others, as if imagined by Kafka. And all the new employees needed places to live. Bereft bankers and Democratic office seekers and even tourists filled the hotels. Negroes surged in from the South, arriving by train across the bridge from Virginia, the northernmost reach of the old Confederacy. Many of them hoped to find government jobs in the city where the money was printed, but they wound up as maids and chauffeurs. As the 1930s went on, the federal workforce almost doubled and the city's population bulged by a third.

Morris understood this. One winter's evening, at a dinner meeting at the Ambassador Hotel, he addressed the executives and salesmen of the revived Cafritz Construction Company. Washington's economy, he declared, experienced no great extreme of either prosperity or depression. The company built a hundred dwellings in 1931 alone. The next year he joined in on the lushly landscaped Westchester apartments, near the National Cathedral, soon the home for senators and New Dealers. On Nineteenth Street, between K and L, he built an apartment house of efficiencies, each with a Murphy bed and fold-into-the-wall dining table and benches, and as a birthday present for his wife he named it the Gwenwood. He built two yellow-brick high-rises, the Majestic and Hightowers, out Sixteenth Street, and garden apartments off Fourteenth Street, and the Park Crescent, with an oblique view of Rock Creek Park. His architects concealed a utilitarian design with an Art Deco style—aluminum entrances, zig-gurat cornices, wraparound windows, rounded edges, a sense of in-dustrial bulk.

From 1925 to 1941, he built eighty-five apartment houses, in all price ranges and in every part of the city. Across the Anacostia River, on spaciously landscaped grounds, Morris was building seventy-two three-story buildings, the Greenway Apartments, most with one or two bedrooms: the largest low-cost housing venture ever tried locally by a private concern. To protect his three-million-dollar investment, he pressed his subcontractors, who needed the work. He would tell the lowest bidder that someone had underbid him, then work him down in the price. Or he would refuse to pay for extras or in full, or pay them slowly if he thought they charged too much. Working for Morris set up his subcontractors to go broke on the job.

One day, at the site, he arranged to meet his heating and plumb-ing subcontractor, Morris Pollin, who had his teenaged son, Abe, with him. The Pollins arrived in their broken-down car. Morris Cafritz favored pale blue Cadillacs with fins.

"Good morning, Mr. Cafritz," Morris Pollin said.

"Good morning," came the reply. "How're you doing on this job?" By his tone he expected a complaint.

"I'm doing great on this job," the elder Pollin said. "I'm going to make a lot of money on this job."

Morris Cafritz's face fell, as if this prospect had ruined his day.

Real estate was a brutal game, and he excelled in playing it. He was a fierce competitor in everything he did. When he played gin rummy with J. B. Shapiro, they argued about the score, and they played golf as if they were bitter enemies for two dollars a hole. At the gaming tables he played rashly and without limit. He could be charming to employees, remembering their children's names, and fair to them, if they did as he asked. But he was also a taskmaster, who fired his own brother-in-law.

He was every bit as hard on himself. He would arrive at the con-struction site before the workmen and put in fourteen-hour days. He ran his business of two thousand employees from a small corner of-fice on the mezzanine in the Ambassador. In the basement he put in an exercise room, a sauna, and a Turkish bath, as much for himself as for the hotel guests, and entertained his friends. One of them was an aimless young man named Johnny Sirica, who was torn between a career as a professional boxer and the law. On the morning of the bar exam, Morris had persuaded his pal to take it and slipped him twenty-five bucks to take care of the fee. Morris also pitched for the Cafritz Company's softball team in the Realty League, and he sponsored the first-place trophy that his team won three times.

For all of his intensity in work and sports, and in his available time, Morris was an affectionate parent, more so than Gwen. When the nuns at Georgetown University Hospital told Gwen that her first-born, in 1931, was a boy, she cried hysterically. Instead of a Calvin she had wanted a Cynthia. "You can't pretend about something like that," she said later.

Calvin was a blond, earnest boy who liked living in a hotel. "Every day was different," he remembered. Calvin had run of the kitchen and would hang around there, drinking grape juice or the ginger ale bottled exclusively for the hotel. The housemen and the maids became his first friends. A houseman would toss a coin on the carpet and shout, "Look, a dime down there!" and keep the boy searching for more. Calvin mingled with the guests—the northern accents startled him—and rode the elevators. To play outdoors, he crossed Fourteenth Street to Franklin Square, where rotted trees and overgrown brush had given way to saplings and bird baths and spruced-up walkways. The groans of the city were never far distant. The streetcars screeched across K Street, with its mansions and Victorian town houses that were turning into rooming houses and offices.

Morris acquired a Great Dane and named it Caesar. ("Morris names all children, horses, dogs, apartment houses, and everything around here," Gwen said.) The oversized dog descended from the penthouse by private elevator and was led through the lobby to find relief in Franklin Square.

The Depression was making Morris rich. With Gwen pregnant again, he applied for a permit, in the fall of 1936, to build a three-story house at 2301 Ridge Road NW, just west of Georgetown. Morris had built thousands of houses, but this one was to be theirs.

The hilly, winding lane was taking on a new name, Foxhall Road. At Thomas Jefferson's invitation, Henry Foxall had built a foundry nearby to cast the fragile republic's cannons and shells, and he and the Virginian occasionally played violin duets. The beauty of the woods and a view overlooking the city were not all that attracted Morris to the site. The city's nicest neighborhoods were off-limits to him, because restrictive covenants in the deeds forbade the sale to "any Negro or colored person" or to anyone "of the Semitic race," including "Armenians, Jews, Hebrews, Persians and Syrians."

Foxhall Road had no covenants because it had so little development. A few frame houses huddled at the base of the hill, and a reproduction of an eighteenth-century Parisian mansion stood across the road from the ten acres Morris had bought. The property was an operating farm, covered with corn stubble and beautiful fruit trees. Calvin would long remember visiting the fields in winter with his father when he was not quite five years old. He had always lived in the grit of downtown.

"To suddenly find myself out there, after growing up downtown in a hotel, there was so much to explore," he said. "It was a fairyland to me."

Away from the road, the view was magnificent in several directions. The ground sloped sharply into a squat line of trees, and beyond it lay the hazy skyline of a low-lying city. Straight ahead, toward the northeast, the Gothic towers of the National Cathedral rose from a far-off hill. Around to the right, the spires of Georgetown University guarded the glistening Potomac. Between them jutted the square granite tower of the Post Office building, the merest hint of the Capitol dome, and the lonely alabaster peak of the Washington Monument. They glimmered in the distance, as if they had retreated to a nostalgic and unreachable place, as if *this* was reality and the city splayed below was make-believe.

The same pair of architects who had designed Morris's apartment buildings tried their hand at a mansion as an indulgence in Art Deco, with almost three dozen rooms and a dozen baths. The true designers, however, were Morris and Gwen. They had been inspired by a house in Mount Kisco, New York, that the modernist Edgar Durell

Stone had designed, combining a stark geometry in steel and concrete with the rounded rooms of an ocean liner.

Morris and Gwen built their house out of bricks, 270,000 of them, painted white. Three oblong boxes, end to end, and a rounded entranceway followed the contours of the curved driveway, resembling a freight train about to derail. Ambitious but unnervingly functional, the house was shorn of shutters or ornament. The only concession to irregularity was the two-story bulge at the back, defining the two rooms that Gwen would love best—the dining room and her bedroom.

The house was designed for entertaining. Its soul was in the public rooms downstairs. The dining room comfortably seated twenty-two, with the hostess holding forth from the prow. Her foot on the servants' buzzer under the table would galvanize the three adjoining kitchens. The vast living room, with its rosewood, satinwood, and California redwood floor, looked out across the back. It led out onto a wide terrace that ran along the house, confined by a metal railing in rectangular swirls. Few places in the capital had such a magnificent view.

The spare exterior, with its geometric purity, gave way inside to curves and a syncopated symmetry. The door to Gwen's rounded bedroom was dotted with circles of smoked glass to suggest portholes. A stereo system in every room could play any of the city's four radio stations. The nightclub in the basement had an intimate feel, with its sinuous benches of synthetic leather, the bar top of industrial plastic, and the miniature dance floor of opaque glass, lit from below. Whimsy reigned down the corridor in the game room, where the linoleum walls had linoleum cutouts of a couple lunching in the garden and rows of men cheering the home team.

The most astonishing room, and the smallest, was the first one that visitors saw. The foyer was rounded in a perfect eclipse. The floor of a radiating marble was inlaid with eight figures in brass, including a polo player, a conga drummer, a couple dancing the rumba, and the back of Albert Einstein's head. The spiral staircase had a handrail made of Lucite and extruded brass. The light in the gold-leaf ceiling shone red or white or silver or gold, depending on the dress Gwen wore. (As a child Calvin believed that that ceiling was the route to heaven when you died.) At night, under any light, the white marble in the back wall looked translucent. The elevator, which had not been part of the original plans, added twenty-nine hundred dollars to the mansion's already outrageous cost of fifty-five thousand dollars.

The décor, more than the structure itself, gave the mansion its sense of self. The satin silk wall coverings along the passageway into the living room showed a Dalí on one wall facing a Miró and a Chagall. The living room featured something more shocking than the stainless steel mantel, in the wall-sized murals of Greek maidens, draped in diaphanous white or in nothing at all. The furniture was every bit as modern in sensibility. Eugene Schoen, the Art Deco interior designer, favored bleached woods and sharp corners and astringent, low-slung designs. The indirect lighting was meant to make everyone look lovely; the mirrors were colored to enhance complexions.

All of this was stylish and glamorous, yet there was something cold about it, too. More than anything it was a measure of what liberty could mean. In less than thirty-eight years, Morris Cafritz had risen out of an alley dwelling in the poorest of neighborhoods and into a mansion on Foxhall Road.

Lindy was unaware of the tears that trickled down her cheeks as the president's third inaugural parade passed by. She and her husband, Hale, a congressman for seventeen days now, stood in the cold sunshine at the sharp corner of Pennsylvania and Constitution Avenues, at the apex of the Federal Triangle. Over their shoulders, the rounded monolith of the Federal Trade Commission building looked as brawny as the industrial trusts it had been created to tame.

At the East Front of the Capitol, on this January noon of 1941, they had watched the bareheaded president jut his jaw in the air and declare, "Democracy is not dying." Because the crippled president needed both arms to hold himself upright at the podium, he would punctuate a point with his chin. He alluded to the dangerous dictatorships of Europe and Japan. "The democratic aspiration is no mere recent phase in human history. It *is* human history."

In the parade, the student-workers of the National Youth Administration in their colorful blue blouses and the tanned young men of the Civilian Conservation Corps and the rows of West Point cadets and even the infantrymen with fixed bayonets moved Lindy, but not to tears. The famed Third Cavalry's soldiers followed, with machine guns strapped to their saddles, and the gun-bearing caissons—and then the tanks, clattering along Pennsylvania Avenue at a frightening thirty-five miles an hour.

"That was the worst, when the tanks came, and I realized how close we were to war," Lindy remembered. Not since Wilson's second inaugural or possibly Lincoln's first—it depended on the particular commentator's penchant for drama—had an Inauguration found the capital so uneasy, so ready for war. "We were against war," Lindy said.

That included Hale. He was just twenty-six, and Lindy twenty-four, and both had absorbed the antimilitary sentiments of their generation. They had come of age in the wake of a soul-searing war that had failed, more obviously than ever, either to end all wars or to make the world safe for democracy. Hale had written editorials in college against rearmament and another world war, and he had risen to prominence in Louisiana as an enemy of the political powers-that-be. Now he had joined them.

Lindy had missed Hale's swearing in. Eight days after he had won the Democrats' September primary, tantamount to election in the deeply southern state, Lindy had given birth to their second child. After the hard delivery, Tommy's legs were weak and his breathing became labored when he cried. Then, as Lindy packed up the house for the drive to the capital, she was stricken with a temporary glaucoma, an excruciating case of elevated tension in her left eye.

As Hale raised his right hand along with the 434 other members of the House of Representatives, Lindy could only send a wire. "May you be the fine man you are today," she wrote, "each time you take an oath of public office."

They had met as freshmen at a fraternity dance at Tulane University. He had asked a mutual friend to tap Lindy on the shoulder and introduce him. Hale stood almost six feet tall and was strongly built, with a lean and muscular face, wavy brushed-back hair, piercing blue eyes, and an easy smile. Awkwardly, he swept her around the dance floor, and he said in a mellow baritone, "I'm going to marry you someday."

She prayed for someone else to tap in, and after another young man did, she asked him, "Who is that weird boy?"

Thomas Hale Boggs—the *Thomas* was an afterthought, for need of a saint's name—was a native Mississippian from a respectable family that had fallen on hard times. His mother's father, Thomas Hale, had been the president of the Gulf & Ship Island Railroad; an earlier forebear who owned an island in the Gulf of Mexico in 1814 had sent word to Andrew Jackson that the British fleet was sailing for New Orleans. Hale's father's family leaned toward the literary and aesthetic—that meant they were poor. Hale's father was a writer and painter who by nature was moody and spoiled. He scratched out a living variously as a farmer, a dairyman, and a bank cashier, and as deprivation dictated, moved his family back and forth between the Mississippi Gulf Coast and the outskirts of New Orleans. Hale, the third of six children, could point out numerous places they had moved to in Jefferson Parish, to beat the rent.

Before he turned ten he was earning fifty cents a week to water down Huey P. Long Avenue, in front of the bank where his father worked near New Orleans. When the Depression struck, and banks failed, the family returned to the Mississippi coast—to catch mullet so they could eat, or so Hale exaggerated in later years. Hale held what he called "the usual boy jobs"—pumping gas, soda jerking—"to pay the greater portion of my expenses since my fourteenth birthday." (He elicited a letter of recommendation from the druggist, "To whom it may concern," extolling "a high class boy.") At seventeen he worked as an assistant program director and an announcer for a Gulf Coast radio station.

He also earned a little money in a brainier way. The *Times-Picayune*'s contest to select the biggest news of the week attracted as many as a thousand essays from high school students in Louisiana and Mississippi. Almost every week Hale entered an essay and almost every week he won a prize. First place meant ten dollars for his "splendidly intelligent essay . . . free of all mawkishness"—or so the New Orleans newspaper judged—on the Community Chest and the people dependent on charity ("civilization has become more merciful") and then again for his "smoothly professional" essay on the president's veto of the veterans' loan bill ("condemned by Hoover, prayed for and awaited by needy soldiers"). Or he won seven dollars for second place or five dollars for third—four hundred dollars over the years—or an honorable mention. He won so often that the judges changed the rules, barring a first-place winner from entering again for four weeks.

In high school, the occasional Cs and Ds were supplanted by As. At age fourteen he was reading William Blackstone and planning to become a lawyer and a member of Congress. He represented the Gulf Coast at the state debate tournament, and he won his high school's four-year scholarship to Tulane.

Hale arrived in uptown New Orleans with thirty-five dollars in his pocket and took on two or three jobs at a time. He worked in an ice cream shop (until he was fired, supposedly for eating too much of the profits), as a ditch-digger on the lakefront, and as the emcee at a hotel's rooftop garden. He worked on the copy desk at the *Times-Picayune* and as a campus correspondent at a nickel an inch for the *New Orleans States*. He sold magazines, mail-order seersucker suits—four dollars each—and chewing gum. He arranged for a few of his friends to stop at the drugstore that was closest to campus and ask for Beech-Nut gum; then after a couple of days Hale would enter and offer to supply it.

And somehow he still managed to score high enough grades to earn an invitation from Phi Beta Kappa, and he won the university's medal for debating—the second time a freshman had, though he later claimed it was the first. In his spare time he served as the president of his fraternity and as the editor in chief of the campus newspaper, the *Hullabaloo*.

It was there that he met up again with Lindy Claiborne. She was the weekly's editor for Sophie Newcomb, Tulane's sister school—"and that was the beginning of her working under his leadership," as a ladies' group in Washington put it years later.

Lindy had a sweetness that failed to mask her intelligence. Short but with a colonel's posture, she knew her own mind. Her thin face was not quite dainty, framed by a sharp chin, prominent cheekbones, and dark businesslike hair. Yet the effect was soft and warm. Maybe it was the modulated voice or the steady yet unthreatening eye contact or—yes, more than anything—the perfect, self-effacing manners. There was something unconquerably calm about her. Her ingratiating smile almost concealed her sense of control.

Marie Corinne Morrison Claiborne, nicknamed for her daddy, Roland—Rolindy had shrunk to Lindy—lived first on a sugar plantation, then moved to a cotton plantation after her father died of influenza when she was two years old. As the only child in a household of indulgent adults, she learned to exploit the attention she received. When her mother's beau let Lindy tag along on a shopping spree in New Orleans, she saw a red-haired baby mannequin in a window on Canal Street and wanted it; no explanation sufficed. "I'm just going to sit here"—she found a bench in front of the store—"until you get me that doll." She went home with it.

Lindy was educated by tutors and then in a convent, and she applied to Sophie Newcomb at age fifteen. She had learned from a family friend who taught there that her interviewer revered Shakespeare. So when he asked her point-blank whether she was sixteen, the minimum age to enroll, she answered, "To be or not to be, that is the question, but to thine own self be true, thou canst not then be false to any man.

"No, sir, I'm not sixteen."

She was admitted.

Her self-assurance was the product of centuries. A Claiborne had arrived at Jamestown in 1621 and became the first white settler in Maryland. In every generation since, at least one Claiborne had held public office. Lindy's great-great-great-granduncle, William Charles Cole Claiborne, had perhaps been the most consequential. He entered the House of Representatives at age twenty-three (two years younger than the Constitution decreed) and was serving as Tennessee's sole congressman when the 1800 election deadlocked between Thomas Jefferson and Aaron Burr. The decision was thrown into the House, where each state cast a single vote, and Claiborne waited until just the right moment before deciding on Jefferson. The president appointed him governor of the Mississippi Territory, then of the newly purchased Louisiana Territory, before Claiborne was elected the eighteenth state's first governor.

An act of political guile had given the family its home.

In the early twentieth century the Claibornes had even hosted a president, hospitably enough to overlook the fact that he was a Republican. They had taken Teddy Roosevelt on the 1902 hunting trip (Lindy's daddy, too young to shoot, had stacked the gear) when the president famously refused to kill a mama bear—the reason Lindy's baby photos included a teddy bear. Later the family invited Herbert Hoover to dinner, while he was still the secretary of commerce and not yet president.

Lindy's dreams had nothing to do with politics—she was a woman, after all. Instead she wanted to become another Margaret Bourke-White, the renowned photographer. That was before she fell in love with Hale.

Short of money for dating—Lindy's family was land rich but cash poor—they would split a big sandwich and a malted for a quarter at a soda fountain near Tulane. Both of them had to fend off competition from other suitors. When Lindy swooned over a medical student, Hale put an apple on her desk every day, to keep the doctor away. Hale received notes from "Mallie," who implored him to "write very soon, my love." Lindy never knew about them.

After Hale finished law school, in 1937, they married, and that sent him up a notch or two in social standing.

But always, politics intruded. On the *Hullabaloo*, Hale had been seen as something of a radical at a politically turbulent time. His editorials fastened on a meaty target—the populist turned autocrat, Governor Huey Long. When the Kingfish shut down the student newspaper at Louisiana State University, Tulane took in its editor (later to become Hale's top congressional aide, having covered his campaign for the *New Orleans States*). Hale's fraternity brothers dubbed him "the Senator," and he ran for student body president at Tulane Law School but lost. Soon he took up politics for real.

Even after Huey Long was assassinated, his corrupt machine lived on. Hale joined with other recent Tulane law grads to form the

People's League, to throw the rascals out. The uptown reformers unanimously chose Hale, because of his oratorical talent, as their chairman and public voice. After he organized a rally on the courthouse steps to denounce the district attorney for impeding an inquisitive grand jury, the district attorney resigned. The People's League had more committees than members, but the movement caught fire, beyond anyone's imagining. Its slate of candidates swept into office as governor, lieutenant governor, attorney general, and a majority of legislators.

Hale had already made up his mind to run for Congress. In 1940 he challenged Paul Maloney, a mild and competent five-term incumbent, a House Ways and Means Committee member personally untouched by scandal but backed by the Long machine. Hale took to the stump in a white linen suit and assailed the congressman in a rich, booming voice as "the tool of the Long dictatorship," as someone who had not authored a single law in his decade in Washington, as a politician who had left the nation unprepared for war.

The newspaper photograph of the smiling candidate and his fifteen-month-old daughter, Barbara, carried the caption *Hale Boggs and Boss*. He took his campaign slogan—*Mr. Boggs Goes to Washington*—from the recent hit movie starring James Stewart as Senator Jefferson Smith, a pure soul of democracy in a capital of corruption.

Hale won by a comfortable eight thousand votes.

He did not intend, however, to follow the fictitious Mr. Smith, who was naïve and idealistic, a crusader. Hale had no affection for lost causes, and as the youngest Democrat in the Seventy-seventh Congress, he was smart enough to know how little he knew.

"I'll have plenty to learn," he told a reporter shortly before leaving for Washington. "I'm not going to stick my neck out."

Even before arriving, Hale Boggs showed a knack for Washington's ways.

One morning, Gwen Cafritz received a telephone call from Cissy Patterson, who asked to visit her on Foxhall Road and showed up that afternoon. Gwen knew this was an audition.

"She heard me speak somewhere," she recounted years later. "Cissy saw I had potential."

Cissy Patterson was the keen-witted, willful editor and now also the publisher of the *Times-Herald*, the sassy merger of the city's two Hearst papers. With her family fortune and her redheaded flamboyance, she gloried in her own unpredictability. Her whims became crusades. She expanded the *Times-Herald's* society pages, launching a separate section on Sundays, and used them to topple the old guard. Evalyn Walsh McLean was fading in health, and besides, Cissy loathed her. She decided it was time for somebody new.

Evalyn Walsh McLean had inherited the mantle of the capital's premier social hostess from her mother-in-law and had reigned unchallenged since President Harding's day. (Indeed, her husband had been a minor accessory after the fact in the Teapot Dome scandal.) She was a kindly eccentric, who kept a llama on her lawn and a monkey in her bathroom, and during the Depression she wandered around the city handing out five-dollar bills. But no one else would plan a party the same time that she did. She could draw all of the capital's officialdom to a single gathering, out to her estate along Wisconsin Avenue. Her dinner parties were lavish, often with a movie afterward, as were her Sunday night "entertainments" or her seated luncheons for 150 or more. She might wear the Hope diamond, which she had purchased, despite its curse, because she wanted it.

A Tin Lizzie had killed her son, her husband had gone mad, and now Cissy Patterson wanted her dethroned.

Gwen Cafritz was bound to appeal to Cissy, who had once been married to a Polish count. How intriguing Gwen looked, how foreign, with her Continental manners as well as intelligence and wit. She had other necessities, too—an abundance of money, a palatial home, a potent ambition. She wanted to do more than ride horseback before breakfast.

Friends of Cissy's thought her foolish to choose a Jewess, but undoubtedly that was part of the point—to tweak the conventions of society, to act as she liked, because she could.

And there was something else she liked about Gwen—her husband's advertising dollars.

Gwen greeted Cissy in a silk tea gown and served caviar and champagne, then gave her a tour of the house and its lovely views.

She was anointed.

When the *Times-Herald* launched its Monday feature, "Beauty of the Week," the seventh week belonged to Gwen. "She's an exotic type with heavenly white skin." The caption below the oversized photograph found her "vivacious . . . dynamic . . . stunning." Cissy dispatched her top social reporter to Gwen's parties. Her face showed up on the newspaper's daily photo page, her name in the society columns—"always so smart and exquisitely groomed."

Morris increased his advertising in the *Times-Herald* without being asked.

Lindy Boggs steered her Pontiac south along Connecticut Avenue from their apartment on Tilden Street. It was the only route she knew to the Capitol, south on Connecticut, then east on Constitution, until she could see the Capitol dome and find her way to it.

Self-possessed brick apartment houses, ornamented with bas-relief and contrasting trim, lined both sides of upper Connecticut Avenue. Past the zoo, she crossed over Rock Creek Park on a long graceful bridge, guarded by concrete lions, and swept down the hill. This was as civilized a city as New Orleans but without the abandon. Lindy approached Dupont Circle, proud of herself for having navigated the geometrically perplexing city, which had never been designed for cars. Three avenues and two crosscutting streets converged at the circular plaza, named for the Civil War general who had failed to capture Charleston Harbor. Lindy followed the traffic into the circle and partway around it.

A streetcar was heading straight at her.

She swerved and missed it. Too shaken to keep on her way, she stayed in the circle and continued around it and veered back onto Connecticut Avenue, heading north. She drove six blocks before she could turn around. Then she drove south again, as slowly as she could with the horns honking behind her. She looked for a sign that warned of streetcars driving the wrong way and saw none. She survived Dupont Circle and had never been so grateful to glimpse the Capitol dome.

The moment she arrived, she stormed into Eddie Hebert's office, next door to Hale's, and bemoaned her near-wreck. The former city editor with owlish glasses and a liking for lovelies and liquor had been elected with Hale as a New Orleans reformer.

"Lindy," he said, "everybody knows that Cissy Patterson lives on the other side of Dupont Circle, and she doesn't want those streetcars going in front of her house. What's wrong with that?"

"When I heard that," Lindy said later, "all I could do is say, 'Yay, Cissy.'"

Cissy lived in her late mother's mansion on the eastern rim of Dupont Circle. Stanford White had designed the fan-shaped forty-room palace of marble and mahogany. The Coolidges had rented it while the White House was being repaired, and Charles Lindbergh had slept there after returning from Paris. The streetcars screeched as they passed her house, and Cissy prevailed on the privately owned streetcar company to route even its northbound streetcars along the opposite side of the circle.

"What's the matter with you?" Eddie Hebert added. "You're not familiar enough with Washington to know that?"

Washington looked simple enough at first, a one-industry town, its rules of engagement inscribed in the Constitution, a city no more bewildering than diagonals imposed on a grid. But as Lindy learned while trying to drive, the city was far more complicated.

For one thing, it combined a political artfulness with a cultural provincialism, a certain backwardness. Washingtonians of taste traveled to New York to watch a play, to Philadelphia to attend a concert, to Baltimore to have lunch or to shop for clothes. In the summer, men wore white linen or seersucker suits and Panama hats; women's hats had broad brims for the shade. Most restaurants specialized in everything deep fried.

More confusing, Washington, D.C., was two cities in one, the national capital of marble and monuments, and the local, corporeal city—Washington *and* D.C. The two crossed paths in the unlikeliest, even the most literal, of ways. Once, as Lindy was parking the car to shop on Connecticut Avenue, near Tilden, she hit the bumper of a luxury car. She went looking for the driver and when she saw he was colored, she assumed—was she not still in the South?—that he was the chauffeur. But the car was his.

When he noticed her congressional license plate, he said, "Don't worry, dear; I won't tell your daddy about it."

Local and national was not as simple as black and white. Crossover was uncommon between the races, and yet the boundaries between D.C. and Washington were labyrinthine, occasionally porous, and always in flux. Many people inhabited both places at once, their workday in the capital and their life in their neighborhood. Cabinet officer or janitor, on all sides they owed their presence in D.C. to the fact that it was the capital. This was how the city had grown, for fourteen decades now—by accretion. Contrary to reputation, it was not a transient city. People went there to work in the government or to serve those who did, and then, more often than not, they stayed. After a generation, at most, the capital became their home. It was a warm community, an easygoing society, as long as all of its members understood their place in it.

As the city grew, its anthropology became ever more intricate. Block by block and street by alley, the residences of black and white made a mosaic. Colored people accounted for just over a quarter of the population, more than in any American city its size, with schisms and gradations of their own. The white majority was divided into tribes. Greeks, Italians, and Jews settled in pockets. Protestants from Appalachia were drawn to Anacostia, and the Irish Catholics congregated in Swampoodle, north of Capitol Hill, and worked as cops and firemen and streetcar conductors. The professional denizens of the federal city divided themselves socially into occupational groupings, of lawyers, journalists, military men, businessmen, diplomats, civil servants. Families who stayed enough generations, and showed sufficient breeding, became known as "cave dwellers," because they generally kept to themselves for the six or seven months each year that Congress was in session.

Lindy, however, had an entrée into the cave dwellers' world. A friend from home, a distant relation by marriage, had been living in

Washington because an uncle insisted that she make her debut in the capital. "Almost immediately I was thrown into the do-good, charitable, cultural activities of the city," Lindy said. She and Hale gained introductions to another sector of the city through Paul Wooton, the *Times-Picayune* correspondent who would achieve a trifecta of sorts, heading the National Press Club, the White House Correspondents' Association, and the Gridiron Club. He knew of a temporary vacancy at Tilden Gardens, an apartment house of a dark and dignified brick, the grounds given to brick walkways, magnolias, and ivy. Hale and Lindy and their two babies moved in.

Others guided Lindy through the arcane customs of the tradition-bound capital. Since before the Civil War, the wives of high government officials had practiced a rigid system of calling cards. They formally called on one another in the late afternoon once a week—on Mondays for the Supreme Court, Tuesdays for the House of Representatives, Wednesdays for the Cabinet, and so forth. Within each institution, the junior wives visited their seniors; because parking was forbidden on many D.C. streets from four o'clock to six, visitors could keep the engine running, leave their card, and go on their way if the recipient was "not receiving," even if physically at home. Lindy was senior to no one, but the wives of three southern congressmen only slightly more senior to Hale broke protocol and called on *her*. She was relieved to see others so young. She was destined to remain friends for decades with all three women, married to Albert Gore and Estes Kefauver of Tennessee and Lyndon Johnson of Texas. Sixty years later she would be taking August vacations with Lady Bird Johnson.

In a city of an understandable—indeed, a constitutional—self-importance, Lindy also learned the uses of pretension. Hale phoned one morning in 1941 to suggest that she hurry down to Capitol Hill for a committee hearing. The passions unleashed by President Roosevelt's wily Lend-Lease proposal to deliver military equipment to the British, for a war that Lindy still hoped to avoid, filled the hearing room and lengthened the line for a seat. She had thrown a jacket over her sweater and skirt and approached the guard at the door and told him that her husband served on the committee and expected her inside.

"Oh, sure, honey," he said dismissively and turned away.

She needed to gain entrance. Then she remembered something a socialite in New Orleans had told her.

Lindy rushed back to Tilden Gardens and put on kid gloves, a black Davidow suit, and a black velour hat. Then she stopped by Palais Royal, a department store at Eleventh and G, to buy a purple veil to drape over her hat. Nothing looked more sophisticated—this was the advice—than a purple veil.

When she arrived back, before the same guard, she slowly peeled off her gloves and announced, "I'm Mrs. Boggs. I'd like to be seated, please."

"Oh, yes ma'am. Come right in."

It had taken some time but her new world was starting to feel familiar. When Tommy cut his first tooth on the day of a garden party at the White House, she rushed in late—a violation of protocol—just as the first lady was leaving. Lindy poured out her apologies and explanation, and she understood her audience. Eleanor Roosevelt extended her empathy to individuals as well as to masses.

"Can you believe that this child has a baby old enough to be cutting a tooth?" the first lady trilled, as she swept Lindy through the receiving line. "I'm glad someone has her priorities straight."

Hale, too, was starting to make himself felt in the Capitol, where success came harder and seniority reigned. He needed no reminding of his lack of power. He had been assigned at first to four minor committees, dealing with war claims, administrative spending, and the like, and squeezed into distant offices in the House Office Building. For a white-tie reception at the White House for new members of Congress and their wives, the five freshmen from Louisiana hired two limousines to drive them the two blocks from the Hotel Washington restaurant. As they waited for President Roosevelt to regain his strength to stand, supported, for another spurt of handshakes, they debated which affairs of state to raise with him.

Summoned into the president's presence, they were rushed past him, with barely a word. Eddie Hebert called back to the others, "Impressed with our views, wasn't he?"

Within months, however, Hale had been promoted to Banking and Currency. The speaker of the House already had his eye on him.

Sam Rayburn, incorruptibly honest and astonishingly guileless, was always on the lookout for young men who had brains, political judgment, and a willingness to obey—"to get along, go along," he liked to say. As a Texan he was also partial to southerners.

When Hale celebrated his twenty-seventh birthday, six weeks into his term, Sam Rayburn sent him a congratulatory note, signed, "Sincerely your friend," a rare gesture by the shy House Speaker. Hale had become politically reliable on the leading issues of the day. The world had changed since he had assailed rearmament and the military draft at Tulane. Most of Europe had fallen to the Nazis, while Britain spent its blood, sweat, and tears. Hale was for preparedness though not for sending American troops overseas. He favored Lend-Lease, and that August—rarely had Congress met so late in a steamy summer—cast his vote to extend the military draft.

"I am a member of this generation of draftees," Hale declared on the floor of the House. "For my part, I would rather be wrong about this than have the responsibility on my shoulders of giving away the liberty and the security of my country." By a single vote, the draft was extended.

Hale understood reality, political and otherwise, and as a result a coveted invitation arrived early on. Around 5:30 P.M. on Tuesday, Wednesday, and Thursday evenings, after the House had finished its work, Rayburn convened a small group of congressmen at his "Board of Education," named for the legislators who received instruction from time to time about their wayward voting. Usually the education consisted of an hour or two of drinking, card playing, scheming, and swapping of political gossip. Room H-128 of the Capitol, the speaker's hideaway, was a small room with a marble fireplace and a vaulted ceiling ornately painted. Rayburn had added the Seal of Texas painted high on the wall, old easy chairs, a leather sofa, and a concealed refrigerator. Occasionally the speaker asked promising freshmen to join in.

After Hale's first time, he went often. Rayburn, nearing sixty, "had no family, no son, no children"—this was Hale's explanation years later—"and he more or less adopted me." The Speaker ordinarily drank bourbon and branch water. The freshman preferred scotch.

If Hale worked late into the evening, Lindy would drive to the Capitol to pick him up. She loved to look at the Capitol dome in different lights—a mawkish white in the sunlight, pearly against a dark sky, pinkish at sunset, luminous at night.

One night, she was standing on the Capitol lawn waiting for Hale and gazing up at the dome. She sensed someone beside her.

"Isn't that the most beautiful sight in the world?"

She turned toward the deep, soothing voice and saw a craggy skull as bald as the dome. It was Sam Rayburn. Even after twenty-eight years in Congress, he still found himself drawn to the Capitol lawn for inspiration.

On December 7, 1941, the 27,102 fans at shabby Griffith Stadium for the final game of a disappointing football season remained unaware that the world had turned upside down. George Preston Marshall, the headstrong owner of the Washington Redskins, explained afterward that team policy forbade the use of the public address system for any news other than sports. Generals and admirals kept being paged to report to duty, and newspaper reporters and delivery boys to theirs. As "Slinging Sammy" Baugh's right arm rescued the Redskins in a fourth-quarter victory over the Eagles, 20–14, the rumors spread through the crowd.

On Foxhall Road, directly across from their home, the Cafritzes gladly attended a Sunday reception at Mrs. Edward Stotesbury's limestone mansion. The grande dame had thrown birthday parties at her Palm Beach estate for Gwen, who entertained ambitions of her own. They heard the news at the party.

At Tilden Gardens, Lindy Boggs had wedged Barbara and Tommy into heavy layers of clothing for the block-and-a-half hike to Rock Creek Park, to visit the ducks. December's dreadful weather had kept the children cooped up, and Lindy had asked Hale to take the buggy up in the elevator so that fourteen-month-old Tommy could be strapped in without two-and-a-half-year-old Barbara scampering off.

The telephone rang. It was Paul Wooton. He told Hale of the sneak attack.

"He means Manila, doesn't he?" said Lindy. "How could they get all the way to Pearl Harbor?"

She had been suspicious of the team of Japanese negotiators in Washington. "Those people are just in town to distract our government," she kept telling Hale.

"You're never suspicious of anybody," Hale replied.

He switched the radio on. The children were bundled up and the Pontiac had a better radio. "Let's get in the car and go down and see what's going on," Lindy said.

The silence in the city was startling, as on an ordinary Sunday. They passed the Japanese Embassy, on Massachusetts Avenue, where crowds watched the smoke rise from diplomatic cables burning in the back garden. They drove by the White House, where two or three hundred people had gathered, staring up at the high, lit windows behind which the president was planning a war. When they interfered with the official cars pulling into the driveway, the police moved the throng across to Lafayette Park, then closed Pennsylvania Avenue to traffic.

Hale and Lindy had driven to the Capitol, staring at the dome, when suddenly the floodlights switched off. They wondered whether bombs were about to fall. Military guards were already in place.

Overnight, Washington turned into a wartime capital. Helmeted guards patrolled the Potomac bridges. Soldiers with submachine guns secured the White House lawn. Cots were wheeled into the Munitions Building, at Nineteenth and Constitution, for military officers.

The familiar air of leisure was gone, never to return. "A sense of hurry," as James Reston wrote in the *New York Times*, had taken its place.

More than two thousand people milled around the Capitol the next morning and roared as the president's limousine arrived for his twelve-thirty address. His eldest son, a marine captain, escorted the president into the House chamber. Prolonged applause turned into cheers. In the gallery, Eleanor and the Cabinet wives wore black.

This was the people's House. Dark suits and white shirts filled the semicircles of benches, in the subdued lighting and solemnity. The commander in chief stood erect at the podium. *A date which will live in infamy*—it was his single rhetorical flourish, in his opening sentence, as he asked for a declaration of war. Hale voted with his colleagues, all but the gentlewoman from Montana, Jeannette Rankin. Afterward she was trapped in a telephone booth until the police escorted her to safety.

At eleven that night, as an experiment, lights all over the city were dimmed. Policemen stopped many of the deputy air raid wardens, as they roamed the darkened streets without official credentials. Sometime during the night, vandals with handsaws sliced through four of the thickest Japanese cherry trees near the Jefferson Memorial, which was under construction.

Hale tried to turn this new and darker world to his advantage. His newspaper ads in his 1942 campaign used his youth—"A Young Man's Challenge to a Young Man's World"—as a contrast to his sixty-six-year-old opponent, Paul Maloney, the man he had defeated two years before. Maloney had served ten years in Congress, Hale charged, "and failed to understand the menace of Hitler."

Yet it was Hale who failed to understand something. He had ridden into office on a reform movement that, having been so successful, lost some of its steam, and the regular Democrats sought revenge against the self-confident young incumbent. Because Congress had stayed in session almost constantly, even over weekends, Hale had spent too much time in Washington and not enough at home. He had left his political base untended.

When the results came in, Lindy said later, "I was not surprised."

Hale vowed to run again in 1944 and announced that he would probably enter the navy when his term expired, though he took longer than that.

In a shimmering silver gown, Gwen Cafritz paused on the landing between the round wide pillars at the Shoreham Hotel and posed. A diamond-encrusted *V*, for *Victory*, rose from the back of her raven hair. The tea and fashion show was to raise money for Bundles for Britain, which sent knitted garments to soldiers overseas. At the Shoreham, a redoubt of restrained opulence on a hill overlooking

Connecticut Avenue, Gwen swept down the staircase, into the ball-room, and along the runway—the grand finale. Charitable work had its rewards.

Gwen was becoming practiced at it, as so many society matrons were. She had hosted a garden party for the women's auxiliary of the Metropolitan Police Boys' Club, one of Morris's favorite causes, and she had opened her house (along with eight others on Foxhall Road) to raise money for the Home for Incurables.

War provided ever more opportunity. On Monday nights she volunteered at the Stage Door Canteen, and she sold war bonds in a booth at the Carlton Hotel. As the chairwoman of special events for the Special Recreation Services of the Metropolitan Office of Civilian Defense, she suggested an age-old idea to bolster everyone's morale.

Gwen insisted on meeting personally with Eleanor Roosevelt to enlist her support as honorary patroness for the program she called (after a 1938 madcap comedy starring James Cagney, Pat O'Brien, and Ronald Reagan) "Boy Meets Girl." "We could get an answer to this without an interview being necessary," a social correspondent for the first lady privately complained, "but it seems Mrs. Cafritz still wants the interview." In the spring of 1942, she organized a dance for five thousand servicemen and Government Girls at the cavernous Uline Arena, behind Union Station, which had seen more wrestling and minor-league hockey than the jitterbug. Arthur Murray himself judged the eleven o'clock dance contest.

In June, at Griffith Stadium, she tried something more ambitious, described by a sports columnist as "the most colossal job of match-making in history." Only vaguely had Gwen heard of Bob Feller, once baseball's highest-paid pitcher and now a chief petty officer and captain of the Norfolk Naval Training Station nine. His team was to take on soldiers from Camp Lee, Virginia, including the Nats' former first baseman batting cleanup. The lower grandstands were reserved for men in uniform and young women who worked as wartime civil servants, in alternating seats.

The new chief of the Manpower Commission was to throw out the first pitch, but he had been detained elsewhere, and Gwen took his place. Clark Griffith, the Nats' white-haired old owner, stood by her side in the grandstand. In her floppy straw hat and a summery frock, she grasped the unfamiliar baseball in her right hand and arched her arm.

She threw like a girl.

Though the tickets were free, only twelve thousand of the thirty-two thousand seats were filled. As everywhere else in wartime Washington, more women than men showed up. Still, while Feller's men romped, a date or two was arranged for Saturday night.

All four of the city's newspapers distributed tickets to the ballgame and publicized it, the *Times-Herald* most of all. Cissy Patterson's ten-edition-a-day newspaper commanded the grandest circulation in Washington, with its abundance of local news and chatty columns. The news pages showed a photograph of Gwen "'Pinch-Hitting' for the President," as the caption avowed, over a headline about the "Big Success." The sports section judged her "considerably more than extremely ornamental."

Gwen gloried in the publicity. She needed it, for the customary routes to social prominence were closed to her. She was a past president of her synagogue's sisterhood, and her uneducated husband gave lavishly to Jewish causes.

"Old Washington was very anti-Semitic," Gore Vidal, the novelist and a frequent guest of Gwen's, said later. "She was not, as they say, invited anywhere at the beginning."

"Oh, *her*," the cave dwellers would say.

Once, while lunching with a friend, she went over to chat with a table of society women, only to be snubbed.

"How can you do that?" her friend commiserated upon her return.

"It doesn't matter," Gwen replied, though it made her mad as hell.

In time, she would prove herself right.

When Gwen threw a glamorous party for the actress Gene Tierney, whose brother-in-law was a *Times-Herald* society columnist, the newspaper rhapsodized that in her black-and-white taffeta dress, "Mrs. Cafritz was like something from *Vogue*." The story spread that the matrons of society had balked at attending until Morris spoke up at a meeting of the Riggs Bank's directors. He said he hoped they had received their invitations and could attend. All of them did, their wives in tow.

———

Carol Andrews worked the swing shift at the War Department, at a long row of desks in one of the grimy gray cement-and-asbestos "tempos" along Constitution Avenue. Hot in the summer and cold in the winter, they were purposely ugly—this was the president's idea—so as not to last as long as the tempos that had been built during what was now distressingly denoted as World War I. World War II had doubled the government's civilian employment, and Carol's job, like most of them, was boring. She checked the name, rank, and serial number of soldiers killed, wounded, or missing in action against those in their War Department records. Then she stapled the matching documents together, located the name of the next of kin, and passed the paperwork along.

"My mama didn't send me to school four years for this," Carol complained. Then she learned that the civil service exam she had taken in Dallas, the only one available to Negroes, confined her to the lowest of clerical jobs.

"I quit," she told her supervisor.

"No, you can't quit," came the reply. "We paid your way here." Her train trip from Dallas had been an expensive one (Negroes slept in a pricey "roomette" because Pullman cars were only for whites) that she had to pay for unless she worked at least six months.

Still slender but no longer so gawky, she had an intelligent and kindly face, with a shy smile and yet a mind of her own. By sweeping her hair back off her forehead, she accentuated her serious demeanor. She was only twenty years old but seemed older. Carol was uncompromising about religion and matters of right and wrong; when she set a goal for herself, she would not be deterred.

She had moved back to D.C. during the war not to take a mindless job but to pursue a master's degree in sociology at Howard University. She had graduated from a black college near Houston, but because no university in Texas would grant a graduate degree to a Negro, the state subsidized its separate-but-equal policy by paying the difference between tuition in state and elsewhere, and paying for transportation.

"So for one year, I was making out like a bandit," Carol said.

She had resisted her mother's entreaties to try Howard as an undergraduate, out of fear that her skin was too dark. Howard University took itself ever so seriously, and perhaps had a right to. Founded by Congress just after the Civil War to educate freed slaves, and named for the white Civil War general Lincoln had appointed as the Freedmen's Bureau's founding commissioner, the university liked to describe itself as the capstone of black higher education. Its spacious campus of clean-lined, colonial-style buildings fostered its nickname as "the black Harvard." So did its quality. Howard attracted many of the nation's finest Negro scholars, whose alternatives were few, living in the dignified brick row houses in nearby LeDroit Park, a backbone of the city's black elite.

Howard's academic striving produced social pretensions, so that another student who was a Pullman porter's daughter said to Carol, "Do you have a fur coat?"

"No."

"You can't make it at Howard without a fur coat."

But she wanted to live near her brother, and at Howard there were inklings that the white-envy culture was changing. The fall Carol arrived, the students elected the first brown-skinned homecoming queen.

When school began, she arrived at the War Department at seven-thirty in the morning, worked six hours, then caught a streetcar out Seventh Street to the Howard campus. After classes she worked a second job, as a researcher for the famed Negro sociologist E. Franklin Frazier.

He had shocked her the first day in his class when he asked the students, "How many of you come from free issue?" She had never heard the term, but numerous hands shot up.

"How many of you here are related to Thomas Jefferson?"

A few redheads and two girls with greenish eyes raised their hands.

"Don't think you're so great because you could trace your white ancestors," the professor snapped. His expansive forehead and rimless glasses underscored his sternness. "That just means your mama or your grandma was raped."

Professor Frazier—he found "Doctor" too common—was a dark-

skinned, henpecked man whose wife's light-skinned family had protested their marriage. He had written an award-winning book that
traced the Negro family's woes to slavery and a decade hence published *Black Bourgeoisie*, blaming the status-driven behavior he had
seen at Howard on "a deep-seated inferiority complex" among light-
colored Negroes who had lost their cultural roots.

The greasy spots on his tie and the dandruff that speckled his
coat collar showed his scorn for the bourgeoisie. He berated Carol for
being "unsophisticated" and for bathing too regularly. ("Europeans
don't bathe every day," he told her. "It takes all the oils out of your
skin.") She helped to research his books, proofread his manuscripts,
bought his cigars, and took a streetcar to Anacostia to pick up lemon
pies for his wife's bridge club.

Not all of his students disliked him. Carol's best friend thought
that he demanded more from black students than from white ones
because he knew they needed to excel in order to succeed. A few
years later, when the American Sociological Society chose Professor
Frazier as its first colored president, he arrived on the freight elevator
to address the group at the Shoreham.

Of the nine old men on the Supreme Court who had so frustrated the
president that he wanted to appoint several more justices, eight had
died or resigned by the fall of 1943. Their youthful, intellectually vig-
orous successors—Frankfurter, Douglas, Black, the others—looked
down from the mahogany bench in the marble-pillared courtroom
upon twenty-nine-year-old Hale Boggs. To Hale's left, in the frieze
high on the wall, near the figure of Blackstone, Napoleon represented
the civil code that Louisiana had taken as its own.

This was perhaps too technical a case to goad the revivified
Court to passion. As the chief counsel for Louisiana's conservation
department, Hale was defending his commissioner's authority to
force a wildcatter to produce natural gas from his neighbor's holdings
as well as his own, in the interest of efficiency. Just three weeks later,
the Court ruled Hale's way.

But Hale had accomplished something even more practical on

the train ride north to Washington, when he was seated beside a retired admiral with a kindly countenance. Telfair Knight had been
pressed back into his nation's service, as the man in charge of training merchant marines at the new War Shipping Administration. The
two men talked and talked during the round-the-clock trip, and by
the time they pulled into Union Station, Hale knew what he wanted.

After his forced departure from Congress, he had looked for an
administrative, legal, or public relations job in the War Department
but had been unsuccessful. He had moved the family back to New
Orleans, renting out the tidy brick colonial they had purchased on
maple-lined Stephenson Place, a few blocks from the Maryland line.
Hale did not expect to stay in Louisiana long. Finally, a commission
in the Naval Reserve—New Orleans was a navy town—had come
through, because of Eddie Hebert's and a Louisiana senator's efforts.
While waiting he had been working for the commissioner of conservation and practicing law with Marion Epley Jr., a future Texaco
chairman. He was slated to leave for Patrol Torpedo (PT) school in
Rhode Island after Christmas, and Lindy was pregnant with their
third child, due in mid-December.

Why not return to Washington instead? Hale met with navy officials before going home to New Orleans and was told they would
probably honor a request from the War Shipping Administration for
his services. Hale wrote to Telfair Knight, the admiral turned bureaucrat, on his return: "I am extremely anxious to become associated with your organization." Within two weeks, the arrangements
were made.

When the navy ordered him to duty on December 1, his new patron allowed him to report in New Orleans, then in Washington, at
the start of 1944.

Every night, as the children recited their prayers, Lindy would
say, "And please, God, send us a healthy little baby."

"Girl," four-year-old Barbara would add. Then she would sock
Tommy. "Say 'girl.'"

"Girl."

Two days after Christmas in 1943, Barbara got her way. When
Tommy tried to pronounce "Corinne"—the baby's full name was

Mary Martha Corinne Morrison Claiborne Boggs—it came out "Cokie."

Hale set out by automobile on New Year's Eve, leaving Lindy behind with three tots and, she discovered, no checkbook. Hale had not intended to take it.

"It's a good thing the littlest one is so strong. She has a lot of competition," Lindy reported to Hale in one of her long, frequent handwritten letters. Barbara had a tummy, she said, and "Tom's as round as he is tall. They're wild as little bulls." Cokie refused Similac or anything other than Lindy, who was not able to sate her. She still had trouble from time to time with her left eye (there had even been a fear of losing its vision), and said she'd eaten herself out of her clothes. And money was tight. She diverted fifteen dollars of grocery money to pay the nurse and borrowed money from her family for food.

Lindy admitted that she was feeling lonely and low. "Am busier than the proverbial bee," she wrote to Hale, "and in just about as stinging a humor (horrors, did I say that?)."

Hale was staying with the Coulons, friends from back home who lived near Stephenson Place, while he settled in at the War Shipping Administration. Office space was tight all over the city, especially for an embryonic bureaucracy. Hale wound up on the seventh floor over the National Theatre, which faced Pennsylvania Avenue.

As the legal officer for the agency's Training Organization, Hale negotiated contracts involving millions of government dollars at bases all over the country and had his staff draw up the leases for coastal cabins and motels in which the sailors-in-training might stay. He had other undertakings to pursue. Telfair Knight was aware of Hale's insider knowledge of how laws were made and appropriations passed, and of the men crucial to both, and he had another job in mind for Hale—as a lobbyist, to "represent us on the Hill." For this Hale was released from active duty and joined the Maritime Service as a lieutenant (senior grade).

"At your rate of advancement," his brother wrote to him from the Philippines, "you should be admiral before too long."

The change in his military status opened the possibility of politicking again. Friends from home sent him news clippings that suggested he could run for public office. The *Times-Picayune* "practically announced" his candidacy for 1944, Lindy wrote, and she was urged to campaign in his stead.

"I will not leave my post of duty," he announced.

He acted as if he were still in Congress—or intended to be. He wrote flattering notes to the new Federal Communications Commission chairman, to the new federal prosecutor in New Orleans, to a retiring justice of the state's Supreme Court. He helped a fraternity brother who wanted a navy commission, a kinsman in need of an immediate passport, a once-and-future constituent who sought a physical waiver to attend purser's school.

The most poignant request, in the summer of 1944, was from Hale's patrician-looking, floundering father. William Robertson Boggs had moved away from banks and into the Office of Price Administration—undoubtedly with Hale's help—as a supervisor of rent inspectors around New Orleans. But the rent controls might "peter out in 6 months," he wrote to his son, and besides, he wanted "a better job." He was interested in the Reconstruction Finance Corporation—"so I was wondering if you know any of the higher-ups in the R.F.C. that you could speak to about getting me in."

It was a family in which the true father was the son.

Lindy and the children had moved back to Washington, to the brick colonial on Stephenson Place. Late one afternoon the following spring, she rushed onto the bus with her ration books and the five children it was her turn to watch, hoping to reach the Safeway on Connecticut Avenue before the red meat was gone.

She was waiting for her number to be called when she heard the news. It was unimaginable—a strut had been kicked out of place.

The president was dead.

"Oh my Lord," Lindy wailed. "What are they going to do?"

"Don't cry, Lindy," one of the five-year-olds assured her. "We'll get another president."

Three

TRUMAN

To earn her fellowship at Howard, Carol Andrews supervised the social science laboratory on the second floor of Frederick Douglass Memorial Hall, at the farthest end. The spring that Jackie Robinson broke the color line in baseball, students gathered in Carol's office and listened to games on the radio.

One day, Carol looked out into the drab-tiled corridor and pointed to a dark, tightly muscled man who was conversing with someone she had known in college.

"Do you see that man standing there?" she asked a friend.

"Yeah."

"I'm going to go out and get a drink of water, and he's going to ask the fellow he's talking to to introduce him to me, and we're going to get married."

He was neither tall nor husky, and his features were unremarkable. But his mahogany skin had a luster, and he carried himself with pride. "Excellent carriage," thought Carol. He wore a dark olive-green slipover jersey, and she admired his smooth, clean-shaven complexion. "He was the most handsome thing I'd ever seen."

Carol went into the hall and leaned over the water fountain. Then the bell rang and both young men rushed off to class.

Later, Carol ventured into the stairwell and found him looking for her.

His name was Julius Hobson. He asked her what she did in the lab.

Help students with their research, she replied.

"I have a paper to write," he said, "because I'm working on a master's. You're supposed to help me." His Alabama twang betrayed an intensity.

He asked whether he could go by her home sometime, except that he worked every day but Wednesday. He told her he repaired radios, though he was packing groceries at the Giant.

"Well, today is Wednesday," Carol said.

They arranged to get together that evening. When she learned she needed to babysit for her nephew, he tagged along.

Julius Hobson had started at Howard the previous fall on the G.I. Bill. After the war he had finished his undergraduate degree in electrical engineering at Tuskegee Institute, but he had no wish to return to segregated Birmingham, his hometown. Even with a college education, a colored man in Birmingham had a choice of three careers— in the steel mills, the post office, or the classroom. Julius was too bright and ambitious to feed a furnace or to carry the mail, too impatient to teach, and too angry to stay in his place.

Later he would say that he had been born angry, and perhaps quite literally that was true. Julius eventually told his daughter that his mother, Irma, was pregnant with twins, and when her labor went awry in the spring of 1919 the closest hospital refused her admittance. The ambulance drove on, and by the time a hospital was willing, only he survived. Irma was never quite right after that.

He was given his father's and his grandfather's name, but his father vanished when Julius was an infant. His mother raised him with his cousins in the spic-and-span frame house that *her* mother, the daughter of a slave, ruled with a firm yet benevolent hand. He addressed his grandmother as "Mamma" and his mother as "Irma."

Julius was a solemn little boy with an oversized head who always looked mature beyond his years. In high school he went to parties but would leave early and stayed away from drink. (Mamma forbade it, along with tobacco and coffee.) Julius would sit on the deep front porch with a thick book and read. His mother, a thrice-a-week churchgoer, was a teacher and then a grammar school principal who had given him a taste for poetry. Though he had a job sweeping out the library he was not allowed to borrow books, and so one day he dropped a thirty-nine-hundred page anthology of poetry out the back window and took it home; he kept *The Home Book of Verse of the English-Speaking World* at hand all of his life. He could recite Kipling's "Gunga Din" almost by heart and liked the Victorian poets—Byron, Keats, Shelley, Wordsworth—best.

In high school he grew interested in politics and society and began to think in radical ways. "He questioned everything, and then questioned the answers," a cousin who lived with him said. "He knew that things weren't always what they appeared."

The routine cruelties of Birmingham could not be concealed. "Your everyday living," his cousin recalled, was "knowing what your place was." Some downtown stores served only whites; in others, white customers rode on segregated elevators and were served first. His mother was called by her first name at the local school board. Once, while his uncle was changing a tire on his boss's car in front of the house, policemen stopped and questioned whether it was stolen; when he was slow to stand up straight enough, he was beaten and taken to the station. Another time, a white salesman in a corner store was describing his Florida vacation when he pointed at young Julius and said, "I got almost as black as that little nigger there." Julius never forgot the humiliation.

"Scratch any black," he said later, "and you'll find a hurt child."

When he was called "nigger" in 1941, as an electrician at the Birmingham Paper Company, he punched his coworker and was fired. He enlisted in the army the following spring.

Julius had wanted to join the Tuskegee Airmen but was not accepted and was also rejected by Officer Candidate School. "Why have I failed so often?" he wrote to his mother. "I don't run around with bad women, I don't drink and gamble nor do I get loud & foolish, but still I fail. What is the secret of success? Some say, 'failure is not so bad, it's low aim that counts against a person.' Well I aim high every time. . . . I won't quit mother, dear, ever. I will make you happy & proud."

He was sent to Italy as an artillery spotter, on thirty-five missions aboard a Piper Cub, and was awarded two Bronze Stars. In his off-hours, he passed up the taverns for the opera, and he made sure to visit Florence and Rome. On the way home he stopped at Flanders Field, the Belgian battlefield, to witness "the crosses, row on row," immortalized by a poet of the previous world war.

Later he said he despised the army. He was a staff sergeant in the segregated Black Buffaloes, but the army was his first experience with integration. Sharing bathrooms with white men, he learned how much easier it was for them to shave. (He had his mother ship him boxes of "Magic Shaving Powder," full strength, to deter hairs from curling under his skin.) He was astonished that the same blood and plasma was used for everyone, yet he watched white soldiers refuse to help blacks on a military mission, and the reverse.

When he returned home, dealing with Jim Crow was even harder than it had been before the war. Torrents of black southern soldiers traveled north. Julius wrote to Oberlin College, in Ohio, in the hope of pursuing graduate work, and was told that his prospects were "very meager indeed." After finishing his last credits at Tuskegee, in the spring of 1946, he fled the South. "I hated whites, I hated myself," he said later. "I was ashamed to comb my hair in front of whites."

He took a train to New York—"the promised land, where everybody was getting rich and so forth." He lived in Harlem and worked in a plastics factory in Brooklyn. He told Carol he had enrolled at Columbia, though the university kept no record of this.

He moved to Washington and found a place to study economics at Howard.

That night he walked Carol home the two blocks from her brother's apartment on Girard, past the shuttered shops along Georgia Avenue, formerly Seventh Street extended, then west along Gresham, past the painfully plain-faced duplexes with patches of yard.

As they walked side by side, Julius proposed marriage.

Carol was expecting this, and she accepted. "It just seemed like something that was supposed to be," she said later.

Her brother told her the next morning, "Well, you've brought me a man."

Several months after the war came to a close, the directors of Riggs Bank gathered for their regular meeting in the vault of a building across from the Treasury Department on Pennsylvania Avenue just west of Fifteenth Street. The mahogany-and-leather boardroom of the city's wealthiest bank looked like everything a real bank should be. Morris Cafritz had been a director for five years now, as a reward for all the business he had transacted with Riggs—and as a reason to do more.

"Mother piggy bank," Gwen called Riggs.

Morris was called out of the meeting, causing the bank's intimidating chairman, Robert V. Fleming, to stare over his pince-nez at what he considered a sacrilege. An absent director had telephoned Morris with an urgent message. Charlie Tompkins was a onetime choirboy and then a concrete contractor and now a slab-faced developer who had drawn Morris into Riggs. Over the years they had done many deals together, as two gentlemen, Episcopalian and Jew, and they had never had a beef with each other.

Tompkins was interrupting the meeting to say that if they could raise one million dollars within an hour—this was the emergency— the Temple Heights property was theirs.

The Masonic Grand Lodge had bought the ten-acre wooded hillside along Connecticut Avenue, just north of Florida Avenue, in 1922 for a huge temple that was never built. On it stood the Treaty Oak, where (legend had it) local Indians had come to terms with the earliest settlers over what would become the capital. Morris had first tried to buy it nineteen years before. In 1940, Frank Lloyd Wright had designed a series of buildings for the site, which would have been the most grandiose project in the modernist architect's career, an aggregation of glassy high-rises—apartments, hotels, a movie house—and a thin, tapering tower. It was to be called Crystal Heights—or as the newspapers dubbed it, Crystal City. War and neighborhood opposition had quashed it.

Today, once again, the site was for sale.

Within an hour Morris Cafritz and Charlie Tompkins presented a check, and within two hours, the deal was closed.

Commercial development had not ventured north of Dupont Circle before—zoning did not allow any north of Florida. Yet Morris saw promise in Connecticut Avenue. It had already been widened several times, and the growing traffic and the grinding of gears were wearing away its residential flavor.

The collaborating developers proposed a further audacious erosion: "I would like to see another Radio City on that site," Morris announced. "We all know how badly Washington is in need of something like that." They proposed building several legitimate theaters and an opera house, along with an office building, a hotel, and a garage, on what Morris described as the last undeveloped parcel of such size within easy reach of downtown.

"It took a sense of adventure and real faith in the city," his son Calvin said later.

Calvin was fourteen years old when his father drove him out to the site one sunny morning. From Connecticut Avenue, they turned onto a dirt road up into the woods. At the top of the knoll they got out. Morris asked Calvin what he saw.

"Well, I can see the Potomac River," Calvin said, "and I can see the Anacostia." Through the trees, the sunlight shined off the water.

"That's what the Indians saw. This used to be their campsite. In the morning they would check to see where the herds of animals were feeding and drinking along the river, and the hunting parties would go down and they would select their targets and ride down the hill toward the water."

Morris took one or another of his sons to work from time to time, sandwiched in the backseat between men smoking cigars. At fifty-eight he was too old—more a grandfather than a father, with sons six, eight, and fourteen years old—and yet threw too hard to engage them in sports. But he was fun-loving with Calvin, and they often took the Great Dane out for walks in Glover Archbold Park in the mornings before Morris went to work. His youngest son, Conrad, sat with him in the mornings over breakfast and the newspaper. Every September he took all three boys to Atlantic City to watch the Miss America pageant.

He was a good father, at least when he was around. In the evening he and Gwen went to a cocktail party or two and to dinner. Afterward, he dropped her off and, still in his tuxedo, stopped by the Ambassador Hotel to chat with the employees and examine the bookings for the following day. The Hi-Hat Cocktail Lounge would be in full swing, a place for lonesome men to find an evening mate.

At home, Gwen adhered to a wealthy European's notion of rearing children. "She had sort of an affection toward us," Carter, the middle son, said later, "but no real contact with us." Servants took the responsibility for raising them, mainly a nurse, an English disciplinarian who believed that children need fresh air daily regardless of weather. (There were also a cook, two maids, a laundress, a butler, and a chauffeur.) The boys ordinarily ate dinner in the kitchen, only occasionally with their parents. The philosophy was that they were to be seen but not heard.

"It was not the kind of household where kids sit at dinner for an hour and talk about their day," Calvin said. "Nobody did that with us."

Gwen slept late in the mornings and played favorites. "My best child . . . the smartest one," Gwen said publicly of nine-year-old Conrad after a judge added him to the family trust. His older brothers did not let him think he was the best when they stuffed him into a chest of drawers.

"She damaged all of them," said one of Conrad's future ex-wives. "She wasn't very affectionate, she wasn't approving—she was jealous of them."

Gwen also kept Morris's family at a distance. She invited his relatives over only once a year, in July, and she kept the boys away from the Passover seder at Nussen's. At his family's functions, Morris typically showed up alone. The boys remembered meeting their paternal grandfather only once or twice before he died in 1942. The younger ones attended Sunday school at Washington Hebrew, though they were confused about why, and none of them had a bar mitzvah.

As he was with his workmen and with himself, Morris was demanding with his sons. He thought Calvin would benefit from riding his bicycle to school and back, with hills both ways. Saint Albans School for Boys, the city's toniest prep school, was the stone Gothic embodiment of the capital's Protestant elite. It stood next to the Washington National Cathedral, the Episcopal high church, at one of the city's highest points, where Wisconsin crossed Massachusetts. It was a hard enough place to attend for the son of a nouveau riche Jewish family whose mother liked her name in the newspapers, and arriving by bicycle instead of by a grander transport made it no easier. Once, a taxi collided with his bicycle outside Alban Towers, an apartment house near the school.

Calvin flipped over the handlebars, into the front fender of the cab, "but the important thing was," he said, "the bicycle wasn't hurt and I made it to school on time."

Morris made it clear he wanted his sons to pursue careers in real estate, and it never occurred to them not to. Calvin started working summers at age fifteen, first as an office boy, then as a timekeeper at a construction site, then as manager of a parking lot at 1625 I Street. While he was in college, at Washington and Lee, he worked summers in construction and in the purchasing department. "Dad wanted me to have a variety of experience," he said later, "and had me do anything and everything." Carter hung doors, kept time, checked materials, and in his early twenties was given a project of his own, a tiny warehouse that was built in three weeks. Then he built some houses and offices on his own, and some with Conrad.

Morris and Charlie Tompkins were the first D.C. developers to require timekeeping; even their office workers had to punch in and out for lunch. Morris wanted everyone to work as hard as he did, but he asked no more of others than he asked of himself. He was skilled at picking people and treated the best of them like dukes. He helped his brilliant stuttering engineer, Gus Ring, put up buildings of his own, including the Westchester apartments. A shrewd and careful businessman, Morris kept the only key to the liquor cabinet at the Ambassador Hotel and forbade his engineers and estimators to let a contractor pay for their lunch. He was well organized, could handle big crews, and was among the first in the city to understand the impact of taxes on his business.

He took out a blind help-wanted ad in *The Washington Post* headlined "Tax Man," and hired a tax economist eager to leave the Treasury Department. Martin Atlas was an easygoing but thoughtful lawyer who had taken the lead before the war in designing the pay-as-you-go system of withholding federal taxes from paychecks. He believed that Morris's desire to structure his business to avoid confiscatory taxes had the virtue of honesty; he prompted Morris to create a separate corporation to own each project, with a holding company over all.

Morris had begun building houses again, once materials became available after the war. He put up 221 garden apartments for white working families in the most distant tip of Anacostia. But the rising prices in D.C. plus the continuation of the city's wartime rent controls prompted Morris to think beyond its borders. One morning in 1946, a land broker took him to see several properties in northern Virginia. The last one, nearly two hundred acres of brickyards, stood opposite the Pentagon. Morris was unimpressed until he drove back into town—in only five minutes—to Fourteenth and Pennsylvania.

He phoned Charlie Tompkins and they summoned up $1.5 million, one of the richest land transactions near downtown Washington in years.

At about the same time, Eugene Meyer, who had bested Cissy Patterson in purchasing the *Post* from Evalyn Walsh McLean's husband, sold Morris a plot of land at 1625 I Street, a block south of K Street. (The city's grid lacked a J Street because, in L'Enfant's day, J was considered a consonant version of *I*.) I Street was lined with three- and four-story brick town houses with bay windows and peaked pediments. At the corner of Sixteenth and I, two blocks north of the White House, stood the Motion Picture Association of America's many-gabled, ivy-walled mansion.

Morris had something other than housing in mind. The city had never seen such a boom in office buildings. The rents on office space, unlike on housing, were controlled only by supply and demand. And demand was rising, from trade associations, corporations, labor unions, law firms, and insurance companies that needed representation in Washington. Most of the city's office buildings lined Fourteenth Street and the numbered streets toward the east. Morris gambled that, soon, these would not be enough.

On the northern side of I Street, midway between Sixteenth and Seventeenth, Morris struggled with his deep, oddly shaped lot. For an ordinary office building, that would mean an awkwardly long distance from the lobby to the offices at the rear and internal courtyards that consumed too much space. His architect, LeRoy Werner, suggested an imaginative solution—building a garage up through the center of the ten-story building, with the offices arranged around it, along the outside walls. A spiraling, two-way ramp a half-mile long could deliver more than four hundred cars to twenty-seven levels of parking, so that employees might park near their desk. Morris called it a "Park at Your Desk" building. That, and something else: the Cafritz Building.

He broke ground in the spring of 1949, without having any tenants signed. Within weeks, union carpenters went out on strike against the Master Builders Association, and after twenty-two days Morris and three other builders agreed to a raise of ten cents an hour. By the next summer, the real estate editor of *The Evening Star* heard passengers on a city bus gasp about a building with a highway winding through it. When he arrived with a photographer, they found Morris in a natty blue suit and black-and-white shoes. He offered to drive them to the top.

"As we took the curves," the daunted journalist wrote, "we began to wonder whether Mr. Cafritz ever had been a daredevil driver at a county fair."

Before the building opened, the Korean War had broken out, and military suppliers became desperate for space in Washington. General Motors moved offices into 1625 I Street, along with Hughes Aircraft, Bell Aircraft, Bechtel, Western Electric, *Time* magazine, and the Republican National Committee. The Cafritz Building filled up so fast that Morris kept his own office at the Ambassador Hotel, on K Street. "I can't afford the rent," he said.

Hale Boggs had passed up politics in 1944, but by the spring of 1945 an elaborate rumor spread that a three-cornered deal had been struck. Hale would resign his navy commission after the war and temporarily become the postmaster in New Orleans. Then Paul Maloney, the congressman, would be named as the city's port tax collector, the incumbent collector would become the postmaster, and Hale would succeed Maloney in Washington.

Two days after Japan surrendered, Hale asked to be released from the War Shipping Administration. Telfair Knight thought it over and refused, because of Hale's knowledge of the contracts that now needed to be undone. It was early 1946 before Hale returned to New Orleans and helped to elect Chep Morrison, Lindy's cousin, as a reform mayor.

Soon Paul Maloney announced his retirement, and Chep Morrison, who was building a political machine of his own, anointed Hale as the reform candidate for his old seat in Congress. The Old Regulars put forward a colorless ex-prosecutor, who accused Hale of having spent the war as "a swivel-chaired officer who was in command of a complement of stenographers." Hale defended himself on the stump by reading a telegram from the head of the War Shipping Administration that recited Hale's "meritorious" navy promotions, to the rank of commander. Hale behaved as if *he* were the incumbent, and he won in a waltz—"another milestone," he proclaimed, "in the march of Louisiana toward the perpetuation of good government."

Hale missed his swearing in because Lindy had given birth to a baby boy in New Orleans. William Robertson Boggs cried lustily at first but within hours the doctors noticed that he was retaining fluid in his lungs. Two days later the baby was dead.

Lindy, too, was fighting for her life. "I had a very, very difficult delivery," she recalled, "and nearly died myself." Hale had to bury their fourth and last child without her.

In the evening, Julius Hobson tiptoed into his infant son's room and lifted him out of his crib, even as he slept. Julius carried Hobby, as they called him, into the living room, rested him in Carol's arms, turned out all the lights except one lamp, switched on the radio, and listened to Sam Spade.

"That's my family," he said.

He did this again and again, and those were the only times, Carol said later, that she ever saw him truly content.

Julius had always wanted a son, and he named him Julius W. Hobson Jr.—actually, Julius W. Hobson IV, though the boy would be a high school senior before he learned this. Having hardly known his own father, Julius harbored what Carol thought of as romantic notions of fatherhood—"what I would call a *Ladies' Home Journal* idea of what a father's supposed to do. He's supposed to make the money and take care of the house, direct everything."

Who could doubt his devotion as a father and husband? "Nobody loves you like I do," he said repeatedly to Carol. "You say your mother loves you. You say your sisters and brothers love you. Nobody loves you like I do." At home he ran the vacuum cleaner until everything was spic and span—Sergeant Hobson, she called him—and he insisted on breaking the bars of Ivory Soap in half. Every morning he ironed the creases out of his shirt. Very gradually, he discouraged Carol from having friends of her own. If someone telephoned, he would say, "Well, Carol's busy—don't you have a family of your own? Don't you have a child to look after?" If she talked on the phone he would pick up the extension and say, "You're not through yet?"

He began buying some of her clothes, showing exquisite taste that was more expensive than they could afford. After a while he was laying out her clothes while she showered, including a girdle if he thought she should wear one. He would not let her wear low-heeled shoes, even at home. When she cut her hair, he stopped speaking to her.

They moved to Mayfair Mansions, a collection of low-slung apartments deep in Northeast. Their apartment was across the walkway from Carol's brother.

"I saw your lights go out last night," Richard sometimes teased Carol. "What are you-all going to do, sleep your life away?" He volunteered to babysit with Hobby so they could attend a formal dance.

"Did you have a good time?" Richard asked when they arrived for Hobby.

"Yes," they replied.

"How many different men did you dance with?" he asked Carol.

"Nobody but Julius." Everytime another man had come near, Julius danced her away.

"You could have saved all that money and stayed home," Richard said.

Julius retorted, "I don't want a man putting his arm around my wife."

For the most part, Carol acted as her husband wished, as well-raised women knew to do. "He had all these deep insecurities, where he had to hold everybody real close," she explained years later. Over time her marriage began to feel more and more like a prison.

His temper had already ended his academic career. Julius had started graduate school at Howard on academic probation because he had taken so few economics courses at Tuskegee, but soon he was earning mainly Bs. He took the standard courses in finance, comparative economics, statistics, and the like, but economic theory became his passion. Veblen's *The Theory of the Leisure Class* was one of his favorite books, with its critique of capitalism and the cult of "conspicuous consumption." Julius found a mentor in a visiting professor from New York University, Otto Nathan, a German-born Jew who was an avowed Marxist. He provided Julius with a form and a context to what he already believed, that it was the cruelties of capitalism as well as the racial underpinnings of the political system— the system more than the individuals in it—that were responsible for society's woes.

"I was interested in why I acted like I acted," he reflected later. "Did I hate whites because they were white? It had to be more than just looking at some guy and hating him. What the hell is the reasoning behind it? And I found that social science, economics, political science, history, psychology, and sociology led me to conclusions about the whole thing which were very interesting."

Soon Julius considered himself a Marxist too.

His adviser, Dr. Edward Lewis, preferred drearier academic concerns. He was a brilliant economist, with three degrees from Columbia, who was working on a path-breaking book on a fresh subject—methods of statistical analysis. This was all the more impressive because he suffered from a motor disease that caused him to limp and drool; saliva ran down his chin; chalk flew out of his hand. Yet he was a wonderful lecturer, and as many professors at Howard did, he involved himself in his students' personal lives. When Carol had become engaged, Franklin Frazier stormed, "I'm telling you right now, don't become a little m-a—a mama—before you get your big M.A." After Hobby was born, in June 1948, Dr. Lewis said to Julius: "I can see that you're starting a family. Graduate school is very serious work, and I just think you need to drop out."

Julius exploded.

He was not at Howard to win friends and influence people, Julius shouted at the crippled professor, but to get an education, and as a white man Dr. Lewis had no business giving him advice. Julius accused him of wanting everyone to think that an interest in black people had attracted him to Howard. But he was really there because, with his medical condition—Julius had a merciless tongue—no comparable white institution would hire him.

Dr. Lewis never forgave him. The university barred Julius from taking courses and later expelled him. Carol and others pleaded with Dr. Lewis to relent. Carol never heard Julius apologize for anything. This time, it probably would not have sufficed.

"Some things aren't forgivable," Dr. Lewis told Carol.

Julius, with a family to support, applied for a job at the Library of Congress, in its Legislative Reference Service. Congress, now in Republican hands, wanted to pull back some of the legislative initiative—the power—that Franklin Roosevelt had seized, in part by bolstering its own sources of information. The Legislative Reference Service had only two black professionals who were doing analysis; to hire more of them it turned toward Howard, for a pool of researchers who had few other options.

Ordinarily a master's degree was required. But Julius was hired as a GS-5, a junior professional, at a salary of thirty-one hundred dollars—"an accomplishment for a black man at that time," he boasted later. Most of the researchers rated a GS-9 or higher.

Each of the service's seven divisions—Julius's was economics—occupied its own stretch of high-ceilinged space on the first floor of the imposing Library of Congress, behind the Capitol. Vast unshaded windows provided natural light for a building that dated from the dawn of the electrical age. The researchers sat at metal desks, lined up two by two, similar to an unending schoolroom. A linoleum aisle down the center was wide enough for library carts to roll by. Julius's desk stood by the aisle, on the Independence Avenue side.

The work was relentless. Congress submitted twenty-three thousand inquiries a year, and Julius drafted reports and speeches on myriad topics—rent controls and the fluoridation of water, seizure of the nation's coal mines and injection of female hormones into chickens to make them plump. (He would not eat chicken for years.) He learned the essence of a researcher's work—to assemble facts, in a meticulous and detached manner, and to conduct analyses of volatile subjects that a lawmaker of any philosophy might accept. This would be useful to him later on.

Julius was quiet and kept to himself; he did not speak until spoken to. His colleagues found him pleasant to work with. Often he ate lunch with them at a Japanese restaurant on Pennsylvania Avenue. The white researchers felt sure that the different races got along; the Negroes did not.

Julius quickly received a promotion to GS-7. But when he pressed for another, to GS-9, his superiors judged his work deficient, because of errors in grammar, spelling, and statistical tables. When two other Negroes were denied promotions, Julius saw discrimination. Other researchers had better assignments, he believed, because they were white.

"His feelings were very easily hurt," Carol explained years later. "He could sense, within the smallest way you could measure, if you were belittling him. And if he felt that, he could strike out. He could smell prejudice around the corner."

Only thirty-two hours had elapsed since Perle Mesta had been sworn in as America's minister plenipotentiary to Luxembourg, in the summer of 1949, and Gwen Cafritz was making her move. That was the way the gossip sheets played her latest, splashiest party—"Gwendolyn Cafritz Makes Her Bid," was the headline in *Life*'s five-page photo spread—and they were usually right about matters like this. In Washington, parties of such potency rarely happened by accident.

The cave dwellers regarded both hostesses as vulgar upstarts—too wealthy too recently, and too obvious about it. In a city such as Washington, however, they had a chance. With the continual infusion of socially connected people from the nation's political tides, two or three generations' residence made a family an antique. This created a society without a traditional hierarchy, so that almost anyone who had money and ambition and even a pretense of breeding could rise.

Perle Mesta was a rather homely middle-aged woman who neither smoked nor drank, an oilman's daughter and a Pittsburgh industrialist's widow who had changed the spelling of her name (from *Pearl*) after her husband died. She was exuberantly American—plainspoken and amiable, deft at making people enjoy themselves. Her parties relied on unadventurous food, plenty of liquor, and dependable fun. It was no wonder that Harry Truman, the midwestern president, the onetime haberdasher, liked her so much. Over the years she had entertained four vice presidents, and now the fourth one had moved into the White House. She had raised money for his come-from-behind victory in 1948, and within a short period she had the president, the chief justice, and the entire Cabinet to dinner, all at once.

She had *so* arrived, in fact, that she was leaving. The president wanted a woman to serve as Washington's first envoy to a grand duchy too minor to matter, and Perle thought it over and accepted. (In a year she would be the subject of a Broadway musical, *Call Me Madam*, starring a friend of Perle's, brassy Ethel Merman, as the "hostess-with-the-mostes'" who became the ambassador to Lichtenburg.) No ambassador had ever had such a glamorous swearing in. Alben Barkley, the folksy vice president, attended, in an uncharacteristically sober necktie and a dark blue suit, along with Dean Acheson, the starchy secretary of state, and more than two hundred others. A "party-for-the-party-giver," as the *Post*'s society writer called it, followed at the Mayflower.

If a hostess from the heartland had seen the charms of the man from Missouri, a woman of European demeanor and sophisticated tastes had, understandably, cold-shouldered him. "Sometimes I think he deliberately set out to deceive me," she said. "I used to see him at parties when he was in the Senate and he was dull, dull. So naturally I never invited him or Mrs. Truman to my parties because I was sure they wouldn't be interesting guests. Who would have thought he'd ever get to be president?"

That had given Perle Mesta the edge. Her rivalry with Gwen supposedly dated back at least to the president's inaugural ball, early in the year. Perle was cochair, and when Gwen requested some tickets for friends, Perle said she had none to give. The feud fed on itself.

After Perle had moved to Foxhall Road, Gwen telephoned and said, "Now that you're a neighbor, I suppose I'll be seeing more of you."

"I suppose not," Perle was said to have replied.

The bad feelings would have emerged anyway, given what was at stake. It was an article of faith that the capital had room for only one top hostess at a time, and now that Evalyn Walsh McLean was dead (and Cissy Patterson too) preeminence was up for grabs. The cave dwellers had their own, understated aspirants. Yet attention fell on the rivals who never hesitated to take reporters' telephone calls: the hausfrau from the heartland, her manner warm and direct, versus the exotic Hungarian with a glamour from between the world wars and an air of mystery that made a bystander want to know more.

Gwen was coy, of course. Her big party was for her twentieth wedding anniversary, just two days away. "My real ambition is to be a member of the board of the National Gallery of Art," she announced—"not that I know if a woman could attain that."

The invitations were engraved: *Gwendolyn and Morris Cafritz Cordially Invite You for Mint Juleps, Steak (Charcoal Grilled), Dancing.* The evening was a glorious one for July in Washington, cloudless and not terribly sticky; the summer air had lost its feel of wet crinoline freshly ironed. As the darkness gathered, the soft blue lights by the edge of the terrace offered a glow beneath the disk of the moon, and the candles fluttered in the hurricane lamps on the tables across the rolling lawn. Even when the city was breathless, there was always a hint of a breeze behind the Cafritz mansion.

The Alger Hiss jury was still out deliberating, giving the 120 guests something to buzz about, a topic for heartfelt speculation without the discomfort of hard facts to hem anyone in. The men wore white dinner jackets and the women their chic gowns. Everyone stood around the outdoor fireplace, by the rough stone chimney, and waited patiently for the Delmonico steaks. The crowd included denizens of both political parties, or neither. General Eisenhower showed up with Mamie—nobody knew *what* he was, currently the president of Columbia University after he had spurned the pleas of leading Democrats in 1948 to run in the unpopular president's place. The Omar Bradleys had arrived, and also Robert Jackson, the stout Supreme Court justice and former prosecutor at Nuremberg; no longer did the men in black robes feel the need to keep socially aloof.

Drew Pearson, the king of the city's syndicated columnists, who had briefly been Cissy Patterson's son-in-law and then her enemy, chatted on the lawn with a mint julep in his hand. Gwen had invited a slew of ambassadors, to use her languages (French, German, and Italian, besides Hungarian and English, plus a little Latin and, recently, some Spanish). The Cabinet was well represented, and the president's counsel, Clark Clifford, was there, along with several senators, a few of whom had earned their air of self-importance—Lister Hill of Alabama, and possibly Estes Kefauver of Tennessee or Claude Pepper of Florida, and surely balding, bespectacled, ordinarily standoffish Robert Taft of Ohio, Mr. Conservative, the son of a president and possibly a president himself someday. Gwen skimped, however, on the House of Representatives. "I always invite senators to my parties," she explained, "but I seldom play around with the lower House."

Taft was her greatest catch until Vice President Barkley had invited himself, that afternoon. The seventy-one-year-old widower spent most of the evening wooing a thirty-eight-year-old widow, a houseguest of the Cliffords he had met the night before while gliding along the Potomac in the president's yacht. (Inside of four months, they would return to this house for a reception honoring their marriage.) This explained his exceptionally high spirits, as Gwen seated herself at a table between the smitten vice president and Senator

Taft. When a strolling guitarist stopped by, the populist and the blue-blood, Democrat and Republican, the pudgy Kentuckian and the intellectual with a walnut-shaped face, harmonized on "The Good Old Summertime." The vice president downed mint juleps and shouted, "Skoal!"

Gwen, making her peace with the administration, looked both radiant and demure. At the last minute she had changed from a yellow taffeta dress into a gown of white chiffon, brocaded in purple and silver. Morris's anniversary gift had arrived. He enjoyed Gwen's parties and encouraged them—invitations to local officials helped him with rezoning—but he stayed in the background. In May he had secretly attended an estate auction for Mrs. George Drexel, the late queen of Philadelphia society, and purchased seventy-eight thousand dollars' worth of necklaces, bracelets, and brooches rich with diamonds, emeralds, and pearls. He had intended to give them to Gwen one at a time, for birthdays and Christmas, but a Philadelphia reporter got wind of the sale and telephoned Gwen. Morris gave her everything that evening. The thirty-eight-thousand-dollar necklace with forty-six graduated diamonds set in platinum was breathtaking against her ivory skin. She may have felt self-conscious in her plunging neckline, for she kept adjusting the shoulders of her gown.

More than her necklace sparkled as she circulated among her guests on her triumphal evening, from the tiled swimming pool across the manicured lawn and up to the terrace. The pastel flowers on the tables cast off a sweet perfume.

"The moon has a special polish on it tonight," remarked Julius Krug, the interior secretary.

The vice president chattered so long with his beloved that protocol delayed everyone else from sitting down to eat. It was long after dark before all the guests had been served. Champagne and wine, or ice-cold beer for the gentlemen who preferred it, eased the wait. After dinner was the dancing, out on the terrace and also on the translucent floor in the ballroom. The dancing continued into dawn.

The party was a magnificent, and conspicuous, success. Still, it was whispered, July was a time when the rival hostesses were away and many of the men were summer bachelors. The cave dwellers wondered whether Gwen's acceptances of summer would occur again in the fall.

Cokie Boggs peered through the forest of knees to the front of the House chamber, which buzzed with conversation and half-sincere pleasantries. She had just turned five years old and wore a dress of Christmas velvet, with her Mary Janes and white stockings and gloves. After two years of pushing for flood insurance, protecting the sugar industry, and issuing high-minded calls for a United States of Europe, Hale had rolled to reelection. The three Boggs children stood near their father on this January noon in 1949 as 435 right hands hovered in the air and Hale was sworn into the Eighty-first Congress.

This was Cokie's first swearing in. She listened as the clerk called the roll and the members responded: *Mr. Rayburn, Mr. Rayburn, Mr. Martin, Mr. Rayburn, Mr. Martin, Mr. Rayburn.* She asked her daddy why so many members shared the same name. He leaned down and explained about the election of a Speaker.

The Boggs children soon grew accustomed to life around the Capitol. When the president declared the foreign policy doctrine that would bear his name, in a speech to a joint session of Congress, seven-year-old Barbara watched from the House floor. Whenever the president delivered his State of the Union address, the children sat in the family gallery. And sometimes they were taken out of school to watch important congressional debates. They often ate lunch or dinner at the Capitol, and Cokie spent many an hour riding back and forth by subway, in the old-fashioned open car with wicker benches, between the Capitol and the Senate office building.

On the morning of her seventh birthday, Cokie woke up excited, because now she could sit in the public gallery and, even better, lead tours around the Capitol on her own. Her birthday party that year— ice cream, cake, children in hats—took place in the Speaker's Dining Room, a lovely little room with a marble fireplace and elaborate chandeliers.

Hale Boggs took his children very seriously. At the dinner table, when the conversation turned to politics and arguments, everyone's opinion was considered valid. Once, after Hale and Lindy had gone to the White House the evening before, five-year-old Cokie asked as they sat down, "Daddy, what's a tuxedo?" The conversation meandered before Hale could answer, and Cokie raised her hand until her father said, "Yes, Corinne?"

"Getting back to the tuxedo . . ."

That, Lindy liked to say later, was when she realized what line of work Cokie would pursue.

The children piped up even when "the pooh-bahs," as Cokie later called them, arrived to dine. Hale and especially Lindy understood, as any southerner would, that the socializing and the informalities of Washington could be useful in making their way. More than that, they enjoyed it. With little or no notice, Hale often took home four or five people, fellow congressmen or conversationalists, at the end of the day. Lindy learned to keep capers, caviar, olives, canned artichoke hearts, and Louisiana spices on hand, to fancy up a meal. Eddie Hebert and the other Louisianans frequently stopped by, and Jamie Whitten of Mississippi, an up-and-comer on the House Appropriations Committee, lived with his wife around the corner from the Boggses.

Hale and Lindy also saw quite a lot of the Gores (their daughter, Nancy, was about Barbara's age, and Al Jr. was four years younger than Cokie) and drew closer to Lyndon and Lady Bird Johnson. Hale and Lyndon, both protégés of Sam Rayburn, struggled to balance their southern constituencies with their national ambitions. Lady Bird said later that she spent "some of my best times" at the Boggses'. Cokie and the Johnsons' older daughter, Lynda Bird, who were three months apart in age, took dancing classes together at the Congressional Club, an organization of spouses.

When Lindy felt starved for company as she recuperated from hepatitis, contracted from a blood transfusion during childbirth, Hale took home a congressman who was just recovering from it. Jack Kennedy was a gangly yet handsome thirty-year-old Democrat from Massachusetts who had won a House seat the same year that Hale returned. Hale had known Jack's father, Joe, who had been the maritime commissioner and the ambassador to Great Britain. But as did others he found the son "not too impressive" at first, in his careless dress—often, khaki trousers and a nondescript jacket—and his customary unwillingness to comb his hair. (These would improve once he married Jacqueline Bouvier, the *Times-Herald*'s inquiring photographer, whose family Lindy had known in Louisiana.) Yet the two young congressmen hit it off. Both loved to read history—Hale later spent a summer plowing through Winston Churchill's tomes—and together they took an Evelyn Wood speed-reading course.

"He was the kind of fellow that you would enjoy just sitting down and talking with," Hale said later. "This man had great intellectual charm."

The children liked him too. When the boyish Kennedy stopped by for a drink or a meal, "he would kid with you," Cokie remembered, "in the nicest of ways."

As they grew older, the children became involved in Hale's political campaigns. The girls in particular loved the life of politics. Barbara said later that she had learned to read precinct lists upside down from her stroller. Feature by feature, Barbara resembled Hale most, with her strong face, broad forehead, and lively eyes. She was tall and ungainly as a girl, not pretty so much as handsome, combining her mother's warmth with her father's gregariousness, a natural at his craft. Cokie, too, started making speeches "when I was a little bitty girl" and found it thrilling to visit polling places on Election Day.

"It was a great way to grow up," Cokie said.

Tommy liked it less, fearing embarrassment before his friends. If his sisters wanted to enter politics, he announced when he was ten or eleven, "I'd better be the one to make some money."

It was not a household in which the father arrived home for dinner each evening at six and then the family gathered around the television set. Sometimes Hale and Lindy were off campaigning, and even in Washington the children had to share them. Decades later Cokie still fumed at her mother for putting out a mass mailing and missing a Christmas concert, because "she didn't know I had a special part." But Hale and Lindy made the children feel as if they were around more than they were. They tried to eat dinner, at least part of it, with the children every night and succeeded two or three times a week, Lindy more often. Hale attended Cokie's father-daughter field days and one or two of Tommy's football games each fall.

"We had a total family life," Cokie recounted.

Much of the day-to-day child rearing was left to the housekeeper. Emma Cyprian was a tiny, wiry, well-educated granddaughter of slaves—"as old as my time and a little older than my teeth," she liked to say. She believed in cleanliness, good grades, and discipline. "There was nothing warm and fuzzy about Emma," Cokie said. Her distaste for men (a legacy of her own late husband) made a target of Tommy. When something was broken or missing she would say, "I don't know who did it; I don't know who did it. Now, Mr. Hale's not here, and of course Lindy didn't do it, and the girls didn't do it. I don't know who did it."

"Emma was terrific," Tommy remembered.

Lindy ordinarily left with Hale by eight or so each morning, to work on a charity event or an activity for congressional spouses or to report to her desk in Hale's office. As did many congressional wives, she added to her husband's $12,500 salary a congressional stipend of her own, occasionally drawing accusations of nepotism. She helped to keep his offices in Washington and New Orleans running in tandem, and represented him or Speaker Rayburn at outside functions. In 1948 she began to coordinate his political campaigns, serving as the front person, gathering volunteers at her dining room table, handling the logistical details, listening to constituents. There was no one else Hale could choose who did not belong to a political faction, and she had the patience to soothe the egos that Hale had riled.

"Everybody loves Lindy"—this became a refrain that reflected a political truth that was proving crucial to Hale's career. They were becoming a team.

On Capitol Hill, the speaker welcomed Hale back into the Board of Education and invited him into another inner sanctum. The House Ways and Means Committee touched every American's wallet—levying taxes, crafting loopholes, tinkering with Social Security, shaping foreign trade. Its Democrats wielded even more power, functioning as the committee on committees, deciding on every House member's assignments—and political fate. Yet again Hale had proved his political reliability to a national party, during the Democrats' agony at their presidential nominating convention in 1948. When Strom Thurmond led the southerners out of the hall, Hale had joined them. But then he returned with Lindy (though she was not a delegate) and Russell Long, Huey's senatorial son, and lifted Louisiana's standard back into place. The following January he joined Ways and Means.

With a rude jolt, however, he was made to realize that his political future was confined to the House of Representatives. Persuaded to run for governor of Louisiana in 1951, Hale was vilified by the state's segregationists as a communist. In Washington, Joe McCarthy had touched off a crusade that continued to spread. Hale's involvement at Tulane with the American Student Union, condemned by the House Un-American Activities Committee, haunted his campaign. He finished third, disabused of any prospect for political success statewide.

"He understood," Cokie said years later, "that his life was going to be here, not there."

Hale had another reason to commit himself to a future in Washington. Lindy and the children had always spent six months in Washington and six in New Orleans, following a congressional calendar that often ended in the summertime. Barbara and Cokie found this tolerable. They went to a Sacred Heart school in both places, with identical curricula, except that Cokie missed learning long division. Both fifth grades elected Barbara as class president. When Cokie's schoolmates in New Orleans taunted her for Hale's loss, a nun pulled her aside and showed her a photograph of the snow-covered hills she had known at Stone Ridge, her school in Bethesda, out past the Maryland line.

"Darling, this is what you'll be going back to." It was a lush campus, with Georgian architecture and twin gazebos. Cokie understood that the nun was telling her: This is your home.

She loved Stone Ridge, though like Barbara she was not the most deferential of students. When Cokie was eight or nine, a nun had put a hand over her smart-alecky mouth. Cokie warned, "Do it again, and I'll bite you."

She would remember a chalky taste.

Yet it was a wonderful place for the girls—"a much more private, safe, loving atmosphere," in Cokie's mind, than Tommy faced.

He shuttled between overcrowded parochial schools, using the desk of whoever was absent, switching schoolwork twice a year. But Tommy found this fun, especially the yearly move to New Orleans, because he had already learned the first four months of schoolwork in D.C. As he entered seventh grade, Georgetown Prep began accepting day students his age, for a classic Jesuit education. Once a part of Georgetown University, the school had moved out to Bethesda while it was still countryside, onto ninety-two acres of trees and brick that any college would envy. Tommy was required to enroll, however, for the entire school year.

It became obvious to Hale and Lindy that if they were to live in the capital year-round, they had outgrown the house on Stephenson Place. On the vacant lot next door, Hale's garden featured the only fresh-grown Louisiana okra in D.C. When Hale used nets to protect the peaches from baby squirrels, Cokie sat on his lap and rapped her little fists into his chest and shouted, "Mean old daddy." But they lived on top of one another in the teeny rooms (even without the houseguests who stayed and stayed), and the dining room was too small for entertaining.

Lindy went looking for a house with a spacious dining room and a back staircase. On weekends she took the children, then took Hale to see the ones she liked best. On a winter's day in early 1952, she drove out Wisconsin Avenue, by the low-slung brick storefronts of downtown Bethesda, past the large Victorian houses and stretches of nothing along the four-lane thoroughfare, narrowed by parked cars. She drove what seemed a long way. All over Montgomery County, farmland was becoming subdivisions, for the young families with a veteran's mortgage to buy a tract house on their own sixth of an acre. Woodward & Lothrop had recently opened a Bethesda–Chevy Chase branch, its first in the suburbs.

Bradley Boulevard swept west off Wisconsin Avenue. A mile along, on the right, a long driveway led to the house she had gone to see. Two huge weeping willows at the entrance resembled (if Lindy squinted) live oak trees with Spanish moss. The white brick house was a typical center-hall colonial, with two departures—a half-acre of cloistered grounds, enough for privacy and a vegetable garden, and the white columns across the front, from porch to roof. This was powerful to Cokie because even at age eight, she loved *Gone with the Wind*.

"It looked like Tara to me," she said.

Lindy inspected the house with the real estate agent while the children scurried around. When she reached the living room, Cokie was sprawled on the floor in her snowsuit.

"I want to live in this house, Mamma," she declared.

"But, darling, it doesn't have a back stairway."

"I don't care."

"The bathrooms are much too small."

"I don't care."

"The dining room is small, too. It would be hard for us to have a big family meal, much less give a dinner party."

"I don't care."

"There isn't enough closet space for us."

"I don't care what you say. I love this house. I'm gonna tell my daddy to buy me this house."

The real estate agent phoned Hale the next morning and told him what Cokie had said. When Hale asked Lindy about the house she had not mentioned to him, she described its shortcomings.

They bought it, for $52,500.

The house was close to the children's schools, and the Capitol was not a much longer commute than they were used to. They had left D.C., venturing a mile and a half (as the mosquito flies) beyond the Maryland line. Yet it was the capital that had grown, all but cartographically, beyond its constitutional measure.

Something else had changed. For Hale and Lindy, Louisiana was still their true home and would continue to be. But for their children, other than summers in Louisiana, the nation's capital had become their home. Even living in Bethesda, they were truly Washingtonians now.

Four

EISENHOWER

Before dawn the telephone jangled by the bed, and Lindy Boggs answered it. A cultured and resonant baritone asked to speak with Hale. She said he was asleep.

"This is Adlai Stevenson."

"Good morning, Governor Stevenson. This is Eleanor Roosevelt," Lindy said and then hung up.

The phone rang again.

"Lindy Boggs, this really *is* Adlai Stevenson!"

She awakened Hale.

Hale did not meet the Illinois governor until a month before the 1952 election, when the divorced, debonair Democrat who had been nominated for the presidency traveled to New Orleans to solidify the wavering South. He was a witty intellectual whose grandfather had been Grover Cleveland's vice president, and Hale was an obscure though influential congressman overshadowed by his neighbor, Eddie Hebert, who liked Ike. Yet Adlai Stevenson and Hale had much in common, in their subtle minds and their personal charm. The congressional secretaries had recently voted Hale the "most charming man on Capitol Hill," because he told every woman she was beautiful.

When Hale was introduced to Stevenson, he began, "Governor, I'm Congressman Boggs."

"Oh, sit down, charming," Stevenson replied.

Hale was smitten. When the nominee suggested that he tag along to Miami, Hale left without a toothbrush. He continued on to Tampa and Nashville.

Hale had always had a knack for making himself useful to his elders, and in a capital ruled by hierarchy, nothing mattered more. Washington was a land of giants A handful of men ran the government. In the Capitol, the likes of Sam Rayburn, Carl Vinson, Richard Russell, Arthur Vandenberg, Robert Taft, and LBJ ruled. Hale understood how to work his way toward the front.

One evening Hale called from the Hill to say he had invited an exhausted Sam Rayburn home for dinner. The speaker was a shy and lonely man, who had survived a brief and mysterious marriage many years before. He lived alone in a gloomy apartment near Dupont Circle and on Sundays walked for hours through the city's deserted streets. He would adopt families, as almost his own. He had done this with his fellow Texans, the Johnsons; he would go to breakfast on Sundays with Lyndon, Lady Bird, and the girls and read the newspapers in their apartment all afternoon. Taciturn to a fault, he seemed more comfortable with children than with adults. Lynda Johnson once threw him a birthday party and invited nobody older than six.

Now he was building the same relationship with the Boggses. The speaker would have a home-cooked meal, and he and Hale would go fishing together, the young man letting the older man talk. ("God, what I would give for a tow-headed boy to take fishing," Rayburn had once written to a friend.) Lindy—and Tommy, too—always thought of Mr. Sam as their "buddy."

The adults relaxed on the screened-in porch, drinks in their hands, looking out on the backyard at Hale's garden, which was filled with lettuce, broccoli, asparagus, beans, beets, onions, radishes, corn, turnip greens, and tomatoes. The children huddled out by the fence, until Cokie scrambled across the yard and up the steps to the porch, in tears. She rushed past her parents and clambered onto the rocking chair, into Mr. Sam's lap.

"You've got to come out and see about Tommy Boggs," she cried.

"What's the matter, darling?" said the Speaker, in a tender growl.

"He's being disrespectful to Charlie Chicken!"

"Disrespectful to Charlie Chicken? How's he being disrespectful to Charlie Chicken?"

"He's digging his grave, and when he puts the shovel in, he's humming that tune from *Dragnet. Dum-de-dum-dum.*"

Tommy and his pal, Charlie Coulon, had given Cokie the undyed chicken the day after Easter. It had cost the boys a dime at Woolworth, plus eleven cents for the food. Cokie named it Charlie Chicken, after Tommy's friend—to torment Tommy, who so enjoyed tormenting her.

Lindy's mother, who was visiting, had built a coop, which was in the garage, and Charlie Chicken had the run of the yard. He greeted Cokie every day after school. He was "a nice chicken," she recalled. But one day Emma Cyprian had to pry it from the mouth of the family's cocker spaniel, Governor, a gift during Hale's doomed campaign. After that the two pets learned to get along. Governor rounded up Charlie at night, and the chicken lost its fear of dogs.

That morning, when the girls had left for school, Emma Cyprian chased the stray dog away—too late—and carried home the carcass of Charlie Chicken.

That afternoon after school, as Cokie danced up the long driveway, Lindy was waiting. No chicken greeted Cokie.

"I wonder how Charlie Chicken is," she exclaimed.

Silence.

Lindy took Cokie up to her bedroom. On her mahogany four-poster bed Cokie saw something she had yearned for but had given up on ever getting—a poodle skirt. Her school, Stone Ridge, required uniforms, and Lindy sewed the girls' dress-up clothes, so they owned almost nothing in between. (Cokie dreaded the one day each month when uniforms were forbidden, because she had to wear her only outfit again and again.) But now the flared and fashionable skirt was hers.

Then Lindy scooped Cokie into her lap and told her.

"I was undone by Charlie's death," she remembered. "He was the first pet that was just mine."

To console her, Lindy suggested an elaborate funeral, just as soon as Hale got home. Tommy used his jigsaw in the basement to turn a cigar box into a coffin and to fashion a small wooden cross. Barbara lined the casket with pink satin and lace.

Then Lindy told them that Mr. Sam was tired and the children would have to conduct the funeral on their own. As twelve-year-old Tommy dug a grave by the back fence, he taunted his little sister until she cried.

Mr. Sam soothed Cokie.

"That's not very polite," he said of her big brother's behavior. "Perhaps if I go out and see what's going on, do you think your father and mother would accompany me?"

Lindy wondered how she could have underestimated him or thought he was too tired for the children. She loved his kind soul, which was concealed behind his gruff silence.

They filed outside in the dimming light, to the high back fence. And there the powerful and self-contained Speaker conducted a proper Baptist funeral, to lay a Catholic chicken to its eternal rest.

On the Saturday before the Ace Wrecking Company went to work at 1701 K Street, the eighty-two-year-old mansion was opened for antiquarians to pick among the marble mantels or the sliding doors of maple and burled walnut. The previous tenant had been the Washington Club, which had already moved into Cissy Patterson's palace on Dupont Circle.

This was the last of Shepherd's Row, the three adjoining limestone-faced mansions done in Second Empire opulence, stretching from Seventeenth to Connecticut. Boss Shepherd, a crony of President Grant's, had dominated D.C. in the 1870s and had the streets paved, sewers installed, Center Market rebuilt, sidewalks laid, parks put into place, sixty thousand trees planted, and the smelly canal that had once been Tiber Creek filled in, to make B Street, now Constitution Avenue. He spent three times as much as Congress had authorized, enough to grease his friends' palms and to build for himself a home with satin-upholstered walls and Brussels lace in the high windows.

However, antiquarians with open wallets stayed away. The only interest was that of the wife of an investor in the building that was to rise in its place. Mrs. Jacob Kotz asked that the mantels and the stone doorway be reserved for the house that she and her husband were building at the edge of Rock Creek Park.

Dr. Kotz, the first local surgeon to perform an appendectomy through a short incision, had financed the new office building with another prominent surgeon, Eddie Cafritz. Morris had put his younger brother through medical school at George Washington University. Morris, too, was an investor—and the builder.

"Washington's busy builders"—*The Evening Star* lauded the city's developers, beneath a photograph of a new building's skeletal frame—"gradually creating a new Nation's Capital from the old."

As early as 1929, while he was driving to the Ambassador's construction site, Morris had seen the promise in K Street. Only Sixteenth Street, East Capitol Street, and a few of the avenues were wider than K Street. L'Enfant had intended its 147-foot breadth as the route from the Georgetown waterfront, to deliver into Washington City the bulkiest of supplies. He had also envisioned it as the boulevard with carriageways and gracious residences, lushly lined with trees, that it had become. By the century's turn it was known as the Park Avenue of Washington. Admiral Dewey had died behind the bay windows at 1601 K Street, and William Howard Taft was living next door, in the short squat house at 1603, when he learned of his nomination as president. At 1730 K, with its green stone basement and flat mansard roof, Frances Hodgson Burnett wrote *Little Lord Fauntleroy*.

Morris was not the first, however, to imagine K Street as something else. In the 1880s, when Leland Stanford lived at 1701 K, the tycoon-turned-senator had predicted it was destined to become the city's commercial thoroughfare, once F and G Streets grew congested. "A street can't be a big street unless it can grow," he had said.

K Street was already changing. The lines of elms had been cut down in 1939, and hotels kept going up. Two blocks west of the Ambassador, the Statler had opened in 1941 at Sixteenth Street, across K from the Carlton. Restaurants, travel agencies, and steamship lines had followed. West of Sixteenth, elegant town houses had become

apartment houses, medical buildings, and lawyers' haunts, and between Twentieth and Twenty-first, across from the old horse fountain, stood the Western Market.

Morris had hired an architect who had imagination. Yet within
the city's limitations on building heights, there was only so much that
any architect could do. The wider the street, the taller the buildings
were permitted to stand, but even on K Street the limit was 130 feet.
The purpose was to keep the national monuments predominant;
other than the Washington Monument, nothing stood higher than the
Capitol dome. To maximize the office space at the corner location,
Morris's architect designed a boxy twelve-story building, its exterior
in horizontal ribbons of limestone and glass.

The limestone showed some flair, in place of the steel that
builders had been using instead of brick, as a hard material meant to
lend the buildings a formal, modern look. The stripped-down, unornamented International style was popular all over Europe and increasingly in the New World as well. Another office building, also
striped in limestone and glass, was rising next to Morris's, at Connecticut and K. Its developer had spurned Morris's suggestion that
they build them as one, to cut costs.

Gus Ring, Morris's protégé, had put up an earlier office building
west of Fourteenth Street, in 1946, a flat, squat tan building at Eighteenth and M. The neighborhood was convenient, close to the White
House and government departments and the hotels. It also offered
developers what they valued more than anything else—available
land, toward the north and the west. Within months an office building would rise at the southwestern corner of Connecticut and K, and
then at the northwestern corner.

Bulky, boxy, profitable buildings kept going up. Architectural critics thought of them as ice cubes spilled on the street. Morris finished
the brick-and-concrete Continental Building on Fourteenth Street,
just above K, about the same time as the building at 1701 K; at a ceremony in July 1954 he accepted gold keys to both.

He leased his buildings as quickly as he constructed them. Even
before he began, K Street had attracted the National Association of
Frozen Food Packers, the Burley & Dark Leaf Tobacco Export Association, the U.S. Wholesale Grocers Association, the National Insti-

tute of Public Affairs, and others who had an interest in what the government did. At 1701 K, he leased the fourth floor to the *New York Times* for its correspondents, part of the fifth floor to the printing trades union, part of the sixth floor to the American Machinery and Foundry Company and the remaining parts of the fifth and sixth floors, as well as the seventh and twelfth floors, to law firms. Lawyers had everything they or their clients needed nearby, except the courthouses, and the capital's lawyers bothered less and less with those.

The city's center of commerce remained in the old downtown, over by F Street, east of Fifteenth. But by 1953, of the sixteen office buildings in the business district put up since the war, twelve stood west of Fifteenth Street. Any doubt about the rise of a new downtown faded by late in the year, when the Washington Board of Trade, the business community's instrument in making its wishes felt, left *The Evening Star*'s building on Pennsylvania Avenue and moved into 1616 K Street, within a glance of Morris Cafritz's redemption of Shepherd's Row.

Julius Hobson often complained to his colleagues at the Library of Congress that his wife made more money than he did. It seemed to make him feel worse about his own prospects.

Carol *was* lucky—"I'm just very, very blessed," she marveled years later. But she was the sort of bright and engaging person, forceful but not overbearing, who made her own luck. She had carried her master's degree into the Census Bureau, and in 1953 when it cut back its workforce, she paged through the federal directory of statistical personnel and phoned agency after agency to ask about a job. A woman at the Bureau of the Budget suggested she try to get a position with Herbert Spencer Conrad at the Office of Education.

A mild-looking man with thinning gray hair, Herb Conrad was the pushiest of bureaucrats in snatching budget and staff. He had turned the government's statistics on education—which could only be requested, never demanded, from states and localities—into data that were regarded with respect. She also found him "the nicest man in the world."

Soon after starting, she said to him, "You know, this is a temporary appointment and Christmas is coming up and my son wants a bicycle. Is my appointment going to be renewed?"

"Get him the bike," he replied.

He also protected her from the racial prejudice that permeated the Office of Education. Carol was the first Negro woman to work as a professional in the research and statistics branch. The cafeteria was segregated and all of the messengers were black. Racial jokes were told within her hearing, in the high-ceilinged room that the branch's secretaries, clerks, and professionals all shared in a vast limestone building on Independence Avenue, southwest of the Capitol. The most valued civil servants sat by the windows or—as a tribute to a genuinely accomplished career—beside the drapes. Every morning, the most senior men took out rulers to determine whether the cleaning people had moved the desks overnight. One man sharpened his pencils and arranged them by length. The agency's highest-ranking Negro, Frederick Douglass's grandson, was a special assistant to the commissioner for Negro education.

Herb Conrad made sure Carol drew interesting assignments. She compiled tables and added up figures and pleaded with school districts to part with facts about themselves. She coauthored an annual survey of public school enrollment and teachers, state by state, and wrote a report on the segregated education of Negroes in the South, including D.C. She started at a desk by the doorway and worked her way to the middle of the room.

"I see you wrote a letter and signed your name," a coworker told her one day.

"Yeah."

"Do you know how many years *we* worked here before they let us sign our own name to a letter?"

With their two government salaries, Julius and Carol bought a frame house with a covered porch and a white picket fence around a yard where Hobby could play. Myrtle Avenue, deep in the city's northeastern quadrant, almost to the Maryland line, had a touch of countryside, with its shade trees and drab shingled houses. But the houses were closely spaced and the Doric columns that held the porch roof betrayed its pretension. The neighborhood was not quite poor, though it was short of comfortable.

Each morning, Julius drove Hobby to kindergarten, but not around the corner to the handsome brick schoolhouse with the elaborately carved limestone entrance. That was the white school, Woodridge Elementary. He dropped Hobby off a mile away at the smaller, shabbier Lucy Slowe Elementary, named for a Negro tennis champion who became the first principal at Shaw Junior High (and later the dean of women at Howard). Slowe was overcrowded, whereas the student body at Woodridge was less than half as large as the school could hold.

Whenever Julius passed Woodridge, he became angry. In September 1953, he took Hobby into the school and they sat in the principal's office, to no effect. The principal had once testified to Congress that she had heard of a black first-grader who had raped a white kindergarten girl.

Then Julius tried going through channels. "That was just about the first fight I got involved in," he said later, after many more.

Representing the Slowe school's Parent-Teachers Association, he read a prepared statement before the city's Board of Education at its last meeting of 1953, arguing that Woodridge should be shifted from white to Negro. "A close scrutiny of the elementary schools in the areas under discussion here," he told the six white members and the three Negroes, "will show that if an elementary school in the Woodridge–Brookland–Michigan Park–Edgewood areas were transferred to Division 2, the children of Division 1 would still have more than adequate accommodations." He offered facts and then the larger context. His request, he said, was merely "a move toward a temporary solution to the problems inherent in the constitutionally questionable dual school system of the District of Columbia."

A month later, the school board turned him down.

Julius's allusion to a constitutional issue was not an idle one, because two months earlier the Supreme Court had heard the rearguments in its landmark case about desegregating the nation's public schools. *Brown v. Board of Education of Topeka* centered on the Fourteenth Amendment's dictate that states assure their citizens equal protection. But D.C. was not a state, and a parallel case, *Bolling v. Sharpe*, depended on the Fifth Amendment's broader guarantee of due process of law. A twelve-year-old boy who wanted to attend the brand-new, all-white John Philip Sousa Junior High School, beside a golf course in Anacostia, was sent an endless streetcar ride away, beyond the old downtown to Shaw Junior High.

The court decided both cases the same day, in the spring of 1954, both unanimously.

That night, the D.C. recreation board voted to desegregate the city's playgrounds immediately. The next day President Eisenhower suggested that the capital serve as a "model" for the nation in desegregating its schools.

So Hobby started first grade the following fall around the corner, at Woodridge Elementary. At the opening meeting of the racially mixed Woodridge PTA, after the principal prattled on about the difficulties ahead, Julius spoke up. To the fearful white parents, he offered no apologies or pleas for acceptance.

"My boy washes with the same Ivory soap your kids use," he said. "He brushes his teeth with Colgate, just like yours. His color won't rub off, and he's coming here for the same reason your kids do—to get an education."

Julius Hobson was starting to make a name for himself.

A few months later, at the school's Christmas play, Carol noticed that the white girls played angels and the black children wore devil masks.

The witness he was following had pleaded the Fifth Amendment, so Morris Cafritz seemed cooperative, even loquacious, in comparison.

"No, it wasn't a windfall, no sir," Morris said.

He was addressing pudgy-faced Homer Capehart, the chairman of the Senate Banking and Currency Committee. Having made millions by popularizing the jukebox, the senator was in his second term as a Republican from Indiana, a Joe McCarthy kind of anti-Communist. In fifteen days of Senate hearings, he was pursuing twenty-seven rental apartment complexes, including three in the Washington area, that had allegedly reaped windfall profits from Federal Housing Administration loans.

"What was it?" he asked Morris. He meant the $552,000 extra that Morris had received in a federally insured mortgage, beyond the

three million dollars that the generously landscaped garden apartments in Anacostia had cost him to build. Morris had invested part of
the difference in a shopping center.

"Why, it was just good management," Morris replied—the six
hundred units would have cost another builder 20 percent more. He
said: "A windfall is something that you get for nothing. This money
had to be paid back."

With an air of injured innocence, he wanted everyone to know
that the government had approached *him* about building Parklands
Manor, because of the Negroes' need for rental housing. He was the
first white developer to build housing for middle-class Negroes. "I
don't like the idea of government in private industry," he had told the
newspapers, "but I went ahead and built the project. Then, instead of
calling me up and saying, 'Well done, Mr. Morris Cafritz, you did a
great job,' they shout 'windfall.'"

But now the tone grew sharper when the committee's counsel
mentioned the benefits that would accrue to Morris's three sons.
Morris had bought the hilly hundred acres a dozen years earlier, for
sixty-nine thousand dollars, and put it in trust for his sons; he now
claimed the land was worth $422,000.

"But isn't it true," the counsel pressed, "that after the mortgages
are paid off out of rental income, your sons will own properties now
valued at $7,200,000, from which your only contribution was the gift
of the land?"

"That is correct, probably."

"Now, if a man . . ."

"Do you want this for a newspaper statement?" Morris flared. "Is
that why you were trying to build it up?"

Ordinarily a man had to earn twenty million dollars, the counsel
replied, if he hoped to bestow seven million dollars upon his children.

"Everything I have ever done," Morris countered, "has been one
hundred percent within the law."

"Well, we don't have to decide that this morning."

The local newspapers were entirely too enthralled with the hearings, from Morris's perspective, and his role in the scandal had
piqued the interest of the Federal Bureau of Investigation.

Her husband's being a target in a Senate investigation did noth-

ing to impede Gwen's social plans. In fact, she could help him. When
she threw a lawn party for Generalissimo Franco's daughter and son-
in-law (Gwen had been a guest at the Spanish dictator's summer
palace), she invited Senator Capehart and his plain wife. It happened
that they were out of town, but they sent a huge vase to the door at
2301 Foxhall Road, with two dozen large yellow roses. The Senate
chairman who put the developer under oath before the cameras could
still be a pal after work.

"Now first, sir, which party spent the most money in the elections of
1952?"

Hale Boggs looked at his questioner with a sly smile. He had a
square jaw and wavy pomaded hair. His sinewy face had taken on a
trace of fleshiness.

"Mr. Huie, the Republican Party spent considerably more than
the Democratic Party in the elections of 1952," he growled in a be-
mused drawl.

"That's a factual answer, and the fact that you're a well-known
Louisiana"—William Bradford Huie pronounced it *Looziana*—
"Democrat had nothing to do with the answer, I assume?" The editor
and publisher of *American Mercury* flashed a smile. He was one of
the two questioners this evening in 1953 on *Longines Chronoscope*,
the fifteen-minute show ("A Television Journal of the Important Issues of the Hour") broadcast live on CBS three times a week, sponsored by "the world's most honored watch."

"Nothing in the world but the cold figures," Hale replied, slow as
an August afternoon.

Hale had a knack for the fledgling medium of television. Understated and wry, he spoke patiently, melodically, in a deep and resonant voice. His succinct answers offered facts but not too many.
(The Republican congressional committees had spent $1.8 million,
the Democrats "about" eighty-two thousand dollars.) With a persistent half-smile, he glanced at the camera, as if to make sure the viewers were in on the joke.

He understood the political uses of broadcasting. Before Christmas every year in New Orleans, he and Lindy and the children had put on a radio show. In the recent election, television counted as the greatest single cost to campaigns—sure to rise, Hale was now telling a national audience, as the number of stations multiplied.

"You might eventually reach the point," he prophesied, "where only a man who has considerable money or who has connections to people with a lot of money would be able to offer himself as a candidate for public office." He promised to introduce legislation to revise the "inadequate and antiquated" laws on financing campaigns, by allowing congressional candidates and political parties to spend more while requiring any group trying to influence a federal election to file a financial report.

Hale owed his national TV appearance to his chairmanship of the Special Committee to Investigate Campaign Expenditures. It was an unpleasant legislative duty—it offered untold opportunities for upsetting his colleagues and almost none for earning their gratitude—but the Speaker needed it done. If Sam Rayburn was turned down for a favor, he never asked again.

Hale was enthusiastic about legislative tasks. Later he chaired a special subcommittee of Ways and Means that designed the highway trust fund as a politically invisible means of paying for the interstate highways, proposed by a logistics-minded president to unite a far-flung nation. As the chairman of the Ways and Means subcommittee on foreign trade (and a port city's representative) he became an early advocate of a united Europe and a permanent delegate to the Inter-Parliamentary Union. The speaker credited Hale's arguments on the House floor with swaying fifty votes against a protectionist bill, to produce "a smashing victory" (this, from Paul Wooton in the *Times-Picayune*) for the president's five-year freer trade bill.

He had already reaped a reward for his skill and loyalty. When Sam Rayburn needed a new majority whip in 1955, Hale was one of the people he considered. But there was a problem. John McCormack, the majority leader, was a Catholic, too. The speaker remembered all too well the resistance in Baptist-disposed Texas in 1928 to Al Smith, the Catholic presidential nominee. Instead he chose Carl

Albert, whose Oklahoma district adjoined Rayburn's. An orator and former Rhodes scholar, Albert was the shortest man in Congress, an expert in the parliamentary rules yet so passive that he would do whatever Rayburn wished.

But Hale was not left out; the speaker created a new position, that of chief deputy whip, and named Hale to it.

The point of the whip operation was to count Democratic noses and to keep them in line. But the Speaker did that himself, leaving little for Carl Albert to do, and even less for Hale.

Still, Hale showed a knack for persuasion. He learned to confront predicaments right away, to let a grumbler vent. He could twist arms with a smile, and he was one of the few who could change colleagues' minds with a speech. Shortly after joining the leadership, during a debate on foreign trade, a Dixiecrat lambasted "the fantastic dreams of the one-worlders and the do-gooders."

Hale took exception. "I hear people using that phrase 'do-good' all the time," he remarked. "Well, I do not see why that is such a bad thing to call a man. Suppose you call him a 'do-badder.' I just wonder what a do-gooder is. Some say when you want to say something real bad about somebody you call him a do-gooder."

Jim Wright, a young freshman from Texas, was awed. "He destroyed that fellow's argument entirely, reducing it to absurdity," he recalled years later. "After that, I decided I wanted to follow him."

Drew Pearson reported on Hale's "sharp-eyed" interruption at Ways and Means when the president's assistant budget director urged that the excess-profits tax be extended.

"Say, aren't you the same man," Hale jumped in, "who was around here in 1950 telling us the excess-profits tax was a horrible thing and ought to be repealed?"

The former bank lobbyist flushed and gave a wan smile.

"Yes, Congressman, I recall talking to you, among others, about it."

"What caused you to change your mind?"

"Oh, I still think it's a bad tax," he stammered, to guffaws. "But it's a matter of timing"—the budget situation had changed.

"Well, the budget was out of balance in 1950 also," Boggs said. "Let us just say that your position is governed by where you happen to be."

So was Hale's, really, except that his political circumstance situated him simultaneously in more than one place. He was struggling with the art of political balance, on which his survival—as well as his ambitions—depended. It was not so challenging for an accomplished politician to support sugar and oil, to back the New Deal and the Fair Deal, and to protect himself against further accusations of unpatriotic opinions by offering paeans at every opportunity to the House Un-American Activities Committee (HUAC) and the FBI. "Your constant support of this Bureau is indeed a source of encouragement to my associates and to me personally," J. Edgar Hoover, the FBI director, had once written back to Hale, who inserted the two-sentence letter into the *Congressional Record.* Hale signed a statement, witnessed by Rayburn, that he was not and never had been a Communist.

Another balance was harder, however—between the electoral demands of his Deep South constituents and his national ambitions. His position as chief deputy whip put him on the ladder to becoming the Speaker of the House. Unlikely ever to attain statewide office (or, as a southerner, the White House), he could realistically hope to attain no higher position. But to reach that point he would have to make himself acceptable to the mainstream of his party, while still persuading Louisianans to keep him in office.

The peril of a misstep could be more than political. In 1956, all but three of the 105 southerners in Congress signed the Southern Manifesto, which condemned school desegregation as a Communist-inspired path to perdition. Hale had always stood with the South on civil rights, and he signed. The three dissenters—Lyndon Johnson, Albert Gore, and Estes Kefauver—had national ambitions and had become family friends with the Boggses.

When Hale arrived home that night, his children locked all the doors and refused to let him in. Lindy could have intervened but refrained. Her devout Catholicism had made her an advocate of civil rights, and besides, Cokie said later, "What would be the mileage in stopping us? We were going to express these views, and it was important for him to know how passionate we felt." The children had seen racial discrimination firsthand, the times they had driven back to New Orleans with Emma Cyprian in the car and finding a place to sleep had been daunting.

Hale usually handled his children's argumentativeness with equanimity, even at the end of a tiring day, though occasionally he would explode. This time, when they let him in at last, he did neither. He tearfully explained that the Southern Manifesto would prevent a walkout by southern delegates at the Democratic convention that summer. It would be better for black people that he sign the statement and remain in Congress, he told his children, than that he lose his seat to a real segregationist. Cokie remembered that "everything was always put in those terms."

For the second segment of CBS's popular show *Person to Person* on a Friday night in 1955, Edward R. Murrow visited by live camera from his studio in New York the living room at 2301 Foxhall Road in Washington. This was where the capital's social season was to begin unofficially on Sunday with a cocktail reception for four hundred, marking the opening session of the Supreme Court the next morning, the first Monday in October.

"You see, Ed, I was born and reared in Europe, and to me that lovely ideal of equal justice for all means so much," Gwen Cafritz explained. Her sharp whiny inflection showed a Continental flatness and flair. "And then I followed the workings of the court for so many years. In 1935 I was there when Chief Justice Hughes handed down the decision favoring TVA, and that was the first time that energy was ever devoted to the public good, and I think that I can sort of—or anybody could—draw a direct line from that to the Geneva conference when American genius called this meeting to decide on beneficial uses of atomic energy."

Gwen's raven hair glistened as she waltzed across the room in her black-and-white sheath dress, her heavily made-up eyebrows plunging like pelicans. She lowered herself into an armless chair beside Morris. As she kept moving, he sat stiffly, his hands between his legs. Behind them, on the wall, long gauzy dresses draped the bare breasts in the bas-relief murals of Greek maidens, to suit the present administration's prudishness.

"Good evening, Mr. Cafritz."

"Good evening, Ed."

"How would you describe your contribution to the social affairs in your home? We'll get around to your business in a moment."

"I think Gwen, generally—she does all the work and planning." Morris spoke with a raw accent and a gravelly self-consciousness. "Sometimes she confers with me regarding certain parts of it."

"So then you compromise and do as she wants to do. Is that it?"

"Right." Both Cafritzes laughed uncomfortably.

The newsman asked Gwen how many cocktail parties she attended in an average week.

"I would say about three a day, but they are not what you would really call cocktail parties," she said. "I think that's a misnomer and it's unfair to Washington. They really are receptions, or what the French would call *salons*."

"Uh-huh." Murrow sounded amused.

"You meet the most famous people who have gained recognition all over the world—diplomats, government officials, leaders in science and in industry." She spoke breathlessly. "It is something that makes our life in Washington so fascinating."

As she led the camera into the dining room, past the Dalí, she described her preference for dinner parties for twenty-two people, so that she could "really chat" with her guests. Rigid protocol dictated the seating (after the Supreme Court justices were the Cabinet officers, the ambassadors, the senators, and only then the lowly representatives), and a strict schedule governed the evening. For each party she wrote a six-page script on a yellow legal pad and rehearsed the timing, to leave nothing to chance.

The guests were to arrive promptly at eight o'clock and sit down for dinner at twenty past, after imbibing at most a cocktail and a half. "If you give them more," she said, "somebody is apt to get woozy and spill soup down some dowager's back." The soup, fish, and meat courses—sometimes she served five courses or as many as ten—each with its own rare wine, were all precisely timed, as specified on a scratch pad in the pantry. She would start on the menu ten days ahead and use imagination—partridge and pink champagne was a favorite combination. Caviar canapes, consommé terrapin, whole trout and filet of beef, crepes Suzette—there was no telling what might appear at Gwen's table. She started the fad of serving punch in a bowl with dry ice, to give off clouds of steam.

After dinner, the ladies retired to the drawing room and the men, in black tie, to the library for brandy and cigars. The guest of honor left promptly at ten forty-five and the others followed—"so you can go out five nights a week," Gwen informed CBS's viewers from coast to coast, "without any great hardship on the men, who all work very hard."

More important than what she served was who accepted her invitations. Gwen understood the art of the guest list. She would start with an appealing couple, perhaps the chief justice or a prospective senator or an ambassador from a chic country, with his wife. Once it was the children's author Roald Dahl and the actress Patricia Neal. The president regarded cocktail parties as "abominations of the devil," but Gwen had entertained the Nixons (before he became the vice president), the Nelson Rockefellers, the Walter Lippmans, even Senate Majority Leader Lyndon Johnson, who rarely did anything but work. Bob Hope showed up, and Frank Sinatra. Once, her son Calvin was watching a Tyrone Power movie upstairs and wandered into the basement and found the actor at the bar with Gwen. The newspapers charted the comings and goings of the "effervescent young" trial attorney Edward Bennett Williams, or the new Mrs. Jack Kennedy, whose dress (*The Evening Star* bubbled) "simply shouted Paris."

Gwen reveled in what her guest of honor once described in a toast—to laughter—as the "fascinating city of Washington, where everybody is prominent or wants to be."

She struck the necessary balances in assembling a guest list. "If you have enough pretty women and clever men at your party," Gwen noted, "then you can afford to invite a homely Cabinet officer and his wife." She would never invite an *ex*-Cabinet member—"When they're out, they're out," she decreed. "I always invited one Democratic senator and one Republican senator, or reasonable facsimile thereof. I can have the same respect for Fulbright and Saltonstall."

Gwen was believed to be a Democrat and Morris a Republican,

though nobody knew for certain. "I'm bipartisan," she said. Once she described herself as neither a Democrat nor a Republican but an intellectual—"I carry my intellectual integrity like a shield."

She disdained the after-dinner movies that Evalyn Walsh McLean liked to show, and the square dancing at the cereal heiress Marjorie Merriweather Post's. Gwen had higher purposes in mind. One was to foster a feeling of community in an impersonal capital. A new senator from Arizona who received his first invitation from Gwen was standing on her terrace, admiring the city spread below, when "I first realized that Washington has some fine, upstanding people," Barry Goldwater reminisced. Her parties eased personal relationships and softened the city.

"They get a chance in the atmosphere of a home to discuss their problems," Gwen explained to Edward R. Murrow, "and by the time they leave, they are much friendlier and understand things much better."

Gwen's conception of her mission was grander still. Between the salad and the dessert, she would rise to her feet at the rounded end of the dining room and offer a toast to the guest of honor and then make a short speech—on whether to recognize Franco's Spain, perhaps, or to approve of the latest pact between Turkey and Greece—to get a discussion going.

"Now about these dinners," Gwen told the viewers, "the conversation is usually perfectly marvelous. I think the thought in the back of everybody's mind is preserving civilization. It always has been. Before the last war, during the war, afterwards, I mean that is the underlying thought."

Julius Hobson thought he was having a heart attack, like the ones that had killed his father and grandfather. At the hospital, he learned that in addition to high blood pressure, he had pericarditis, an inflammation of the sac around the heart. When he went home he told Carol that the doctor had said she must not disagree or argue with him.

But the scare served its purpose. He switched from Camels to a pipe and quit his second job. He had been working evenings and Saturdays in rundown Rosslyn, across the Potomac from Georgetown, as a draftsman in a factory for optical character recognition equipment.

It also made Julius think. "They say that between the ages of 35 and 50 a man begins to examine himself"—he penned a ten-page letter to his mother in his lucid script. "I guess I have started a little early. I do not like what I see of myself. Oh I am not worried about money or degrees. Any fool can acquire those. It's the courage of living. The usefulness of life which worries me. I feel as though the world will have been no better off by my having been here.

"I'm tired of my snug security, my warm and comfortable life, and my endless process of acquiring more and more. I feel ashamed when other men have sacrificed, gone to jail, or even been executed for mankind. . . . [T]he injustice, suffering and cheating and all of man's inhumanity to man seems to be my personal problem. I cannot divorce myself from it. I will be ever unhappy if I cannot do something about it. I just hope this heart will last long enough for me to strike one blow at all the things around me which I detest.

". . . I know having a family to support is important but it seems to be dimmed by larger problems."

Julius struggled between his family and his mission. Later it would be said that he had "a messianic itch," which was fueled by a desperation to make something of himself. He also craved being a good father, having never really had one. Julius would take Hobby to the movies (both of them liked westerns, which Carol hated) and play catch with him in the yard and occasionally take him to baseball games. When astronomy caught Hobby's interest, Julius bought a globe with a light inside that shined the heavens all over the boy's bedroom ceiling and walls. Before Easter each year, Julius would take Hobby downtown to be fitted for a suit, at the row of tailors along D Street, between Sixth and Seventh—always made too big, so Hobby could grow into it for five or six months. Still, with a pointed white handkerchief in his breast pocket and a child-sized fedora on his head, the boy looked sharp. Julius had been known as the best-dressed student at Tuskegee—his mother had instilled in him the importance of looking one's best—and in turn he instilled in Hobby a belief in an immaculate appearance.

"He was a devoted father and family man," Carol said later, "until he hit the street"—that is, until his mission in civil rights overwhelmed his need for a family.

When Carol told Julius she was pregnant again, he exploded. "I was an only child," he said, "my father was an only child, my grandfather was an only child—you have ruined tradition." The doctor reminded him that Carol had not become pregnant by herself.

Their daughter, Jean Marie, was born in the summer of 1956.

But by then, Julius was away from the house more and more. He often had meetings at night, of one or another of the organizations he had joined. The Woodridge Civic Association handled neighborhood issues for Negroes (the white residents formed parallel "citizens' associations") and by 1955 he was its president. Then he became active in its citywide counterpart, the D.C. Federation of Civic Associations, and was soon the second vice president. He led the federation beyond its usual neighborhood concerns, into cosponsoring a conference on Negro employment he organized at Howard.

"Julius was nobody's vice president," said a friend.

By late in 1957 the civic federation formally commended Julius for his work with the National Association for the Advancement of Colored People (NAACP). The local chapter of the nation's oldest and most successful civil rights group was using Julius's research to goad the police force to abandon its own practice of segregation. Negroes were excluded from six of the eleven detective squads, from three of the four traffic squads, from three precincts entirely, and from all ranks above corporal. His dry facts proved what everyone knew.

He became the secretary-treasurer of the NAACP's Citizens Committee against Defamation, which analyzed desegregation's benefits in D.C. schools. Julius published an article on the difficulties Negroes faced in finding jobs in the capital. "The large department stores, the chain food stores, the public utilities, and hundreds of smaller businesses," he wrote, "do not hire colored District citizens in any except the lowest paying jobs."

He joined the local NAACP's executive committee and then the Washington Urban League—"each organization theoretically becoming more radical as I went along." He began to deliver speeches around the city. At the monthly meeting of the Mount Pleasant Neighbors Association, he worried over the social degeneration that resulted from clearing slums and building roads. "Progress cannot be left to experts alone," he said.

Something gradual yet dramatic—and unprecedented—had happened in D.C. In 1957, the demographers believed, a majority of the city's residents were Negroes, a first for a major American city. They had continued to arrive from the South, while the desegregation of schools had driven frightened whites to the suburbs. This made Julius part of a powerless majority in a city that could not rule itself.

Even in his own life, Julius too often felt powerless. When he heard one of Carol's coworkers inquire why she had not worn her spring coat on such a mild morning, he rushed over to Kann's and bought her one of peach cashmere. She returned it and paid the mortgage instead.

"That's the way he conducted his life, his whole life, according to what people thought about him," Carol said. "He had this image that he wanted people to think about him."

When his mother visited, she said to him, "Julius, your schoolmate is living down the street in a brick house. What are you doing living in a frame house?"

So they bought a sturdy brick colonial, on a corner in the predominantly white neighborhood of Brookland, on Queens Chapel Terrace NE, just a block from the Maryland line. Not long after they moved in, their white neighbors dumped trash in their yard and broke the radio antenna on their maroon Mustang and punctured its tires.

A nicer house meant a larger mortgage, and they had already been feeling the pinch. Hobby was "wearing last Easter's brown and white shoes to school," Carol wrote to her mother-in-law. "Trying to get out of this economic stranglehold that has had us psychologically imprisoned now for over 7 years. Just must get our heads above water."

When the Library of Congress kept refusing him a promotion, Julius looked for another job in the government. In 1959 he found an opening for a GS-9 at the Social Security Administration, though at the agency's headquarters in Baltimore. For almost a year he commuted the thirty-five miles each way.

"I am a bit afraid on this new job," Julius confided to his mother. "I have not told Carol, but the change and all after having been at the Library for 11 years is tough."

Julius was destined never to hold a job that he loved.

Perle Mesta was still serving as the minister to Luxembourg when a letter from California arrived at the central post office by Union Station, addressed only to:

CAPITAL'S NO. 1 HOSTESS
WASHINGTON, D.C.

It was delivered to Gwen Cafritz without a day's delay.

Partygoers and readers of the society page shook their heads at the latest "Gwendolynisms," as her wandering sequiturs were dubbed. "Oh, there'll be millions of ambassadors and some desultory food and caviar walking around." Or, "It's nice to have a European background, especially if you're from Europe." Or, "I know we are approaching the posterior of the afternoon." Or, "My dear, you look positively strategic." And, "Darling, I just couldn't bother with Mrs. Mesta—I go with girls my own age."

Even when Perle returned, the rivalry continued. Neither had ever hosted the other, though Gwen issued invitations. "I have no feeling about her," Gwen said. "It's just that she has a distinct allergy to me." The only parties that both attended were put on by Marjorie Merriweather Post. Lesser hostesses took pains to anger neither of them while preventing an inadvertent brushing of elbows near the caviar. "This soft-shoe jostling for position," the gossips winked.

Only it was not always soft-shoe. "She's not a hostess in the usual sense. She's a showman," Betty Beale wrote of Perle Mesta in *The Evening Star*. "Few professionals know how to direct and time a production like Perle."

Sometimes Perle threw a party for pay, such as the one on a March evening in 1957 to open a Sheraton Hotel in Philadelphia. What took place there could never have happened in Washington.

In a sequin-studded emerald green satin gown, Perle stood in the receiving line. Zsa Zsa Gabor attended—money was to be raised for Hungarian relief, after the Soviet invasion of the year before—as did Ginger Rogers, George Jessel, and Joe E. Brown. Xavier Cougat conducted his orchestra.

Perle noticed the photographers beginning to cluster near the door. A commotion stirred the receiving line, as the announcer proclaimed, "Mrs. Mesta, Mrs. Cafritz." The Sheraton Corporation had invited Morris Cafritz, a director of its Washington subsidiary, and his Hungarian-born wife.

The two hostesses had barely touched hands when Perle spun away, as if she had heard someone call her name.

Gwen waited and dropped her handbag. Its contents spilled onto the floor.

As two gentlemen helped collect her belongings, Gwen said, "Isn't this what happens when I come to a Perle Mesta party? She walks away and I drop everything."

When Perle returned, the two women shook hands, to the photographers' delight. The next day's *Post* showed a pudgy-faced Perle turning angrily away from Gwen, then greeting her with a grin.

Gwen sashayed in triumph toward the ballroom, to drink and to dance.

On Fridays, the egg man clattered through the corridors of the Longworth House Office Building, also peddling freshly killed chickens and homemade sausages from his cart. A dry cleaner stopped by the office to pick up laundry. The House and Senate carryouts served some of the best southern cooking in the city. From spring until fall, Hale Boggs took basketfuls of vegetables from his garden to his staff; the sweet corn was a favorite.

Hale's garden had become his refuge. The busier he grew on Capitol Hill, the less reliable a partner for tennis or golf he became. Gardening became his exercise and relaxation. He would awaken an hour early to weed and rake; in the evening he would move the hose in his tuxedo. Once, when a visitor mistook him for the gardener, Hale ran to fetch the congressman, his polished self, who returned well-scrubbed.

At the Capitol he operated out of his hip pocket. He dashed in and out of his office and made decisions—about his schedule, staff assignments, legislative judgments—on the fly. Nothing significant was known by the staff. When an aide suggested staff meetings, Hale glared and stalked out.

Hale's charm, his devil-may-care laugh, could instantly turn abrasive. He had a tart tongue and a temper, even with colleagues. He might dismiss them by walking away or, even more irritatingly, shake hands with one lawmaker while staring over his shoulder at another. "For chrissake," Dan Rostenkowski, sixteen years his junior, would tell him. "How about eye contact, Hale?"

Lindy helped. She smoothed matters over for Hale with his staff and constituents; even his colleagues she could invite to her table and thus into her spell. She had developed a network of friends and well-married allies. In 1954 she served as the president of the Democratic Congressional Wives Forum, and in 1956 she headed Operation Crossroads, which dispatched congressional wives around the country in four caravans of loudspeaker-equipped station wagons, to plump for Adlai Stevenson's second doomed campaign. (Seventeen-year-old Barbara christened the lead car with a bottle of TVA water.) Hale served as the campaign manager in the South, and speculation had it that if Adlai won, Hale might wind up in the Cabinet or as party chairman; he was already a vice chairman, representing the House.

Lindy, too, was becoming a presence in Democratic circles, by virtue of the Woman's National Democratic Club. A legacy of the suffrage movement, the club sought to involve women in politics, mainly by educating them at luncheons twice a week. It had acquired its own clubhouse, a rambling mansion on New Hampshire Avenue beyond Dupont Circle. After terms as the finance chairman, then as the first vice president, Lindy began a year's term as the president in the spring of 1958. She lined up well-known speakers—dear egg-headed Adlai, presidential aspirant Jack Kennedy, Albert Gore, Drew Pearson, cartoonist Herblock—and attracted new members to the club. She made it into "one of the better organizations in Washington," judged a new congressman, George McGovern, whose wife watched Lindy at work and began to think of her as the woman in Washington she would most like to be.

The club grew in part because of an influx of congressmen's wives. More lawmakers had been moving their families to Washington since the war, as the housing market eased and the voters grew more forgiving. The prevalence of central air-conditioning kept Congress in Washington through the summer and made it tolerable for wives and children to stay. These women got to know one another, at backyard barbecues or in carpools.

Stone Ridge School of the Sacred Heart put Barbara and Cokie in contact with the world beyond politics, the daughters of dentists, doctors, developers, insurance executives. Yet the children of politicians gravitated toward one another. Gene McCarthy's daughters and Bobby Kennedy's girls and Sargent Shriver's later attended Stone Ridge, and Cokie became close (and lifelong) friends with the daughter of Congressman Bill Miller, a Republican who would become Barry Goldwater's running mate two elections hence. Cokie's boyfriend's little brother was best friends with Chris Dodd, a Connecticut senator's son—and later a senator himself—who was also Tommy's "little brother" at Georgetown Prep.

Hale's prominence meant perquisites for his family. Barbara reigned as a Cherry Blossom princess. As high school seniors, both Barbara and Cokie were crowned as queen of the capital's Mardi Gras ball. Later, as queen of the President's Cup Regatta, Cokie was crowned at the Shoreham with a wreath of white gardenias and made small talk with the actor Robert Goulet.

Once, when she was twelve, Cokie returned from England with her parents, where they had met Queen Elizabeth and attended the opening of Parliament, and went immediately to watch Tommy play football at Georgetown Prep. "This is just too weird," she thought.

Hale helped foot his three children's tuition bills by occasionally writing articles for publications such as *Reader's Digest* and *Look*, to augment his $22,500 salary and Lindy's smaller one and the campaign cash that oilmen would slip into his hands—quite legally, and all too customarily in Washington—over lunch.

Money had always been a struggle in the Boggs household, more intensely as the family's expenses grew. Hale was thrilled when the nuns asked Cokie to skip a year, because it saved a year's tuition. As the children got older, they worked at odd jobs. Tommy lugged milk cans at a dairy in the summertime and ran an elevator in Longworth. Lindy sewed the curtains as well as most of the girls' clothes.

"We never had any money," Cokie said.

Besides the tuition and the considerable cost of making a family presentable in circles of eminence was the expense of entertaining. There were impromptu dinners, but Hale and Lindy also undertook a far more ambitious project, though involuntarily. "Blind Tom" O'Brien, nicknamed for his inattention to evil, had been the sheriff of Cook County during Al Capone's heyday and now ranked one seat ahead of Hale in seniority on Ways and Means. In early 1958, he mentioned to Hale and to Charlie Davis, the committee's chief counsel, that his eightieth birthday was three months away.

"Oh, that's wonderful," they replied.

When he mentioned his birthday twice more, they caught on.

The Boggses proposed a garden party at their home, and the guest of honor insisted that they invite the committee, the leadership, the press corps, the Cabinet—fifteen hundred people, before the list was done. "We invited everybody," Lindy said, "and everybody came."

A racetrack, Blind Tom's passion, adorned the icing on the gigantic cake. Fourteen-year-old Cokie and Walter Little, a wiry Negro who worked for Ways and Means, picked up the box with the cake so they could slip a tablecloth underneath. What they failed to realize was that the box had only part of a bottom. Walter instructed Cokie to hide the cake with her skirt while he rushed to the kitchen for a glass of hot water, to repair the breach.

The following year Tom O'Brien mentioned his birthday five weeks in advance, and again they obliged, and yet again with vats of gumbo, rivers of bourbon, a New Orleans jazz band. A few years later, when Blind Tom died, Hale and Lindy were saddened but relieved.

Then the phone calls from people who wanted to know why they had been removed from the invitation list began.

"I think we're going to have this garden party," Hale said, "whether Mr. O'Brien is here or not."

And so every spring, on Bradley Boulevard, the famous garden party went on. The newspapers always covered it, and the rain always stayed away.

For years Morris Cafritz had used the slogan "Watch Washington go to a million" in his newspaper ads. The city's population peaked in 1950 at 800,000, but the suburbs kept surging, so he changed to "Watch Washington go to two million." In the metropolitan area, this was happening.

New York City had proposed a World's Fair in 1964, but that did not pose "the least of the threats" to Washington's plans for one in 1963. That was the boast of the Board of Trade, which was leading the drive to lure fifty-five million visitors to what was now a lazy crossroads out in Largo, Maryland, just beyond the circumferential highway under construction. Morris sat on the finance committee. "As a builder, I can see the tremendous advantages a fair would be to business as a whole in the entire metropolitan area," he said, though when he announced plans for a thousand-room hotel on Temple Heights, he promised to build it whether the World's Fair happened or not.

He was reputed to be the wealthiest active businessman in the city, worth as much as twenty-five million dollars. The city had enriched him, and he wanted to reciprocate. He offered to donate Keith's Theater, the old vaudeville place at Fifteenth and G, for use as an opera house and legitimate theater. For years he had headed the Community Chest and the Metropolitan Police Boys Club as well as the Jewish Community Center (though when wealthy Jews had gathered to raise money for the *Exodus*, he stayed away). He had started a small foundation in 1948, after years of keeping track of his philanthropies on scraps of paper.

His real estate interests stretched in every direction. He proposed a Town Center of shops and service establishments in Southwest, where the city's worst slums had been razed, but lost out to a developer from New York. On his land near the Pentagon, he proposed a tripling of the mammoth apartment houses, four sprawling office buildings, and a shopping center.

"My dreams for Pentagon City are not just dreams," he declared. "I'm not just a dreamer."

His empire centered, however, in the new downtown. He put up cookie-cutter office buildings at 1725 K, 1725 I, and 1735 I, and on the northwestern corner of Seventeenth and L. "There is more real wealth in new buildings on K Street, between Fourteenth and Twentieth Streets," he said, "than on any other street in the city." He predicted that once the underpass was completed beneath Washington Circle and connected to the planned freeway along the Potomac, K Street would rank as "the main artery through the central business district." In real estate circles, Morris was known as Mr. Office Building.

When John Hechinger stopped in one day for advice about a new location for his family's burgeoning chain of lumber and hardware stores, Morris was blunt. "John," he said, "there isn't a piece of real estate worth a damn east of Fourteenth Street."

The old downtown was dying, and a new downtown was rising in its place, just as the worn, provincial city was giving way to something shinier and new.

Five

KENNEDY

Lyndon Johnson, the Senate majority leader, entered the elevator and realized he had left Speaker Sam Rayburn's office holding a not-quite-empty tumbler of Cutty Sark. Tommy Boggs, in college at Georgetown University, had been promoted from running an elevator in the Longworth House Office Building to operating Rayburn's private elevator, behind the House chamber. Tommy worked there weeknights from five o'clock until the Speaker left, rarely before nine.

"Tommy, I can't take this around the Capitol," Johnson said. Tommy had known him most of his life. "Why don't you take this from me?"

"Mr. Leader, you could leave a little more scotch in there," Tommy said. He meant the next time.

A ritual was born.

Tommy's introduction to scotch plus his conviction that Johnson would make an effective president prompted him to travel the country doing advance work when the Texan ran for the White House in 1960. Others in the Boggs family were torn. Lindy regarded all seven of the major Democratic candidates as close friends: Adlai Stevenson, the quartet of senators (Hubert Humphrey, Stuart Symington, and John F. Kennedy, as well as LBJ), the diplomat-politician Chester Bowles, and Bob Meyner, the governor of New Jersey. She had worked with several of their wives on charity or congressional functions and refrained from taking anyone's side. So did Hale, though "he loved Kennedy," Tommy said later, and believed that the senator from Massachusetts had the best chance of winning. Hale stayed neutral, however, in the hope of being chosen as the nominating convention's chairman.

As the Democrats prepared to gather in Los Angeles to choose a presidential nominee, Rayburn decided not to preside over his fourth straight convention so that he could openly support his fellow Texan. If a congressman was named to preside in his stead, the gavel would make him the seventy-eight-year-old Speaker's heir apparent. Rayburn wanted Hale appointed, and so did Johnson, Kennedy, and Harry Truman. But Paul Butler, the party's chairman, a Catholic, feared having a Catholic preside over a nationally televised convention that was likely to nominate a Catholic for the White House. (Leroy Collins, Florida's moderate governor, was chosen instead.) Many of Hale's friends suspected that the true reason he was passed over was his legislative opposition to civil rights.

Yet his friendship with both leading candidates, and with Sam Rayburn, put Hale at the center of events at the Los Angeles convention. The morning after the presidential nomination, Hale received a telephone call from a party insider. Tommy ("the Cork") Corcoran, the onetime FDR brain truster and now a renowned Washington fixer, invited Hale to the hotel where the top candidates and Rayburn had suites.

When Hale arrived he learned that Johnson had been offered the vice-presidential nomination. But Johnson would accept only if Sam Rayburn thought it wise, and he did not. Corcoran wanted Hale to change the Speaker's mind.

Rayburn feared that as a Catholic, Kennedy was certain to lose and that Johnson, whose Senate term was up, would lose with him.

Hale's rebuttal consisted of a single name: Nixon. The only way to prevent the sitting vice president from entering the White House, he argued, was for Johnson to join the Democratic ticket and help Kennedy win.

With that, Rayburn relented.

The choice of party nominees ended the Boggses' divided loyalties, and the fall campaign became a family affair. Hale organized the campaign in Louisiana and delivered speeches for the national ticket all over the country. Lindy planned the campaign's kickoff dinner in Washington and was one of six southern women who traveled in advance to drum up support in the places LBJ would pass through on his whistle-stop tour across the South. Twenty-year-old Tommy handled the advance work for Johnson's first campaign foray into New York and then for other trips too.

American voters, by the narrowest of margins, elected both a president and a vice president whom the Boggses counted as friends of long standing. Two decades earlier Hale and Lindy had started out as opponents of the established political order. Now they dwelt at its center.

Lindy's role was a delicate one, as cochairman of the 1961 inaugural ball. Beyond the logistical details and the juggling of egos, the hardest part for Lindy was handling the unceasing requests for tickets, to most of which she had to say no.

"The desirable thing would be to have an open list, so everyone could come," she said, "but the practical facts are, you can't have a ball of such proportions."

Fortunately, nobody was better at salving bruised egos than Lindy Boggs. And the pressures eased when a second ball was added and a third, then two more.

In the middle of everything, she flew home to New Orleans, to attend Tommy's wedding just after Christmas to Barbara Denechaud, the daughter of Lindy's closest college friend. ("The only arranged marriage in the twentieth century," Tommy's older sister liked to say.) Then Lindy immediately plunged back into the inaugural planning.

No one could have planned, however, for the almost eight inches of snow that struck Washington on inauguration eve, causing the worst traffic jam the city had ever seen. Drivers abandoned nearly three hundred cars on the George Washington Parkway. From the inaugural headquarters overlooking the Tidal Basin, Lindy gazed down at the traffic stalled on bridges across the Potomac and gave up hope of getting home to Bethesda. At two in the morning, she trudged a mile to the Mayflower Hotel, dropped off tickets for the Johnsons' guests, then retraced her steps.

The next morning she sat in her office, as people continued to scream about tickets. Near noon she remembered to switch on the television and watch as John Fitzgerald Kennedy was sworn in as the thirty-fifth president of the United States—passing the torch to her generation. Hale delivered her ball dress, a floor-length sheath she had designed herself. It was made of Japanese silk brocade that Hale had bought at an Inter-Parliamentary Union meeting in Tokyo.

There was no mirror in the office, so she applied her makeup by looking at her reflection in a spatula. "I liked the way I looked in a spatula," she said—"sort of shimmery."

On Inauguration Eve on Foxhall Road, Johnny Carson, the shyest man in the Cafritzes' mansion, stood uncomfortably in the corner. Gregory Peck, Carol Burnett, Julie Andrews, Rudolf Nureyev—celebrities filled every room, reflecting the glamour of the incoming administration.

The next evening, Gwen stopped off at the Uline Arena, behind Union Station, in her turquoise gown and purple stole, to look in on the dance she was officially cohosting for the twenty-seven hundred military academy cadets who had marched in the inaugural parade. (She had also invited two thousand local teenaged girls.) Then she and Morris continued on to the Mayflower Hotel for an inaugural ball. Gwen Cafritz and Lindy Boggs had sat on charity boards together, and Lindy had gone to events on Foxhall Road. She thought Gwen was "not only a nice woman—she was a good citizen," always ready to lend her house for charity.

The Mayflower's ball, the third to be arranged, was the first that President Kennedy and Jackie (along with the Johnsons) attended. The Cabinet appointees and their wives had been announced and ushered to their seats, followed by Adlai Stevenson and Sam Rayburn, both greeted with cheers, and the cochairs of the balls—Lindy and the chief of protocol—with their spouses, and last, the Harry

Trumans. Two thousand celebrants gazed on the tanned, smiling president and (as *The Evening Star* described her the next day) his "storybook queen."

The stylish couple in the White House restored a sparkle to the capital's social life. By living on N Street, past Thirty-third, they had helped to make Georgetown fashionable again, with parties that became Washington salons, mixing professors, politicians, and movie stars. Now the Kennedys shifted their purposeful socializing to center stage. "Jackie and the President," Lindy said, "were very good about having social events at the White House that were helpful in creating support and easing tensions." Jackie's tasteful redecoration, her pillbox hat, the cellist Pablo Casals in the East Room, the president's wit and wordplay—the capital was discovering sophistication. Its social life had never seemed so grand.

For their first Easter in the White House, the president and his family went to Florida (his father had suffered a stroke), and his brother, the attorney general, took his family skiing in Vermont. Most of the New Frontiersmen stayed behind, and several of the shrewdest sought to understand the intricacies of Washington better by accepting an invitation to the Cafritzes' annual reception on Easter afternoon.

The postmaster general, the secretary of the army, and the deputy special assistant to the president for national security, Walt Rostow, stole past the two caged white bunnies in the entrance hall on Foxhall Road. So did the first lady's stepsister and *her* half-brother, Gore Vidal (who would later include a social-climbing Jewish hostess as a character in his novel *Washington, D.C.*), along with ambassadors, justices, senators, and—invited from the lowly House—Hale and Lindy Boggs. The cherry trees were in bloom in the garden while the hundreds of guests huddled indoors in the cold.

The next morning, Justice Felix Frankfurter telephoned the Rostows and left a message: "The Cafritzes are Old Frontier."

He was wrong, of course: They only tried to be.

The intimacy between the capital and the world of celebrity reached a new level of confusion on a September evening in 1961, at Tregaron. The imposing mansion on wild grounds behind the zoo had belonged to Marjorie Merriweather Post and her third husband, Joseph Davies. She had bought him the ambassadorship to Moscow by bankrolling FDR's campaign for a third term. After their inevitable divorce, and his death, the house had fallen into disrepair, so that its conservatory needed to be furnished before it could host a fictional Washington party, during the filming of *Advise and Consent*.

The star-studded movie was based on Allen Drury's blockbuster novel about the Senate's nomination struggle over a secretary of state. "Socially, it isn't correct," Gwen had said of the book. "The man has never been to a good party." That night she wore a peau de soie gown, in peach, as she arrived with Morris around seven o'clock, among the more than three hundred society people invited (and paid twenty dollars apiece) to appear as extras in the five-minute scene. The Reverend Martin Luther King Jr., the young civil rights leader, had been cast as a senator from Georgia, though the part never materialized. "Just because there is no Senator at present who is a Negro," Otto Preminger, the director, had explained, "doesn't mean there couldn't be a Negro Senator in the future."

The socialites took their assigned places on the dance floor outside. Peter Lawford, in real life the president's brother-in-law, played a senator who winked at Gene Tierney, the hostess, as she ambled by.

Eighteen times they ran through the klieg-lighted scene, while the band played the same twelve bars of "Just One of Those Things." Otto Preminger glowered and kept filming until past one o'clock the next morning, when finally he was satisfied. Gwen and Morris had already left, in what the *Post* described as "a pique of aggravated boredom." Nine nights later, they had recovered enough to host the stars (Henry Fonda, Walter Pidgeon, and Lew Ayres, besides Gene Tierney) at a dance on Foxhall Road.

Gwen was at the top of the Washington social scene, but her own celebrity had yet to peak. The following spring she was planning a dinner party for the president's favorite foreign ambassador, Lord David Ormsby Gore of Great Britain, and his lady, when the embassy phoned and asked whether they might bring houseguests. Gwen added a "small" dance after the dinner and dispatched two hundred invitations by telephone, to honor the duke and duchess of Windsor.

Soft Spanish music strummed in the little ballroom with the translucent dance floor and in a larger room for dancing nearby. It was a magical evening. The droopy-faced duke, who had given up the throne for the Baltimore-born divorcée he loved, tried to dance the twist with his commoner wife, but she stopped him. She stayed with the two-step and the waltz, as an old family friend of Gwen's swept the duchess around, so light in his arms.

The fortunate guests marveled at the jewels, at the azaleas and Easter lilies, at the mix of American royalty proud of its presence— the Clark Cliffords, the Heinzes of Pittsburgh, senior military men and their wives, a senator or two, even Perle Mesta.

It was still early when the duke had begun to look bored, but people would talk about the glorious evening for years.

In 1960, Julius Hobson had run for secretary of the NAACP chapter on an insurgent ticket and lost. Soon he emerged with a position that suited him better, when he received a telephone call from Paul Bennett, a Negro physicist who led the local chapter of the Congress of Racial Equality (CORE), which was looking for a new president.

"I tried to explain," Julius said later, "that if I adopted the philosophy of nonviolence it would be on a pragmatic basis, as a technique, and not as some mystical way, as an article of faith."

The Congress of Racial Equality had been founded twenty years earlier by students, black and white, inspired by Gandhi's confrontational nonviolence. A D.C. chapter established in 1958 had fallen idle by 1960, then was revived. Julius had a model in mind for the strategy he planned for CORE to pursue in civil rights—a "selective patronage" campaign that Negro ministers had tried the year before among merchants in Philadelphia.

"When I started out with picket lines," he said years later, "a black clerk was as rare as a white crow."

He launched his "merit hiring" campaign at Hecht's in March 1961. The middle-range department store, at Seventh and F, had introduced escalators, credit cards, and photos-for-a-quarter booths to Washington. Hecht's had long welcomed Negro shoppers, but if the managers considered themselves as thereby immune to charges of discrimination in hiring, Julius turned the logic inside out: Any store that did so much business with Negroes should also hire them—and would make itself vulnerable if it refused.

First, Washington CORE would investigate Hecht's, "to determine as accurately as possible the nature of the hiring practices," he told the members. The available information suggested that the store engaged in token hiring, placing its few Negro employees in strategic positions to suggest that there were others. A careful counting found that Negroes made up 44 percent of the shoppers—47 percent on Saturdays—and whites accounted for all but 5 of the 270 salesclerks at the downtown store, all twenty store managers, all eight credit office clerks, and every parking lot cashier, but just two of the fourteen stockmen and none of the janitors, cooks, or maids.

The picketing, or its prospect, persuaded the department store to hire thirty-five Negro salesclerks and an assistant buyer. Not a word appeared in the city's daily newspapers, which relied on department stores for advertising in bulk.

"CORE can't break any downtown department store," Julius explained. "They have too many resources. They have money and personnel that we don't have."

Hahn's was next. The chain of ten shoe stores swore that it did not discriminate in hiring. Julius gave the company a week to agree to hire all employees on the basis of merit and to state this policy in its help-wanted ads—or face picket lines.

For years Julius would treasure a photograph of the first Negro salesman at Hahn's putting his hand on a white woman's leg.

Julius typed a letter to the Board of Trade, warning of picketing and "other means"—boycotts, he explained—that would be used against stores that discriminated in hiring. "We intend to take them on one by one," he wrote.

The members of CORE, more of them white than black, met at the All Souls Unitarian Church on Sixteenth Street. They should start with the "easy targets," Julius told them. "We are not going after the big ones until we get a few more victories under our belt."

Letters went to the Mann Potato Chip Company, whose president was the mayor of Alexandria, and to the Wilkins Coffee Company; both hired Negroes as driver-salesmen and clerks. At its thirteen movie houses, the Warner Theaters hired eight Negroes as managers and six others as ticket takers and candy vendors.

Julius would claim four hundred members or even seven hundred, though the number was probably closer to fifty. Occasionally the mere threat of a picket line was enough. Every Saturday, CORE organized a picket line in front of a merchant on F Street or nearby. Without warning, as many as three or four dozen picketers or as few as a half-dozen showed up on the sidewalk and marched in an unrelenting ellipse. The national organization instructed that the men dress in a suit coat and a tie, and the women in a skirt, stockings, and high heels, and that everyone carry enough money for a meal and a bus ride home. Julius gave the picket captains a list of fifteen rules— to space the demonstrators six feet apart, to make sure they use CORE's own placards and refrain from arguing with passersby. A majority of the picketers were white, and many Negro shoppers crossed through, to take advantage of Saturday sales.

"I had no troops," Julius said later. "Had a few stringy-haired white boys from Silver Spring. The blacks in this town never walked in a picket line."

Julius's own clean image helped. He never appeared without a fedora and a narrow tie. He drank no alcohol (for fear that anything he did, he would overdo) and he was respectful toward women. "The Deacon," a colleague called him.

In September, Lerner's dress shops (with its stores as far north as New York) agreed to hire 130 Negro office clerks and salesclerks. In December, CORE published a Selective Buying Guide, to publicize which places of commerce discriminated in hiring and which did not.

Just before Christmas, Julius scored his most satisfying victory yet. The previous spring Woodward & Lothrop had agreed to hire four colored salesgirls. That was not enough. Woodie's mattered not only in the volume of business it conducted but also in the precedent its policies might set. Starting three Saturdays before Christmas, picketers took up their places on the sidewalk along F Street with signs: *Money Spent Here Purchases Discrimination*. On the twentieth of December, the city's oldest department store relented. Woodie's promised to hire fifty-six Negroes as salesclerks and office clerks and another as a buyer-in-training, and to place an order with Howard University's business school for a junior executive trainee.

It was a lovely present for Carol.

Lindy Boggs never learned whether Sam Rayburn received the sassy postcard she had sent from London. In October 1961 he checked into the hospital with lumbago, and doctors discovered he had an incurable form of cancer. Six weeks later he was dead.

Hale had once described Mr. Sam on the House floor as "more or less a father to me," and he eulogized the speaker as a man of "rugged honesty—he despised the phony. No one ever thought of questioning his word." Rayburn's task of leadership as the speaker for twice as long as any before him was "to translate the mood of the House," Hale said, "which we know reflects the mood of the nation."

For Hale, tragedy also offered opportunity. John McCormack, a dignified but elderly ward heeler, became the Speaker, and smaller-than-life Carl Albert was promoted to majority leader. Hale also moved up, without open opposition, to the position of majority whip.

The job was now important, absent Rayburn's sensitivity to the slightest trembling in the legislature's pulse. McCormack was remote from House members—he ate dinner with his wife every evening without fail—and Albert was, too. Hale liked to spend hours on the House floor, walking around, chatting with colleagues, measuring their hesitations, feeling out their concerns.

As the deputy to the disorganized Albert, Hale had energized a system of regional whips, and Danny Rostenkowski now went to him with a suggestion. The barrel-chested young congressman from Chicago was, like Hale, a big-city Democrat with national ambitions; the two often shared red meat and drinks at Blackie's House of Beef on Twenty-second Street, at the Rive Gauche in Georgetown, or at the Sans Souci on Seventeenth, a half-block from the White House. "You know what I think we ought to do?" Rosty told him. "I think we ought to get a network of whips, where we just have a network of guys who can feed us information and they would get information, make them important on the floor." They could meet weekly, to discuss a legislative schedule. Every Thursday morning, Lindy woke at five and baked two coffee cakes from scratch, using a different recipe each week. Hale then carried them, while they were still warm, to the Capitol, with jugs of juice and milk. Maybe ten of the nineteen regional whips typically showed up, representing all sections of the party, for more of a social gathering than a meeting with a formal agenda. In Hale's spacious office, with the huge bottle of Tabasco on his unused desk, they exchanged scuttlebutt and political intelligence and forged a united front for confronting Speaker McCormack. There was never any coffee cake left for the staff.

But Lindy did more than bake. She kept a loose-leaf notebook to track legislation and went almost daily to Hale's office, where she kept Hale's schedule, sat in on discussions of strategy, and represented him with constituents he preferred to avoid. She was more organized than he was and was a steadier, regulating force. "Hale could get on a high horse and Lindy would settle him down," someone who worked with them said. "It was like burping a baby."

Hale was a large man who radiated a sense of confidence and command—"kind of an egocentric guy," said Rostenkowski. "Especially if he took a drink or so, he was very direct, very direct." In an institution "lubricated with sugar and bullshit," another colleague said, Hale was more frank than most, and he held few illusions about human nature. He was also fun to be with, a storyteller with a sly sense of humor—and a man of his word. Most of his colleagues liked him, unless they saw him as competition.

Lindy thought of him as a figure in a nursery rhyme. "When he was good, he was very good," she paraphrased, "and when he was bad, he was horrid."

As Hale grew older and the pressures heightened, he was becoming more cantankerous. His job as party whip was to keep southern Democrats in line for a White House that was in northern hands. His collaboration with Kennedy's plan to expand the House Rules Committee, so that it could break the South's parliamentary chokehold, drew hisses from home, but Hale held firm. He made himself a

man of the New Frontier, guiding an ambitious trade bill to enactment, supporting the president's initiatives to smooth other southerners' way.

As Hale took his place as the truest of insiders, politics was becoming the family business. During the summer of 1962, while
Lindy tended to Hale's reelection in Louisiana, Cokie kept house in
Bethesda. She had finished two years at Wellesley College and was
taking a summer school course at Georgetown University. Each afternoon she stopped by the House gallery to catch her father's eye, and
he held up fingers to show how many guests he expected for dinner.

Barbara had wound up with a job in the White House. She had
campaigned for Kennedy in 1960, and after graduation from college
the next year, and with her father's influence, she started at what she
joked was the only place in Washington that would hire her. (She
could not type or take dictation.) Her job was to write presidential
messages and proclamations for the special assistant to the president
in charge of correspondence.

"I thought you were going to go get married," the president told
her one day.

"I can't leave the simple joys of maidenhood," she said, alluding
to the hit Broadway musical with a medieval plot called *Camelot*.

She neglected to say that her father had broken up her engagement. Allard Lowenstein was an intense young activist she had met
first through the National Student Association and later during the
campaign to create a domestic Peace Corps.

"I just don't get it," Cokie railed at her father as they drove
through Rock Creek Park. "This is going against everything you've
ever believed and everything you've ever taught us."

"It has nothing to do with him being Jewish—you've got to trust
me on this," Hale replied. "I just don't think he'd ever be there for her."

When Lowenstein later married and traveled to South Africa on
a political mission when his first child was born, Hale was vindicated.

The breakup left Barbara with plenty of time for her White
House duties, and a little mischief. As the House majority whip,
Hale joined the Tuesday morning breakfasts that Kennedy hosted for
congressional leaders, and when he was asked on the *Today* show
about an economic policy decided in confidence at one, he changed

the subject. "Don't ever go to one of these breakfasts because the food isn't any good," Hale replied. "The eggs are Boston-style, dry and uninteresting." The coffee lacked chicory and there was no Tabasco sauce or grits.

The following Tuesday morning, at the White House, the waiter carried in a small silver coffeepot and a demitasse cup—everyone could smell the chicory. He passed quickly by the president and placed them in front of Hale. Then a silver bowl of grits arrived, and red-eye gravy in a gravy boat, a bottle of Tabasco in a silver holder, and biscuits. Barbara remained concealed behind a screen.

"I finally got him around to serving grits," Hale said of the president at a Jefferson-Jackson Day dinner over in Arlington, the nearest corner of the Confederacy. "But I can't get him to eat them."

Kennedy needed Hale, because he needed the South. When Hale faced a difficult reelection in 1962 because of his support for packing the Rules Committee, he prevailed on the president to visit New Orleans—"he came really because I asked him to." When Kennedy heard reports that he would be booed, he sought out Hale in the Washington senators' dugout during a rain delay on Opening Day.

"If the time ever comes when the President of the United States can't go to any city in the United States," Hale said, "then our country has ceased to be the hope of mankind."

"Well, I'm going," the president replied.

The following October, after Congress had adjourned, Hale went deep-sea fishing for the first time in a year. He was nine miles out in the Gulf of Mexico, the red snappers biting, when he noticed a military helicopter circle overhead and land on an oil rig nearby. Then a navy plane dropped a plastic bottle with a red flag attached. Inside was a note: "Call Lawrence O'Brien, White House. Urgent message from the President of the United States."

The helicopter flew Hale to shore and he boarded a jet fighter to Andrews Air Force Base near Washington. He shaved and changed clothes on the way, then arrived at the White House with the other congressional leaders. There they learned of perhaps the gravest crisis in the history of civilization, triggered by the discovery of Soviet nuclear missiles in Cuba.

During the next thirteen days, the congressional leadership was repeatedly briefed at the White House. Hale said later that he saw the president practically every day until the crisis was resolved, "and the calmest man in the whole United States of America was John F. Kennedy."

Just days after the world stepped back from the abyss, Tommy took his firstborn son to the White House at Barbara's behest to celebrate his first birthday. As Thomas Hale Boggs III, known as Hale, lurched along a corridor, the president's two-year-old son, John-John, wobbled toward him. The two toddlers collided and embraced.

Barbara took her nephew to meet Larry O'Brien and Kenny O'Donnell, two of Kennedy's aides.

"I want to introduce all of you," she said, "to the real Hale Boggs."

Kenny O'Donnell looked at the majority whip's one-year-old namesake and joked, "No telling what will happen to a fellow scrunched down in a jet fighter for two hours."

Julius Hobson walked into Bruce Hunt, the fine men's haberdashery on F Street. A lieutenant accompanied him, and fifty members of CORE were waiting on the sidewalk.

"I want to see the manager," Julius said.

"Who are you, sir?"

"My name is Julius Hobson. I want to see him now."

"Mr. Hobson, he's not here now."

"Well, who's managing the store while he's away? You the man? Well, let me talk to you. I'm looking behind the counter and I don't see any black folks. You do sixty-five percent of your business with black folks."

"Well, Mr. Hobson, that's the way things are. We don't want any trouble. Can we help you?"

"No, I'm here to help *you* eliminate your discriminatory practices."

"Well, Mr. Hobson, what would you have us do?"

"I want you to hire some black people."

"Mr. Hobson, I can see you're an educated man. You can understand, we're a business, and we can't afford to antagonize our public."

"Most of your public is black. You think they're going to be antagonized?"

"Well, we have to consider the entirety of our . . ."

"I got fifty people out there now, I'm coming back Monday, and if I don't see some black, thick-lipped, broad-nosed, nappy-haired folks behind that counter waiting on everybody, I'm going to close you down."

Picketers, black and white, showed up at lunchtime every weekday—*Don't Buy Where You Can't Work*—and on Saturdays. The daily newspapers ignored the campaign but the twice-weekly *Afro-American* covered it. Business dropped off; charge accounts were canceled.

Around two weeks later the manager telephoned Julius and offered him a job as personnel manager for Negroes.

"I ain't no employment manager," he answered. "I'm the cat's going to close your business down. Now I still don't see no black folks there."

Soon he did.

As Julius's successes grew, he waged psychological warfare behind closed doors. He would take Paul Bennett, his predecessor at CORE, into negotiation sessions with the timorous merchants. Bennett was a beatnik of sorts, who wore unlaced boots, smelly clothes, and a World War I airman's helmet that buckled under his chin. He also suffered from sinuses that caused him to honk and spit into his handkerchief. When a deal was about to be struck, Bennett would leap up and shout, "Julius," and call him an Uncle Tom.

"This worked very well on Raleigh Haberdashery," Julius remembered. "It worked very well at Bond Clothing Company; it worked beautifully on Drug Fair and one or two other stores."

At Lansburgh's, Kann's, National Shirt Shop, University Shop, Safeway, Giant Food, A&P picketers descended, negotiations ensued, complexions behind the counter darkened. More than eighty picket lines yielded sixty settlements and five thousand jobs. Julius never divulged where the picketers would show up next.

His creative tactics, his audacity, assured a reaction. CORE was ready to distribute 400,000 stamps in perforated sheets—WE BELIEVE

IN MERIT HIRING—for customers to paste over the keypunched holes in their utility bills, until the Potomac Electric Power Company rushed to court and obtained an injunction.

Would he obey it? "We do not intend to act like Governor Ross Barnett of Mississippi," Julius said.

Sometimes he overreached. When picket lines appeared at Rich's Shoes on F Street, Frank Rich, the owner, was incensed. There were already two or three Negroes selling shoes in his women's department, one in the men's department, and another in his Chevy Chase store, and more were being trained. He had recently stopped asking for customers' race on their credit applications. After a day's picketing, Frank Rich sought an apology from Julius that took him fifteen years to obtain.

Julius fought not only with the white merchants but also with people of his own race. In the spring of 1962, Julius took on his mightiest target yet, Capital Transit Company, the bus company owned by self-made, self-promoting silk-shirted O. Roy Chalk, with his ice-pick mustache and elevator shoes. Only forty-two of the nineteen hundred bus drivers, and none of the clerks, stenographers, typists, switchboard operators, or receptionists, were black. The vice president for personnel explained that the drivers, who were mainly southerners, had threatened to quit when the company once proposed to hire colored drivers for the Benning Road line. CORE's call for a boycott of the buses prompted negotiations. The company agreed to hire forty-one Negroes as driver trainees.

Only then did a group called the Community Committee for Jobs and Justice, cosponsored by the NAACP and the Washington Urban League, step in. The chairman was Walter Fauntroy, a cherubic Baptist minister who had been jailed in the South with the Reverend Martin Luther King, Jr. The third-generation Washingtonian, a product of Yale Divinity School, looked younger than his twenty-nine years. The short, stocky son of a Patent Office clerk and a churchwoman was what every colored mother could want in a son—bright, handsome, cheerful, deferentially polite, yet ambitious. He went public with the opinion that the settlement was "unsatisfactory," prompting O. Roy Chalk's negotiator to wonder about "two groups battling each other." Charles Diggs, one of four Negroes in Congress, wrote privately to Fauntroy to rebuke him for "a grave tactical error."

"Sorry second-guessing," the *Afro-American* railed, chalking it up to "the confusion of personal leadership rivalry."

The episode only intensified Julius's general distaste for men of the cloth—"preachers whose only objective," he said later, "is to get themselves a Cadillac and get some personal creature comforts."

It also reflected an enduring division among the city's Negroes, arising from the sort of city that Washington was. Because of the near-absence of factories and the stability of government employment, D.C. offered a higher standard of living for Negroes than any city in the country—or the world. Many had migrated from the South and found work at the Government Printing Office or the Bureau of Engraving and Printing or the Navy Yard or some other federal agency, or as teachers or city workers. A dependable job with insurance and benefits promised a decent livelihood, a family's future, and thus more to lose than to gain by racial upheaval. Nobody looked more middle class than Julius did, but his boycotts, his picketing, his open anger threatened to disturb the comfortable arrangements of the Negro middle class, even though it was middle-class Negroes who stood to benefit.

Washington was a company town, where, according to a fourth-generation black Washingtonian, even the Negroes accepted "the whole notion of don't-rock-the-boat. The sanctions are great for stepping out of line, and the rewards limited for stepping out of line, so there's really no incentive for being innovative, challenging, assertive. All the rewards are for sticking by the rules, and you get rewarded at the end of your career with a very nice pension. That's really the culture of Washington."

The resentments that Julius stirred up sidled into his home. Hobby flunked biology and geometry in his first semester as a sophomore at McKinley High School—because his teachers "hated my father," he said.

"You're lying," his parents told him.

After a PTA meeting, they went home and said, "Well, you're right."

Being Julius Hobson's son was hard. "He is a peculiar son," Julius wrote to his mother when Hobby was ten years old. "I can't figure him out. Guess his softness will fade as he grows older." Julius tried to make sure of it. He was strict with his son and namesake. If Hobby so much as forgot to take out the trash, Julius spanked him or took out his belt. Hobby trimmed the grass on his knees while his father was pushing the lawnmower.

The less Julius was home, the more chores—fixing, cleaning, mowing—came Hobby's way. Only once after Hobby was twelve years old did his father watch him play baseball (a game in which he injured his elbow), and Julius never saw him play tennis for McKinley or march as the drum major the year the McKinley band won the citywide cadet competition. "When you're growing up, there's certain things that you want your parents to see," Hobby said, "and he didn't see any of them."

Years later, when he was facing a similar Hobson's choice, Hobby said, "You've got a choice between walking the picket line and fighting to get more black people jobs and, say, taking your kids roller skating and to the movies. To an extent, you can explain away some of that to the children, but after a while they begin to resent it."

The older he got, the more Hobby pushed back. Father and son argued over whose shoe polish Hobby was using or whether his combo could practice at the house. When Julius decided that Hobby's girlfriends in high school were not pretty enough, he took home a *Jet* calendar of girls, stood in the dining room with his son, and turned the pages.

"You see Miss January?" he said. "You see Miss February, you see that? That's the way I want my daughter-in-law to look. I don't want any ugly grandchildren."

When he got to Miss December, he said, "Now do you understand what I'm talking about?"

"Yeah," Hobby replied. "When men get old they look at pictures."

Then he jumped up and ran.

With Jean, Julius was different—he spoiled her.

"In my father's eyes, I could do no wrong," Jean said years later. "If I wanted something, he would get it."

When she played in the creek behind the house on Easter morning and muddied her new dress, Carol had a fit but Julius paid no mind. He never spanked her, even when she deserved it. When Carol told Julius to take Jean upstairs for a spanking, he closed the door, got out his belt, and slapped the legs of the chair. "He always felt that little girls or women should have pretty legs," Jean said, "and spanking them would just mess their legs up. He never raised a hand to me, never hollered at me."

Naturally, the cherubic, summer-freckled girl became demanding and difficult. She would blame things on her brother so he would get spanked. Once, when Jean lied to her father that Hobby had hit her, Julius backed his son into a corner, pulled a blanket over his head, and started to strike him. Hobby reached for a baseball bat in the corner, but before he grabbed it, he broke free and fled the house.

Beyond Julius's temper and his lack of time, exacerbating the distance between father and son was the compulsion of his public image. He would rush for the newspaper each morning to see whether it mentioned his name. The Sunday that Hobby stood and made a profession of Presbyterian faith to join the Church of the Redeemer, Julius stayed home to paint the front of the house. He had publicly declared his atheism—the newspapers quoted him quoting Marx, calling religion "the opiate of the people"—and wished not to be contradicted.

Yet his father's prominence also meant privileges for Hobby, notably in the people he knew. Dick Gregory, the comedian and political activist, often visited the house. Julius hired as a babysitter for Hobby a Howard student he had met during the Freedom Rides, while dispatching young civil rights workers by interstate, court-desegregated bus to Mississippi. The handsome, lanky, cocky Trinidadian had a dark complexion, large bright eyes, and the unlikely name of Stokely Carmichael. He became one of the few people outside the family to call the boy Hobby instead of Julius. Stokely arranged a tour for him of Howard's architecture school and hosted him at the university's high school day. They played pool in the basement of Queens Chapel Terrace, where Hobby listened to Stokely and his radical friends talk about politics, strategy, and women.

"Sometimes," Hobby remembered, "you see a discussion turn into an argument and realized that it's not so much about the issue—it's personal, damn it."

From upstairs in his bedroom, Hobby could listen to the activists through the air ducts. "I didn't particularly like what I heard. They're supposed to be down there planning how they're going to further the cause of black folks, and what I'm hearing coming through the vents—ego arguments, who should be in charge."

He was learning never to count on any single fallible individual.

As the summer of 1963 heated up, the rash of racial demonstrations and outbreaks of violence around the country, North and South, took even some of the Negro leaders by surprise. Conditions, after all, had improved. A Negro could eat in any restaurant in Washington or attend any school or watch *Lilies of the Field* at any movie house (though the latest films still opened both downtown and on U Street) or try on a dress before taking it home.

Perhaps it was the progress that made the exceptions all the more galling. Joseph Gawler's & Sons, the eminent funeral home out Wisconsin Avenue, refused to remove the body of a four-year-old Panamanian boy who had drowned in the swimming pool at the presidential adviser Chester Bowles's home in Georgetown. ("There are several very fine colored funeral homes in the city," William Gawler noted.) Only near the end of 1962 had the exclusive Cosmos Club admitted the historian John Hope Franklin as its first Negro member; its earlier blackball of Carl Rowan, a deputy assistant secretary of state, had prompted administration officials to resign from the club.

Worse, the housing patterns were becoming ever more segregated, and as a result so were the schools. The Supreme Court had abolished the restrictive covenants in 1948, and yet the lines between white and Negro neighborhoods had grown ever more rigid. Negroes were leaving Georgetown, unable to pay the rising prices, as whites abandoned Anacostia and Northeast. The ghetto was growing. CORE campaigned for a fair housing ordinance, to forbid landlords to discriminate on the basis of race.

Julius Hobson and CORE needed a symbol of the city's segregated housing, and they found one on Foxhall Road. Morris Cafritz controlled 5,359 apartments around the city. Who was a bigger or more obvious target?

On an unseasonably warm March night in 1963, while Morris hosted more than 150 businessmen for the United Jewish Appeal, twenty-six picketers marched in an orderly fashion five hundred feet away, on both sides of the mansion's grounds. They carried placards stating *Segregated housing is morally wrong*. Negroes were barred from two of Cafritz's apartment buildings, Julius told a reporter from the *Post*, the Majestic on Sixteenth Street and the Parkview, out in Brookland. Julius said that he had requested a conference with Mr. Cafritz two weeks earlier but that his letter had not been answered.

In an editorial titled "Morris Cafritz's Plantation," the *Afro-American* minced no words: "As much as any single man, Morris Cafritz is responsible for the vicious racial ghettoes which have been built up in the nation's capital."

He was hardly the only landlord in Washington who discriminated in housing—all of them did. How many other white developers had built apartments for Negroes? Morris had even fired the manager of a new all-Negro building out Bladensburg Road for putting up signs that said, "Integrated" in the hope of renting to whites. Julius was far from satisfied. "This appears to be still another example," he said, "of the shameful segregation policy practiced by the Cafritz Real Estate Company."

CORE picketed during business hours at 1625 I Street, the Cafritz Building, where Morris had moved his office, in what Julius called a "continuous sit-in." The picketing spread to the Cafritz apartment buildings, where Julius tried a "dwell-in," a tactic borrowed from New York. A white volunteer signed a lease, and a Negro moved into the Miramar, at Fifteenth and Rhode Island, and then into two other Cafritz buildings. The company was "completely unaware" of the protest, a spokesman said, and planned no response.

Morris still refused to meet with Julius Hobson or to speak with the press. He ended practically all advertising of his apartments.

Then the city government became involved. The three D.C. commissioners had decided to move the city's Public Utilities Commission (PUC) out of the District Building, at Fourteenth and Pennsylvania, to make room for the Alcoholic Beverage Control Board. The president had appointed the first Negro commissioner, but this did not discourage the city's authorities, a month after CORE's protests began, from approving a five-year lease for space in the Cafritz Building, starting in May.

Generosity toward Morris Cafritz became an opportunity for Julius Hobson.

"A slap in the face of the District's colored community," Julius declared. "We, along with the NAACP, are going to continue to picket this citadel of bias that the commissioners chose to house the PUC." Congressman Diggs spent fifteen minutes on the picket line and announced, "I wanted to associate myself with the protest against the biggest bigot in D.C."

The PUC moved in on schedule, but its chairman refused to cross the picket line. "If the Cafritz Company does discriminate," he said, "it should be brought to the public's attention." The vice-chairman also declined to enter.

One morning, Julius and several others from CORE sat in the company's reception room and demanded to meet with Morris Cafritz. But they were told he had gone home sick.

The impasse lasted four weeks more. Then Morris issued a statement to the press.

"I have lived in and have loved Washington all my life," he said. "I deplore the reputation that Washington has, both in this country and in other capitals of the world, as a city of discrimination in housing. I think that it is right and proper that this Nation's Capital should be free from such accusations."

This, he professed, would take an act of Congress or an order by the D.C. commissioners, which Morris endorsed. "As soon as such a law is enacted or such an order issued, I will be the first to open all apartments which I control within the District of Columbia to all persons regardless of race, creed or color."

Carol Hobson stood with a contingent from her church, closer to the Washington Monument than to the Lincoln Memorial, along the south edge of the Reflecting Pool. The Wednesday afternoon was sunny and not as sweltering as August in Washington could be. Hobby was with her and Julius was somewhere nearby.

"It was the first time I'd ever seen that many people," Hobby said.

Surely this was so for everyone there. Never before had so many Americans marched on the capital to petition the government—as the First Amendment guaranteed—for a redress of grievances, not in support of the suffragettes or of the Ku Klux Klan or of the Bonus Army. The national leaders of the March on Washington for Jobs and Freedom spent the morning on Capitol Hill, lobbying for legislation to allow people of any color or creed to be served in a place of public accommodation; no minds were changed. More than one hundred thousand people had gathered around the Washington Monument by eleven o'clock, and twice as many by eleven-thirty, when the march (such as it was) to the Lincoln Memorial began a half-hour prematurely. The leaders hurried to get in front of the sea that followed behind. People sang and clapped and waved placards, almost every one of which included the word *NOW*. Harry Belafonte, Marlon Brando, and Burt Lancaster, with Charlton Heston, Sidney Poitier, and Robert Ryan led a three-abreast procession of movie stars, separated from their well-wishers by cordons of police. Dozens of demonstrators fainted, packed too tight; only three were arrested. Volunteer marshals fanned through the throng with walkie-talkies, as helicopters whirred overhead.

At the Lincoln Memorial, a sweet-natured crowd of a quarter of a million people or more gathered to hear the speeches. Dressed as if they were going to church, people kept on their best behavior; they lined up patiently at the seven thousand portable toilets, and boys of one race boosted boys of another into the branches; black and white legs dangled in the Reflecting Pool.

Carol had met Martin Luther King once before. He had spoken at the Church of the Redeemer, on Girard Street, while she served as the secretary of the D.C. chapter of his civil rights organization, the Southern Christian Leadership Conference (SCLC). She had shaken his hand and spoken with him and saw that "he had a very beautiful spirit and soul. That was obvious. He didn't require a lot of toting to"—unlike, she had found, James Farmer, the founder and national chairman of CORE. "People who have a great deal of inner security don't require a lot of obeisance. King didn't. He was just Martin Luther King. I'm sure he enjoyed it, but he didn't require it."

King and Farmer and the national chairmen of the other cosponsoring groups formed the Big Six that led the March on Washington. The heads of the groups' respective D.C. chapters made up the Washington Coordinating Committee, to work with the local authorities. Walter Fauntroy headed the SCLC in the capital and emerged as the spokesman for the local organizers, then as the chairman. Julius Hobson was in charge of the marshals, the nonofficial arrangements to control the crowd. He lined up local volunteers and worked with the New York policemen who had organized the security. Two weeks before the march, at Union Hall on U Street, Julius met with more than five hundred prospective marshals and impressed on them the need for nonviolence.

"You must use nothing but friendly persuasion," he exhorted. "Under no circumstances should you touch anyone. You must not even use harsh language."

Still, Julius had his doubts about the march. He thought too much white money was behind it, and he resented the organizers' insistence that all ten speeches be reviewed for inflammatory language. More than anything, he was upset by his circumscribed role. When the organizers briefed the police, *The Evening Star* photographed him at Fauntroy's shoulder. He felt as if he had been passed over for attention.

Maybe that was why, unknown to the other organizers, Julius disclosed some of the advance planning to the FBI—"pertinent information," the bureau believed.

All afternoon he worked from the command tent on the Washington Monument grounds, where the marshals picked up their orange armbands and the walkie-talkies kept Julius informed. But he worked his way down to the steps of the Lincoln Memorial while the speeches were under way.

He thought Martin Luther King was "a nice, clean-cut colored boy." King mounted the podium last, because nobody wanted to speak in his wake.

Everyone had been looking forward all afternoon to hearing the thirty-four-year-old preacher from Georgia with the prophet's intonation. Even a fifteen-year-old such as Hobby understood the importance of the vast and peaceful march and sensed King's eloquence as the climax. By the time the speech began, however, Hobby was worn out. During the long afternoon the Reflecting Pool offered no shade and indeed reflected the Sun's heat. Years later Hobby remembered little about the speech, except all that he had learned about it since.

On a Tuesday morning near the middle of November, Hale Boggs had breakfast with congressional leaders at the White House. Lindy had said she wanted to stop by afterward with her mother and mother-in-law, to see Jackie's refurbishing of the mansion. Hale mentioned it to Evelyn Lincoln, the president's secretary, and so she was looking for them and ushered them into the Oval Office.

It was a sparkling fall day, and President Kennedy showed the three ladies and Hale the redesigned Rose Garden and pointed beyond to the magnolia that Andrew Jackson had planted. The chrysanthemums were in bloom, along with the marigolds and the dahlias.

"Lindy," the president said, "how long do the chrysanthemums bloom in Washington in the fall?"

"Well, until the first frost," she replied.

"Oh, I hope the first frost comes late this year."

Then he showed them the Cabinet Room and spent fifteen minutes or more with them, before he asked Evelyn Lincoln to summon a photographer.

The following week, at the congressional breakfast, Hale brought up the Democratic feuding in Texas that the president hoped to repair in his impending trip.

"My, you are going into a hornet's nest," Hale said.

"Well, that'll add interest," the president answered. And then he said, "Things always look so much better away from Washington."

Those were the last words he ever spoke to Hale.

The week was a busy one for the House majority whip. Speaker McCormack was burying a brother in Boston, and Carl Albert had accompanied the president to Texas. Early afternoon on Friday, during a committee meeting's two-hour recess, Hale was downtown on his way to the bank because his account was overdrawn.

Somebody screamed, "The president's been shot."

"The whole place was in pandemonium," Hale remembered. "You couldn't get telephone calls through! You couldn't get taxicabs! You couldn't get anything."

Lindy was in her husband's quarters in the Capitol when someone from the Speaker's office phoned and told her to switch on the television. "Nobody knew whether it was a coup or what," Lindy recounted, "what the assassination was all about, so of course the police and the FBI and everybody moved into the Capitol." The telephone lines jammed. As the only person in the building remotely related to the leadership, Lindy invited in the security people, who arranged for guards at every entrance to the Capitol.

By the time Hale returned, the Speaker had also arrived, along with the Secret Service agents who had moved to protect the gaunt, white-maned man now next in line for the presidency. Already McCormack was complaining about their presence.

They would stay with him, Hale told him, whether he liked it or not.

Hale issued a statement to the press blaming "the radicals and haters in politics and elsewhere" for the assassination. He had made clear whom he meant when he encountered William Colmer, the segregationist congressman from Mississippi, in front of the newest House office building, named for Sam Rayburn.

"Your people, your Ross Barnetts," Hale blurted, "are the people who crucified this man."

Soon word arrived that the airplane bearing the slain president—as well as newly sworn-in President Lyndon Johnson—was to land just past six o'clock at Andrews Air Force Base. Hale accompanied the Speaker and the dean of the House, Carl Vinson of Georgia, out to the Maryland countryside southeast of the capital. On the tarmac he stood beside Charlie Halleck and Everett Dirksen, the House and Senate Republican leaders, as the casket moved past, into a battered ambulance. Jackie opened the ambulance door, her pink suit still stained with blood.

Hale joined eight other congressional leaders at the White House around seven-thirty, to meet with the new president. At first they could not find him. They tried the Oval Office but it was empty, and so was the Cabinet Room. Hale went into the Fish Room and found Ted Sorenson sitting alone.

The speechwriter was watching the playback on television of his final handiwork, delivered only that morning—so long ago—in Fort Worth.

"They wouldn't even let him have three years," he muttered to Hale.

At last the congressional leaders found the new president next door, over at the Executive Office Building, in the vice president's suite.

"I am president in a way that no man would ever want to become president," the tall, sad Texan told them, "but I am president."

He asked for their help, and they pledged it.

"God bless you, Mr. President," each of them said, filing past.

Hobby was throwing a football with a neighbor in the backyard. The high school sophomore, off for a teachers' training day, heard somebody shout that the president had been shot. He went inside, turned on the television, and froze.

The next day, his mother asked him to get something at the store. He was sure that nothing was open—nothing should be. He walked to the end of Queens Chapel Terrace, to Michigan Avenue, and waited to cross. The cars rushed past.

"Nothing's stopped; everything is business as usual," he marveled to himself. "The president's dead, but the whole world's still going."

Six

JOHNSON

Lady Bird Johnson knew that she should give Jackie Kennedy the time she needed to move out of the White House with her children. Lindy Boggs helped Lady Bird pack up the house where she and Lyndon had been living while he was vice president. They had bought the dignified French-style house in the exclusive Spring Valley neighborhood from Perle Mesta, and it had given them privacy and space. They had added air-conditioning, a swimming pool, a built-in hi-fi system, and marble over the bathtub tile. "That's the nicest house I ever lived in," Lady Bird said. They had surprised Lindy with a birthday party, a seated dinner for forty.

Even the Johnsons' daughters thought of Lindy as a friend. When Lynda Bird, the older, wanted to sneak away to Mardi Gras, she stayed with the Boggses' close friends, the Kohlmeyers, while her boyfriend, the actor George Hamilton, slept at Hale's brother's. Both girls married while their father was president. Hale read an epistle at Luci's wedding, and he and Lindy threw a party for the bridesmaids and groomsmen before Lynda's, to Chuck Robb, a marine guard in the White House.

These joys were yet to come. A few days after President Kennedy was laid to rest at Arlington Cemetery, in its serenity overlooking the capital, Hale sat in the homey den on Bradley Boulevard and conversed with the new president by telephone. The two men were friends but also competitors, with similarly outsized personalities.

People would surely start asking dark questions about the assassination, Hale told the president—about what had really happened and why. He suggested that Johnson appoint a blue-ribbon committee to investigate.

"Okay," the president replied—"you're on it."

This happened early in the Thanksgiving holiday, the week after the assassination, and the secrecy-minded president began planning for a commission that would be sufficiently august to lay the public's suspicions of conspiracy to rest. A pall had spread over the nation, of an innocence breached, as Americans watched the caisson carrying President Kennedy's mortal remains creep along Pennsylvania Avenue, past John-John's salute.

The day after Thanksgiving, Representative Charles Goodell rose on the House floor. When the Republican from upstate New York warned about hasty inquiries, Hale could not resist telling what he knew.

"I can say on the highest authority that this matter is going to be the subject of an inquiry, and that it will be a very high-level inquiry, and that it will bear no resemblance to partisanship."

When Johnson learned of this, he was furious. He hated to have his plans disclosed. "He's talking all the damn time," he groused to Abe Fortas, a Washington lawyer and confidant. "Talking to the leaders is just like talking into a big microphone."

Still, Johnson appointed Hale as one of two Democrats on a seven-member commission headed by Chief Justice Earl Warren to investigate who had murdered President Kennedy and why.

Hale found the ten months of work emotionally draining. He joined in the commission's hearings (Lee Harvey Oswald's widow had "a sweet, feminine smile," he wrote in notes to himself), participated in the closed-door debates, and looked through the piles of evidence. He visited the Texas School Book Depository, lifted Oswald's rifle to his shoulder, and aimed through the telescopic lens, as an automobile rolled below. He went home shaken. "It was like I killed Jack," he told Lindy.

The investigation of a murder used all of Hale's legal training (the other six members were lawyers as well) and called on the strength of his supple mind. Gerald Ford, a fellow commission member and the leader of the activist Republicans in the House, later recalled the "pertinent questions" that Hale posed to witnesses.

Hale also applied his skill at political compromise. The commission's staff recommended a flat statement that there had been no conspiracy. But when the principals deliberated, "we showed better judgment," as Ford remembered. He and Hale and the Senate's giant, Richard Russell—three of the panel's four working politicians—proposed a conclusion that would be easier to defend, that no evidence of a conspiracy had been found. Chief Justice Warren later told Lindy, over and over, that Hale had suggested the precise language (that the conclusion had been reached "according to the testimony presented," thereby excluding the rumors and casual allegations) that assured the commission a unanimous vote. Hale never doubted, however, that Lee Harvey Oswald had acted alone.

Hale's proximity to power yielded pleasures as well as historic duties. Barbara's wedding was planned for January. "In some ways I got her on the rebound," the groom acknowledged. Paul Sigmund was a mild-mannered professor of political theory at Princeton, ten years older than she, an anchor for her ebullience, and also a Catholic. Hale insisted on a backyard wedding—"We do things in our backyard, we don't do things in a country club"—under a heated Arabian Nights sort of tent.

The wedding became the capital's first outsized social event following the assassination, an emerging from mourning.

At the Shrine of the Most Blessed Sacrament on Chevy Chase Circle, Barbara wore the veil used in Lindy's mother's family since 1848. President Johnson skipped the ceremony, so as not to outshine the happy couple. But he went to the Saturday reception at the Boggses' and danced with the bride. "Everybody was there, every politician you ever heard of," said the groom. The traffic jammed along Bradley Boulevard. In her modest kitchen Lindy had done all of the cooking, with help from friends, for fifteen hundred guests. The heads of all three branches of government attended.

"I'm awful glad I was invited," the president said, to laughter.

Not everyone in the household, however, was impressed with the president. For years Johnson had been trying to get Emma Cyprian's recipe for a half-fricasseed chicken dish. Under protest, Emma had furnished the recipe more than once, but some crucial ingredient was always missing.

"Emma," said Lindy, "Mr. Johnson is now the president of the United States. You must give him the recipe for your chicken."

But Emma refused to allow her recipe to be prepared anywhere else, even the White House. "If he wants my chicken," she said, "he has to come to my kitchen."

Many of Julius Hobson's friends joked that the white news media had anointed him as "the GNL"—the Great Negro Leader. He was often invited to local radio and television stations, and his hosts always hoped for a scoop.

In March 1964, Julius appeared on WTOP's *City Side*, which aired on channel nine on Sunday at noon and that night on the radio. As the interview started, Julius was asked about a possible boycott of the city's public schools, and he proposed one for April 20.

"This is the first I've heard of this," his interviewer said—"is this the first announcement of a boycott date?"

"We just decided this, really, a couple of days ago."

The one-day boycott was to touch off a week of protests, featuring sit-ins at the school board, picketing by CORE and the Student Nonviolent Coordinating Committee (SNCC), and two days of busing children from overcrowded schools to schools with extra room.

"I'm not in favor of just scattering children out for the sake of integration," Julius explained on the show. "What we're worrying about is quality of education." The white neighborhoods, he said, simply had the best schools—"They have libraries, they have science laboratories, they have all kinds of extracurricular activities, and they are under-capacity comparatively speaking, whereas in the lower economic areas, which are primarily Negro, where the schools are primarily Negro, they have none of these things."

The date for a boycott was news not only to the press and the public but also to members of CORE, who had not been asked. Eleven Negro leaders (from the NAACP, the Urban League, the SCLC, and other groups) met with the school superintendent and then summoned reporters to Walter Fauntroy's church, at Ninth and S, to denounce the boycott as a tactic to be used "only when progress has stagnated or when communication has broken down. Neither of these conditions is present at this time in Washington."

Julius called this act of defiance "Uncle Tommery," and he accused his rivals of undercutting CORE. He said, "It should be named the National Association against CORE Projects rather than . . ." At a meeting on the school boycott, he argued that his organization's very weakness left it no choice but to try gadfly tactics. "CORE has to act as in guerrilla warfare," he said. "CORE can't do anything but raise sand."

Julius arranged his own session with Carl Hansen, the superintendent of schools. Hansen was a balding Nebraskan with unstylish eyeglasses who had spent seventeen years as an administrator in D.C. schools. As an associate superintendent, he had drawn up the plan to desegregate the neighborhood schools, which civil rights leaders hailed as a model for the nation. But, a journalist explained in *Saturday Review*, "policies that seemed liberal during the 1950s in what had basically been a Southern town seemed very conservative ten years later amid the rising tensions of a Northern ghetto." Julius presented fourteen proposals to equalize the resources in the city's schools. Over two hours the superintendent agreed to study twelve of them and rejected two: that the city pay for buses to transport children away from overcrowded buildings and that police officers be removed from schools in the ghetto. Those, said Julius, formed the "heart" of his recommendations.

The next night he told the members of CORE what had happened. The meeting was held at All Souls Unitarian Church, at Sixteenth and Harvard Streets, a Georgian-style brick church (modeled on one in London's Trafalgar Square) that offered a biracial breath of freethinking in a stodgy and still segregated city. The absence of decoration in the white sanctuary was meant to focus the mind beyond temporal things. This time it failed.

After a heated debate, a majority voted to "suspend all boycott activities" for a week, the deadline (at Julius's insistence) for the superintendent to complete his response.

Julius also made an announcement: When his term as CORE's chairman ended in May, he would step down.

"I'm tired," he told the *Afro-American*. "I've been neglecting my home. If a hundred percent of the membership signed a petition, I would not stay."

A week later, the boycott was canceled and Julius announced that he was running for chairman again.

The dissension within CORE went deep. Julius was convinced a disruptive force was at work, and not only in Washington, pitting CORE against the likes of the NAACP. "I don't know if it's coming from the far left, the far right, or if they are agents of the Confederacy," he said, but "there is a well-organized effort to take over the group and to change the basic philosophy of CORE."

His opponents within CORE, mainly white, pleaded the cause of democracy. They objected to Julius's high-handedness.

"You can't run a revolution with Robert's Rules of Order," Julius shot back.

The discord intensified. Twenty-five dissidents stormed out of a meeting, singing "We Shall Overcome." Several of them formally requested to James Farmer, the national chairman, that Julius be expelled. They submitted thirty-eight pages of accusations: He had initiated projects and ended them without consulting members of CORE, "rudely cut off" discussion at meetings, used ten consecutive tabling motions to stanch a debate, adjourned a meeting without a motion, and otherwise acted in "an arbitrary, non-democratic manner."

CORE had never expelled an active member, but as any organization does, it needed a measure of control over what was done in its name. With Julius in charge, the chapter faced a fracturing.

CORE's higher-ups had to choose sides. The organization's national steering committee listened to both camps and heard too many complaints to leave the outcome in doubt. Julius had edged away not only from CORE's discipline but also from its philosophy.

"I'm nonviolent," Julius said. "It's just not a religion with me." He was also losing faith in the customary tactics. "I frankly believe that limited picket lines, sit-in demonstrations, and big marches have reached their peaks of effectiveness," he wrote a few months later in a letter to the editor. He wanted to turn the attention to the larger problems of schools, slums, and poverty.

When CORE's national steering committee voted unanimously to expel him, Julius announced that he would appeal to the full membership, at the national convention in Kansas City in July.

In the meantime, he kept working. CORE joined the NAACP in picketing at the Washington Hospital Center, which practiced segregation in its semiprivate rooms. While activists congregated in the lobby and conducted a sit-in, Julius ventured upstairs and climbed into bed in a whites-only ward—a lie-in, he called it—until his arrest.

He and his NAACP counterpart threatened to fill the jails until the hospital ended its restrictions by race. Four days later it did.

In Kansas City, Julius spoke to the gathered reporters while he watched the delegates filing in. "CORE is getting to be a middle-class organization," he said. "Just look at those delegates." Most of them were white. "We have to get back to the ghettos and work."

By a vote of 213 to 21, his expulsion was upheld.

The Washington chapter of CORE withered after he left.

The Homestead felt farther from Washington than a four-hour drive. The stately redbrick resort hotel was nestled in the hazy dramatics of Virginia's Shenandoah Valley, by the mineral springs. Visiting there was like taking a trip back in time. A young George Washington had passed through, as the commander of the Virginia militia, and fifteen presidents had visited this reminder of plantation days, known for its painstaking service and manicured grounds.

No wonder the D.C. Bankers Association chose the Homestead for its annual convention. Its elegance and pampering suited the image the bankers had of themselves.

Morris Cafritz, as a director at Riggs, attended, with his wife.

Still svelte and athletic at age fifty-four, Gwen was determined to enjoy Homestead's elaborate facilities. At home she was known to swim any distance, paddle on the Potomac, exercise for a half-hour each morning, and even water-ski and fence. Morris, at seventy-seven, preferred golf, but it had not been so many years ago that he won a five-dollar bet by doing fifteen push-ups.

The evening's event was a dinner to honor the association's outgoing president, a Riggs vice president, and Morris was in high spirits. He was waltzing Gwen around the dance floor when he said he felt ill. They stopped dancing and Morris went to "get a pill."

Minutes later, friends found him in an adjoining room, dying.

A rescue squad arrived but could not revive him. In his jacket pocket was a photograph of him and Gwen in bathing suits.

His death was less than a shock. Morris had suffered a mild heart attack a year before, and the pain from his angina had grown worse. There was nothing he could do but take nitroglycerin tablets.

His three sons drove down from Washington and arranged to have their father's remains shipped home. Friends called at Joseph Gawler's & Sons and the funeral took place at Washington Hebrew, on Massachusetts Avenue, on acreage that Morris had donated. The builder's faith in the future, the rabbi eulogized, "soared to eloquent heights when he spoke of Washington." A senator, a Supreme Court justice, three ambassadors, the city's police chief, and the columnist Drew Pearson served as honorary pallbearers.

Gwen's mother and sister had recently died, and now Morris. They were the three people she cared about most.

His death was front-page news. "Cafritz Shaped City's Skyline," headlined *The Washington Post*. On Temple Heights, Morris had just completed the Universal North Building, in tandem with the Universal Building he had finished eight years earlier, marking the northernmost edge of the new downtown. He and Charlie Tompkins had sold the rest of the plot to Conrad Hilton, for a hotel.

The Evening Star profiled Morris as "Civic Leader, Builder," as if to rearrange his legacy. But Morris had already done the rearranging himself. His philanthropy had been earnest. Three days before leaving for the Homestead, he had met with seven local businessmen and wangled another thirty-five thousand dollars (beyond his own generosity) for a hospital being built in Anacostia. When it opened, two years later, it bore his name.

His estate was valued at twenty-three million dollars. He willed a quarter of it to his sons, to whom he had already given property. Another quarter went to Gwen. The other half of everything he had earned in a lifetime was bequeathed to the Morris and Gwendolyn Cafritz Foundation, to give back to a city that had given him so much.

The ribbon cutting for the final twenty-five miles of the Capital Beltway took place on a sweltering August morning in 1964, near the New Hampshire Avenue exit, in the rolling hills of Maryland. The smell of the fertilizer on the banks and median strip mingled with the automobile exhaust of drivers who kept the air-conditioning turned on. Thousands of cars were parked on the new roadway, two or three or four abreast, for more than two miles in both directions.

As early as 1928 the capital's planners had suggested a "by-pass" around the city to relieve the highways of congestion; nothing happened until the federal government started footing the bill for interstate highways. The twenty-two miles in Virginia had opened in April. Soon, commuters would marvel at how many minutes they saved—eighty minutes a day between Alexandria and Fort Meade, forty-five minutes at night from Falls Church to College Park.

The circumferential highway, which took its name from the two-year-old Baltimore Beltway, had already started to reshape the capital's metropolitan area, socially and economically. Wholesalers had begun to locate nearby, and suburban shopping centers showed up on drawing boards. Mike Causey, a reporter for the *Post*, coined a phrase—"inside the Beltway"—to characterize the separation of the government from the people it governed.

"A huge wedding ring for the metropolitan area, uniting all of its suburbs"—the Federal Highway administrator waxed metaphorical in addressing the dignitaries and spectators. After Governor Millard Tawes of Maryland wielded the golden scissors, everyone tried to leave at once, creating the Beltway's first traffic jam.

One hundred protesters and forty policemen showed up at the Rat Relocation Rally in the tangled triangular park at Florida and First NW. There was talk of rats, threats of rats, but no rats.

Julius Hobson had attached a cage to the top of a station wagon and threatened to drive the rats caught in the poor neighborhoods over to Georgetown and set them loose. But for now the rats they had caught and not yet drowned in the river were in birdcages at the Florida Avenue row house that served as the headquarters for Julius's new group, the Associated Community Teams, or ACT.

Julius had attended ACT's organizing session the previous spring near Philadelphia, along with Malcolm X, Dick Gregory, and Adam Clayton Powell, the congressman from Harlem. The loosely federated network of "hard-hitting, militant" groups, as Julius described it, was "designed and run by Negroes for Negroes." It was meant to include poor people in its ranks. It professed a belief in nonviolence but also in self-defense, "not a civil rights organization in the classical sense," Julius declared, "but a revolutionary one in the American tradition."

Julius had vowed to take CORE's members with him into the new group, and supposedly sixty of them went, though only fifteen or twenty people typically showed up at a meeting—a "paper tiger with teeth," he said, "that could hold its convention in a phone booth." Yet that was enough, as long as the newspapers covered its activities, as they had been more and more. "Maybe I shouldn't say it, but the strength of the whole damn civil rights movement in this town is the press," he acknowledged later. "It wasn't me—I had no way of communicating."

The Rat Relocation Rally was an inspired idea, meant to publicize the diversion of the city's rat eradication funds away from the ghetto and into the neighborhoods where white people lived and tourists roamed. (Rats had been seen scurrying from beneath bushes by the Washington Monument even in daylight.) Julius demanded a meeting with D.C. officials to show them medical records of "thirteen or fourteen" children bitten by rats, and he offered volunteers to help kill rats, if the city supplied the know-how and the poison.

"I don't think Julius would have deliberately turned them loose," an associate said later. "He was pretty ethical—there were certain lines he would not cross."

This time he did not need to. The *Post*'s account of the Rat Relocation Rally ran alongside a report "that there are as many rats as people in the District," with the problem worst in "slums or deteriorating neighborhoods."

The city soon shifted its extermination program into Northeast.

Julius knew how to draw attention. He built a parabolic microphone like the wireless ones that football coaches used for listening to the opposing quarterback and swiveled it out of his car, which had signs—*Cop-Watching Wagon*—on the side. He followed police cars on weekend nights and played two or three tapes for the chief of police to hear the abusive language used in making arrests. That, plus the articles and editorials, provoked a directive that the cops change their ways. Or Julius would bluff the authorities into believing that Stokely Carmichael was planning to attend a demonstration, so that police motorcycles would congregate and draw a crowd. He would stick a finger in a policeman's face and demand to know whether he had ever fired his gun, whether he had killed anyone, maybe a black man.

"What he was doing was teaching us," said a sidekick, "you don't have to be afraid of these cops, as long as there's enough of you."

Julius held to his own strict standards of right and wrong, and he allowed himself to act as he needed when he felt sure he was right.

Early on a Saturday morning in August, Carol watched from a second-floor window as a man who had rung the doorbell a few minutes before walked away. She knew he was from the FBI, because she recognized his name from the time somebody had threatened to blow up the house and from when they had been charged for an expensive subscription and stacks of phonograph records they had never ordered.

Then Julius returned upstairs with one hundred dollars in his hand and said, "Pack your things; we're going to Atlantic City."

"I thought the involvement with the FBI was for our protection," Carol said later. "He never would tell me anything." Only later did she learn that he had something to sell.

They usually vacationed in Atlantic City during the summer with the pastor of Carol's (and Hobby's) church. This year money was tight, but politics had proffered an opportunity. As the Democrats convened on the New Jersey shore to nominate President Johnson for a term of his own, issues of race took the forefront. The dark faces of the Mississippi Freedom Democratic Party sat huddled on the Boardwalk and sought seats in the hall. The leaders of ACT had designated Julius to pick out places for demonstrations, the best intersections for tying up traffic, which in a beach-hugging community was easy to do.

The FBI considered what Julius told them "important information concerning the meetings, plans, and proposals for demonstrations of racial groups such as CORE and ACT in Atlantic City."

Hobby and Jean slept at the pastor's rental, while Julius and Carol stayed at the hotel in which Dick Gregory and the other protest leaders lodged. After the mosquitoes drove Carol to join the children, the family got together once. When Hobby ordered chicken in a seafood restaurant, Julius exploded.

One day, as Carol and the children walked up from the beach, still in swimsuits, wrapped in towels, Julius drove up. He stopped and said, "Get in the car."

Carol asked, "For what?"

"We're going back to Washington."

He had already packed their things.

As they drove out of town, Carol heard on the radio that Julius Hobson had threatened to bring in horse-drawn wagons and tie up traffic. Her questions brought no response.

Back at home, the FBI phoned. For another two hundred dollars, Julius left for Atlantic City again.

To mourn Morris's death, Gwen Cafritz flew to Rome, on an expired passport.

"I'm still in a state of shock," she whispered to Earl Wilson, the gossip columnist, by the pool at the Rome Golf Club.

"When will you feel comfortable giving a party again?"

"It depends on my soul. Probably not until fall." But the time, she knew, would come. "My husband wouldn't have wanted me to change my way of life."

The Supreme Court, however, opened its session in October without a reception on Foxhall Road.

Gwen planned a party for November. Only after she had mailed the several hundred invitations did she realize to her horror that she had scheduled it for the twenty-second, the first anniversary of Camelot's collapse.

She had never met the postmaster general before, but she telephoned him. John Gronouski gallantly agreed to have the invitations retrieved and for his trouble received one, for the twentieth.

"I guess it's not my year—I'm not thinking right," Gwen confessed to an inquiring reporter. "I'll think right in 1965."

The party was a triumph—"THE party of the year," *The Evening Star* gushed. Barry Goldwater, tan and confident, as if the president had not crushed him in the recent election, held court in a corner of the living room. J. Edgar Hoover got caught in the entrance hall by waves of congratulations for his three-hour press conference with women reporters. A photographer snapped the FBI director, rarely seen on the social circuit, in a two-handed clasp with his weary-looking hostess.

After Morris died, "she was terribly sad," her eldest son said, "like a ship without a rudder. They had worked very closely, and she depended on him in many ways. After he died, something went out, in terms of her sense of herself."

Yet she kept trying. Gwen threw another large party in December and an even splashier one two nights before the inauguration, after the star-studded gala. A line of long black cars snaked along Foxhall Road after midnight and disgorged the stars—Alfred Hitchcock, Rudolf Nureyev, Barbra Streisand, Harry Belafonte, Johnny Carson, Woody Allen, Gregory Peck, Carol Burnett, Ann-Margret, Bobby Darin, Dame Margot Fonteyn. Political luminaries were there, too: Lynda Bird and the vice president–elect and Mrs. Humphrey. Hubert danced downstairs on the glass floor with Carol Channing until two fifteen. And the Gronouskis were invited again.

Gwen wore more jewelry than usual to the Inaugural Ball, including a diamond choker that indeed seemed to choke her. She had taken her jewelry from the safety deposit box at Riggs for the week's parties. Carter, her middle son, was living at home and went through the house, which was ordinarily unlocked, and secured every door. Gwen was concerned about a string of robberies in the neighborhood.

Three nights after the Inauguration, Gwen's chauffeur drove her to a party in Georgetown, at the Alaska Airlines president's home, and then dropped her off to dance at the stark new German Embassy at the foot of Foxhall Road.

A half-hour past midnight she was snacking in her kitchen when Carter walked in the back door. He had celebrated his twenty-eighth birthday with dinner at his younger brother Conrad's and a cake at his older brother Calvin's. Carter was a loose and likable young man, short and stout as his father had been. As he returned the silverware used for the cake, Gwen groused at its having left the premises.

Carter wished his mother good night and went up to bed.

After Gwen went to her bedroom, fifty feet from Carter's, she locked the door, laid her dress on a chaise lounge, and put on a robe. In the dressing room, she returned her jewelry to the boxes on the windowsill.

As she returned to the bedroom, the lights went out. Somebody grabbed her rather gently from behind, an arm around her neck.

"Carter, don't." She thought it was a joke.

A man told her to be quiet or be killed.

She was pushed and held down on the bed—by four Negroes, she believed. She stopped herself from screaming, out of fear that Carter would burst in.

Her eyes were taped shut, her wrists bound.

"Give us your money!"

She had none, she said, for she carried only small amounts of cash.

"White bitch," they growled, slapping her. They told her "niggers" would rape her and so would their "boss" if she did not open her safe.

They pulled her across the bedroom to the cedar closet that held the safe. Her blindfold was removed, her head kept pointed toward the wall. The men wore leather gloves and held pencil-thin flash-lights. She thought one of them was wearing her blue flowered shower cap.

She asked for her reading glasses. Someone gave them to her and she opened the safe.

The burglars dragged her through the dressing room and laid her facedown on the floor of the bathroom. She was hogtied with wet clothesline and lashed to the drainpipe of the sink.

She moaned that she would die on the cold marble floor and asked for a Turkish towel.

A man asked what that was, then took a comforter from her bed and several pillows and a glass of water—"You know you white bitches drink scotch." She was gagged with her own silk scarf.

They warned her to stay still and promised to tell the police where she was.

For fifteen minutes she obeyed, then she took a half-hour to wriggle her hands free. She crawled to the dressing room. With a pair of manicure scissors she unbound her feet.

Rope dangled from her wrist as she banged on Carter's door. He telephoned the police and then the FBI.

Police cars converged on the house. "The cops," said Carter, "all wanted personal tours of the house." After dawn the detectives combed the grounds and found that the intruders had climbed a trel-lis onto the balcony by Morris's old bedroom, broken a pane in the French door, reached through, and unlocked it.

Eighteen pieces of jewelry were gone, including the $100,000 necklace of forty-six diamonds, and other necklaces, brooches, and earrings that Morris had given to Gwen for their twentieth anniver-sary. Everything was insured for $264,940 but worth as much as $600,000, counting the $50 taken from Gwen's purse. Police called it the richest Washington house-breaking in memory.

J. Edgar Hoover instructed his Washington field office to make the heist a top priority. FBI agents stayed at the house for more than twelve hours, interviewing Gwen, her sons, and the household staff. In the course of the morning, Gwen drank two or three medium-sized tumblers of scotch, and more during the afternoon. "Mrs.

Cafritz has been in the habit of consuming great quantities of intoxicants," the agent in charge reported to Hoover. "Her narration of events was less than coherent and frequently punctuated by digressions concerning the very many prominent people she has known in Washington social life."

She told the agents she suspected someone on her household staff was involved—how else could intruders have known the location of her safe? The only firm evidence turned up a few blocks away, on Forty-fourth Street—the shower cap, with a single strand of hair, an undyed brown, from a Caucasian. FBI investigators expressed "considerable doubt" that the intruders had been Negroes.

Two months later Gwen phoned the FBI to say that she was no longer certain that Negroes had robbed her. She believed she knew who the "boss" was, though he had never spoken—so that Gwen would not recognize his voice, she realized now.

She said she must have recognized a "Cafritz grab," in first thinking it was Carter. The boss, she now presumed, was someone who had supposedly been promised one million dollars in Morris's will but had been disappointed: Dr. Eddie. Clearly, she was imagining this. Edward Cafritz, an executor of his brother's estate, was seventy-one and ailing.

Neither the jewelry nor the burglars would ever be found.

One evening in 1965, four generations of Boggs and Claiborne women lingered over dinner on the back patio at Bradley Boulevard. Hale and Lindy; Lindy's grandmother and mother; Hale's mother; Cokie and her fiancé, Steve Roberts, and some of their friends gathered around the table. Hale liked having young people around. They found him intimidating but not standoffish. There was also something magnetic about him, with his easy laugh and his aura of power.

The conversation turned to the voting rights bill, which was up for a House vote the next afternoon, the fourth day of debate. The police bullwhips and tear gas in Selma, Alabama, had compelled President Johnson, who was usually so awkward on television, into an emotional plea before Congress and the nation to assure Americans of any color the right to vote.

All four generations prodded Hale to break with his region and his past and to throw his support behind the voting rights bill. He told them he had already decided to vote for it, no small concession. In 1962 he had proposed a constitutional amendment to return control of problems in schools to the states. At Lindy's urging, he had almost voted for the path-breaking Civil Rights Act of 1964, but in the end he opposed it, fearing the political risk.

This time, however, the balance of political risks had shifted. For one thing, the substance of the issue was easier for Hale. He regarded the right to vote as fundamental, as the instrument for acquiring every other civil right. Besides, it had become more dangerous for him to oppose the bill. Hale understood that his ascent within the national party depended on his willingness to act as a national Democrat. On most issues he already did. As early as 1960 he had endorsed a federal program to finance medical care for the elderly, and he had reliably supported the New Frontier and now the Great Society. Federal aid to education, housing for the poor, the War on Poverty—these were popular in a city as poor as New Orleans. That left civil rights. He could see where the South was heading and hoped to lead it there. He also recognized that Democrats from the North and West would stymie his rise within the House—surely, to the speakership—unless he joined them on an issue so pivotal.

For the women, simply voting for the legislation would not suffice—he also had to speak on its behalf.

"You've got to do it," Cokie argued. "First of all, you're a leader in the House. Secondly, as long as you're going to vote for it, let your voice be heard; give the reason you're doing it."

"Look, don't push me any further on this," Hale exclaimed. "I'm going to vote for it—leave me alone." Any statement in public would only provoke his opponents at home.

The next day, all over the Capitol, a crackling charged the air, a feeling of great moment. The Senate had scheduled a final vote on Medicare, the grandest social legislation in a generation, while the House faced yet another climax in the nation's century-long pursuit of an ever-truer democracy.

The House chamber was dignified by its cream-colored ceiling and its fabric-covered walls. Ordinarily it was empty on a Friday afternoon, but reporters, tourists, and lawmakers' families had crowded into the galleries. The members of Congress scurried around the floor, resembling an undisciplined colony of ants.

Joe D. Waggonner strode down to the well and asked to be recognized. The third-term congressman hailed from northern Louisiana, a land of scrub pines and good ol' boys. He assailed the bill for discriminating—not against Negroes but against Louisiana, which stood to fall under Justice Department jurisdiction because fewer than half of its nonwhite citizens had registered to vote. "We cannot justify this discriminatory legislation under the guise of erasing discrimination," Waggonner proclaimed. There was no need for such a law in Louisiana, he said, because no discrimination was taking place.

This was too much for Hale. He asked for five minutes to respond. He had nothing prepared.

"Mr. Chairman," Hale began. "I had not intended to talk at this stage of the debate. I am constrained to do so now only because of the remarks made just a moment ago by my distinguished colleague and dear friend, the gentleman from Louisiana."

The House had hushed. Hale was an orator in an age of oratory, when the logic and majesty of a speech might still occasionally influence votes. The word would go out in the Capitol—*Boggs is up*—and people would flock to the House chamber to listen. He spoke in a quietly self-assured drawl, a patient rumble, from the diaphragm. He could speak softly or sharply, but always strongly, fluctuating his rhythm and pitch.

"I love the South," he declared. "I know it as well as any man in this body knows it." His grandfather had been on Robert E. Lee's staff, and his great-uncle—"God rest his soul"—had surrendered the last Confederate army in the field, six weeks after Appomattox. "I wish I could stand here as a man who loves my state, born and reared in the South, who has spent every year of his life in Louisiana since he was five years old, and say that there has not been discrimination," he said. "But unfortunately it is not so." Just south of New Orleans, in a jurisdiction with three thousand Negroes, fewer than one hundred had registered to vote. And elsewhere, too—"Can we say there has been no discrimination? Can we honestly say that from our hearts? I ask the gentleman that question. He knows it is not so."

His voice dropped. Hale's passion lay less in the words than in the context and courage. Lindy had arrived in the gallery halfway through, fearing he would vote against the bill.

"So, Mr. Chairman, I take this rostrum really more out of sadness than anything else. I love my state. I love the South with every part of me, and I love my country. I shall support this bill because I believe the fundamental right to vote must be part of this great experiment in human progress under freedom which is America."

As he sat, his colleagues stood and applauded. Many considered it the finest speech of his career.

That night, the landmark legislation passed, 333 to 85. Of the eighty-seven southern Democrats, twenty-two said, "Aye," compared to the seven who had voted for the Civil Rights Act of 1964. Gradually the South was becoming part of the nation.

Julius Hobson smoked his pipe as he sat in the Board of Education chairman's chair. The school board was about to convene at Thirteenth and K, across the park from the Ambassador Hotel, in the old Franklin School, where Andrew Jackson's children and Chester A. Arthur's had practiced their cursive. How profoundly the city had changed, for Julius and two other Negro protesters to have seized the seats of the school board's three Negroes, accusing them of voting "against the best interest of black children."

The city's nine-member school board, appointed by the federal judges in D.C., had called the meeting to explain to the indignant citizens why a white woman had been appointed to run the city's predominantly Negro elementary schools. Julius had another complaint: the academic track system that D.C. schools had instituted after desegregation to deal with the disparity in the quality of the white and colored schools. Children were assigned to one of three tracks as early as first grade and to one of four in high school. Once in a track, a child rarely left it. Jean had been placed in the lowest, "basic" track and was stuck there.

Julius announced that the sit-in was aimed at "three Uncle Toms as a protest from the black community," as the start of a "drastic, direct action campaign against the school board."

At two o'clock on Monday afternoon, when the school board was scheduled to convene, Wesley Williams stood at Julius's shoulder. The board's first Negro chairman was a distinguished-looking attorney, a lifelong Republican, a member of All Souls.

"I'm asking you like a gentleman," he told Julius.

Julius stared at the table and vowed to sit until the police took him away.

Reporters crowded behind. The committee of ministers in attendance to protest the racial imbalance among school administrators dissociated itself from the sit-in. "We were as surprised as the school board," a spokesman said.

A policeman stepped over to Julius. "Will you move out of his chair?"

Julius's pipe jutted from his mouth as he gazed up at him.

Wesley Williams said he could run the meeting from his feet, but the other members demurred. He asked Julius whether he wished to say something to the overflowing crowd.

Julius sat silently.

A shouting match erupted between Colonel Hamilton, whose seat had also been usurped, and a minister in the audience.

"Liar!" the retired colonel yelled.

Julius and his two companions were arrested for disorderly conduct. It was Julius's third arrest, but no more unpleasant than the others. The police treated him with respect—"Mr. Hobson," they called him—probably because he respected them. He did not regard individual cops as "pigs," as they were soon to be tagged, but as the instruments of a wicked system.

"I don't want to meet the chief of police," Julius once said—"I might like him."

The ACT arrestees requested a jury trial—"We couldn't ask for a better forum to air our complaints," Julius said—and hoped to subpoena the school board's records and members.

They wound up before a judge, to argue that the school board had caused the disorderliness. Julius testified he had contributed "only a smile" to the confusion.

Found guilty and slapped with five days in jail or a ten-dollar fine, Julius chose to go home.

No president had ever uttered the word *beauty* in an address to the nation, or so Lady Bird was told before her husband delivered his State of the Union message in 1965. Nor had any previous first lady, even Eleanor Roosevelt, joined in meetings on legislative strategy or buttonholed members of Congress, as Lady Bird did in securing enactment of the Highway Beautification Act.

The secretary of the interior, Stewart Udall, suggested that she fashion the capital into a garden city, as a model for the nation. At the second meeting of her Committee on Beautification, in the Yellow Oval Room upstairs in the White House, a slide show began with L'Enfant's vision of the Mall, then pictured the steam plant that rose from its one-time wilderness. Too much of L'Enfant's beautiful city, with its clean geometric lines, had become a jumble of slums. President Kennedy, during his inaugural parade, had been disgusted by the pawn shops and boarded-up storefronts along Pennsylvania Avenue. Lady Bird's committee broke into factions that favored different parts of the city to be beautified—its monumental core or the neighborhoods beyond, Washington *or* D.C.

Lady Bird insisted on both.

Starting in the rundown neighborhood now known as Shaw, near the junior high school, children and adults were enlisted to clean up trash and control rats, to apply paint to playgrounds and housing projects, to plant grass, shrubs, and flowers. Nine cherry trees and ninety-three hundred azalea bushes were planted along Pennsylvania Avenue, in addition to the 100,000 daffodil bulbs along Rock Creek Parkway and the 175 dogwoods near Key Bridge in Georgetown.

Lyndon Johnson said later that the tulips in Washington bowed whenever his wife passed by.

Lindy Boggs had helped get the president's Head Start program off the ground, by organizing volunteers to educate disadvantaged children in the nation's neediest three hundred counties, many in the rural South, using the contacts she had made while planning the Lady Bird Special, the first lady's whistle-stop tour during the 1964 campaign. Now Lindy traveled the country giving speeches on beautification. "Every time Mother had a project," Lynda Bird recalled, "Lindy was roped into it," for her organizational skills.

Lady Bird paid particular attention to the Mall. A master architect suggested a sculpture garden just west of the National Gallery of Art, across Constitution Avenue from the National Archives, on fallow acreage called L'Enfant Square. A benefactor—a benefactress—was found.

"There were quite a few other projects on the agenda," Gwen Cafritz said, "but this is the one I wanted."

The Morris and Gwendolyn Cafritz Foundation promised eighty thousand dollars to buy statuary, classical and modern.

Gwen's interest was natural. She had always loved art, and William Rogers, the former attorney general who had become Gwen's lawyer and confidant, was on Lady Bird's committee. But it was more than that. Her interests were changing. Without Morris, she no longer enjoyed hosting parties. In effect, she was shifting careers.

"I'm through with my social period now," she announced. "From now on I'm going to have fun with the arts in my beloved city—always cooperating with the White House, of course. I'll do anything Mrs. Johnson asks me."

She also offered to commission a major piece of sculpture, though she insisted that the White House announce it, even as she invited two hundred guests one evening in 1966 to meet Alexander Calder, the world-famous sculptor. The white-thatched Philadelphian who resided among the Parisian avant-garde had invented the mobile, as a playful exploration of flat planes in motion. When Gwen and Morris visited the Brussels World's Fair in 1958, they loved the sleek black Calder in a fountain by the American pavilion, glistening with droplets that Gwen likened to diamonds in the sunlight. Now the sculptor was Gwen's houseguest for ten days. Over lunch he promised preliminary plans in two months for a "stabile," with its planes at angular rest.

He would return for the dedication. Calder was a bear of a man, seventy-one, with an incorrigible shock of hair and a rumpled suit, a red shirt, and the fat purple knot of a loosened necktie. His stabile was six times taller than a man, its riveted slices of black battleship steel slanted like the prows of a fractured armada. It stood at Fourteenth and Constitution, in a circular pool, by the Smithsonian's Museum of History and Technology, in line of sight to the Washington Monument.

"Washington has suffered in the past from sameness," said S. Dillon Ripley, the Smithsonian's impresario.

Calder delivered an un-Washington-like, one-sentence speech.

"I call it the Cafdolyn," he declared.

No one could hear him because of the trucks and a plane overhead.

He repeated, "I call it the Cafdolyn."

Still his listeners were puzzled. Had he not intended to name it the Gwenfritz? Gwendolyn Cafritz understood that he had changed his mind.

"I like the Gwenfritz," she said firmly.

The Gwenfritz it became.

"I had my old man get me a job on the Joint Economic Committee," Tommy Boggs would recall with a laugh. "It was that easy."

Hale ranked third among the House Democrats on the committee, which possessed no authority except to issue reports. "This is no secret," Hale told a reporter once his son's daytime tenure on the committee staff became publicly known in 1963. He had started as a research assistant, at eight thousand dollars a year, and then as one of five staff economists, for nearly ten thousand.

Tommy had started attending Georgetown's law school at night in 1961 and had a family to support. He loved economics, his undergraduate major, but as a career, economics offered few options. He thought about combining economics and law, for with a law degree he could hang a shingle wherever he liked.

His night school class at Georgetown included two future senators and three congressmen to-be. His classmates enjoyed his irreverent sense of humor—"And we were impressed with his dad," said Steny Hoyer, who would go on to a House leadership career of his own. Tommy hit it off the first day with Jim Jones, a self-described "poor kid from Muskogee," and they studied together at Hale's office in Longworth or while babysitting little Hale at Tommy's house in Chevy Chase. (Decades later, young Hale became Jim Jones's law partner.) "Neither of us prepared that well," the Oklahoman said later, but they earned respectable grades.

At the Joint Economic Committee, the chairman, Paul Douglas, took awhile to trust Tommy. The senator from Illinois had been a high-minded economics professor who enlisted in the marines at age fifty to slog through the Pacific in World War II. Tommy adored him (even naming his second son Douglas), but the principled senator had been suspicious of any congressman's son, the president's young friend, until Tommy wrote a report on the shipping industry that was sufficiently critical that it earned his father's footnoted dissent. The unmasking of discriminatory pricing by European cartels prompted an investigation into the way American shippers set their rates. Tommy was a force behind the hearings.

"I tell you, we destroyed the shipping industry," Tommy jested years later. "Just three kids running wild." The other two were Nicholas Johnson, the thirty-year-old head of the Federal Maritime Administration, and thirty-one-year-old Tim May, the managing director of the Federal Maritime Commission.

Tommy was still with the committee when he helped with the advance work for President Johnson's antipoverty tour of Appalachia in the spring of 1964, and again for the president's opening trip of his fall election campaign, to the capital of Pennsylvania. When a Harrisburg newspaper quoted Tommy's announcement of the details of the president's visit, Tommy's telephone rang in the hotel room at six that morning.

It was Lyndon Johnson: "*I'm* supposed to announce what I'm doing, not you." No one could work near this president without being yelled at.

After the president won a term of his own, Tommy went into the White House. Officially he was special assistant to the director of the

Office of Emergency Planning, assigned to keep in touch with governors and mayors. But in reality he did whatever the president wanted him to do, which meant a lot of advance work.

"I was a glorified helper," Tommy said.

Yet he was amazed by the extent of the White House's day-to-day power. Once, while preparing for a presidential trip, he was able to overrule a small-town mayor's objections and have a tree uprooted because it interfered with the view from the podium.

This was fun, but he had been doing things like this for years, and his salary of $10,500 or so hardly sufficed for a family with two children, soon to be three. He started at the White House in January 1965 and stayed for fifteen months, leaving before he got locked into a second term.

"It wasn't hard for me to walk away from," he said.

His father longed for Tommy to join a major law firm, in Washington or New York, because of the pay. Hale had always scratched for a living, much as his father had. The salary for members of Congress had recently risen to thirty thousand dollars, but the capital was an expensive place to live, especially if entertaining was one's duty or pleasure. For the Boggses, it was both.

With Hale's help, Tommy lined up interviews at seventeen law firms—"because of my brilliance, of course," he remembered with a laugh. What law firm wanted to annoy the House majority whip? Tommy was a catch. With his political lineage and his time on Capitol Hill and in the White House, he knew everyone in government worth knowing. In his bones, he understood the dynamics that other twenty-four-year-olds could only read about.

"I had a ridiculous level of self-confidence," he said.

He went to see Clark Clifford. The Truman intimate had managed the presidential transitions of the man who was now in the White House as well as his predecessor. His hushed tones and silken elegance and, more than anything, his closeness to the giants of his time had made him a lawyer and lobbyist of the highest order. A client's problem might be fixed in a phone call, for a goodly fee. Rather than law books, "he uses the Mayflower Hotel menu instead," or so the gossip-mongers of *Washington Confidential* had said.

He offered Tommy a place in the firm, but on a condition—that he first improve his skills as a lawyer by laboring for two years at Hogan & Hartson, one of the city's largest law firms, which was located in the same Connecticut Avenue building across Lafayette Square from the White House. Tommy was impressed that Clifford could arrange this.

"I shouldn't tell you this, Tommy," a friend at Clifford's firm told him as he left, "but you've seen Mr. Clifford more in the past two weeks than I've seen him in two years."

Tommy fielded offers from a dozen law firms in Washington alone. One in particular intrigued him. Barco, Cook, Patton & Blow, a four-year-old, five-lawyer firm with offices in Washington and New York, specialized in international law. That was Tommy's domain at the Joint Economic Committee, and a subject that Clifford's firm ignored. Years later, Tommy struggled to explain the attraction. "I guess I felt more challenged," he said, "trying to create something with a couple of guys."

And there was something else. "I liked Jim Patton," Tommy said. "He liked me."

Jim Patton had been a rebel at stuffy Covington & Burling, the city's most distinguished law firm, where lawyers were criticized for mistakes but never praised for success. Patton was a ruggedly handsome, impeccably tailored southern gentleman—his father was a judge in North Carolina—and a one-time Central Intelligence Agency (CIA) man, a veteran of two years in Saigon. He collected fine wines and had acquired paintings by Jasper Johns and Roy Lichtenstein before they were famous. He was a conservative Republican and a social liberal, alternately charming and moody, a man of guile.

As the lead partner in Washington, Patton was looking for a particular kind of help. He had finished negotiating a deal for the world's largest steel mill, in South Korea, when a heavyweight American company applied political muscle to persuade the U.S. government's Export-Import Bank to shift its support to a competing venture, causing his client's to collapse.

"I'm not going to let it happen again," he vowed.

Jim Patton went looking for a lawyer who could prevent such a thing, who could cater to clients with problems that the government could solve. In the embarrassment he had suffered, he caught a glimpse of what his law firm might become.

When he told an economist he knew on the Hill of his search for a lawyer who understood the political arena, the suggestion he got was Tommy Boggs.

"It was a stroke of genius, because it made the future of the law firm," said a lawyer who soon joined the firm. "Patton understood the potential of Boggs in terms of the connections, Tom's deep involvement in the political life of the city. He grew up with all these people, he knew all these people, they were all hanging around his father's house." He fathomed why politicians acted as they did, what they found consequential or trivial, what they feared and craved.

Patton was willing to let Tommy remain as a consultant to the Joint Economic Committee, an arrangement that more than doubled his first-year pay, to eighteen thousand dollars. Patton sensed another reason why Tommy accepted the tiny firm's offer: "It gave him a chance to go off on his own. He could say, '*I* did this.'"

When Tommy told his father in the spring of 1966 that he was joining Jim Patton, Hale replied, "Who?" Then he accused his only son of stupidity.

This was Superintendent Hansen's second day, his ninth hour, on the witness stand, at the mercy of Julius Hobson's lawyer. William Kunstler was a showman even with dry facts. His long gray hair flying, he pranced around the courtroom, rat-a-tatting questions in his gravelly mien. The civil rights lawyer was highly competent, full of himself, emotionally committed, and—for Julius, best of all—willing to work for expenses.

"You testified yesterday that you had given depositions in *Bolling versus Sharpe*; is that correct?"

"That is correct." The superintendent became wary at the mention of the school desegregation case.

"And do you remember in those depositions being asked any questions with reference to whether it was more or less desirable to have separate or integrated schools?"

The school board's lawyer jumped up. "I would like to ask the relevancy of that question, Your Honor."

J. Skelly Wright was a federal appeals court judge in D.C., presiding over a district court case. All of the lower-court judges had recused themselves because Julius's wide-ranging lawsuit sought, among its other ambitions, to end their authority to appoint the city's school board.

The judge asked Kunstler.

"The purpose, Your Honor, is to show a predisposition towards separation of Negro and white children in the school system and a feeling that Negroes in separate systems could get just as good an education."

"All right. I will overrule the objection and he may answer it."

"My recollection," Hansen replied, "is that I wasn't asked the question."

Nor did Kunstler bother to ask, but his point had been made. As any good actor would, he knew his audience. Skelly Wright, modest and shy, had once ordered the desegregation of schools in his native New Orleans, prompting a cross burning in front of his home and a shunning by many of his friends (though not the Boggses). When southern senators objected to President Kennedy's plan to appoint him to the federal appeals court in New Orleans, he wound up in Washington instead.

Julius never cared much about integration per se, for he failed to see the benefit to a black child of learning beside a white child. Besides, in Washington it hardly mattered anymore, in the wake of white flight to the suburbs. Because of the paucity of working-class families forced to stay in the D.C. public schools, within a decade of desegregation 90 percent of the city's students were black. What mattered more to Julius was the disproportion of resources—textbooks, libraries, well-paid teachers—between the integrated schools and the poor, black ones.

He had approached the NAACP, the Urban League, and numerous lawyers before Kunstler took the case. The son of a Jewish doctor, he had once drafted a will for Joe McCarthy but had gone on to defend the Freedom Riders and conduct legal work for Martin

Luther King. Nobody else had believed that Julius could win. The theory of the case was a provocative one—that the rigid track system and the imbalance in the distribution of teachers and resources among the schools constituted illegal discrimination by race. Julius called it a "system of programmed retardation," one that consigned black children to "the junk heap."

"It's a deliberate attempt to push Negro children to lower categories," he had charged—"just another word for 'nigger.'"

At the trial Julius furnished statistics to prove his point. He had computed them, he testified, by using the same statistical techniques he applied at the Social Security Administration to analyze workmen's compensation claims. A scant 1.7 percent of junior high school students had moved between academic tracks during the 1963–64 school year, and just 8.3 percent of high schoolers; only 16 percent of Negroes attended schools that even had an honors track, compared to 70 percent of whites. He synthesized the school-by-school figures on enrollment and expenditures with demographic data. The more affluent the neighborhood, his ten charts showed, the more money spent per pupil. The child psychiatrist Robert Coles and Christopher Jencks of Harvard's Graduate School of Education offered expert testimony in the first lawsuit outside the South to challenge de facto segregation, based on the racial patterns of housing.

For Julius, the stakes were higher still. He and Carol had put Jean into a boarding school in Virginia, as an escape from the basic track and from their deteriorating marriage. They shared a house but led separate lives, since Julius had disconnected his political life from his personal life. Marriage counseling had failed. Night after night during the trial, Julius and Kunstler competed in reciting poetry, at the home of Patricia Saltonstall, a former reporter for *The Evening Star*, who had become involved in the lawsuit and given Kunstler a place to stay.

A couple of times Kunstler told Julius, "Hey, don't you think you should go home and spend some time with your family?"

To Carol, the lawsuit was the final straw. They had long felt strains over religion, so vital to Carol and repellent to Julius. He had never discussed with her his intention to include Jean and Hobby—

and himself—as lead plaintiffs, so that the case became known as *Hobson v. Hansen*. "Nobody else was going to be the lead plaintiff," Pat Saltonstall remembered. "He wanted to be the star."

Carol felt protective, especially of Jean. "I just felt that this was a movement of vanity on his part," she said. "With as many plaintiffs as they had, it was unnecessary for him to use his own child, with the possibility that her life would become an open book."

Soon they separated, and she filed for divorce. Unable to find a black lawyer who would handle a case against Julius Hobson, she hired a white one instead.

Jean, as it happened, never testified in the case or saw her privacy disturbed. Yet her circumstance imbued the proceedings, as Kunstler continued to interrogate Carl Hansen, who had personally developed the track system in 1956, the year Jean was born.

"And is it your testimony," the lawyer said, "that at that time the amount of Negroes in, say, the basic track was considerably more than the amount of whites in the basic track?"

"The number was considerably more, yes, sir," Hansen said.

"Is it not also true, Dr. Hansen, that the number of whites in the honors track was considerably more than the number of Negroes in the honors track?"

"That is correct, but there were also Negroes in the honors track. I do have a recollection that there was a proportion, a fair proportion, of Negro students in the honors class and a significant number of white pupils in the basic track and that therefore this curriculum or-ganization was not designed on a racial basis."

Kunstler pressed further.

"But is this a fair statement that I am making, that the number of Negroes in the basic track in the tenth grade in 1956 was substan-tially larger than the number of whites?"

"To my recollection, it was."

"And would it be a fair statement also to make that the number of whites in the honors track was substantially higher than the num-ber of Negroes?"

"This would be fair to say."

Later, Kunstler would recall that *Hobson v. Hansen* resulted in the single most gratifying decision of his career.

Steve Roberts was grateful to Al Lowenstein, who had almost married Cokie's sister, Barbara, in 1962. It "really paved the way for me," he remembered. Steve's long engagement to Cokie Boggs produced plenty of tears, mainly Cokie's, as they wrestled with their difference in religion. Lindy and Hale worried about the complications of a marriage between Catholic and Jew, but it was Steve's parents who found the prospect far harder to accept.

Steve liked to say later that he first fell in love with Lindy. In 1963, as a Harvard undergraduate from northern New Jersey, he had gone to Washington for a conference on a domestic Peace Corps that Barbara was conducting and was staying at the Boggses' house when he developed a hacking cold. Deep in the night, a knock on the door ushered in Lindy, in a flowing peach negligee, a hot toddy in her hand. Steve had never seen such a charming apparition. He had already met Cokie at a National Student Association conference at Ohio State between their sophomore and junior years, but it was at Barbara's gathering that they became sweethearts.

When they finished college in 1964, Steve moved to Washington as a research assistant to James Reston, who was then a columnist at the *New York Times*. Don Graham, whose father had been the publisher of the *Washington Post*, had held the job the previous summer and suggested that Steve, a friend on the *Harvard Crimson*, apply for it. Steve was smart and pugnacious, with tightly curled hair. He had a New Jersey edge and, to family and friends, a genuine warmth.

"Steven is my sweetest child," said Lindy.

"Not much of a contest, Mom," Cokie would respond.

The *New York Times* had its Washington bureau at 1701 K, in the building Morris Cafritz had put up a dozen years before. Steve would eat lunch across the street, out in Farragut Square, and dream about the day that he would cover Congress for the *Times*.

Cokie moved back to Bethesda to be near Steve. Through Wellesley's placement office, she found a job with Altman Productions, owned by an alumna, to work on two television shows. Cokie had appeared a couple of times as a teenager on one of the shows, called *Teen Talk*, in which the participants mulled over various issues. (The show's main purpose was to help channel four meet the federal requirement for public-service programming.) Now she was the one who picked out topics and found teenagers to discuss them. On *It's Academic*, she wrote questions for the competing high school teams and helped in other cities that aired their own shows.

Then a bigger break occurred. When channel four wanted a replacement for *Teen Talk*, Altman Productions created *Meeting of the Minds*, which featured foreign journalists in discussions with an American public figure. Looking for a moderator, the producers asked Cokie to try. Even before she was old enough to vote, she was hosting the Sunday morning show that often aired in the capital just before *Meet the Press*.

Steve's impending transfer to New York to start working as a reporter for the *Times* prompted them to set a wedding date. Lindy had wanted a church wedding, but she understood the pain that Steve's Grandpa Abe, in particular, would feel.

Cokie said to her, "Could we be married in Daddy's garden?"

Hale's brother, a priest, would officiate, and they searched for a rabbi to join him. "It was like looking for an abortionist," Cokie remembered. She knew of a rabbi who moonlighted in the White House and phoned him.

"Rabbi," she began.

"I'll call you back from a pay phone."

He did, but he also insisted on officiating alone—not with a priest.

It turned out that the only rabbis who were willing to help conduct an interfaith wedding had their calendars filled. At last Steve's mother said, "This is getting silly." A rabbi presided as an elder, after all, not as a cleric. "Why don't you just get a learned man who is a friend of the family, which makes so much more sense—like, say, Arthur Goldberg."

Steve's parents did not know the labor secretary turned Supreme Court justice and now the ambassador to the United Nations. But Cokie's did. In fact, when Hale and Lindy had gone to a Passover seder at the Goldbergs' and joined in on singing old labor songs, Steve made sure that his parents heard about it.

Goldberg agreed.

Quickly the invitation list got out of hand. The night Lindy asked Hale which House members to invite, he had no desire to decide anything.

He answered, "All of the Democrats."

After the Democratic landslide of 1964, that alone meant 295 guests and their spouses. Add some friendly Republicans, half the Senate, the entire Cabinet, several Supreme Court justices, journalists of all descriptions, the extended families, and, oh yes, the bridal couple's friends, the guest list exceeded fifteen hundred. Again, with the help of friends, Lindy did all of the cooking—turkeys, hams, red beans and rice, shrimp creole—this time in the new, huge kitchen that had been the garage. The wedding cake, from the Senate Dining Room, arrived in a truck.

Only a day before the wedding, set for September 10, 1966, did Steve and Cokie remember they needed a marriage license. Ordinarily a license required a forty-eight-hour wait. They phoned Hale, who called Tommy—"It doesn't get more humiliating than that," Cokie thought—who phoned a Maryland judge he knew from local politics, and the legal requirement was waived. Hale's press secretary found the story so amusing that, to Cokie's mortification, he told the wires.

Five minutes before the ceremony started, at eight o'clock on a Saturday night, President Johnson arrived, with Lady Bird and Lynda Bird. They sat on the bride's side, in the second row. A gigantic tent covered the yard. Sprays of white jasmine decorated a latticework that served as a Jewish chuppah, with an altar beneath. Barbara was the matron of honor, Steve's twin brother the best man. One of the ushers was a friend of Steve's from high school, a perennial graduate student at Harvard named Barney Frank.

Tommy's three-year-old daughter, Elizabeth, carried the flowers and four-year-old Hale, the rings. The ribbons on the satin pillow loosened and the rings tumbled into the grass. A Secret Service agent borrowed a flashlight from the president's physician and crawled around until he found them.

Hale's brother conducted a Catholic ceremony (without a nuptial mass) and then Arthur Goldberg spoke. He had written his remarks on a notepad from the Waldorf-Astoria, the U.N. ambassador's residence. His black-framed eyeglasses lent him a look of learnedness, and perhaps a glint of self-consciousness about his stature among his people.

"In my tradition," he stated to Cokie, "a home has rarely been a castle. Throughout the ages it is something far higher, a sanctuary."

The reception was a mob scene. Guests pushed and shoved; a long line formed at the shrimp creole. Gwen Cafritz, among so many others, passed through. Out back, the chauffeurs were given sandwiches and beer. The tent became a dance hall.

Cokie had fun, and Steve felt overwhelmed. They barely left the receiving line, and Lindy never stopped working. "When you watch Lindy Boggs in a setting like that, it's like watching Heifetz play the violin," the best man told the groom. "You're watching someone do something that no one else in the world does any better."

President Johnson circulated through the crowd but took his leave at ten minutes to nine, for fear he was distracting attention from the newlyweds.

Julius Hobson had reason for optimism, beyond the merits of his case. Lawyers for the school board learned too late of Skelly Wright's earlier article in the *New York University Law Review*, condemning de facto segregation of the schools as unconstitutional. The judge refused their plea to disqualify himself from *Hobson v. Hansen*.

His opinion, issued in June 1967, was 183 pages long and concluded that D.C. had "unconstitutionally deprived Negro and poor public school children of their right to equal educational opportunity." The *Post* described it as perhaps the most important court decision on schools since the 1954 *Brown* case.

The judge showed how segregation in housing had grown in D.C. since 1940, when every neighborhood was at least one-third white, and especially since 1954. He explored the inflexibility of the track system and its "tendency of resegregating the races within the individual school." He culled the statistics on predominantly white versus Negro schools, comparing per-pupil spending ($392 versus

$292), teachers' experience, ratios of library books to students, age of the buildings, and availability of kindergartens.

"Separate but unequal," he judged.

More than with statistics and legal arguments, Skelly Wright wrote with his heart, of the "cancerous squalor" in the slums; of the Negro child's "sense of worthlessness, of inferiority, of fear and despair"; of how "racially and socially homogeneous schools damage the minds and spirit of all children who attend them—the Negro, the white, the poor and the affluent—and block the attainment of the broader goals of democratic education." So effusive was his opinion that the *Harvard Law Review* bashed "its unclear basis in precedent, its potentially enormous scope, and its imposition of responsibilities which may strain the resources and endanger the prestige of the judiciary."

His passion explained the breadth of his remedy. He left the system of neighborhood schools intact but decreed that their faculties be integrated and that money be spent evenly among them. Students in overcrowded schools were to be bused, voluntarily, to the fancier, emptier schools west of Rock Creek Park. His most dramatic step was unprecedented: He abolished the track system.

When the school board refused to appeal, Superintendent Hansen resigned and filed an appeal on his own. On every point at issue, he lost.

For Julius this was getting expensive, having to defend against the appeal on top of everything else. He took a pauper's oath so that he could mimeograph rather than print his brief on a part of his lawsuit, about the method of selecting a school board, that had been bucked to a higher court. Neither of his lawyers charged legal fees, but they counted eleven thousand dollars in expenses, besides the long-distance telephone bills, the rented office equipment, the costs of statistical research. Pat Saltonstall let Kunstler stay at her house for five months, and she also conducted research, donated money for legal expenses, and raised the rest.

Julius had contemplated a lawsuit, but it was Pat Saltonstall who conceived of it as a constitutional case. She was a member of an underfunded branch of a blueblooded New England family (the Republican senator who graced parties on Foxhall Road was her father's first cousin), but her name had always opened doors for her. She was an attractive and lively brunette who had become a society reporter for *The Evening Star*. She telephoned Julius and met with him at a Howard Johnson's in Northeast, a section of the city unfamiliar to her; they ate from a tray that was hung from the window of his green Mercury. Soon she left her job to work on the lawsuit full-time.

Within six months her involvement with Julius was more than statistical or financial. "It was obvious to me that he really liked white women," she said later. "He liked their freedom." But he was anxious at first about being seen at a restaurant with her, and so was she, for fear that her Dixiecrat ex-husband would challenge her custody of the youngest of their three sons. Julius went to her house in the evening, and he took Jean over to play, but he never spent the night.

When he asked her to marry him, "There was no way—we weren't anywhere near marriage," she said.

More and more, she disliked his habit of lying, whether about the fanciness of the car he drove or the documents he was to produce for the lawyers or his promises to Jean for the weekend. Once the lawsuit ended, they drifted apart, though not before she performed one last benefaction.

She was seeing a psychologist to help her break away from Julius, and told him. He was amazed that she would reveal something so personal, and the next time he saw her, he said, "I would like to learn how." He had tears in his eyes. "Can you teach me to tell the truth?" He asked her to find a doctor for him.

The first time he visited the white psychiatrist in the lovely Kalorama neighborhood, he left pretty shaken up. But he continued off and on for quite a few months.

Late in 1967, Julius invited Tina Lower to dinner at his apartment in Southwest. She was an outspoken ash blonde ("a white divorcée who is extremely attractive," as the FBI described her later) and a Stanford University graduate who had moved to Washington six years earlier as a single mother of three boys. As an unhappy suburban housewife, she had broken free, she said, from "a nice house, good neighbors, and a lovely dichondra lawn." A swept-back bouffant hairdo set off her chiseled yet delicate features and deep-set eyes. Her fluttery demeanor, a birdlike earnestness, concealed a strong personality and a streak of stubbornness.

After bureaucratic stints at the Department of Labor and the Peace Corps, she had joined a nonprofit organization, the National Institute of Public Affairs. The Ford Foundation financed the program to invite police commissioners, city managers, and other officials in riot-prone cities to Washington for three or four weeks to learn how to cope with social afflictions. As if to prove that its idealism was rooted in the practical political world, the institute leased its headquarters at 1825 K Street, in a recently constructed Cafritz building.

Tina organized the program's People's Day, which started with coffee at a housing project, followed by a discussion with a slumlord, an hour in an all-black school, then lunch with Julius Hobson. His description of his lawsuit always wowed them. Every group that went through considered him the best speaker.

"Your audience has problems determining whether you are a total saint or a total sinner," she wrote to thank him, enclosing a modest honorarium, "and this makes for a more lively conference and sometimes a good deal of antagonizing thought."

He had spoken over lunch for her program a half-dozen times when he said to her, "Why don't you come over to my house for dinner? I'll cook."

Julius lived in a fastidious studio apartment in Carrollsburg Square, an eight-story apartment complex of dun-colored brick in almost treeless Southwest. "I don't want to live in the ghetto," he had explained to a reporter. "I just want to keep people out of it."

He cooked barbecue for Tina—"People think I have a special barbecue sauce," he laughed, "but frankly I just throw anything I have in it"—along with baked potatoes, broccoli, and sliced tomatoes, all meticulously prepared. They drank wine, and he quoted poetry.

"He was an absolutely perfect gentleman, very fascinating," she recalled.

Tina had moved from Arlington into an inexpensive apartment in

Georgetown, at Q and Thirty-first, after the youngest of her sons died of cancer. Julius drove her home.

In the front room of her apartment, Julius proposed marriage.

"I want you to know that I'm serious," he said, "that I'm not just being facetious about our relationship. You can take me seriously." He was deadpan—and not yet divorced.

Tina was shocked. They had not even kissed.

Julius did not ask for an immediate answer, and she had none to give him.

Hobby's parents pressed him to attend Hampton Institute, a fine Negro college deep in Virginia.

"I wanted to stay home," he said—because he liked the food, because he felt comfortable, possibly because he felt he was needed. He applied to George Washington University, but a photograph was required, and it was obvious that he would not gain admission. (Even the Negro valedictorian at McKinley was rejected.) So Hobby enrolled even closer to home.

Howard University, as were so many universities, was undergoing a political upheaval as Hobby arrived in the fall of 1966. The snootiness of his mother's experience was giving way to militancy. Leopold Senghor, the president of Senegal, spoke on campus about his philosophy of Negritude, as more of a cultural than a political concept. Stokely Carmichael, now SNCC's national chairman, returned to his alma mater to expound on his new, intimidating political slogan, Black Power. Adam Clayton Powell had used the phrase first, but Stokely had caught the public's attention when he shouted it in frustration at a rally in Mississippi the previous June, and he developed it as a political philosophy—and a way of life. Martin Luther King and the mainstream civil rights leaders denounced the slogan as antiwhite, but Julius considered himself Stokely's political godfather.

"We're talking about black men directing their own destinies," Julius told William Raspberry, the *Post*'s black columnist. "We're talking about a black woman wearing her hair natural. We're talking about black skin being beautiful—not like twenty years ago, when a

Negro's social position could be determined by the fairness of his wife's skin."

The week Stokely appeared, Howard students pursued a crusade of their own, in the most traditional of collegiate activities. The five candidates for homecoming queen included a D.C. native on a full scholarship (and the dean's list) who was a field secretary for SNCC. She looked unlike her rivals in one respect: Her hair was natural, with all of its kinks. Across the brick-and-leafy campus, her candidacy became a rallying cry—Black Is Beautiful. "And she stopped subjecting herself to the searing heat of the straightening comb and other head melting devices"—this, a tribute in the campus newspaper, after Hobby's vote and others had delivered her a victory.

Otherwise, Hobby professed little interest in militancy. Julius had complained to Pat Saltonstall that Hobby showed no interest in civil rights and that he seemed embarrassed by Julius's activism. Hobby understood that his father's prominence required careful conduct. If he smelled marijuana at the door to a party, he would turn back. When a friend asked why, he explained, "Because if the police came in here and arrested everybody, my name would be the only name in the newspaper. I don't need that."

In a class of fifty, the professor would read down the roll and invariably glance up at his name. He joined the Reserve Officers' Training Corps (ROTC), which occupied classrooms in the basement of Douglass Hall, where his parents had met. His study of military history suggested to him that a tenth of the population, the nation's blacks, could never succeed by taking up arms against everyone else.

He also had to work for his tuition and books. He was embarrassed to learn that Pat Saltonstall had signed one of his tuition checks. His part-time job at Safeway, at Third and Rhode Island, paid him $2.31 an hour, almost twice the minimum wage. He was a checkout clerk and he cleaned the supermarket's floors on Sunday nights, and later night-stocked the frozen food.

He was working at Safeway on a balmy Thursday evening in April 1968 when the news arrived from Memphis that Martin Luther King had been shot. After eight the word arrived that he had died. The supermarket closed as usual at nine.

The calm that descended on the city felt "ominous," a white newswoman noticed, "like before a hurricane strikes."

It had long been assumed that Washington, unlike Watts or Newark or Detroit, was immune to the self-mutilation of a racial riot. In a city of government jobs, the poverty was not so grinding. Nor was the power structure so white, since the president had appointed a Negro, Walter Washington, as the city's mayor the autumn before. Among the middle class, at least, the city seemed on the brink of a genuine integration. Blacks and whites ate dinner at one another's homes. Racial relations seemed smoother, occasionally even un-self-conscious.

But around the time that the Safeway was closing, Stokely Carmichael, in his green fatigue jacket, strode with a crowd of young men into Peoples Drug at Fourteenth and U, in the congested heart of the black city, a corner familiar to shoppers, moviegoers, bus riders, and prostitutes, and demanded that the store be closed. The manager complied. They went to the next store, then the next, south along neon-lit Fourteenth, until Walter Fauntroy caught up with them at T Street. He and Stokely had debated black power at Howard the previous fall.

The dulcet-toned preacher, a head shorter than his self-possessed rival, grabbed Stokely's arms and said: "Let's not get anyone hurt. Let's cool it."

"All we're asking them to do is close the stores," Stokely replied. "They killed Dr. King."

Satisfied, Fauntroy returned to the SCLC's office adjacent to Peoples Drug, when he heard the drugstore's windows shatter.

The night produced looting and burning—Stokely exhorted, "Burn, baby, burn!"—and the sirens shrieked along Fourteenth Street. When the president received a report that Stokely was organizing a mob to burn Georgetown to the ground, the Texan smiled at the prospect of the sophisticated neighborhood he had loathed and envied rising in flames: "Goddamn, I've waited thirty-five years for this day."

It was only a rumor. Stokely dropped from sight so that the authorities would have no grounds to arrest him.

Carol's divorce had become final the day before. She begged Hobby to skip work the next afternoon.

"Oh, Mama, I'll be all right." He told her the supermarket planned to close early; that worried her more.

By one o'clock on Friday afternoon, when Hobby arrived at Third and Rhode Island, Stokely had been waving a pistol at Howard University, on the steps of Douglass Hall, and the Safeway on Seventh Street was already in flames, with the smoke blowing east. Before the riots ended, five Safeways would burn.

Carol could see the smoke from her office window, just south of the Mall. She told her boss she had to pick up her son. On the way she saw people steering grocery carts full of merchandise they had taken from stores.

"What are you doing here?" Hobby said.

"Let's go pick up Jean." The eleven-year-old was staying with her teacher, a friend of Carol's, out Eighth Street, almost to Maryland. "We've got to get home—this town's going to blow up."

"They're going to close the store in about twenty minutes," Hobby said.

"I'm not leaving until you leave with me."

Downtown, Hecht's and Woodie's closed after bands of black teenagers ran through the aisles and taunted the salesclerks, sending customers and workers into the streets. Soon cars crammed the roadways, as more white workers left. Black shop owners painted *Soul Brother* on their front windows. At Rich's Shoes on F Street, the looters preferred Ferragamos. Seventh Street was burning and Fourteenth Street yet again and then the shops along H Street NE and in Anacostia—five hundred fires, more than the British had set, and this time by the inhabitants' own hand.

A crowd collected outside the Safeway at Third and Rhode Island. The manager had locked the doors. He was a Negro who could pass for white, and he owned a brand-new car that Hobby offered to move to a safer place.

"I was so angry with him I didn't know what to do," Carol said.

Carol's nerves sent her to the ladies' room, using one of the keys on a miniature broomstick. When she returned, bricks and boulders were sailing through the supermarket's front windows. Young men poured in behind.

"Where are my keys?" the manager was shouting, wanting to unlock the wall that slid up at the back of the store. The keys rattled in Carol's hand. She stood there and watched a man point a gun at her son. Hobby was putting the money from the cash registers into the safe.

Hobby shoved the money inside, shut the safe, and spun the dial.

"That's white folks' money," Carol wailed at him later "You took a chance on your life to put that money in that safe."

The rioters filled shopping carts with more meat and vegetables than any refrigerator could hold. Hobby wondered why they passed up the canned foods, the dishwashing soap, the costlier goods that would last.

Carol was nearly hysterical, and Hobby asked a coworker to move his mother's Ford LTD around to the back.

Going home, however, meant passing through the rioting. So they drove to their pastor's instead, out Sixteenth Street, and spent the night.

Julius found Carol by telephone that night. He and Tina had been on a plane to Jamaica when they heard the news.

Tina had said, "Julius, do you want to go back?"

"No, there isn't anything I can do."

The next morning, Carol and her children passed through an eerie quiet as they ventured back across the District, to Queens Chapel Terrace. Curfews and soldiers in helmets ruled the capital for the next seven days. Hobby's Safeway reopened within three weeks, though burned-out lots would remain vacant for decades.

All day, Hale Boggs was nervous. Gary Hymel, his administrative assistant, had to accompany him everywhere around Capitol Hill, even into the bathroom, to calm him down. Legislation to forbid discrimination in housing was up for a vote on the House floor that afternoon, and Hale fretted about how a "yea" would play back home.

With good reason. His support for the 1965 voting rights bill had

not sabotaged his reelection the following year. But 1968 was different. Presidential election years were always harder for Hale, when he
had to share the ticket with a national Democrat. (Had this southern
president not predicted, in signing the Civil Rights Act of 1964, that
the Democrats would lose the South for a generation?) Hale had opposed an open housing bill in 1966, but the turmoil that followed the
King assassination and the deaths of Negro soldiers in Vietnam had
persuaded him, he said, to change his mind.

He also understood that a "nay" vote would squelch his ascent
within Democratic ranks. Yet Hale never cast such a painful vote on
civil rights, for a law that wielded so little real-world impact but
stirred such intensity among voters at home.

The benefits of voting as a national Democrat soon became apparent. Johnson had become a victim of his own endless war in Vietnam and had dramatically abandoned his hopes for another term. But
he was intent on keeping his control over the political party that had
spurned him. He handpicked Hale, a hawk on Vietnam, to chair the
platform committee at the nominating convention in Chicago and
told him bluntly that the final language would be decided in the
White House.

This put Hale in between the president and his prospective successor, the vice president, whose electoral interest lay in backing
away from the war. Hale and Lindy had known Hubert Humphrey
since his days as a graduate student at LSU. On his way home in the
evening, he often stopped off at Tommy's house, just east of Connecticut Avenue in Chevy Chase, to chat and see little Hale.

Big Hale had supported Humphrey since the president's withdrawal from his reelection campaign. He and Lindy were also
friendly with the McCarthys, who had lived on Bradley Boulevard.
Gene McCarthy's political insurgency had driven the president into
retirement, but the high-minded senator from Minnesota was too
impractical, too poetic, for Hale's hard-headed taste—more like
Hale's father than like Hale. After his antiwar crusade faded, his
wife, Abigail, bequeathed Lindy an extra on-the-road wig and a fluffy
top-piece.

Humphrey's most dangerous Democratic opponent was Robert

Kennedy. But Hale mistrusted the very trait that Lindy had found appealing in JFK's younger brother—his tendency to view the world in black and white.

"Jack is Rose's son," Hale would say. "Bobby is Joe's son."

And then he, too, was killed.

In Chicago, the party's platform occupied the battlefront for the emotional convention. Hale named the cohost of his garden parties (Charlie Davis had left Ways and Means to become a tax lawyer in Chicago) as the committee's chief counsel. Tommy was the staff coordinator, whose job was to serve as his father's liaison to the party's institutional liberals and to make sure the platform's twelve thousand words actually were written. For a week and a half, Tommy slept no more than two hours a night.

Carl Albert, the convention chairman, caught the flu. When Tommy went to his hotel room, the House majority leader was propped up in bed, shoes off, reading from a stack of first editions he had borrowed from the Library of Congress. Hale's task was to prevent the convention—the party—from splitting apart over Vietnam. He negotiated a compromise with the vice president's advisers that the antiwarriors could accept, for a halt in the bombing of North Vietnam without the conditions that the president had decreed.

President Johnson summoned Hale back to Washington, in the wake of the Soviet invasion of Czechoslovakia but really for a discussion of Vietnam. The president gave Hale a cable—"carefully chosen portions," as Clark Clifford, the new defense secretary, later divulged—from the U.S. commander in Vietnam, warning that a bombing halt would help the enemy. Hale took it back to Chicago, to push the president's hard-line language through the fractured committee, and he insisted that no amendments be permitted on the convention floor, foreclosing any chance of compromise.

While he was in Washington, the committee incorporated the entire Kerner Commission report on racial riots into the platform, and Hale sought to remove it. When the liberal governor of Vermont argued for keeping it in, Hale retorted, "Look, I know a lot of things wrong went on and we can't solve them all here. But that slave trade just wasn't my ancestors having slaves, it was your ancestors manning those ships that brought them over here." The governor backed off.

On all sides, the pressures mounted. Hale's staff found micro-phones concealed beneath a radiator cover that everyone suspected the FBI—or was it one of the networks?—had installed. Hale per-suaded Johnson not to celebrate his sixtieth birthday in Chicago, making his case to the White House chief of staff, Tommy's old friend Jim Jones. Carl Albert had encouraged a birthday visit, Jim Jones recalled, but the president "highly respected Hale Boggs for his political judgment."

Some of the strains of the riotous convention proved more per-sonal. As the police clubbed demonstrators in the streets, Barbara screamed at her father: "You don't know what's going on out there. You've got to pay attention to what's going on out there." She and Cokie had once stalked out of "21" in New York after arguing with him over the war—"And much to our horror," Cokie recounted, "the whole place clapped." Now seven months pregnant with her first child, Cokie swung around to any policeman who prodded her with a night stick and warned, "Do it again and I'm going to have this baby right here, right now."

Steve Roberts still worked on the city staff of the *New York Times*, but he had begun to cover national stories. His first political exclusive was due partly to his in-laws' connections. When he had filled in to cover the McCarthy campaign for a couple of days during the spring—"It was my first national political assignment, I was ab-solutely petrified, I didn't know a thing"—the candidate walked to the rear of the airplane on a flight from Omaha to Milwaukee, after Bobby Kennedy had entered the race and Johnson had withdrawn. He saw Steve and sat down beside him and started to vent about Kennedy and denied that party leaders were rushing RFK's way. "Bobby's campaign is like a grass fire—it will just burn off the sur-face," McCarthy said. "Mine is like a fire in a peat bog."

Steve made the front page.

The *Times* sent Steve to Chicago to cover the demonstrators out-side the hall, because he had met the leaders of the antiwar move-ment through student politics. (Al Lowenstein had slept on his couch the night the activist announced the Dump Johnson move-ment.) Turbulence in the streets became the convention's predomi-nant story, and the twenty-five-year-old reporter wrote article after article, including two on the front page, with some graceful writing and compelling quotes.

"All through that period was odd for me," he said later, because he knew the protesters and yet he had also "married into this Establishment family, worked for an Establishment newspaper." His family connections helped, but they also produced complications. When he was admitted to a closed-door session of the platform committee, he was spotted and the press corps jeered. "A mistake on my part," he said later. "I was a kid." Before the convention opened, he had learned through Tommy and others on the staff of a secret meeting on the Vietnam plank and wrote something brief that mentioned Hale as representing "the southern point of view." The next morning, Lindy telephoned and sobbed to Cokie, "Why does Steve think Hale's a racist?"

As for Hale, "he was under such terrible pressure from the convention, that terrible pressure cooker," his other son-in-law remembered. "Psychologically he never sort of had peace after that."

He found none in facing the voters back home. The Ku Klux Klan had once burned a cross on his lawn, and after his vote on open housing he stopped attending private parties in New Orleans because, Lindy said, people were "so ugly to Hale." At the polls he faced, for the third time, a buttoned-down, boring Republican, a repackaging of racial conservatism in a presentable tone. Dave Treen had drawn 45 percent of the vote in 1964, and a redistricting had snatched Hale's two staunchest jurisdictions.

Still, Hale held a lead of twelve percentage points in opinion polls ten days before the election. That was when Treen began to broadcast a black-and-white television spot of a moving van pulling up to a house in a new suburban subdivision. Two beefy white men open the van, revealing only an old sofa and a chair; concealed behind it, an old station wagon holds a dozen black children and two grandparents who walk to the door of their new home.

"Hale Boggs believes in open housing," the announcer declared. "Dave Treen does not."

Had the ad started running a week earlier, Tommy said later, Hale would have lost. George Wallace, Alabama's segregationist governor, captured Louisiana's electoral votes for the presidency, and Hale eked out 51.2 percent among his district's voters.

Hale was drinking too much as the campaign staggered toward its suspenseful conclusion. After the election, he and Lindy traveled to England and stayed awhile. When he returned home feeling better, everyone concluded he had merely been exhausted.

Julius Hobson had announced he would run for the school board if people wanted him to. "The poor need somebody to represent them," he said. "On the other hand, maybe people are getting sick and tired of so-called leaders like Julius Hobson."

Even an elected Board of Education would have no more power than the existing one. Julius's lawsuit against the appointed board had reached the Supreme Court when Congress acquiesced to the judges' plea to be relieved of the obligation to make such controversial appointments and approved elections in 1968. (Southern conservatives found even the appointed board too liberal.) The superintendent would still make policy, the appointed City Council would draft the budget, and Congress could still meddle in the capital's schools to suit its whims.

Julius had second thoughts about running, because of the book on *Hobson v. Hansen* he intended to write and what he regarded as an uninspiring field of candidates. But the lawsuit had raised his stature and his sense of himself. "The school case gave him the credibility and the respectability he didn't have before," Pat Saltonstall said. He had accomplished as much as he could on the streets and in the courtroom. Now he would try to change the system from inside.

On a sweltering Saturday afternoon in August 1968 he invited reporters to a banquet room at the Washington Hilton, high on Connecticut Avenue, at the farthest edge of the new downtown. The gleaming white hotel squatted on a slope overlooking the city, though the unbroken lines of office buildings and residences blocked any glimpse of a river in the distance.

"I have no ambitions for myself," he announced. "If elected to the board, I will work in the interest of the children."

Julius embarked on a campaign to become an elected official, to join a political Establishment he had always scorned. He addressed civic meetings, sought out reporters, and led a slate that called itself the Committee for Excellence and Equality in Education—Triple-E. He spent no more than five or six hundred dollars, for provocation was free. He vowed to run on a "law and order" platform—"I am campaigning on the enforcement of the Judge Skelly Wright decision"—as Richard Nixon was doing in his Republican pursuit of the presidency. Julius called for democracy in the schools—for community control, for student selection of their teachers and teacher election of their principals.

"When I get on the school board," he said at a press conference, "I am going to give the board fifteen minutes to see if it is going in the same direction as the present school board, and if it is, I'm not going to be a member."

Residents of the capital had first cast their votes for president in 1964 (courtesy of a constitutional amendment) but ninety-four years had passed since they had last elected a local official. Nine candidates competed for the three at-large positions on the school board and fifty-three people pursued one of the eight ward seats. The electorate, however, showed precious little interest. Candidate forums around the city drew hardly anyone but the candidates. Few of the candidates raised as much as four hundred dollars, not enough to mail a flyer to every voter in a ward. On the issues, the candidates barely disagreed.

So Julius made himself the issue. As the best-known candidate, he defined the campaign. His years of referring to "pasteurized Negroes" had made him an object of loathing among the black elite, but his obsession with aggressively educating poor black children emerged as the central issue of the campaign, which everyone addressed.

He also resorted to political theater, in creating a villain. Anita Allen, an incumbent, vied with Julius for an at-large seat. The daughter of a night-shift laborer at the Government Printing Office, she was a large-boned, light-skinned Negro—high yellow, in the vernacular— with a prim manner, perfect diction, a master's degree, and a taste for oversized hats. Julius despised her. He not only insulted her on the stump (she was "running like hell from her blackness") but also sued her, alleging a conflict of interest because of her administrator's job at the federal Office of Education.

"He's in the same department I'm in, you understand," Anita Allen pointed out. The Social Security Administration was also a part of the Department of Health, Education, and Welfare.

He lost in court, but he succeeded in the newspaper coverage.

The Evening Star hoped that Julius would lose, for fear he would disrupt the workings of the board. The *Post* conceded the danger but endorsed him as "an invaluable gadfly, puncturing cant, challenging complacency."

On Election Day, long lines formed at the city's 128 polling places, mainly so voters could join in a landslide for Hubert Humphrey in the majority-black city. But nationally, it was the Republican, Richard Nixon, who sneaked into the White House.

In the local election, only a single candidate was declared elected without a runoff. Poor blacks and white liberals disgusted with the crumbling of the schools gave Julius Hobson most of his 60,842 votes, which amounted to 16.9 percent of those cast for at-large candidates, two-tenths of a percentage point more than required. He finished first in every ward except the two with white majorities. Anita Allen finished two-tenths of a percentage point short.

"I'm flabbergasted," Julius said upon becoming the city's first elected official in nearly a century. "I'm so damn excited I really don't know what to say."

Wednesday was payday at Safeway, and people in Brookland knew where Hobby worked. He drove home after dark to Queens Chapel Terrace, carrying his paycheck and a few dollars in cash. As he approached his house, a car took off and an unfamiliar man ambled along the street. Hobby locked the door and stayed in the car until the man passed by. When Hobby stepped out, the man turned around, a pistol in each hand.

"Give me all you got," he said.

Hobby handed him eight dollars, then a cherished two-dollar bill and a transistor radio. He was almost accustomed to this. Just two months before, six gunmen had entered the Safeway a few minutes before closing, as he was taking money from the safe.

Near the opposite edge of the city, eleven nights after Hobby's earlier robbery, five days before a new president was to take office, Gwen Cafritz and her escort returned to Foxhall Road shortly before ten o'clock. They had dined at the Army-Navy Club, on I Street, next to Morris's original "Park at Your Desk" building. Eugene Myers was a retired air force colonel who was the dean of the Corcoran School of Art, part of the gallery that received the Cafritz Foundation's largesse. He was one of several escorts—the Chilean at the World Bank, the interior designer at W&J Sloane, the gallery owner in McLean—arranged by Gwen's assistant at the foundation.

At fifty-eight years old, Gwen had no intention of remarrying. "I am too old, too tired, and too busy," she said.

These days she hired her chauffeur by the evening. He dropped them off at her front door and Gwen handed her house key to Colonel Myers. As they stepped into the entrance hall, they were grabbed by two masked men who had guns.

The four white men of medium build had arrived at the house almost three hours earlier. The security guard hired after the 1965 robbery was walking toward the garage to change a lightbulb when he was slugged in the face with a gun. The sixty-five-year-old butler was ambushed in his room. Neither man knew how to deactivate the burglar alarm on Gwen's safe; they were bound with tape and left in separate rooms. When the housekeeper and Gwen's personal maid returned from shopping, the burglars took a diamond ring and thirty dollars.

When one of them asked not to be bound so tightly, she was told, "Don't worry; you'll only be tied up until Gwen comes in."

The burglars took Gwen and Colonel Myers into the dining room. He was bound with tape hand and foot and relieved of a gold wristwatch and a money clip with $170. Gwen was made to lie on the floor. She begged them to give her brandy and a pill, and they did. When she told them the combination to the safe was written in Hungarian, she was struck in the face, called obscenities, and dragged upstairs.

She deactivated the alarm to the safe and read the combination to one of the burglars, who opened the safe. She was left bound on the bed. Into two small pillowcases they stuffed thirteen pieces of jewelry, including a $200,000 diamond ring, a $190,000 diamond necklace, a $150,000 pair of diamond-and-emerald earrings, and a gold cigarette case with a diamond clasp. They also took three mink coats and a Somali leopard-skin coat. With property worth nearly one million dollars, they escaped.

The FBI devoted "preferred continuous and intensive handling" to Gwen's repeat of horror, and with the same utter lack of success.

She was no longer willing to stroll alone into her own breathtaking backyard, and she had the swimming pool filled in, for fear a grandchild would drown.

Two weeks later a letter arrived at Foxhall Road.

Dear Gwen,

I was shocked to read that you have again become the victim of a major robbery. You have all of Pat's and my sympathies, and I want you to know that we are going to make a major effort to reduce crime in the nation starting with Washington, D.C.

With warm regards,
Sincerely,
Dick Nixon

Seven

NIXON

The Old Senate Caucus Room, its Corinthian columns of swirling marble, its ceiling of gold decorative trim, had seen so much history unfold—the Teapot Dome hearings, the Truman Committee's investigation of wartime spending, the Army-McCarthy hearings, most recently Senator J. William Fulbright's scrutiny of the quagmire in Vietnam.

On the twenty-seventh of January in 1969, at noon, the august chamber was to witness the nation's first black Supreme Court justice swear in the capital's first elected Board of Education. At last, self-government was starting to return to the soul of the nation's democracy.

The seven Negroes and four whites stood shoulder to shoulder, as Thurgood Marshall administered the oath. The lawyer who had argued *Brown v. Board of Education* before the Supreme Court was now a member, an outsider who occupied a position of power. Julius Hobson had wanted a venue that would be more comfortable for his supporters, but he consented to attend as long as the public was admitted. As his ten colleagues bowed their heads in prayer, he stared off to the side.

Later that evening, dignity was gone in the wood-paneled auditorium at the Department of Commerce, as the new school board met to organize itself. Its main duty was to elect a president, as the latest successor to the D.C. school board's original president, Thomas Jefferson. Julius was considered the odds-on favorite, by himself and by everyone else. He counted six votes, a bare majority.

The first decision was whether ballots should be cast in public or in secret, and the result was a vote of ten to one. Only Anita Allen preferred secrecy. She had looked elegant at the swearing in, in a smart suit and a bulky wraparound hat. She had been vice president of the outgoing board and hoped she would move up, but she lacked the votes.

"I knew that I wasn't going to win," she said years later.

The Reverend James Coates was nominated before Julius was. This was a surprise. He was a capable, soft-spoken thirty-eight-year-old black Baptist pastor in Anacostia who also ran an antipoverty center. He differed from Julius not on educational policy but in his nonconfrontational style.

Julius realized that his opponents were serious.

He knew for sure when John Treanor cast his vote. The representative from Ward Two, the renewed Southwest, was a white ex-prosecutor who had worked for the presidential campaigns of both John and Robert Kennedy. Julius's slate had endorsed him, but when the first vote was cast, he raised his hand for Coates.

"Shame on you, John Treanor!" a man in the audience shouted.

The vote was five to five.

"Somebody's not voting," the board's executive secretary exclaimed. "Mrs. Allen, did you vote?"

"No."

A second ballot had the same result. Anita Allen moved that the board take a five-minute recess.

Abstaining had been her older brother's idea. She dearly wanted the vice presidency, if the presidency were unattainable. Coates had been unwilling to vote for her, so she withheld her vote from him.

People swarmed onto the stage. Partisans on all sides buttonholed the board members, as reporters swooped by.

Anita Allen's brother took her aside to suggest that she offer Coates a deal, that they vote for each other.

Coates assented.

The meeting resumed and the members voted again. Six hands went up for Coates, five for Julius.

"Recount!" came shouts from the audience. "Sell-out!"

Charlie Cassell grabbed a television microphone. The goateed associate of Julius's in CORE and ACT was a black architect and an amateur actor with a cultured voice, who had lost the runoff for the school board from Ward One, the center of the city. "The people declare that the election has been a fraud," he cried. "Shame, John Treanor."

Thirty or forty black spectators stood and chanted with him. The jeering and clapping continued until Julius Hobson slowly rose from his seat. His sure, solemn countenance helped to quiet his supporters.

"Let Mr. Coates be chairman," he said, "and let's get about our business. I have been making bricks without straw for so long it doesn't matter." He said he did not resent any of the votes against him except John Treanor's. "This is not going to amount to a hill of beans. We're going to turn the school system around three hundred sixty degrees."

Surely he did not mean that the schools would finish where they had started.

"Uncle Tom!" people in the audience shouted, as Coates took the gavel. The next business was to elect a vice president. Julius nominated one of his two white supporters to face Anita Allen.

Coates did not cast a vote. Anita Allen drew six votes, a majority, without it.

Afterward, Julius seemed almost relieved by his defeat. "It puts me back in the old Hobson position of raising hell without being responsible," he told a reporter. "The rabbit's back in the brier patch."

He wasted no time in demonstrating that.

The school board's next public meeting took place just days after the appeals court upheld Skelly Wright's decree. As a plaintiff and now also a defendant in the lawsuit he had filed, Julius proposed that the administration furnish the school-by-school data he had found so hard to collect, and the board ordered the new superintendent to do so within forty working days.

This was the calmest part of the four-hour meeting. Students showed up and clapped and heckled the school board and demanded that it create courses in black history, Swahili, speed reading, and sex education and end compulsory phys ed. One thousand students, black and white, had met in an unauthorized assembly earlier in the day at Western High School, in Georgetown. The board appointed a committee to meet with the students.

"No, no, no," forty students chanted. They stood on chairs.

"Why can't we have action tonight?" one of them yelled.

"Now!" screamed another.

"Right now!" shouted a third.

Julius proposed that the board accept the students' demands.

With two dissenting votes, including Anita Allen's, it did.

In the ensuing weeks Julius proposed a tribute in the schools to Malcolm X (who "made 'black' a respectable word") and objected to the inequity in textbooks (three-to-one between Wilson and Cardozo High Schools) and to their racial tone ("Jefferson Davis seems to have had a deep and humble sense of responsibility"). After the board adopted Julius's proposal to stop suspending students until the disciplinary procedures were consistent and fair, grateful youngsters set off firecrackers, squirted fire extinguishers, and hurled milk cartons at teachers. At three junior high schools the teachers walked out, until the board suspended its suspension of suspensions.

"I intend to be an agitator on the school board," Julius stated. "The history of civilization is the history of development borne of friction. If we're going to have civilization in Washington we need more friction."

Julius provided some, outside the school board, in the glory of the capital's early spring. Georgetown University had never held a Black Awareness Week before—"needless to say," the student newspaper snickered, in charting "the Catholic school's helter-skelter rush into the sixties." Julius was invited to deliver the second of the week's five lectures, and he spoke for an hour or more. At least one hundred students, most of them white, filled a third of the Hall of Nations, a hard-surfaced room lined with flags. His ostensible topic was the D.C. school system and the way it damaged black children, and these were matters he addressed. It was when he suggested remedies that he piqued the authorities' interest.

D.C. students "have nothing to lose by raising hell," Julius declared, even if "they take over, control, occupy the schools. . . . They have nothing to lose but their ignorance."

He did not stop there, in plumbing the causes and cures of society's injustices. He said he was personally a socialist—"I believe in the social-economic theories of Karl Marx"—and thought that "the destruction of capitalism is essential to ending poverty. You can't have political democracy without economic democracy." America's system of free enterprise, he said, "must be overthrown by force and violence."

Students in the audience questioned his advocacy of violence. "We are the most violent nation in the history of mankind," Julius answered. "It's our way of life."

The four-sentence account of his speech in *The Evening Star* and the thirteen paragraphs in the *Post* touched off a furor on Capitol Hill. Former FBI agent Larry Hogan, a Republican congressman from suburban Maryland, rose on the House floor and asked his old agency to investigate these "treasonous" remarks. Joe D. Waggonner urged the Social Security Administration to fire Julius. Joel Broyhill, a Republican from just across the Potomac, who was an unctuous bully toward D.C., started searching for a recording of Julius's remarks.

"I would remind those boys of the Constitution," Julius said.

The FBI needed little persuasion to make inquiries, and J. Edgar Hoover informed his agents that he was "personally interested in this case." Just two months earlier, the bureau had promoted Julius from its Agitator Index onto its Rabble Rouser Index. Now he ascended to the Security Index.

The FBI also tried, but failed, to find a recording of Julius's speech. The *Post* reporter refused to turn over his notes and *The Evening Star*'s man said he would, if only he could find them. Agents checked on Julius's credit rating (satisfactory) and on his police record (lengthy but benign). Interviews with students at Georgetown turned up witnesses who said Julius had stated that the house at 1600 Pennsylvania Avenue ought to be burned and that rioters might have to "shoot a few people" on their way downtown.

Agents also sought out Carol, but if they hoped to get dirt from her about her ex-husband, they were disappointed. Julius suffered, she told them, from "the mark of oppression." He had put his desire to help the underprivileged ahead of his family, and that had caused their divorce. But Carol regarded him as clean-living and moral—the most honest man she knew. She had voted for him for school board and would do the same if he ran for mayor, as he had recently said he might, should Congress grant greater democracy to D.C.

A week after his troublemaking speech, Julius made a quieter appearance. He was now the coauthor of a book, *Black Pride—A People's Struggle*, which McGraw-Hill targeted at sophisticated school-children, as a primer on militants from Nat Turner to Malcolm X. Pat Saltonstall had ghostwritten the chapter or two that Julius contributed, and a white Long Island housewife active in civil rights had written the rest. William Raspberry marveled in the *Post* at the book's dispassion—"no odious comparisons, no name-calling (at which Hobson is expert), almost no editorial comment at all." The journal *Grade* named *Black Pride* a "don't-miss" title.

Even the FBI bought a book, and Julius said, "If I thought Congressman Broyhill could read, I'd send him a copy."

Surely his most gratifying reception was the one advertised in the newspapers, accompanied by a photograph of Julius with his pipe: "Come to our autograph party for Julius Hobson." It was held on the ground floor at Woodward & Lothrop, on F Street.

He was now a welcomed guest in the store he had picketed not so many years before.

On October 16, 1969, FBI agents showed up at Hale Boggs's majority whip's office, in the extended East Front of the Capitol. Tommy had already arrived at the well-appointed, high-ceilinged office, and

Hale said he wanted his son to sit in, for he had some knowledge of the facts to be discussed. The agents acquiesced.

In their formal description of the congressman, next to "complexion," the agents typed, "Florida." The agents portrayed the fifty-five-year-old Hale as six feet tall, two hundred pounds, his wavy black hair turning gray. When they told him they had the authority to put him under oath, Hale said, "Let's just go ahead for a while."

This was their second such conversation in little more than a month, and on the same subject—the suspicions of bribery that surrounded the five million dollars in cost overruns on the Rayburn House Office Building's vast underground garage.

John Mitchell, Richard Nixon's law partner and campaign manager and now the attorney general, had specifically requested the investigation. The case grew out of the bribery conspiracy investigation of Senator Daniel Brewster, a skilled practitioner in Maryland's politics of quiet corruption. A politically ambitious prosecutor, Steve Sachs, opened the books of a short, balding Baltimore contractor, Victor Frenkil, who had beguiled his way into political favor with campaign donations and his parlor trick of twisting dollar bills into politicians' initials—*LBJ, HHH, THB*. The contractor had partied in the garden on Bradley Boulevard and had once hobnobbed with Hale and Lindy at the Preakness.

Hale told the FBI agents he considered Victor Frenkil a "name-dropper" and a "positioner."

One day the contractor had stopped by Hale's office to solicit his help in approaching the architect of the Capitol for reimbursement. Hale advised him—yet again, he told the agents—that Frenkil pursue his claim with the General Accounting Office.

"It so happened," Lindy said later, "that Mr. Frenkil came into his office the next day, or maybe that day," just as Lindy was receiving bids from contractors for converting the one-and-a-half-car garage on Bradley Boulevard into a kitchen, with a bay window where the garage door had been. Hale acknowledged to his interrogators that he had once asked Frenkil to recommend a local contractor, but Lindy had used the Yellow Pages instead. Hale showed Frenkil the plans and asked his opinion of a $18,900 bid, in a range that went to $22,000.

A good price, Frenkil replied, but he knew some of his old work-men who might do this sort of job for less.

Hale told the FBI he did not recall any such meeting. What Frenkil considered a meeting, he pointed out, might have been only a chance encounter.

Lindy was surprised when a crew showed up at the house and started to work. She rushed to Rockville because the men had not bothered to obtain a Montgomery County permit, and she was less than happy with the work. The workmen could not build the fireplace where she wanted it, and they used brand-new bricks—"with no patina," Lindy objected—instead of old ones.

Hale told the men from the FBI that he too had found the work unsatisfactory, especially the air-conditioning and the "terrible" paint job. Nor had he liked the final bill of twenty-one thousand dollars.

And, no, he knew nothing about the contractor's true costs, as calculated from Frenkil's books at $45,082.95.

Tommy examined the records of the renovations and found the costs of materials about right but the labor costs maybe 50 percent too high.

The grand jury proposed to indict Victor Frenkil for trying to re-cruit a half-dozen Democrats in Congress, including Hale Boggs, to his cause. Steve Sachs wanted to sign the indictment, but John Mitchell overruled him, because there was insufficient evidence. When a federal judge released a summary of the grand jury's secret recommendation that mentioned Hale by name, the story wound up on front pages.

"You can't know what embarrassment is," Lindy said, "unless you've experienced it yourself."

Julius Hobson accompanied Tina to antiwar rallies, usually as a speaker and often as the only black face. He was less concerned for the suffering of the Vietnamese than for the surfeit of young black men being drafted and killed. Black activists accused him of spread-ing himself too thin, but he viewed Vietnam as an extension of civil rights.

His critics, however, had a point. He was one of fourteen people arrested in a fist-flying, chair-throwing melee when the City Council approved the Three Sisters Bridge across the Potomac, beyond Key Bridge. He joined in challenging the license renewal for channel seven, the ABC affiliate owned by the *Star*, because of its alleged disregard for the black community's needs.

"Most of us can't keep fifteen balls in the air," Tina said later. "He could."

But even while pursuing these causes, he maintained his paramount interest in education. He had taken a year's leave of absence from his job at Social Security, on the strength of a twenty-five-thousand-dollar grant from the Stern Foundation for measuring the success, school by school, in equalizing resources. This allowed him at long last to conduct his activism full-time. Every day he pored over the newspapers (he preferred the conservative *Star* to the liberal *Post* for the lack of editorializing in its news reporting) and decided on his opportunities.

But all too soon he had to face the voters again. In order to stagger the new school board's terms, a lottery had decided which six members would serve for three years and which five would serve for one. Julius had lost.

This time he had a plan, and a grander one than hardly anyone knew. When Julius announced he was giving up his at-large seat, to run instead in Ward Two, he was lauded for his generosity, in opening a second at-large seat for an ally to capture. This was not a matter of altruism but of numbers. If both Charlie Cassell and Bardyl Tirana won, and Julius did too, his supporters would constitute a majority, enough to give him the presidency.

He had something even more ambitious in mind. If he and his allies held six seats or more, they intended to hire a new superintendent of schools: Julius Hobson.

Ward Two was made up of the increasingly white neighborhoods in Southwest and Foggy Bottom and predominantly black Shaw. John Treanor had bowed out, and Julius's main opponent was a plain-looking forty-year-old black mother of four, a secretary at an anti-poverty agency in Shaw. Evie Washington was self-effacing but shrewd. She understood how to turn Julius's strengths against him.

"Mr. Hobson and I both want the same thing—better schools,"

she told the *Post*. "But I'm not so middle class and out of the community that anybody who wants to reach me can't."

At a candidates' forum in the Metropolitan African Methodist Episcopal (AME) Church, downtown on M Street, once a stop on the Underground Railroad, she accused Julius of skipping the meetings that were closed to the press, of preferring disruption to solutions. "Mr. Hobson has had a wonderful one-year career," she said—"before the television cameras."

"I am disruptive," Julius admitted afterward. But he said he saw no other way to change the schools.

Julius had not lost his touch on the stump. He used the cadences of the Baptist preachers he so disdained, invoking the king's English or the language of the ghetto, to suit his audience. When he appeared at the Amidon Elementary School in Southwest, he spoke movingly about a teacher who had made such a difference to him in Birmingham, in whose eye "the sun rose and the sun set in the faces of the children." He had tamed, when he liked, his Alabama twang.

Yet the white liberals had grown tired of black militancy and frightened of crime. If they could vote for somebody black *and* safe, they just might.

Both of the city's conservative newspapers had editorially opposed Julius's election in 1968 but, astonishingly, endorsed him in 1969—"the most exciting . . . personality in the public schools," said the tabloid *Daily News*. Praised *The Evening Star*: "His knowledge of the details is awesome."

The *Post*, however, also jumped sides, because "his tendency to indulge in extravagant rhetoric and to approve of efforts to disrupt school board meetings has reduced his effectiveness as a board member." This hurt him among the gentrifying liberals. An aide to Mayor Washington joined the Democratic Party's national committeewoman from D.C. in a last-minute attempt to defeat him.

The voters showed even less interest in the century's second local election than they had in the first. Candidates' forums drew so few spectators that, at one, the coffee furnished to the speakers was enough to serve the audience, too. The absence of a presidential election was partly to blame, perhaps along with the fractiousness on the weakly led board and a sense of hopelessness about rescuing the public schools. Still, it was startling that fewer than one in six of the capital's registered voters took advantage of the democratic franchise lost for nearly a century. Most of the people who voted were middle class.

Julius and his allies gathered for a victory party that evening at Bardyl Tirana's tan stucco row house on P Street in Georgetown. The at-large candidate was a thoughtful, square-jawed, thirty-one-year-old former aide to Bobby Kennedy, a Princeton-educated lawyer of Albanian and Russian Jewish descent and southern roots. (His grandfather had been a founder of the NAACP.) Two hundred people stopped in as the evening wore on, to swig bottles of Heineken and munch on hors d'oeuvres. Bardyl Tirana was convinced that FBI and CIA agents were spying from across the street.

As the results trickled in, Bardyl Tirana remained comfortably ahead in the race for an at-large seat. Charlie Cassell barely trailed in the other, which he eventually won by two votes.

The outcome of Julius's race was never in doubt.

Bardyl Tirana was saddened but not shocked. Julius had had no inkling. As the precincts reported, Julius grew ever quieter, trying to process the facts.

Tina could see the desperate hurt in his face and was determined to change it. The election results made her mad. She wanted a different headline the following day.

"I hadn't really decided to get married," she said later, but "I was close enough." His loss overwhelmed her. "I couldn't let him feel that nobody cared."

When a newspaper reporter passed by, Tina whispered the news. She wanted to surprise Julius—and she did.

As he announced it to the crowd, Bardyl Tirana poured champagne over his head.

"I wish Mrs. Washington well," Julius went on. "I'm everywhere and always an agitator. I got sidetracked for one year and thought I was part of the power structure. Now I'm back to the old Hobson position—a broken sword and bricks without straw."

The next day, the newspapers reported his loss, 1,170 to 921.

The photograph in the *Star* showed Julius, a pipe in his hand, pecking Tina's white cheek.

Tommy Boggs's first client had arrived courtesy of Clark Clifford. The New Jersey chemical company's problem with its regulators in Washington was too small for the superlawyer to bother with, so he passed the client (and the twenty-five-thousand-dollar fee) along to Tommy.

Tommy attracted other clients through his maritime connections. Marshall Safir had moved from the rag business into ocean shipping, in which the government controlled the rates. He was a flamboyant New Yorker married to an opera singer, the older brother of the president's senior speechwriter (who had added an *e* to his surname, to make the pronunciation plain). In Tommy's eyes, Safir was "crazy as a loon." He was crazy enough to file an antitrust suit against eight steamship companies for colluding against him with retaliatory pricing, to drive him into bankruptcy and out of business. The eventual antitrust settlement totaled three million dollars.

This case drew in a bigger one, when Joe Alioto read of it. The prominent San Francisco trial lawyer was becoming the city's mayor, and he flew into Washington and handed off his client to Tommy.

"The best way to begin as a young attorney is to practice law, and he did," Jim Patton said of Tommy. Less than fourteen months after joining the firm, he was made a partner. The firm had shed its two partners in New York, but its name had been growing again. In mid-1967 it expanded to Patton, Blow, Verrill, Brand & Boggs.

But the sort of governmental practice that Jim Patton had had in mind, to help a company solve its problems in the capital, in any part of the government, was still to emerge. According to Patton, after Tommy arrived at the firm, "Nothing came up with a need for lobbying."

Tommy found his first real lobbying client through a staff member he knew on the House Merchant Marine Committee who recommended him to someone at the trade association for yacht manufacturers. The government played an ever nosier role in telling businesses how to behave, as the Great Society had superseded even the New Deal in its regulatory reach. The Republican who was now in the White House, far from trying to reverse this, created yet another bureaucracy, for environmental regulation, and would even prove willing to control wages and prices. President Johnson had proposed a bill to regulate yachts for safety, and his successor did the same. Tommy represented a frightened industry's interests on Capitol Hill.

An emblem of his success emerged in the macerator chlorinator. Federal concern about water pollution had inspired a directive that any yacht with a toilet have a holding tank installed for the sewage, but the expense and the paucity of pumping stations begged an alternative. As enacted, the law allowed a choice between a holding tank and a macerator chlorinator, a device to grind up sewage and treat it with chlorine.

When he showed up in person one October to register formally as a lobbyist to Congress, he noticed that only sixty-some others had signed their names that year before him.

There had been lobbyists, of course, since time immemorial. The right to petition the government dated to the Magna Carta, and the term *lobby-agent* as applied in the corridors of the New York legislature had been shortened to *lobbyist* by around 1832. Popular accounts traced the usage to President Ulysses S. Grant's epithet for the men who bothered him for jobs or favors as he tried to enjoy a cigar in the lobby of the old Willard Hotel. The role still exuded an unsavory smell, of booze and broads. Since 1946, lobbyists had been required to register with the same government they hoped to influence, as if they were parolees or aliens.

"If you wanted to be a member of the Metropolitan Club, it was better if you were not a lobbyist," recalled George Blow, an international lawyer who had followed Jim Patton from Covington & Burling. The capital's prominent firms, the likes of Covington, disdained such a practice.

Clark Clifford, it was true, and to a lesser extent Tommy Corcoran, embodied a certain respectability. But their very scarcity suggested a more serious limitation. In a capital with so few centers of genuine power, rare was the person with just the right connections who could wield true influence in the White House or Congress. "Washington was run by twenty-five people," Tommy said, which meant almost "three lobbyists for every person who ran the town."

But people knew that Tommy was his father's son and an intimate of Russell Long, the new chairman of the Senate Finance Committee, though he was quiet about it. Tommy was also easy to be around. "He didn't have the same level of intense self-importance that a lot of the old hands had," said a Senate aide he had lobbied.

Clients in search of more than strictly legal help trickled in. He carried the tariff complaints of seven petrochemical companies first to a judge and then, more successfully, to the interior secretary. Central American sugar producers hired Tommy to fight for their share of the import quotas on Capitol Hill; that "made all my Louisiana buddies mad," he said.

"I would like to ask Mr. Boggs one question," a Republican from Iowa began at a House Agriculture Committee hearing. "In your chart A-5, you give a U.S. direct investment figure for Peru of $53.74. I would like to know whether that figure is before or after substantial amounts of direct U.S. investment in Peru were expropriated?"

"Congressman Mayne," Tommy replied, "the question is a pertinent one. The facts are up through 1969, which was, of course, prior to the current policies of the Peruvian government."

Later, Tommy explained that he had "a son's respect for his parents' profession," and he felt a hankering to practice it even more directly. In 1970, when the regular Democrats in Montgomery County urged him to run for the party's congressional nomination from the Eighth District of Maryland, he assented.

"It's in the blood," said Tommy's wife, Barbara. "All three of those children have the smell of the greasepaint, roar of the crowd."

His main opponents were a business-oriented state senator and a bearded ex-minister. All three were dovish on Vietnam and possessed a modicum of money and organization. Tommy was bland on the stump, his father's inferior, though he "got better," he muttered years later. Seeing Hale's connection to Victor Frenkil trumpeted on the front page of the Washington Post was no help. Tommy lambasted the seniority system and kept his father out of sight.

"Voters in the Eighth District are familiar," he said, "with the differences between fathers and sons."

Despite this handicap, his family's connections helped. Lady Bird Johnson's social secretary put on a hundred-dollar-a-family box supper at Drew Pearson's widow's farm in the wealthy suburb of Potomac. The Kennedy family lent its support, notably Senator Ted Kennedy and his Maryland brother-in-law, Sargent Shriver. As the chairman of a national party organization to help Democratic candidates, Shriver made a single exception to his studied neutrality, by throwing a cocktail party at his Rockville home to raise money for Tommy's campaign.

"I intend of course to live up to my commitment to Tom Boggs, who is a personal friend and who has been helpful to me," Shriver said.

The twenty-nine-year-old candidate bought inexpensive black suits to make himself look older and was perceived to be using JFK-like gestures, "speaking occasionally in what sounded like a New England accent."

There was little to separate the candidates on the issues, except for one question: Should the Chevy Chase Club and other bastions of the wealthy continue to be excused from paying property taxes? Tommy proposed to tax them. Tommy saw himself as the most liberal of the three candidates ("This nation must set upon a course of beating its swords into plowshares," he said, to relieve the loss of aerospace jobs) yet also practical. The county Democratic organization endorsed him, and so did Maryland's machine-minded governor, Marvin Mandel.

Tommy's 20,283 votes edged his nearest opponent by 2,455. Barbara wore a wig styled in a flip, as the cameras caught their grins.

The nomination was his, but Tommy was an underdog against the Republican incumbent, Gilbert Gude. The gray-faced, conscientious, independent-minded forty-seven-year-old suited a district dominated by professionals and government bureaucrats who tended to register as Democrats but vote for liberal Republicans. (Only once since 1942 had they sent a Democrat to Congress.) Gude, in his two terms, combined a clean and sober governance with diligent service to constituents, sating their good-government impulses with his proposals for a regional sewage treatment plan and for government-published measurements of auto pollution, model by model, along with his early opposition to the Vietnam War.

He had won 61 percent of the vote in 1968. Everyone liked him, including Tommy Boggs.

Tommy ran a well-organized campaign, one of the costliest the county had seen, and quite a modern one. Three-fourths of his $100,000 budget went to television ads. Senator Edmund Muskie of Maine, the frontrunner for the Democratic presidential nomination two years hence, taped a commercial—"Tom Boggs puts people first"—broadcast in prime time on Washington stations. The two candidates differed little on the issues, so Tommy tried to portray Gude as ineffectual—"Ever hear of the Gude bill? That's because there isn't any!"—and not as liberal as he seemed. Their differences amounted to aggressiveness versus cautiousness, brash youth against middle age.

By 8:25 P.M. on election night, Tommy conceded defeat. He had seen projections from computer-chosen precincts. Gilbert Gude had swamped him, again with 61 percent of the vote.

It took Tommy until the following year to pay off his forty-thousand-dollar campaign debt. He sold his house on Oxford Street in Chevy Chase and took out four mortgages to buy a bigger one, a spacious gabled home of yellow stucco, four blocks closer in.

Never again would Tommy Boggs want to run for office. But he had learned a lot—about what politicians go through to succeed, about the pain of raising money—that he would forever find useful.

One sad morning in 1970, in a vacant lot near the Pentagon, Calvin Cafritz watched his father's primal legacy auctioned off. On the block stood the bulldozers and equipment—the guts and gall—of the Cafritz Construction Company, incorporated in 1922.

"We had to disband the construction company," Calvin said—"let everyone go."

The reason was the philanthropic foundation, which Gwen had made the focus of the family enterprise. At long last Morris's will had gone through probate, freeing the most valuable estate (appraised by now at more than $65 million) ever handled in D.C. The foundation now held half of it, but the Internal Revenue Service (IRS) had forbidden tax-exempt foundations to rely on risky businesses for their funds. Calvin had grown up knowing many of the men and had worked for some of them. Efforts to help them find jobs did not quell his pain at what he later described as the first of many endings.

Within two weeks of his father's death in 1964, the eldest son had been promoted from vice president of the parent Cafritz Company to its president and treasurer. Thirty-three-year-old Calvin completed two of his father's office buildings downtown (the one at Nineteenth and L was nearly finished, and the elevators were being installed at Eighteenth and I) and built one on his own, in black sheathing, at 1825 K. He managed the Ambassador Hotel while probate was under way, at last fulfilling his father's hope when Calvin was a boy that he would take an interest in hotels. He found the rest of the company's operations easy enough, leasing and managing the offices, apartments, and warehouses that the construction company had brought to life.

"I'd worked in different departments," Calvin said, "and knew everyone in the company."

But the company was never really Calvin's to run. He was the president, but his mother was the chairman of both the foundation and the company, which it owned. Who could tell Gwendolyn no? Not her children, certainly. Nor was Gwen the only power. Martin Atlas had stayed on as the executive vice president, to keep the company operating smoothly. Calvin's younger brothers worked in lesser roles, Carter as a coordinator and expediter, Conrad as a service manager.

Without the construction business, however, the nature of the company had changed. Leasing and managing suited Gwen's growing aversion to risk. She depended on the advice of cautious men, tax attorney Atlas and her once-and-future legal confidant, Bill Rogers, the secretary of state who labored in Henry Kissinger's shadow. Calvin would suggest a project and Gwen would initially encourage him; then the next time they spoke she would fret about the risk and change her mind. To whom had she talked, he wondered, in the meantime?

She was distant from her sons. Only occasionally did they visit her. Carter's ex-wife, a heroin addict, was indicted in the spring of 1970 for selling twelve capsules of heroin to an undercover policeman behind the Peoples Drug at Wisconsin and O. Before fall she was found dead, in a sparsely furnished apartment on Twentieth Street.

Conrad was heading toward a divorce from Jennifer, after more than eleven years of marriage. Independent-minded Jennifer was a match for Conrad in intellect, acerbic demeanor, and liberal chic—she counted Joan Baez and Warren Beatty as pals. "Both 'beatnik' types," said an FBI informant.

Gwen had seemed closer to Calvin. She admired people involved in the arts, and Calvin had married an abstract painter, Enid Sanford, who showed her work at local galleries, including the Corcoran. They raised two sons and a daughter in their gutted-and-rebuilt town house in Georgetown, a slit of darkness converted into something light and airy.

But even Gwen and Calvin had a falling out. Ever since Morris's death, Gwen had feared losing her entire fortune, and she was evidently terrified of losing control. How else to explain her action of December 1971?

"I'm forty years old," Calvin announced to the newspapers, "and if I don't strike out on my own now, I never will."

The city's insular world of real estate was stunned. It appeared that his mother had fired him, and all too publicly. His unexpected resignation as the president and a director of the Cafritz Company provoked reports of "differences between mother and son."

In truth, Calvin had submitted his resignation. Once his father's estate was settled, and the foundation shifted to the conservation of assets, he had grown bored with leasing and managing buildings, at having nothing to build.

"My expectations were not in line with hers," he later explained.

That his mother had promptly accepted his resignation hurt him deeply.

The Lone Star emblem was still high on the wall, but Sam Rayburn's vault-ceilinged hideaway had slipped into disuse, ever since John McCormack, a teetotaler and fanatically married man, had succeeded him as Speaker. Then suddenly McCormack announced that he was stepping down after the 1970 elections, though how could anyone tell? Carl Albert, the indecisive and unobjectionable majority leader, was a cinch to become the next Speaker, and so the question became, Who would succeed *him*?

Three days before Christmas, the five aspirants gathered for lunch in the Capitol, in the subdued surroundings of H-128, where the Board of Education had convened. They agreed on ground rules that barred other entrants to the race and would produce a winner by removing the lowest contender in successive ballots.

By the hierarchical traditions of the House, Hale Boggs stood next in line. Traditions required people who believed in them, however, and the old assumptions were giving way, even at last in the people's House. Among his four declared rivals for the majority leader's post, the most formidable was an irreverent westerner. Morris Udall of Arizona was a liberal reformer with a self-deprecating wit whose challenge for the speakership in 1969 had earned him the enmity of insiders.

Hale's chances had looked dim six months earlier. Columnists had groused about his "lethargy and arrogance," and he was accused of inattentiveness as the majority whip. His affection for oil and the Vietnam War distanced him from younger, hipper Democrats. In trying to serve as a bridge between Democratic camps, he seemed to be (in the *Post*'s description) "too liberal for the South, too Southern for the North, too Old Guard for the young liberals."

Hale had another problem. What Udall privately characterized as Hale's "bizarre and erratic behavior" was the talk of the cloakrooms in the summer of 1969. A press conference Hale had called to counter allegations of bribery by a chemical company became a rambling two-hour monologue, with readings from his appointment calendar and the New Testament.

"May I ask a question?" said a reporter.

"Forget it," Hale replied.

Hale was known to barrel by a congressman without a glance, to heckle the Ways and Means baron Wilbur Mills on the House floor, to deliver speeches that mixed brilliance and babble—"and there was *no way* you could shut him up," a colleague remarked. His face looked fleshier, weary. Tommy had been spending time around Hale's office—"babysitting, primarily," he said later. "We actually got to be good friends."

Tommy's role in his father's campaign for majority leader was to count votes—as a whip, in effect, for the whip. Hale's own count was 127, a single vote short of a majority of Democrats. When Tommy followed up by phone, he might get a maybe instead of a yes. His vote count: 103.

A poll by *Congressional Quarterly* gave Udall a comfortable lead, though only half of the Democrats had responded. Hale labored to improve his lot. He threw four garden parties on Bradley Boulevard and charmed syndicated columnists into prophesying his success. He had wired congratulations to the newly elected Democrats and assigned his staff to help them rent homes and find the right schools.

He was fortunate that no other southerner ran. He reached out to northern liberals by voting to require compulsory union membership for postal workers and by furnishing the decisive vote on Ways and Means to reduce the oilmen's beloved depletion allowance.

"I'm not status quo," Hale said, "and I never have been."

He made the most of his leverage as the second-ranked Democrat on Ways and Means, the committee on committees. Shirley Chisholm, the fiery black liberal, wanted a seat on Education and Labor and, in exchange for her vote, got it.

What mattered most in the end was Hale's connections to—as Tommy called them—"the big-city guys." It made sense that he would see eye to eye with the ethnic Catholics from commercial crossroads like New Orleans—Rostenkowski in Chicago, Hugh Carey of Brooklyn, Tip O'Neill from outside Boston.

"They were buddies," Tommy said of his father and Tip O'Neill.

On the first secret ballot, Hale drew ninety-five votes, to Udall's sixty-nine. Two of the lesser candidates withdrew. On the second ballot, Hale's votes soared to 140.

Udall blamed the fifties and sixties liberals who had voted for Hale. "In the House," he lamented, "yesterday's revolutionaries become today's elitists."

The streetwalkers and dope dealers strolled near Thomas Circle, at Fourteenth and M, within a howl's hearing of two bulky churches. Across Vermont Avenue, at the Hotel Sonesta, on this Wednesday night in February 1971, five hundred of Julius Hobson's supporters kicked off his campaign for Congress. They had paid five dollars apiece, in the most affordable of fund-raisers, to watch an acrobatic troupe and to listen first to the soul sounds of the Ashantis and then to political invective.

Julius whirled Tina around the dance floor a few times before walking to the microphone.

"This campaign will be like taking candy from a baby," he said, "but I'm going to take it anyway."

Ninety-nine years had elapsed since voters in D.C. had last been permitted to elect a delegate to the House of Representatives, someone who could participate in the proceedings though could not vote. Norton Parker Chipman, a white lawyer and former colonel in the Union army, had defeated Frederick Douglass for the Republican nomination. He served a fruitful term-and-a-half, prevailing on Congress to extend the Capitol's grounds (by razing houses and saloons) and to appropriate money to build colored schools, before the local government's excessive spending drove territorial self-rule to an early end.

How could Julius not run, and if he won, perhaps gain a national audience? More delicious still was the identity of his chief opponent.

Julius had passed up the Democratic primary, once Congress had reinstituted a delegate's seat for D.C., in favor of a new political party. He had started teaching social problems and the law at American University and assigned students to research the choices of means to obtain self-government in the seat of the national government. A constitutional amendment required a two-thirds vote in Congress and the ratification by three-fourths of the states. But simple statehood, such as Alaska and Hawaii had attained, required only a majority vote by Congress and a president's signature. (The federal district, constitutionally decreed, could shrink to the unpopulated Mall and Federal Triangle.) So the Statehood Party was organized as the vehicle for Julius's campaign, and the reverse.

Julius had announced his candidacy two days after Walter Fauntroy, a city councilman, won the Democratic primary in January with surprising ease. Tina and Hobby looked on as Julius assailed the preacher he called "Little Lord Fauntroy" for constantly invoking the martyred memory of Martin Luther King—"for running in the shadows of a dead man."

He said: "Let's bring out the issues, baby. Let's discuss employment, police brutality, housing, health, schools. Let's not deal with pie in the sky."

This set the tone for an ugly campaign. At a candidates' forum at the D.C. Teachers College, Julius suggested that the choice was between electing "a man or a boy" to Congress.

"If you want a man who will sit next to Joel Broyhill and say, 'Will the gentleman from Virginia please yield?'" Julius declared, "don't vote for me."

He explained his unpolitic approach to politics to an underground newspaper. "I am not a politician," he said. "I want to be elected, but I am not going to say a damn thing for your benefit, or that person's benefit out there on the street, or anybody's."

His opponent seemed oblivious. "His approach was pure Baptist minister," the *Star* said of Fauntroy, who spoke of legislation as "gospel" and likened his campaign to David's against Goliath. At rallies, in his improbable tenor, he crooned "The Impossible Dream." He used his political base in the black churches to organize his campaign in every ward, claiming as many as a thousand volunteers in the precincts. He walked the inner city's streets, portraying himself as a poor boy who had made good and his primary victory as "superbad."

For a while Julius seemed to think he had a chance of winning the election. That was before Fauntroy, on the last day of the campaign, presented Coretta Scott King to tell the moist-eyed crowds about "my husband's trusted friend." Another disciple of Dr. King, a young charismatic preacher from Chicago named Jesse Jackson, also appeared on Fauntroy's behalf and whipped the crowd into a chant, "I am somebody."

On Election Day, the Republican nominee captured the affluent neighborhoods west of Rock Creek Park. Fauntroy swept every ward to the east—more than 58 percent, citywide.

Julius's 13 percent, for third place, was twice what the Statehood Party needed to secure a place on future ballots. But Julius was bitter at the black bus drivers, the salesclerks, the people he had helped, who had forsaken him.

He conceded to Fauntroy but refused to congratulate him. "I hope Washington will not become a rotten borough city," he snapped, "and be controlled by a political machine like Chicago."

Julius also understood, however, what a failure he would have been in Congress. "I would not have been elected," he said, "the second time."

Five hundred men in white tie and tails arrived at the Statler-Hilton, at Sixteenth and K, on a Saturday night in March 1971 and passed between the picketers who protested the Gridiron Club's exclusion of women since President Grover Cleveland's first term. The club's annual dinner, sponsored by the capital's fifty journalistic insiders, was counted as one of the premier events of Washington's year.

Except that this year the president stayed away, in Key Biscayne, to avoid what he privately scorned as "four-and-a-half hours of complete boredom."

Instead, Vice President Spiro Agnew took Nixon's place. He shared the head table in the heavily chandeliered ballroom with seven Supreme Court justices, a few Cabinet officers, General William Westmoreland, Ted Kennedy, the astronaut Alan Shepard, and, far to his left—seated between the Democratic Party chairman and the secretary of the army—Hale Boggs. The new House majority leader was honored not only as a guest but also as a character (played by Jerry terHorst of the *Detroit News*) in a skit about the "Crawfish Mafia." The teasing tone had given the Gridiron Club its name, after an appliance that could singe but not burn, in journalists' backhanded homage.

Hale was anything but bored. The open bar before dinner and the four wines and the champagne served during the seven courses (oysters, terrapin, medallions of filet of beef Rossini) held their own interest. He had hated Richard Nixon for years, because of his history of Communist witch-hunting, and soon he was cursing the attorney general and the administration and the Republicans in general, in loud comments to others along the head table. During the skits and while William Rogers delivered the Republicans' riposte, Hale disturbed the diners nearby.

"That voice of his just carries right across the hall," someone told Nixon three mornings later.

During an early intermission, Hale ran into John Mitchell in the men's room. Hale regarded the attorney general as a bagman for the president. The two had words before the attorney general left.

A former one-term congressman was also in the men's room. Ed Mitchell—no relation to the attorney general—had been sitting at table one, and he was seething. The brawny, sharp-nosed Republican from Indiana was, in Nixon's words, "a loyalist from the word go" and "an old frogman, oh he's a tough son of a bitch." In college Mitchell had boxed three rounds in an exhibition with Max Schmeling; he could still handle himself at age sixty. And like Hale he was susceptible to drink.

When Hale threatened to give him a good whipping, Ed Mitchell swung, and, with one punch, Hale went down. The onetime fighter straddled Hale on the men's room floor, until bystanders pulled them apart.

When Hale finally emerged from the men's room, his white tie askew, he was bleeding around the face and looked drunk, angry, shaken up. He walked unsteadily back to his seat and mocked his adversary as "Jack Dempsey."

Word of the incident hurtled through the hall. It was the talk of the after-dinner parties and within two or three days the subject of news accounts, which so rarely publicized a politician's misbehavior.

Three weeks later, Hale flew to the Florida Panhandle, with Lindy, to appear at a testimonial banquet for a political ally. Congressman Bob Sikes carried a commanding presence, not the least because he was a "cardinal"—in congressional parlance, the chairman of an Appropriations subcommittee, on military construction. Hale and Lindy relaxed in the sun, but the Friday of the banquet, Hale stayed in the hotel room and drank. By dinnertime he was in no condition to deliver one of the evening's four speeches.

Lindy stepped to the podium and told the four hundred celebrants that Hale had fallen ill, and she heralded Bob Sikes's virtues in his stead.

During the banquet Hale barreled into the side room of the banquet hall, loud and profane, obviously drunk, hurling insults at women, threatening to denounce Bob Sikes. Police officers forcibly restrained him and locked the door to the ballroom.

"Gestapo!" he snarled. "Storm troopers." He threatened to sue them.

As the banquet was ending and the doors opened, Hale broke away and entered the hall as it was emptying and mounted the podium. Bob Sikes called everyone back to the tables—"with electric silence," a local columnist reported.

Hale denied that he had been ill—he had been "out on the beach, watching the waves lap against the shore"—and he delivered a paean to his host.

Later, Bob Sikes told reporters, "He was taking antibiotics and you know how they can affect you."

The incidents, and the murmurings, mounted. Reports flourished that he had almost started a drunken fistfight with a congressman at an afternoon reception at the Madison Hotel and that he had grabbed a senator's lapels at a formal dinner and screamed in his face. There was talk of a fight in a restaurant in Baton Rouge and an altercation at the home of a presidential assistant. Speaker Albert canceled trips to prevent leaving Hale in control of the House.

Once, Hale strode into the East Room at the White House, late for a meeting of the president and congressional leaders. He stood in the doorway, with papers wedged between his upper arm and his chest, until the president deferred to him. Hale said something that made no sense and then, "I'm sorry, I have to leave now—I have to return to the House of Representatives."

And then he left.

Dan Rostenkowski drove back to the Capitol with the House Foreign Affairs Committee chairman, Thomas (Doc) Morgan of Pennsylvania, who was also a medical doctor.

"Doc, what the hell's going on with Hale Boggs?" said Rostenkowski.

"There's something wrong with that young man. He's got something wrong mentally."

On the Monday morning after the Friday night fiasco in Florida, the *Post*'s front page carried an article on the "Untouchable Hoover." Despite the succession of FBI lapses (a recent explosion in the Capitol, the theft of FBI documents near Philadelphia) and J. Edgar Hoover's foot-in-mouth characterizations (that a recent attorney general was "a jellyfish," that Puerto Ricans and Mexicans "don't shoot very straight" but are deadly with knives), the director's job, the newspaper wonderingly reported, was secure.

That was only a part of what set Hale off. He had been told that the FBI had eavesdropped on his telephone at home and possibly on Capitol Hill. The summer before, a worker for the Chesapeake & Potomac telephone company had investigated noises on the phone line at Bradley Boulevard and reported evidence of a wiretap, since removed. A former New York City cop who was now in the House, Mario Biaggi, had intended to play tapes on the House floor of FBI surveillance of members of Congress from New Jersey and New York. While Hale served on the Warren Commission, a courier he believed was from the FBI had slipped him compromising photos of a leading conspiracy theorist consorting with prostitutes in New Orleans.

Tommy was in the office at the time and had asked whether Hoover had "done this with other people."

"Oh, yeah," Hale had replied.

Hale and Hoover had danced a minuet over the years, combining public displays of affection and a mutual distrust. An exchange of gushing letters in 1950 had included a complaint on the FBI's internal copy about Hale's "very non-specific" praise. Hoover was advised to refuse a request for a congratulatory telegram to Hale in 1962 because it was "a political stunt" that Boggs would use "to enhance his own political future." The director had declined invitations to garden parties on Bradley Boulevard. Hale lauded the director ("How thorough and how objective this man and his associates are") in the *Congressional Record* while nursing a deeper distrust.

As the House went into session at noon on April 5, 1971, the majority leader rose on the floor to deliver an impromptu one-minute speech. Some spectators said that he seemed drunk or on medication, though reporters who questioned him afterward thought him sober. When he took the microphone and spoke without notes, no one knew what was coming.

> "I apologize for my voice," he began, pleading a cold. "What I am going to say I say in sorrow, because it is always tragic when a great man who has given his life to his country comes to the twilight of his life and fails to understand it is time to leave the service and enjoy retirement. Mr. Speaker, I am talking about Mr. J. Edgar Hoover, the director of the Federal Bureau of Investigation. The time has come for the Attorney General of the United States to ask for the resignation of Mr. Hoover.

> "When the FBI taps the telephones of members of this body and of members of the Senate, when the FBI stations agents on college campuses to infiltrate college organizations, when the FBI adopts the tactics of the Soviet Union and Hitler's Gestapo, then it is time—it is way past time, Mr. Speaker—that the present director thereof no longer be the director.

> "The greatest thing we have in this nation is the Bill of Rights. We are a great country because we are a free country under the Bill of Rights. The way Mr. Hoover is running the FBI today it is no longer a free country."

He finished to a stunned silence.

"I didn't know if Hale was serious or if he was paranoid," said a second-term Democrat who was listening. "I later concluded he was probably serious."

The minority leader immediately stood to reply. Gerald Ford was an affable if unimaginative Republican from Michigan, more agile a politician than he let on.

"Mr. Speaker, I listened with great care to the statements made by the distinguished majority leader," he said.

Congress trafficked in a pointed politeness, so that the sharper the emotion, the more ornate the circumlocution.

"Some of the allegations are a matter of fact, that is, whether certain wiretapping was done or whether it was not done, but there was one statement, if I listened correctly, that I do not think is a fair accusation.

"If my recollection is accurate, the gentleman said that the FBI is turning its operations into Gestapo-type activities." Ford spoke with a whiny Midwestern earnestness.

"I categorically deny that the FBI does carry on such activities. I suggest that the gentleman from Louisiana submit proof before he makes such a charge or to buttress such an allegation by facts in the future."

Newspapers splashed the story across page one. Two of the Democrats' presidential aspirants had called for Hoover's head, but this was a first among the congressional leaders.

Then Hale continued on his way to Robert F. Kennedy Memorial Stadium, for what was destined to be the Washington Senators' final Opening Day. J. Edgar Hoover, too, happened to be in attendance. "I thought there was a bad smell at the Stadium," the thick-necked director scribbled beside *The Evening Star*'s account of the coincidence.

After the ball game, the political turbulence intensified. The president told his chief of staff (who confided to his diary) "that we should attack Boggs on his drunkenness and try to destroy him." The attorney general issued a statement from Key Biscayne that denied any wiretapping and accused the majority leader of reaching "a new low in political dialogue."

Hale phoned reporters that night to call Hoover "incompetent" and to say he had "proof positive" that the FBI had monitored law-makers' phone conversations. The next morning, he was interviewed on the CBS radio network. "I charge categorically that the FBI has had me under surveillance—my personal life," he said. "We're living in a police state."

President Nixon phoned the House minority leader that morning.

"What's the matter with your opposite number?"

"He's nuts," Gerald Ford replied.

"My God, when I read the *Star*. . . . He's on the sauce, isn't that it?"

"I'm afraid that's right."

"Or is he crazy?"

"He's either drinking too much or he's taking some pills that are upsetting him mentally," said Ford. "I hate to say this, we've got to be awfully careful . . ."

"What we tell him," the President finished.

"What we tell him."

"Well, that's the problem."

The president had called Ford about a nationally televised speech he planned for the following evening, to announce he was bringing another hundred thousand American troops home from Vietnam. He had planned a briefing two hours in advance for the Big Five congressional leaders. As for the House majority leader, "he'd probably go off and screw off on that," the President said. "I don't think I can even tell him anything in confidence."

"I think you've got to be awfully careful, anything that's classified."

"I know. Frankly, everything I say is classified. . . ."

The next night, the Big Five became the Big Four.

J. Edgar Hoover phoned the FBI's longtime liaison to Congress, Deke DeLoach, who had become a Pepsico vice president in New York. DeLoach flew to the capital the following day and visited Hale, whom he liked, to ask that he either corroborate his charges or drop them.

"Facts?" Hale replied, in DeLoach's recollection. "I don't have any. I'd had a few too many drinks and was on my way to a baseball game. . . ."

Within a day, the hate mail began. The six thousand critical letters included fifty with threats. Lindy, as instructed, returned a call from a pay phone to a man who claimed to know her but would not give his name, advising Hale not to accuse the FBI of "wiretapping" because other means of eavesdropping were in use.

Hale took to the House floor after the Easter recess to present his proof, as promised. He spoke for fifty-nine minutes but had little to say. Mario Biaggi had failed to come through with the tapes. Hale's only specific allegation of FBI surveillance of members of Congress concerned a tape recorder hidden in an informant's backpack to capture a conversation with a Texas Democrat accused (and later convicted) of bribery. Otherwise, he offered eight senators' assertions and some overwrought prose—"We have established the rule of the dossier. . . . Liberty has yielded. . . . 1984 is closer than we think."

Even Democrats found his remarks rambling and garbled. Speaker Albert sat stonily. There was talk that Hale should not count on another term as the majority leader.

"He was full of contradictions," Lindy struggled to explain decades later, "and he got more and more intense as his life became more and more complicated."

Clearly his career was at stake, and Hale took action at last. He had doctors as friends, including a cardiologist in the Capitol.

Only the previous year the Food and Drug Administration had approved the use of lithium as an unprecedented treatment for manic depression. Hale had frequently been in a manic state and had perhaps relied on drinking to salve episodes of depression.

The lithium, Tommy said later, "clearly made a huge difference."

Soon Hale's drinking eased off, though he still drank a lot, and the reports of untoward behavior faded.

Julius Hobson had suffered a bad back before, from a dislocated disk, so he slipped on his brace. When he contracted pneumonia, he telephoned Tina from George Washington University Hospital. He told her that the doctors had found something else, called multiple myeloma.

"Don't worry about this," he told Tina when she arrived. "It isn't anything that's a real problem." It was not a real cancer, he had understood the doctors to say. Julius had always said he would kill himself if he contracted cancer.

He sent his wife of twenty-one months to the hospital library. She learned that multiple myeloma, a proliferation of plasma cells in the bone marrow, was not a real cancer only in the sense that it did not metastasize. But it weakened the bones from within, so that they deteriorated and collapsed, causing excruciating pain. Sooner or later, maybe in three months or in twenty years, the disease would kill him. There was no known cure, only some hope of slowing its progress. Later he learned that he suffered from the most virulent sort.

He announced the disease from the hospital. "I have never been sick a day in my life," he said. Julius was fifty-two years old and physically fit, 165 pounds on his five-eleven frame. He neither smoked nor drank. His uncle had died of multiple myeloma, but the disease was not believed to be hereditary.

The diagnosis devastated him. "I thought I was a fact of life," he said. He and Tina cried and clung to each other and tried not to think.

Religion was no help. "I dumped Jesus when I was ten," he once said. He remembered his high school graduation, when "we had to sing spirituals—all Negroes sing and dance, you know. The white superintendent, deeply moved by the singing, pulled out his handkerchief, wiped away a tear, and said, 'God must have set aside some place in heaven for you people.' I became an atheist right then and there."

Neither Carol nor their children would ever believe that Julius was truly an atheist. And yet in circumstances known to provoke a search for opiates, Julius professed to finding a certain relief in disbelief.

"Death doesn't frighten me the way it does a Christian," he said. "All it means to me is the end. I don't have to contend with those two doors on the other side and wonder which one I'll be going through."

Yet both Julius and Tina were goal-oriented people. "You don't sit around and mope with him," Tina said later. "Julius had one of the strongest lusts for life I've ever seen."

Their marriage had not been easy. Tina's father, a career navy man, and her sisters had withheld their blessings from the interracial marriage; a brother-in-law suspected Julius of growing marijuana in a closet. Julius's daughter wanted him to marry Pat Saltonstall instead, and Hobby had disliked Tina from the first. "Your father talks black, black, black," his friends at Howard said, "but he married white." Tina sent her own teenaged sons to boarding school in Connecticut, because she could not have handled children and marriage both. "I think my option would have been not to marry Julius," she said. Julius withdrew his retirement money to help her pay tuition.

They kept separate checking accounts but otherwise merged two households and two sets of habits. She would cook over the weekend and he cooked during the week while she enjoyed a glass of wine. ("I can usually outwait him," she said.) He used fresh ingredients in quickly and carefully, though not fancily, preparing meat, potatoes, and vegetables, and maybe an apple or banana pie. On Saturday mornings he would clean the house.

"It's no reflection on you. It's just that I like things a certain way."

"Go ahead," she would say.

They had moved into a light and airy town house, simply furnished, in the sterility of the renewed Southwest. They gave small dinner parties until Julius's jealousy made him miserable if another man so much as helped Tina carry the coffee from the kitchen. But Julius did not try to control Tina as he had Carol; either he did not need to or he knew he could not.

"Julius and I were partners," Tina said.

They ceased seeing each other as belonging to different races. "Frankly, after a while, I didn't even notice he was black," Tina said later. "He was just a very interesting person." And Julius said, "It's hard for me to see her as white." More than anything he was impressed that she never tried to be black.

When he publicly announced his illness, six weeks after the diagnosis, Julius said, "The most wonderful thing about all this has been my wife, Tina. Oh, both of us have had our teary moments, of course. But then she put a stabilizing hand on mine and said, 'Let's continue as we are.'"

The disease could kill him within four years, he told reporters, though half the victims lasted seven. "Everyone knows he's going to die. I just know approximately when." He said, "You can go screaming up the road, but what good would it do?"

He vowed not to traipse around the world to find a cure. He thought about keeping a diary of a fatal illness or writing an auto-biography. "One of the frustrations is trying to figure out how to take this personal tragedy—I guess you can call it a tragedy—and turn it into something useful for somebody else," he said. "That's really the reason I've been doing so much research on it."

Believers might have seen the hand of providence in what happened next. Almost to the autumn day in 1971 that Julius disclosed his awful news, he received a two-page letter from Dr. Benjamin Spock.

"I am writing to ask," the baby doctor began, "whether you would consider being identified with a new political movement, the Coalition, and possibly becoming a spokesman for it by running for office."

Remnants of the Peace & Freedom Party and the New Party, relics of 1968, had joined with newer community-based aggregations, including the D.C. Statehood Party, in horror at the prospect of a presidential choice in 1972 between the creepy, conservative incumbent and a Democratic centrist such as Muskie. Julius was hardly alone in being asked, but he was interested enough to attend the organizing conference in Dallas over Thanksgiving weekend.

The turnout of only two hundred activists, many with long hair and wearing work shirts and jeans, suggested that "the idea of a fourth political party—in addition to George C. Wallace's American Independent party—is hardly a mass movement at this point," reported the Los Angeles–based correspondent for the *New York Times*, its specialist in dissident groups, Steven V. Roberts. But they knew what they wanted. They adopted a name, the People's Party, and found a platform easy to write, calling for an immediate end to the war in Indochina, a guaranteed national income of sixty-five hundred dollars, free medical care, and legalized marijuana and heroin.

But it was far harder, and more important, to settle on a presidential candidate. Ralph Nader was uninterested, and so was the iconoclastic Federal Communications commissioner, Nicholas Johnson. Possibly Gene McCarthy would consent, or Shirley Chisholm, if the Democrats nominated a Muskie or someone to his right.

In the meantime, however, the party needed a stand-in candidate, to qualify for the ballot in at least a dozen states. Who better than Benjamin Spock? Surely the sixty-eight-year-old pediatrician and antiwar activist bore some of the responsibility for this generation of rebels, in his prescriptions of indulgence for children in the seventh-best-selling book of all time.

The organizers wanted a black vice presidential nominee, and dark faces in the antiwar movement were rare. Dick Gregory, who had been Eldridge Cleaver's running mate for the Peace & Freedom Party, may have suggested Julius. In the balloting in Dallas, Julius drew fifty-one votes from among the ninety delegates who remained.

At last he would have a national platform, at least for a while.

The following summer, the Democrats' choice of George McGovern as their most liberal nominee since William Jennings Bryan meant that no established politician sought the People's Party's imprimatur. By acclamation, the stand-in nominees became the nominees.

Julius was on crutches when he followed Dick Gregory to the podium in Saint Louis and delivered a short but affecting speech, which was welcome after the long-winded debates.

"I will die," he said, quoting the poet Edna St. Vincent Millay, "but that is all I will do for death."

"Sir," he was asked at a press conference after the convention, "what is the attitude of blacks toward McGovern?"

"There are twenty-two million blacks in this country," Julius replied, "and I haven't met ten thousand of them."

He promised to campaign as much as he was physically able, and he showed up on crutches in fourteen states. On the University of Pittsburgh campus he criticized the NAACP and the Black Caucus as "pasteurized colored boys." The party located its national headquarters in Georgetown, Columbia, using "the liberated name" for the nation's capital.

In November, the ticket of Spock and Hobson collected 78,756 votes nationwide. They finished fourth, only seventeen electoral votes behind the Democratic ticket of George McGovern and Sargent Shriver.

Tommy Boggs stopped Congressman Jim Scheuer on his way to the House Commerce Committee room, to vote on a harshly contested bill to establish no-fault auto insurance nationwide. Scheuer was a gruff and greasy Democrat from the Bronx who planned to vote yea, in the hope of reducing his constituents' soaring insurance rates. Tommy represented the Association of Trial Lawyers of America, whose members stood to lose a billion dollars a year in legal fees.

He pulled Scheuer into an oversized sterile stairwell near the committee room in the Rayburn House Office Building and argued the issue once again. "We basically had the facts on our side, to be honest," Tommy said later. Scheuer would never be rude to the majority leader's son, and for Tommy, persuading the congressman was not necessary. While their conversation wore on, the balloting was under way. A bill expected to prevail by a single vote came up one vote short.

Tommy had begun to represent the trial lawyers because of a connection he had made during the 1964 presidential campaign. He had done advance work for Lady Bird, and the lobbyist who represented the interests of Lockheed, which supplied the campaign airplane, went along on the trips. In his one-man shop, the lobbyist roamed Capitol Hill also on another client's behalf, the trial lawyers' group, headquartered in Massachusetts. The New England state had recently experimented, successfully, with requiring insurance companies to pay their own customers' accident claims no matter who was at fault. When the concept came alive on Capitol Hill, the trial lawyers quaked—and hired more help.

Tommy concentrated on the House, where he had been deeply involved in his father's campaign for majority leader. He also proposed a tactic for the Senate, the hotbed of sentiment for no-fault. At a strategy session on the forthcoming floor action, he suggested averting an up-or-down vote on the popular bill by referring it to the Judiciary Committee, to bury it. The sleight of procedure might pick up four or five votes among senators scared of riling the trial lawyers back home.

And thus by forty-nine votes to forty-six, the Senate sidetracked no-fault. Tommy understood that in a government of checks and balances, especially with Congress in one party's hands and the White House in the other's, stopping something was bound to be simpler than pushing it through.

Tommy was industrious enough to learn the substance of the issue at hand, respectful enough of politicians to earn their trust, and irreverent and fun-loving enough—he had his father's devil-may-care laugh—for them to enjoy his company. He was hard not to like. He also had an instinct for the way members of Congress made up their minds, and he understood the pressures they faced back home. So he framed his arguments to show that what his client wanted also happened to serve the lawmaker's paramount interest in political survival.

Patton, Blow, Verrill, Brand & Boggs took whatever work walked in the door—"almost everything," said *Washingtonian* magazine, "as long as it's interesting." Its lawyers occupied the next-to-top floor and then two and eventually five floors, in the American Psychological Association's eight-story dirty-white building with reflecting windows on Seventeenth Street, two blocks north of K. They put together international ventures, crafted foreign trade deals, litigated cases, even sprang a political prisoner from a Vietnamese jail. Jim Patton hired Tim May, once Tommy's coconspirator in undermining the maritime industry and then the Post Office Department's general counsel, to hustle up clients (such as *Reader's Digest*) worried about postal rates and rules.

Bill Foster was a pal of Tommy's from the Hill. He was a hard-drinking, high-living Texan with a love of Lone Star history who had drafted bills for Alaska's new legislature and then followed one of its freshman senators to the capital. As chief counsel at Senate Commerce, he had met Tommy at the Joint Economic Committee. Now he was a lobbyist with two clients, Ralston-Purina and a consortium of oil companies that proposed a pipeline across Alaska from the freshly discovered North Slope oilfields. The Alyeska consortium, which needed help in the House on a bill to settle the Eskimos' claims, was aware of Tommy because Hale had cosponsored the legislation that made Alaska a state.

When Tommy invited Bill Foster to join the firm, and bring his client, he accepted.

"My kind of guy," Foster said of Tommy. The two good ol' boys hunted and caroused together.

They also worked hard. Hoping to exempt the Alaska pipeline from environmental lawsuits, the consortium's team of lobbyists— the hired guns and the oil companies' own buttonholers—visited every one of the 435 House members. At first Tommy tagged along with another lobbyist, to learn the patter, and then he went on his own. He chased "the loose balls," in Foster's thinking—the lawmakers none of the other lobbyists knew. What member of Congress, Foster reasoned, would refuse to see the majority leader's son? Tommy made his case to ten legislators a week, a total of fifty. Each day from ten o'clock until four, he and the others pounded the marble floors, jousted with lawmakers, took staff members to lunch, sweet-talked, gossiped, and debated.

Then it was back to the office, for pitchers of martinis and dinner, along with tactical discussions and laughs. They seldom got home before eleven or midnight and liked it that way.

"Wonderful, irresponsible days," Foster remembered. The firm's monthly partnership luncheons started with two or three martinis, followed by wine with lunch, then liqueurs.

But already, the culture of the firm was evolving. Through the 1960s the firm was so small that the partners helped out one another. Pretty much alone, Jim Patton decided on everyone's salary, and George Blow insisted on keeping most of the share he had claimed from the start, though he was no longer considered much of a factor in the firm.

After a couple of years at the firm, Tim May said to Patton, "Jim, let's see if we can't quantify this."

They developed a formula for compensation that, in 1971, was revolutionary. Most law firms relied on seniority for setting lawyers' pay, a comforting system that produced dead wood at the top that every younger lawyer aspired to become. Instead, Patton and Tim May devised a formula that credited a lawyer both for working hour by hour on a client's behalf and, proportionately more, for luring a client into the firm. This was intended as a neutral means of measuring a lawyer's productivity and also as an incentive for an unknown law firm to land new clients. At the time, said a partner, the change seemed "attractive and democratic."

Yet its consequences proved far-reaching—and unforeseen. The eternal rewards it bestowed for drawing in clients—"You eat what you kill," in the vernacular—produced a more entrepreneurial firm. It also prompted infighting among the partners over the credit for recruiting a client (*attribution*) or for expanding the scope of a client's work. Junior partners might outearn their seniors, and lawyers who helped one another ran the risk of provoking arguments over whose client it was.

The compensation formula, according to Bill Foster, "created a whole lot of tension and a whole lot of clients." Another partner recalled that the firm's personality changed—"It lost its collegiality."

In the early spring of 1972, something else at the firm changed: its name. When Tim May became a partner, a sixth name was added to the firm's increasingly unwieldy name, and the capital's Kremlinologists noticed a shift in the order. George Blow, a Virginia gentleman raised in the family mansion where Cornwallis had surrendered, was skilled in a courtroom but too easygoing to solicit clients and keep them writing checks. His name slipped from second to third, and the fifth name took its place. A year later, the last three names were lopped off.

At Patton, Boggs & Blow, the direction of the firm's future was clear.

Tina Hobson went alone to dinner at Bardyl Tirana's. Julius was home in bed, seven or eight months into his treatment. The chemotherapy had made him terribly sick, and his back was crumpling; within a year four vertebrae collapsed and he lost six inches in height. The pressure on vital nerves produced unrelenting pain, which coursed through his shoulders, down his arms, and into his hands. He was taking sixty milligrams a day of morphine, the maximal dose.

Tina had taken Julius's X rays with her. The doctors at GW had given Julius three months at most.

"Call Dr. Spock," said Bardyl Tirana, "and see if he might know anything that might help."

Right away she reached him, and he suggested that she contact his friend at Sloan-Kettering, the famed cancer center in New York.

"We can help him," Dr. Spock's friend told her. A group was starting an experimental outpatient protocol. "So bring him up."

The head of hematology at George Washington University Hospital was incensed. He insisted that the protocol would kill the patient. "If you wanted a second opinion, you should have asked me."

"You would have given me the name of somebody you play golf with," Tina replied. "I didn't want to do that."

Tina knew she would have lacked the nerve had cancer not killed her four-year-old son. Then, she had accepted whatever the doctors told her.

If the hematologist refused to try the protocol on Julius at GW, Tina said, "I'll take him to New York to try it."

The doctor warned that Julius would have to live in a bubble, for fear of infection.

"I want you to try it here," she repeated, "or I will take him to New York."

The hematologist acquiesced.

The experimental chemotherapy entailed forty days of a sequenced permutation of pills, two weeks off, then forty days more. Tina counted out the pills every day.

Julius's bout of paranoia was provoked not by the toxic chemicals he was ingesting, the doctors concluded, but by the morphine. It had been touched off when Tina talked him into selling the town house, which he loved. With Julius sick, they simply could not afford to keep it on her Civil Service Commission salary alone, and they moved into a comfortable though unfancy apartment in a high-rise hyperbolically named Waterside Towers. Julius went to a lawyer and accused her of stealing his money.

"You white people are doing me in," he would say.

Tina was at work, during the second forty-day regimen, when the police phoned. Julius's black nurse had taken him downtown and he had filed charges that Tina was poisoning him. She was, of course—chemotherapy *was* poison. She was assured that the newspapers would not be informed.

"We know he's sick," Tina was told, but "you're going to have to come down. We're going to have to handle this as a complaint."

When she returned home, she discovered that the nurse had helped Julius move into an apartment on the floor below. He announced on the evening news that he was divorcing Tina.

Now she had to venture downstairs to give Julius his pills.

"What saved my life," Tina remembered, "was a lady knocking on the door."

"I am a psychiatric social worker," the black woman said. "I think you need help."

"I think I do, too."

For a year and a half, Tina and the social worker had lunch once a week, to talk about the problems that multiple myeloma and its medicines posed to marriage and to everything else.

Julius was sent to a psychiatrist at GW, and Tina heard them laughing from outside the door. As they emerged, the psychiatrist beamed at Tina and said, "I think everything is going to be okay."

"Everything is *not* okay," she snapped. "You may have been fooled by this man—he's fooled a lot of people—but we have a serious problem here. He really thinks I'm poisoning him."

At a family council, Julius accepted the psychiatrist's suggestion that he live temporarily with Hobby, but Hobby demurred. "There's no way I could have carried that," he explained later.

Tina took Julius out on a balcony and said, "I will take care of you—I am not poisoning you. I don't want to hear about this again, because I can't cope."

Julius moved back upstairs.

He was in the first group to try the experimental protocol and would be the last participant to die.

But he was still in near-constant, crushing pain when he was wheeled into the Cotillion Room at the Sheraton Park, just off Connecticut Avenue, on a Tuesday evening in November 1972. Built of a self-assured but not a boastful brick, a sentry above the mysterious trench of Rock Creek Park, the hotel was formerly the Wardman Park, where a teenaged immigrant named Gwendolyn Detre had lived with her parents. The theater beside the Cotillion Room had been the original broadcast venue, in the early 1950s, for television's *Today* show. In size and elegance, the Cotillion Room was one of the most sought after ballrooms in the city, with abstract brass panels on the side walls and eight grand golden chandeliers, plus a spiky metallic one dubbed Sputnik. The previous week had seen a birthday bash for the vice president.

When local peace activists suggested putting on "An Evening to Honor Julius Hobson," Julius figured on setting up fifty chairs in his apartment and passing out Cokes. The Cotillion Room could seat a thousand and tonight held many more, paying five dollars apiece. Seven members of Congress had signed on as sponsors, along with Dr. Spock, William Kunstler, Nicholas Johnson, William Raspberry, I. F. Stone, a slew of local politicians and activists, even eight clergymen.

Mayor Washington, whom Julius had once described as "colorless, tasteless, and odorless," proclaimed Julius Hobson Day. Half of the testimonial booklet was filled with advertisements from wellwishers—black firefighters, the pastry cooks' union, the Atheist Information Service, the Church of What's Happening Now.

When the guest of honor arrived, the crowd hesitated to react, understandably ambivalent about the reason behind the testimonial. The discomfort resolved itself in polite applause.

"You are not at a funeral," the minister who had married Julius and Tina reminded everyone, for the doctors now gave Julius three to five years to live.

That roused a standing ovation.

Julius puffed on a long thin cigar as he reclined in an invalid's chair, a Scottish tartan blanket over his legs. His mother stood behind him, and Tina sat at his side.

A screen behind Julius showed a documentary of his life. Joan Baez sang and nearly a dozen people spoke. Hobby said he looked out upon "people who worked with him and those who hated him."

"He took his fight into the street, while other people were just talking," Stokely Carmichael, in dark glasses, recalled. "Mr. Hobson can never die."

Tears flowed.

"To the casual ear, it sounded the height of phoniness: all these people pretending to have been with Hobson all along"—this was Raspberry, after the testimonial, in the *Post*. "Well, it wasn't phony, and it wasn't the reaction of pity for a man gravely ill. It was recognition that Hobson, in spite of his abrasiveness, his occasional outlandishness and his near-total unpredictability, had been remarkably consistent—and remarkably right—in his wide-ranging assaults on people and institutions."

To Julius, the evening felt like a wake, one he could watch. He had been amused by the attention, the adulation, he had received since contracting a fatal disease. The *Post* had published a four-part interview with Julius in July, across successive front pages in *Metro*. The newspaper had never given him decent coverage, he grumbled, until he was dying.

At last, Julius spoke at his own testimonial, briefly. He looked shriveled, dwarfed, with a shrunken torso and an oversized head. He mentioned a half-page advertisement in the testimonial program, taken by Walter Fauntroy—"I have always respected you and admired your courage and vigor."

"I attacked him politically," Julius sighed, "but after all Fauntroy is my brother, too. Just say I never expected it all, and thank you."

The following month Julius tried three days of acupuncture, in a motel in southwestern Virginia, hoping to alleviate the pain. Twice a day, a Japanese doctor who had trained as a pathologist at Howard inserted fifteen or twenty needles into his back, arms, and legs—"I just don't like needles," Julius said—and burned young leaves of wormwood all over his body.

By the third day, free of pain for nine consecutive hours, Julius was finished with morphine. Within a few months he could walk without crutches and even drive a car.

"If I've ever lived to see any miracles," he said, "this is it."

The congressional redistricting that followed Hale Boggs's close call at the polls in 1968 meant that he never needed to worry again. The seven other Louisianans in the House, all Democrats, had deputized Hale to rearrange the boundaries statewide, for his district had grown most in population. Gary Hymel drew up a new map and, using Hale's influence in the legislature, pushed it through. Hale added a bastion of Democrats in the French Quarter of New Orleans and shed the white conservatives in the suburbs. The rearrangement was so masterful that he was running unopposed in 1972.

Political security gave Hale time to campaign for fellow Democrats, as a way to collect chits and curry loyalties for a speaker's race someday. A month before the election, Hale traveled to San Antonio for a testimonial to Congressman Henry Gonzalez, a crusty populist prone to stray beyond the party's discipline.

In the audience, the Texas state coordinator for George McGovern's presidential campaign listened hard, then talked with Hale afterward and drove him to the airport. Bill Clinton was a bushy-haired twenty-six-year-old from a dysfunctional Arkansas family, whose talent and ambition had already earned him an elite education. The Boggses had known him since, as a freshman at Georgetown, he was class co-president with Hale's nephew, Charlie Boggs.

As they stopped off for ice cream, the young politico had every reason to learn what Hale knew, to understand how a southerner interested in his political viability might succeed on a national stage.

Hale flew back to Washington for a week before leaving again, for Alaska. Sixteen more campaign appearances crowded his schedule after that, including one in New Jersey on behalf of a novice candidate for the Princeton Borough Council, his daughter Barbara.

The fifty-eight-year-old politician pushed himself hard. The sharp smooth face of his youth was now deeply furrowed. His neck sagged, and his white linen suits encircled a stouter frame. He had been busy mending fences. When J. Edgar Hoover died that spring, Hale led twenty minutes of eulogies in the House ("There is no man who has served this country with greater dedication, with greater love"), even though the press pointed out his earlier disgust. In a closed-door caucus of Democrats, he and the Speaker abruptly turned against the war after seven years, by voting with the majority of doves, yet he was invited to breakfast with the president in the family dining room at the White House. The twenty-one hundred people Hale and Lindy hosted at their garden party in June made for, "without a doubt," said the *Star*, "the largest private party ever held in the area."

During the summer Hale and Gerald Ford had taken their wives to mainland China, only four months after the president's epochal trip, as envoys of the House of Representatives. After a banquet in the Great Hall of the People, in Tiananmen Square, Chou En-lai invited the two leaders back to a meeting room. From nearly one o'clock until ten after three in the morning, they debated Vietnam, traded political gossip, and wondered why hippies lived in Sri Lanka as well as in the United States.

"We have given them the vote at eighteen," said Ford, "so they are now participating."

"I understand you have twenty million young voters," said China's brainy premier.

"Yes," said Hale. "They are preparing to throw us all out."

Before the English was translated, Chou threw his head back and roared with laughter.

"I don't think so," Ford broke in. "Most of them will vote the pattern of their elders."

"You hope," said Hale.

In Washington, before leaving for Alaska, Hale faced an even busier week than usual. The congressional leadership struggled to bring the Ninety-second Congress to a close. That was only the beginning. On Sunday evening he and Lindy attended an at-home at Gwen Cafritz's on Foxhall Road, from six until eight. Lindy and Gwen had been do-gooders together—"Everything you can think of," Lindy said later, "everything that went on in Washington." Lindy found Gwen charming and bright, "And of course I was grateful to her for being interested in doing social—with a small 's'—and charitable things."

Gwen no longer dedicated her October reception to the Supreme Court—"I've given up the Easter bunnies, too," she said. This year she honored Columbus Day instead, with an actor from the Folger Shakespeare Theatre in Elizabethan garb who stood in the foyer holding a replica of the *Santa Maria*. Limousines backed up in both directions along Foxhall Road. People gathered on the terrace to watch the last light of an autumn afternoon steal away from the tip of the Washington Monument.

The next evening, Hale and Lindy joined Tommy and his wife for dinner with the Pakistani ambassador and *his* wife, at the embassy residence, on a quiet stretch of S Street that seemed to hover above the city. "At my request," said Jim Patton, who represented Pakistan. At dinner Patton asked Hale why he was traveling to Alaska to campaign for Nick Begich, a shoo-in for a second term.

As the majority leader, said Hale, "it's my duty."

Bill Foster stopped by the Capitol the next morning to brief Hale on the arrangements for the trip and the fund-raising dinner in Anchorage. The lobbyist for the Alaska pipeline was a Begich booster, a financial supporter, who was hoping to interest the oil companies in the liberal Democrat, to dry up money for potential opponents when, sooner or later, he ran for the Senate. What better way to entice the oilmen than to have a proven friend of Big Oil anoint him?

Hale regarded Nick Begich, an effervescent forty-year-old father of six, as star material. "Just as he had been fostered by Sam," Lindy said, "he did that for younger members." Begich had voted for Udall as majority leader, but for Hale that was a reason to pursue his favor. He had even let the freshman borrow his Capitol office to film a campaign commercial.

Lindy and Pegge Begich had planned to go along to Alaska. That was when Congress was expected to have adjourned for the year. The session refused to end, however, as the White House and Congress wrestled over welfare reform, Social Security taxes, water pollution, and the president's authority to cut the budget. The trip kept getting squeezed, and as the weekend approached, Begich asked Congressman Jim Wright of Texas to take Hale's place if the House stayed in session until its work was done; the oil-minded Texan agreed. Begich had also invited Congressman David Obey, a brash young Wisconsin liberal, to demonstrate to Alaskans that even opponents of the oil pipeline admired him. Obey accepted but contracted flu and stayed home.

At the last minute, the Speaker decided to recess the House over Sunday and Monday, then return to finish up, in part to free Hale for the trip.

Even so, Hale was reluctant. The House worked through the afternoon and evening on Saturday, until after midnight. Hale was to leave the following morning at eight-fifteen. As he wandered around the House floor that night, he stopped to chat with Rostenkowski.

"Goddamn it," said Hale, "Begich got me to promise to go out to Alaska. Sonuvabitch, I wish to Christ I didn't have to do this. I'm trying to get out of it."

On his next circle of the chamber, he told Rosty, "Goddamn it, Begich came up to me, he says, 'We got people coming to that dinner, spend a hundred dollars apiece. You couldn't get a hundred dollars out of any people in Alaska, y'know, with dynamite.'

"Begich has got me going and I don't want to go."

When Hale returned at last to Bradley Boulevard, a batch of black-eyed peas rested on his doorstep. Hale used to stop at a half-acre garden a mile along Bradley Boulevard and watch Marx Leva, a prominent lawyer in the capital, tend his garden. Hale was unable to grow black-eyed peas, beloved of southerners for luck on New Year's Day, but the Alabama-born lawyer could.

Hale awakened Lindy and had her shell the peas and simmer them. He ate a big bowlful and went to bed.

On two hours' sleep, he caught a United flight from deserted Dulles Airport on Sunday morning. He held a reservation to return forty-nine hours later, on Tuesday morning, before the House proceedings were to resume. He also planned to hire the first black for his staff.

Arriving in Anchorage, he had circles under his eyes.

The hotel ballroom was big enough to keep the price for a ticket to the fund-raising dinner to fifty dollars or even twenty-five dollars a plate, so more people would attend. The crowd of 450 included thirty or forty oilmen. With the $250-a-head cocktail party, the evening raised $22,500 for Nick Begich's political future.

At the testimonial banquet, Hale was at his best. His booming voice commanded attention in the farthest corners of the ballroom; his delivery was self-assured, his timing practiced. He lauded the freshman's aggressiveness and legislative prowess—how, step by guileful step, Begich had propelled the Alaska Native Claims Settlement Act through to enactment. Hale recounted how he had asked Begich the likely cost of settling with the Eskimos.

"Not much," the freshman had replied.

Hale had insisted on knowing how much.

He quoted Begich: "Not much more than a billion dollars."

Hale paused in the retelling.

"So we passed it."

Then the Senate considered the bill, Hale continued, and Begich had told him, "I'll call up the whole Senate if you want me to."

Hale paused.

"So the Senate passed it."

And then Begich had gone to Hale and said, "How do you and Nixon get along?"

Hale recalled his own answer: "Why do you ask?"

A long pause.

"Well, he signed it. No one has done as much in as short a time as your congressman has, Nick Begich."

Hale went on to assail Nixon, and even made statistics sound dramatic—"six percent unemployment . . . twenty-five percent of industrial capacity idle." He could shift a low, confiding drawl into a strong and deliberate baritone and always seemed to hold something in reserve. The audience laughed or clapped at his beckon.

Because Hale's Sunday had lasted so long, the congressmen passed up the early-morning commercial flight to Juneau, the state's capital, the site of a second dinner, and chartered a twin-engine Cessna instead.

Shortly before nine that night, eastern daylight time, Lindy had dozed off in the renovated kitchen on Bradley Boulevard. Her correspondence lay unfinished on the kitchen table, as *Laugh-In* blared from the television.

The telephone rang. Cody, the Cairn terrier sleeping at Lindy's feet, did something he had never done before. He leaped onto the telephone table and tried to knock the receiver out of Lindy's hand. Long ago, the night Lindy's father had died, his favorite bird dog had started to howl just before the telephone rang with the news.

Carl Albert was on the phone. He said he had tried to reach Tommy or Cokie, for he hated to tell Lindy the terrible news, but he did not want her to hear it first on television: Hale's plane had never arrived in Juneau. In treacherous weather it was eight hours late.

"Oh, Carl," Lindy gasped, "I'm so sorry you had the duty of telling me."

Tommy and his wife were returning home from a party at Wyatt and Nancy Dickerson's riverfront estate in McLean for the investors in the new Palm Restaurant on Nineteenth Street. A young driver from his congressional campaign was standing in their driveway.

"You probably haven't heard."

"No, I haven't heard," Tommy said.

"Your dad's plane is missing."

Tommy drove to his mother's, two-and-a-half miles away. He arrived the same time as Charles (Mac) Mathias, Maryland's senior senator, a teddy bear of a liberal Republican who lived nearby. Liz Carpenter, who had been Lady Bird Johnson's press secretary, showed up to handle the phones and the reporters. After the ten o'clock news, the house quickly filled up. Friends wandered between rooms and stared at the signed photographs—Hale with JFK, Hale with LBJ.

To Tommy, Ted Stevens was the most reassuring. The first-term senator from Alaska had crashed twice in the untamed state and survived. Ted Kennedy and Hubert Humphrey called to vouch for the pilot, and Pegge Begich phoned to say that once before, her husband had been lost in a plane and turned up nine hours later. The phone rang and rang, until C&P was summoned to install another line. Lindy offered refreshments and soothed everyone's fears.

Lindy overheard a portable radio ("A plane carrying House Majority Leader Hale Boggs has been reported missing") and exclaimed, "It sounds like a nightmare."

The lights on Bradley Boulevard burned all night. Toward dawn Lindy sipped from a glass of sherry in the comfortable pine-paneled den, with the fox-hunting prints and Calder lithographs, and Tommy stretched out on a sofa.

When his mother left the room, Tommy clenched his fists and muttered, "Son of a bitch, son of a bitch."

"The last year and a half of his life," Tommy said later of Hale, "he was a happy man."

The president provided a military jet to fly the family to Alaska, after Cokie had arrived from California. The most extensive search-and-rescue operation in American history involved seventy aircraft, four Coast Guard ships, divers, and mountaineers. Jim Patton suggested the use of a supersonic spy plane and won approval from the secretary of defense, Mel Laird, a former board member at *Reader's Digest*, which was a Patton, Boggs client. Tips from psychics, reports of distress signals, sightings of detritus—every possibility was followed up.

Lindy returned home after four days, and after thirty-nine days the search was called off.

Found in Hale's desk were snapshots of his young children, a U.S. Navy identification card, a ticket to the 1949 inaugural ball, and an application for a certificate of title to a 1954 Chevy sedan.

Julius Hobson Jr. woke up one morning in the spring of 1973 and decided to run for the school board. He did not really know why. He had no interest in a political career. Partly it was related to making a contribution, and partly it involved his father.

"I'm not trying to be exactly like my father," Hobby sought to explain. "But I'm his son and I sure did pick up a lot of traits from him."

Both parents tried to dissuade him. His father recognized the price he had paid for his years in public life and argued hard with Hobby, to no effect.

Hobby had thought to run citywide, but a campaign in Ward Eight looked more manageable. He had lived in Anacostia for two years with his pretty wife, Pat, and their infant daughter, Lynn. (A second daughter, Faye, had been born since.) They could afford a three-bedroom apartment in a modern, unornamented, three-story building along a barren street in southernmost D.C.

"We needed space," he said.

Hobby had dropped out of Howard and was running youth programs at a settlement house in Northeast, a beneficiary of Great Society largesse. He looked older than twenty-five. A well-trimmed Afro and muttonchops overwhelmed his thin bespectacled face. His manner was milder than his father's, though his modishly meticulous dress intimated a blood tie.

In little more than a decade, Anacostia had become nearly all black and predominantly poor, though it still had its tree-lined streets and the occasional hilltop view across the gleaming Anacostia River. The Capitol and the Washington Monument looked startlingly close yet in a distant and unapproachable realm.

Hobby's main opponent, Theresa Jones, was a forty-year-old black mother of seven who served on several community boards, including those of the United Black Fund and the Cafritz Hospital. To Hobby she was "Miss Anacostia."

Hobby hated asking people to donate to his campaign. He joined in candidate forums but, unlike his father, did not dominate them with a scathing tongue. He pursued his own, quieter strategy. He picked the six of the ward's twelve precincts whose citizens had most reliably voted. Every evening and weekend, he canvassed door to door—"really under the radar," he said.

On Election Night, he was less surprised than his opponents. Across the city, the school board campaign attracted less interest than ever before. Barely one in twenty registered voters went to the polls, and that magnified the advantage of having shaken their hands. In five of the six precincts where he had knocked on doors, Hobby won.

Hobby credited shoe leather and something else: his name. "There's no question about it," he had admitted—"it helps."

———

Lady Bird Johnson phoned Lindy Boggs and said, "You know you really must run."

"Well, Bird . . ."

"Lindy, you must run. I'm telling you, you have to do this." Then she added, "But do you think you can do it without a wife?"

More than most congressional couples, Hale and Lindy had truly been a team. She had often been the go-between for Hale and his constituents. If Hale had five social obligations in an evening, each might attend two and they would meet up at the last. She knew most of what he knew—others could never know precisely how much—and the deals he had struck and the promises made in return.

Her children urged her to run. Everyone did. Yet she felt it would be somehow disloyal, as if she were giving up hope that Hale was alive.

Later she could not remember ever deciding. "I just sort of found myself running," she said. If Hale did return, who would be more likely to give up the seat for him? She clung to a belief that he might.

Lindy's campaign slogan was *Let Her Continue*. On her campaign stationery, above *Lindy Boggs*, in smaller print, was *Mrs. Hale Boggs*.

"I wouldn't have run," she said, "unless I had known I could win." Decades of coordinating Hale's campaigns meant she understood the congressional district as well as he had. She dyed her eyelashes so that mascara would not run when she cried.

In the five-candidate primary, she won three times as many votes as her opponents combined. Then she overwhelmed a Republican named Robert E. Lee, whom Hale had defeated posthumously. In March 1973, a Claiborne was sworn in as the first woman to represent Louisiana in Congress, to a three-minute standing ovation.

Her children warned her that legislators lacked a button labeled "maybe." Voting "yes" or "no" was bound to upset people, and Lindy wanted to be loved.

To inaugurate the third season of the John F. Kennedy Center for the Performing Arts, a barge with bunting in red, white, and blue was towed into place off the Potomac shore. A brass band aboard played

Handel, in place of the Marine Corps Band, which had canceled a few days before but never said why.

Inside, along the Grand Foyer, minstrels and musicians performed madrigals as they wandered through the milling crowd. In the Eisenhower Theater, before the curtain went up on *Measure for Measure*, Gwen Cafritz crossed the stage. Her foundation had donated $118,000 to underwrite the monthlong Shakespeare festival, on all three of the Kennedy Center's main stages.

At the podium, she said simply, "There just isn't anybody like Shakespeare."

The Bard was not unknown in the capital. How could he be, given his fascination with the tangles of temporal power? The Folger Shakespeare Library (and its attendant theater) had filled a fortresslike building behind the Library of Congress since the Depression. Nor was high culture unknown. Washington hosted a legitimate theater, a repertory company, an opera, and the National Symphony, besides the free museums.

Yet the city's reputation as a cultural wasteland was largely deserved. Unlike London or Paris, America's political capital was not its cultural capital. Minds that struggle over policy or power are unlikely to love art. It was jarring to witness the philistines in the Cabinet and Congress trying to sit still in Constitution Hall, squirming to Schubert. The first city ever built only to govern lacked the industrialists and titans of commerce who might act as cultural benefactors in hope of removing the stain of their greed. This, too, was left to the government.

"Here in the world's greatest capital we have nothing," John Kennedy had told a luncheon of businessmen, referring to the performing arts, a month before his death. It was perhaps fitting that the center for the performing arts built at President Eisenhower's behest (after years of wrangling, along the Potomac in Foggy Bottom) became the capital's only memorial to his slain successor. Edgar Durell Stone's pitilessly rectangular, unornamented design—the box the Lincoln Memorial came in, went the joke—suited the capital's unimaginative tastes.

Measure for Measure, a dark comedy about licentious rulers who wield power in a tarnished world, ranked low in the Bard's canon. The performance drew harsh ("on the painful side") reviews.

Gwen agreed. "I went home and read the play," she said the next day, "and it was even worse in the reading—sheer death."

The next night she returned to the Kennedy Center atrium for a reception in her honor. She rarely entertained at home anymore. At her last party, the lights blacked out, the phone went dead, and guests were frightened. "How many Pinkertons," she said, "can you have at a party?" She had never replaced her stolen jewelry and swore she never would. "I wouldn't dream of spending the money on clothes," she said, "that Morris spent on me."

But she went to her reception in Shakespearean dress, a blue gown with Elizabethan ruffs at the throat and the wrists. ("I'm not sure, but I think it's an Oscar de la Renta via Saks Fifth Avenue.") In the Opera House, she occupied the Presidential Box to watch the Royal Shakespeare Company perform *The Hollow Crown*, a compendium of speeches, songs, and poems on the follies and foibles of English monarchs from Richard I to Victoria.

The powerful in all their peevishness—it seemed so timely.

"We could feel the audience take a breath at every part of the play which seemed to parallel your Watergate." Sir Michael Redgrave, one of the actors, was referring to the scandal touched off fifteen months earlier with a third-rate burglary in the office building next door to the Kennedy Center. "We intentionally underscored all of those, the allusions of past history to your present."

"Oh, yes," said a bystander, "especially that scene of the trial of Charles the First, who stood upon royal privilege."

Word emerged the next day that John Ehrlichman, the president's adviser, had been indicted in the burgeoning scandal, its pace and plotline worthy of the Bard. Even regicide had started to seem plausible.

FORD

The East Room in the White House was meant for public audiences, with its classic, clean lines and full-length portrait of George Washington—the only object that had survived in the Executive Mansion since it was built. Members of the Nixon Cabinet returned to their seats of an hour earlier, when they had listened to the thirty-seventh president's "maudlin farewell," as it was described the next morning in the *Post*, whose coverage of the Watergate scandal had played a critical role in bringing him down.

Lindy Boggs was among the few Democrats asked to the White House to witness the swearing in of the nation's first unelected president, Gerald Ford, and she was perhaps the only Democrat invited purely because of friendship. Especially after they traveled to China, Ford had begun to regard Hale and himself, partisan counterparts, as "excellent friends—socially, personally, and even to an extent politically," as he remembered. Their wives had worked together on many a charitable event, and both sat on the board of directors at Jelleff's, a ladies' clothes store; both wore size six, a model's size, meaning they could buy the modeled dresses at a discount. Late the previous year, after Spiro Agnew had resigned, Lindy had spoken to the House in seconding her friend's nomination as the nation's first appointed vice president.

She had slipped comfortably into her new role as a member of Congress. As the immediate past president of the Congressional Club, the leading organization for lawmakers' wives, Lindy had cemented friendships with ladies of both political parties, and with their husbands. In her maiden speech on the House floor, she recalled having arrived thirty-two years earlier at a capital of "unsophisticated pace," where Congress met at most for six months a year. In those days a train took two nights and a day to get to Washington from New Orleans. Now, to take her congressional seat, she said, "I arrived by jet aircraft in two hours' time to a physically beautiful, sophisticated, international city filled with cultural performances, with limitless selections of couture, and with an exhausting and varied social schedule."

More had changed than transportation and high culture. These days, lowly legislators had a say. "Unlike 1941," she said, "it is easier now to have a voice in the caucus, in the party councils, in setting our goals and priorities." Even the people's House was starting to resemble a democracy.

Almost without thinking about it, Lindy had retained Hale's personal staff of seven, plus three more in New Orleans. But the slide in seniority forced a move from the spacious Rayburn House Office Building into two small rooms and a third around the corner in the stately but worn Longworth building. The partitions put up for privacy made the space into mazes. Lindy was far more particular than Hale about the staff's work. A constituent's letter deserved a reply not of a stock paragraph or two, but of four paragraphs, with detail. Once, Lindy rewrote a letter to a girl who had asked about the facts of life and added information suited to her age. If a drafted reply stated that she disagreed with a constituent, she would instruct that it "be retyped to say, 'You make a very good point and I think you're right about this, but this is what I'm going to do for the following reasons,'" an aide explained. "You don't disagree, you don't confront people."

She treated colleagues as she treated constituents. "Unlike a lot of freshmen up here," said a friend, "Lindy knows you get things done on the Hill by being on a personal basis with the people in power." A reporter within earshot as she received Louisianans on Bradley Boulevard shortly before she was elected heard, "You're so sweet to come. . . . Oh, I hope the kids are all just fine. . . . Hi, sweetie, how is everything? . . . Thank you, darlin', for all your support. . . . Oh, darlin', do you have to leave now?" She was not being phony but southern—"being southern helped me in Washington, very much so," she said.

EverybodylovesLindy—that was the phrase people used, as if the words ran together. It had followed her through life, and it was accurate.

But the guilelessness that this implied was untrue. She could be sly without seeming to be. Hale's seniority had permitted him to appoint a House page, and when Lindy continued the practice, no one objected. When the Speaker asked her which committees she wished to join, none of the four with a vacancy interested her. She requested Banking and Currency, which had been Hale's first major assignment. She had appealed to the minority leader (now the president) and to Hale's successor as majority leader. Tip O'Neill had sought Lindy's blessing before declaring his candidacy and, when he won, hired Gary Hymel as his executive assistant. The two leaders cosponsored a resolution that expanded the committee by one.

"Purple veil approach," Lindy noted.

She knew how to push without seeming pushy. Lynda Bird Johnson said, "She makes you want to do what she wants you to do." After Tip O'Neill became the Speaker, he confided that Lindy was constantly at his door, that nobody pressed him as hard as she did.

"Charm-plus," said Patricia Schroeder, who was a more confrontational House freshman among the sixteen women in Congress. Or, "charm-plus-plus-plus," she amended, counting Lindy's shrewdness, her knowledge of Congress, and her history with Hale.

She showed a natural interest in flood insurance—if Hale was the father of the federal flood insurance program, she joked, she must be the mother. But otherwise, her legislative interests bore little resemblance to his. During her first year in Congress, she lent her name to compassionate bills on elderly nutrition, runaway children, rural housing, solar heating, home rule for D.C., and a memorial grove for the late President Johnson along the Potomac's Virginia shore.

With a freshman's traditional timidity about delivering speeches, she usually chose a safe subject—for instance, exempting the old *Delta Queen* steamship from the Safety at Sea law to "relive the romance" of the Louisiana Purchase. But not always. She pressed Gilbert Gude, the gentleman from Maryland, to assure Louisiana's fair treatment in an amendment to study carcinogens in the water, and she sprang to the delegate Walter Fauntroy's defense against Joel Broyhill.

Her truest accomplishment, in her taffeta-covered M.O., occurred when the banking committee took up the Equal Credit Opportunity Act of 1974, to ban discrimination in issuing mortgages and credit cards on the basis of race, age, or former military service. As a newly single woman, applying for credit on her own, Lindy had seen the obstacles that women faced. Pat Schroeder was unable to obtain an American Express card separate from her husband's; a senator's ex-wife, a professional, had been refused credit. On every side, her daughters' included, feminism was rising—and demanding a response.

For Lindy this was difficult. As a southern woman of her generation, by temperament as well as by upbringing, she hewed to a feminine reticence. As an every-morning-to-mass sort of Catholic, she was opposed to abortion. Yet she also believed that women were the equal of men—her grandmother had run a plantation—and deserved the same rights. She struggled for a comfortable means of expressing her ambivalence.

When the committee was marking up the bill, Lindy inserted five words in longhand—"or sex or marital status"—on her own copy. Then she found a photocopying machine and distributed her version to her colleagues.

"Knowing the members composing this committee as well as I do," she said in her sweetest drawl, "I'm sure it was just an oversight that we didn't have 'sex' or 'marital status' included. I've taken care of that, and I trust it meets with the committee's approval."

By a vote of forty-seven to zero, it did.

Conrad Cafritz had cold-called Peggy Cooper with a question about someone in the entertainment world who had invited him into a business deal. Peggy served with Conrad's oldest brother, Calvin, on the D.C. Commission on the Arts, and she knew the man in question.

"He's a jerk," she told Conrad. "You'd be nuts to do that."

He asked her to meet him for a drink.

Droopy-eyed, with a perennial five o'clock shadow, Conrad was handsome in an enigmatic way. People thought of him as brilliant, quirky, erratic. He could be quick and engaging, or cocky and difficult, or distant and listless.

"No, it was not love at first sight," Peggy said later.

Conrad was separated from Jennifer. Peggy was an emotional mess. During the summer, while visiting Paris, she had been kidnapped at the Eiffel Tower and gang-raped, so paralyzed with fear she was unable to scream. The American ambassador to the North Atlantic Treaty Organization, Donald Rumsfeld, and his wife, Joyce, took her back to their house in Brussels to recuperate.

Upon returning to Washington, she said, "I was pretty much a basket case." She could not leave her apartment for the store.

This was unlike her. She was bold by nature, even while she seemed sweetly vulnerable. Her great-great-grandfather had been a Seminole chief, and a great-great-grandmother had married a Louisiana governor's brother. Peggy's father was a certified public accountant whose family owned black funeral homes and a burial insurance business headquartered in Mobile, Alabama. She grew up in a huge house in a neighborhood with shacks.

"I was never a humble child," she said. Peggy had never learned to keep her opinions to herself. Her soft, quick voice and her boyish face and figure, the curls to her waist—sheared off now into a close-cropped cut—disarmed the bluntness of what she said. Her father often told her that he wanted her to feel as comfortable in a melon patch as in an audience with the queen of England, and he also "taught me there should be a strategy for each little goal." She could be impulsive or calculating or both.

Her grandparents had gone to Fisk and her parents to Hampton, but it did not occur to Peggy in 1964 to attend a predominantly black college. "I was acutely conscious of the role of politics in national life," she said, "and so I had my heart set on Washington."

When she went for an interview at George Washington University, the dean of women knew who she was. That was odd, Peggy thought, with so many applicants. The darker ones such as Peggy, with her cappuccino complexion, obviously stood out.

"In the course of my interview," she said later, "it became very clear to me that GW would be a social challenge, and so I decided I must go there to try to change it."

She was the only black among the nine hundred women in her dorm. Black men on campus could not take swimming, because the university used the segregated Young Men's Christian Association pool on G Street. Peggy rushed for a sorority, but, along with the other four blacks, she was dropped. She took her case to the Panhellenic Council. "I really would like to belong," she said, though she was less interested in joining a sorority than incensed at the university for condoning a segregated social life.

By her second day as a freshman, she had helped to organize picketing, to attract television cameras. Many protests later, the sororities and fraternities were kicked off campus and were not allowed back until they integrated.

"I became very, very active," she recalled.

She helped to organize the Black Student Union, then planned and directed a Black Arts Festival. She and her boyfriend, Mike Malone, started Workshops for Careers in the Arts, as a summertime program for talented schoolchildren in D.C. Too busy to bother with classes, Peggy flunked out as a sophomore, but appealed for a second chance and was given one.

She had wanted to be a lawyer since fifth grade—her parents imagined her as a Clarence Darrow. During her first year at GW law school, as she awaited her father's visit, Peggy received a telephone call. With his plane ticket on the coffee table and his bags in the car, he had killed himself. The authorities had discovered that he was embezzling money from the capital fund of the burial insurance company to support his six children in the manner to which he had accustomed them.

She moved from her lovely apartment in Foggy Bottom to an inexpensive one in the Adams Morgan neighborhood. Her full scholarship kept her in law school, but "I went from having whatever I wanted," she said, "to zip."

Something about Peggy attracted mentors. She had asked Calvin for an introduction to Martin Atlas, the foundation's vice president, and was soon receiving grants of twenty-five-thousand dollars a year (later, twice that) for her arts workshop, which was growing in ambition year by year. Brashly bright, brimming with ideas and willing to pursue them, Peggy was catnip to white liberals looking for promising young blacks to help along. John Walker, the National Gallery of Art's proudly patrician director who sat on the Cafritz Foundation board, became excited about what she was doing and helped her find grants. Lily Guest was a patron of the arts, the second chairman of the D.C. Commission on the Arts and Humanities, a founder of Friends of the Kennedy Center. She opened doors for Peggy, who considered her "the first truly color-blind person" she had met in Washington. She was introduced to Paul Mellon, the benefactor of the National Gallery of Art, and to Laughlin Phillips, whose parents' Twenty-first Street mansion had become a museum of modern art and who was to become Conrad's first wife's third husband. In 1972, twenty-five-year-old Peggy had been the youngest fellow ever selected by the Woodrow Wilson International Center for Scholars, after Hubert Humphrey asked Walter Washington to suggest a promising young black; she examined the ways that the arts might improve the quality of life in the inner city.

When she met Joe Alsop at a dinner party, even the aristocratic and conservative columnist took an interest. He grumbled to her about how wealth was shifting from the WASPs to the Jews, and he threw a dinner for her at a Chinese restaurant.

Peggy was surprised by how few of the city's influential WASPs Conrad Cafritz knew. When she introduced him to Joe Alsop, the bumptious columnist inquired how much he was worth.

"Joe," Conrad replied, "you know we don't discuss that in polite company."

It was while Peggy was still recovering from the trauma in Paris that "Conrad was extremely kind to me"—patient, understanding—and she fell in love with him.

Beyond the obvious differences—white and black, Jewish and Catholic—Conrad and Peggy had a lot in common. Both were witty, sharp-tongued, intuitive, whip-smart, hip, purposefully provocative, fascinated with politics and culture, and intent on making (and getting) their way. They even looked somewhat alike—slender, with short hair and a swarthy complexion and a predilection for jeans. They felt an intellectual bond, an ability to discuss almost anything and to trade original thoughts.

"Conrad was just mesmerized by Peggy's ability to promote"—herself and everything else. This was Carter Cafritz's assessment years later. "It was never a loving relationship. It was a business relationship from day one. Peggy had Conrad spellbound, because Conrad's a promoter, too."

Carter concluded something else: "I think Conrad saw in her a little element of Mother. Conrad was fascinated with Mother, mesmerized by Mother. His life is patterned after Mother. He likes parties, and he likes to do the social side. And I think Peggy represented the chance to do social things—not with the same crowd that Mother did, but social things."

Conrad moved in with Peggy, into a rented house in Wesley Heights, near Foxhall Road. Even after his divorce, they had no intention at first of marrying.

"There was no distinction between what we have and what is allowed by law," she told a reporter for the *Star*. "It's the relationship that counts."

About the same time, in 1974, Peggy's grandest ambition came to pass. She had known from the start, as a college junior, that the Workshops for Careers in the Arts would become something more. Organizing a black cultural festival at GW had prompted her first foray into the city's cultural scene. That was how she met Mike Malone, a dancer and choreographer, a compact man with a vast forehead and a devilish beard.

"I see all these talented kids," she told him, "but they're so raw, and they don't have any place to go for training."

"Well, why don't you start a school?" he replied.

"Oh, okay."

The idea of a full-time high school for the arts was so audacious that they kept it to themselves. Peggy wrote a three-page proposal for a summer program and took it to Lloyd Elliott, the university's new president. The courtly, forward-thinking administrator wanted to turn a decrepit campus into one with modern buildings, respectable libraries, and a prestigious faculty. He also hoped to change GW's attitudes on race, which until 1954 had been an acceptable basis for rejecting an applicant; even by 1969, black students accounted for barely 1 percent of the university's enrollment. During the riots in 1968, he had taken Peggy up to the roof to watch the distant smoke and to ask her what GW should do.

Not remain aloof from D.C., she replied.

Lloyd Elliott met often with Peggy about her request for funding and at last he answered: No. But she could raise money for a summer workshop by using the university's name and, if she succeeded, its classrooms.

The first summer, the workshop enrolled ninety high school students, rich and poor, taught for eleven weeks by seven teachers of drama, dance, and the visual arts. Then an after-school program was added. After Congress appropriated fifty thousand dollars, in 1970, a warehouse on Georgia Avenue became a part-time school, for students who left their regular schools at noon. Peggy lured Alvin Ailey, Bill Cosby, and James Earl Jones onto the advisory board.

To Peggy, this was truly black power—"black people attaining autonomy and technical skills to make any option they want," she said, "and to circulate freely in any kind of society." She conceded that she was working within the established political system, but added: "How are you going to achieve good if you don't deal with the system? And I mean we deal, operate, and play the game."

They played it well. When she recognized that she could never raise enough money to build a school, she began lobbying the city's Board of Education for a building. But which school building should she request? Four high schools and two junior highs seemed suitable, and Peggy was crafty in choosing. She decided to minimize the potential for protest by seeking the school with the fewest students who lived nearby.

Western High School, at Thirty-fifth and R, on a hill deep in Georgetown, was a once-white brick schoolhouse fronted with Greek pillars so classic they looked self-conscious. As enrollment from families in Georgetown had declined, students from Chinatown, Southwest, even Southeast replaced them.

In the late spring of 1974, the school board voted unanimously on the motion of Julius Hobson Jr. to establish the Arts High School at Western. The following fall, three hundred budding actors, musicians, and painters, half the number who had applied, showed up for classes.

The school took on a new name. Peggy treasured a photograph of her parents taken at the Blue Note in Chicago standing next to the elegant Washington-born jazz composer, who had died earlier that year, in whose social circles her parents had moved. Thus was born the Duke Ellington School of the Arts.

At the third annual convention of the D.C. Statehood Party, the seventy delegates stood and applauded as Julius Hobson was wheeled in. His head, nearly bald now, had sunk into his shrunken torso, as if he were a marionette whose puppeteer was dozing.

The welcome was a tribute but also a celebration. Julius was returning to politics.

The excruciating pain had eased for good and the cancer had abated, because of the poisons Tina had administered. "I'm taking acupuncture and I'm not on dope," he had said. "I may have a few years yet."

Even in a wheelchair his shoes were shined.

He could concentrate again on something outside himself. Home rule, of a sort, had arrived. Ever since blacks had become a majority in D.C., many of the white residents and the business community had opposed self-rule, worried about the hue of a democratically elected government and fearful that Congress might ultimately reduce its financial support, requiring higher taxes. At least a half-dozen times the Senate had approved self-government for the capital, and John McMillan, the South Carolina segregationist who chaired the House District of Columbia Committee, prevented a vote. After an uprising of his black constituents unseated McMillan in 1972, Charles Diggs of Detroit took his place. In skin color he resembled seven in ten of D.C.'s residents.

"Home fool," Julius called the result, because of the compromises made to pass it. The voters would elect a mayor and (as Julius put it) a "so-called City Council," but Congress retained for itself the power of the capital's purse and the right to overturn any laws that the local government enacted.

Julius knew he could never defeat Walter Washington in the mayoral race from a wheelchair, but a quirk in the home rule legislation offered a political opening. Three-fourths of the voters were Democrats, yet no more than two of the four at-large seats on the thirteen-member City Council could be filled by the same political party.

"The way these damn fools have written the law," Julius said to his party's convention, "we can win a seat or two."

He was nominated by acclamation.

Julius spent less, and campaigned less, than most of his sixteen rivals for at-large seats. But 85 percent of the voters knew who he was. In the sparsely attended candidate forums and in "Spaghetti Liberation" dinners in Statehood Party activists' homes, he promised to act as a gadfly if elected. Julius called for lifting the sales tax from food, medicine, and clothing and for petitioning Congress to authorize D.C. to tax suburban commuters. Mainly he spoke about statehood, as a simple matter of dignity. "Only statehood," he declared, "will give us the same rights and powers as other U.S. citizens."

The results in November surprised no one. Democrats placed first and second, and Julius finished a comfortable third, a Republican fourth.

Of the thirteen elected council members, eleven were black and nine had involved themselves in civil rights. "It's going to be a radical council," Julius surmised.

Sterling Tucker saw something else. Overwhelmingly elected by the voters as the elected council's first chairman, he too was a former activist, though of a contrasting style. The trim and bespectacled social worker had moved from Ohio to D.C. in the mid-1950s to run the local chapter of the Urban League, among the tamest of the civil rights groups. Sterling Tucker preferred the boardroom to the picket line. Yet he and Julius maintained a mutual respect. They had first worked together in drafting a charter for D.C.'s Human Relations Council in 1959 and then in organizing the 1963 March on Washington. On many points, they agreed.

But on the members of the new City Council, they disagreed. "People who have been fighting the Establishment," Sterling Tucker said—"now they *are* the Establishment."

"Faggot!"

The demonstrators screamed at Julius Hobson Jr., the vice president of the school board, because he wanted to fire the superintendent. A man rushed to the table and grabbed a microphone and threw it to the floor. A black woman shouted in the board president's face, "You little nigger bitch."

The stink bomb burst later.

Hobby had spent eighteen months on the board. After twelve he had decided he hated elective office. He enjoyed making policy but disliked constituents' phoning him at any hour and being unable to walk the street unrecognized, all for twelve hundred dollars a year.

"I couldn't remember all the damn names," he said.

The board member who sat next to him could. Hobby had never seen as talented a politician as Marion Barry. He seemed to know everyone in the school system and remembered their names and their children's names; almost desperate in his gregariousness, he also knew more about the workings of the schools than many of the administrators. A sharecropper's son from Mississippi, he had been determined enough to become one of the first black Eagle Scouts in Memphis and smart enough to be a dissertation away from earning a Ph.D. in chemistry. Instead he moved to Washington to head the local chapter of SNCC, and he cofounded Pride Inc., a Great Society–subsidized business for moving street dudes into jobs. With the publicity he drew as a dashiki-wearing street activist, he defeated Anita Allen and became the school board's president in 1972.

The superintendent, Barbara Sizemore, sat at Hobby's other

hand. That she was slender and soft-spoken was misleading. Her Afro and her oversized glasses said more about her uncompromising approach. Just after the outgoing board had hired her on a six-to-five vote in 1973, as the city's fourth superintendent in eight years, as the first black woman to run a big city's schools, she said on television, "I know of no change that is not accompanied by chaos."

Marion Barry and Barbara Sizemore agreed on most issues—on decentralizing the schools, on teaching black children their ancestral culture. For Hobby, however, sitting between them was like being caught in a fistfight. Punches would fly from both sides.

Hobby had started to sour on the superintendent three or four months into his term. Put in charge of a committee on federal grants, he read through ten of the school system's proposals and "found all kinds of crap in each one." When he raised questions, Sizemore complained to Barry, who had appointed Hobby to the task. "She decided I wasn't smart enough to do that," Hobby said, "that Marion had put me up to it."

The disputes between the superintendent and the school board had been inconsequential at first—over letting a private school use a public building, over subsidizing a D.C. youth orchestra. Unspoken in both cases was her disdain for institutions she deemed elitist and too white.

In the summer of 1974, after Marion Barry and two other board members quit to run for the City Council, Virginia Morris became the new president and Hobby, the vice president. Only one of the members who had hired Barbara Sizemore remained.

At board meetings, Sizemore made a practice of reading statements that criticized members by name, to cheers from the audience. Her speech to black educators about the "white racist" power structure and its "blueprint" for luring the white middle class back into D.C. upset the board members. So did her unwillingness to cooperate—she sat and read a Bible—as they reworked the annual budget after dismantling hers. Hobby considered her one of the smartest people he had ever met, but inept as a manager and far too ideological and obstinate.

For Hobby, the clincher occurred at a picnic at Virginia Morris's house. As he and the superintendent shared a table, she leaned over to him and said, "Mr. Hobson, if it comes to doing what I want to do or compromising, I will never compromise, ever."

"Oh, shit," Hobby said to himself. "That's it."

By the spring of 1975, the board had secretly started to evaluate her performance and by Memorial Day had approved a bill of seventeen particulars, most of them on a seven-to-four vote. She had failed to comply with the board's directives, to file quarterly reports, to fill important positions. Hobby voted for all the charges except one, that she had not submitted a plan to equalize the resources among the schools in deference to *Hobson v. Hansen*. He had been a plaintiff in the case and now he was a defendant.

A personality clash became a racial clash when Sizemore pointed out that four of her opponents were white and a fifth, Hilda Mason, had a white husband. That left Virginia Morris and Julius Hobson Jr.— "Aunt Jemima" and "Uncle Tom." That was the nicest thing Hobby was called, compared to "nutless, punk, cut your dick off, blow your family up, shoot your ass, run you out of town." He took the threats lightly until a canister of tear gas went off in Hilda Mason's basement and a lighted match was flung into a white councilman's black beard. The school board members asked for police protection at home.

This was democracy at work.

"You're not your father." Over and over, Hobby heard some variant. "Your father would never have done this."

He knew it was true, and it was fine with him. "My father stands on the table and yells, first thing," he said. "That's my last tactic." He seemed to glory in the difference.

"For a long time," he said later, "I thought I needed to do things to differentiate myself—that's my father, but this is me." Yet some of the spectators thought he was showing tough, as if to *be* his father, to measure up.

His father was puzzled by Hobby's opposition to the radical superintendent, though as he began to know her, he changed his mind. After her supporters confronted him in his wheelchair, his feelings hardened.

"She's just destroyed the school system," Julius concluded, "and Johnny still can't read."

Just before the public hearings were under way, Virginia Morris was rushed to the hospital with a mysterious intestinal ailment.

Hobby, the acting president, complained of severe aching in his shoulders and arms.

The first day of hearings started six hours late, as the school board and Sizemore's lawyers argued over the arrangement of the tables, reminiscent of the stalled Paris peace talks that eventually ended the war in Vietnam.

The hearings, once they began, consisted of numbing detail about administrative procedures taken or ignored—"a Burst of Yawns," *The Evening Star* headlined the following day.

The hearings went on six days a week, for nearly a month. No minds were changed.

The management announced that the Ambassador Hotel would close at checkout time on Thursday, March 6, 1975, forty-six years after it had opened. The operator of the rundown hotel had been released from his seven-year lease after two and a half years. There was no real choice.

The neighborhood had deteriorated since Calvin Cafritz had lived on the top floor. Then, apartments and modest businesses—a barbershop, a pharmacy, a cigar shop—had congregated along Fourteenth Street, near K. After World War II the stretch of Fourteenth Street from G Street north to L housed upscale nightclubs, including Benny's Rebel Room, with its Dixieland jazz, and the Blue Mirror, featuring Ella Fitzgerald or Peggy Lee or Nat King Cole. But the 1968 riots just to the north had scared white customers away, and prostitutes and drug dealers and Benny's Home of the Porno Stars had taken their place.

Not that the Ambassador had been so tame in its heyday. Even now, an out-of-town businessman might not mind a hotel near Fourteenth Street, but a family of tourists would. The Ambassador's carpets had grown worn, the walls were lumpy with decades of paint, and plaster was flaking off the walls. The Ambassador had never been a fancy hotel; at its best it offered good value, without pretension. Now it offered less. The revenue from renting barely half the rooms was not enough to remodel them.

After Morris Cafritz's estate was settled, with the foundation restricted in business, the Ambassador was leased (with an option to buy) to a clean-cut thirty-four-year-old hotelier who had run five Holiday Inns around Boston. "We want to change the image of the hotel," said Drew Dimond, into "a simple hotel, plain and clean," suitable for businessmen, bureaucrats, and families. He planned to install color TVs, Astroturf and tables with umbrellas near the pool, and paint the lobby red, white, and blue. He was counting on the nation's Bicentennial celebration to tempt tourists to the capital and save the hotel.

Skeptical banks refused to lend him the $600,000 he needed, and the surge in oil prices after the Arab embargo and the subsequent recession brought tourism low. The Hamilton Hotel, cater-cornered to the Ambassador, had been converted to apartments. Downtown, four other hotels—including, unimaginably, the Willard—had shut their doors. Soon pigeons roosted inside the space where Lincoln had slept.

Customers still slept at the Ambassador, but, without renovations, they rarely returned. The hotel became a home to old ladies who ate at Sholl's Cafeteria, a block west along K.

The Bicentennial was still a year away when Drew Dimond said, "I got tired of fighting."

The announcement that the Ambassador's closing was imminent produced a savior of sorts. Sam Wong owned the Moon Gate in the Ambassador and two other restaurants in Chinatown, where he had served for several years as the unofficial mayor. He and his wife, confident that they could find money for renovations, took over the lease.

A few months later the police, in a crackdown on Chinese gambling, raided the Moon Gate and the Ambassador. The occupancy rate slid even more.

During the summer of 1978 a developer offered to buy the K Street site for an office building. Hundreds of people swarmed into the hotel for the liquidation sale. Black-and-white televisions went for forty-eight dollars, shower heads for three dollars, the two elevators for twenty-four hundred dollars apiece, curtains for a quarter.

"You can't beat this at Levitz or Marlow's," said a woman waiting to pay nine dollars for a nightstand.

Calvin watched the wrecking ball slam into the apartment where he had once lived. "It was very sad," he said.

After the City Council's first ceremonial meeting, several preachers complained to Sterling Tucker that he had not begun with a prayer. At the next meeting, the council chairman suggested a prayer or a moment of silence. He expected no objection.

Julius Hobson spoke up. The City Council was a governmental body, he said, and a prayer would violate the constitutional separation of church and state.

Another councilman suggested inviting ministers to conduct a prayer.

"If you do," Julius snapped, "I'll take you to court."

"I'd welcome it," the at-large Republican, a minister, retorted.

Marion Barry said, "We can pray at home in the morning."

Sterling Tucker called for a moment of silence. "Why start out," he asked himself, "with needless controversy?"

There would be enough of that anyway. The elected council members, activists by nature, made themselves seven times as busy as the appointees they replaced. In their first six months in office, they passed 28 of the 139 bills they introduced, pondered 100 resolutions, published scores of committee reports, and conducted 136 public hearings. They wrangled with the mayor over the budget, shifted a few taxes from individuals onto businesses, extended a moratorium on conversions of rental apartments into condominiums, permitted street vendors to freeze ice cream with dry ice, and declared Gay Pride Day. If they showed more motion than movement, it was in celebration of the novel fact that, as the people's representatives, they could *act*.

Julius shunned busywork. In the first six months he introduced a single bill, to charge a dime's deposit on bottles, and held three hearings. Then he proposed something big, out of his deepest experience: the Architectural Barriers Act of 1975, to mandate that in new and remodeled buildings, the handicapped and the elderly be unhindered by steps or narrow corridors or inaccessible toilets. New sidewalks would have to include curb cuts, a requirement ahead of its time. He enlisted nine cosponsors and exploited his own story. Julius could only enter the District Building when someone shoved his wheelchair up a makeshift, rubber-covered plank across the steps at the entrance. Once, in a rainstorm, his assistant slipped on the way down and the wild wheelchair careened toward the side of the mayor's limousine.

Julius pleaded for a long gentle ramp that he could negotiate himself, and electric doors, but the sixty-thousand-dollar price tag was twice what the mayor spent on a full-time chauffeur. Julius's law would eventually pass, though too late to help him.

He showed a surprising affinity for the etiquette of elected office. He distributed his cache of low-number license plates to political supporters, accepted five complimentary tickets to the Cherry Blossom Parade, and responded to constituents with a bland solicitousness ("I appreciate your bringing your concerns for dental health care to my attention and I shall keep your views in mind"). Over the next couple of years, he introduced bills to ban smoking in restaurants and public places, to keep a rape victim's sexual history out of court, to regulate speech pathologists, to authorize initiatives and referendums—this passed—and to establish a six-step procedure toward statehood. He sent out "Season's Greetings" cards with a blue outline of the capital and a red 51, for the prospective fifty-first state.

Hardly any of his bills became law.

Most of the council members liked him, probably more than he liked them. But he disliked the give-and-take of the political process. Wangling six votes from twelve self-absorbed politicians required endless discussion, coalition building, painstaking compromise, indirection, artful winks. Julius had no patience with political horse trading or back scratching. He expected the others to see his logic and swing his way.

His chairmanship of the Education, Recreation and Youth Affairs Committee gave him and his son "an unusual grip on the school system, past, present and future," *The Evening Star* remarked. Theirs was no conspiracy, however. Before Hobby went to testify in front of his father, he warned his colleagues on the school board that he was not assured of an easy time.

"You don't know my father," he said.

Julius believed so feverishly in whatever he was trying to do that personal considerations melted. Between father and son, their styles and strategies—their souls, it seemed—diverged. Julius would raise a ruckus; Hobby preferred to confer behind the scenes. While Julius issued broadsides, Hobby prided himself on remaining unemotional. Hobby also understood the need for both styles—for the activists who disrupted the status quo, "so that others could come behind them to make the compromises."

The collision between father and son on a January morning in 1976 involved the school budget. They were on the same side, though a casual observer might not have noticed. Imperious in his wheelchair, at the center of the rostrum in the City Council's digni-fied, vaulted-ceiling chamber, Julius Hobson Sr. gaveled the educa-tion committee into session. Two hundred people looked on.

Julius's voice was melodic and strong. "I cannot in good con-science consider the Mayor's level of two hundred six million, eight hundred sixty-three thousand, four hundred dollars," he said in a high-pitched twang. "I would rather consider the level asked for by the Board of Education, two hundred eighteen million dollars, even though I think two hundred eighteen million is too low, and the Board of Education should not be in the habit of asking for less money than it really needs." He was almost haranguing. "If we're go-ing to cut the school budget, let's let the Mayor veto it, and then let the Council override, and you ought to demand that the Council override, and then let it go to the President of the United States and let him in his undemocratic way have the final decision"—Julius's drawl had deepened, the applause was beginning to build—"because we don't have home rule in this city anyway."

The ovation burst, and he allowed it to fade.

"I'm not for cutting one nickel out of the budget for education in the District of Columbia public schools"—applause again swept the room—"no matter how much testimony I get to the contrary. So if you're in favor of shafting the children, you're before the wrong chairman."

He called on the opening witness.

"Good morning, Mr. Chairman," Julius Hobson Jr. began.

The school board's vice president, the chairman of its finance committee, pointed out that the city's school system was facing its third—and worst—budget crisis since 1974, now that the mayor had ordered another year of reductions. In a monotone he hurried through a prepared statement thick with budget figures, personnel numbers, and bureaucratic chronology.

He ended by quoting W. E. B. Du Bois, the black philosopher, one of his father's favorites: "We will fight for all time against any proposal to educate black boys and girls simply as servants and underlings." The school board, he said, "needs at least two hundred eighteen million dollars."

To his prepared statement he had added "at least."

"Thank you very much, uh, Mr. Hobson," Julius said.

Then Julius reminded his son and the spectators about how to treat any promises from the politicians on the podium. "Just to get word that you're going to have support by a member of the City Council," he said, "is not worth the time that it took you to hear it."

And then he called the next witness.

President Ford had hurried over from the opening ceremony for the new Air and Space Museum, on the Mall, where he had delivered the first of six planned speeches during these climactic days of the nation's Bicentennial. (The nation must "keep reaching into the unknown," he declared.) A crowd milled in Statuary Hall, the original House chamber in the Capitol, surrounded by ghostly marble eminences of American history. The president was reaching into a seven-foot-high iron safe and pulling out old photographs and remarkably well-preserved papers.

"Lindy!" the president cried out. "I have a picture of a chairperson."

Lindy Boggs chaired the Joint Committee on Arrangements for Commemoration of the Bicentennial. She loved history—her family had made quite enough of it—and several months earlier she had presided over a ceremony to open the outer door of the Centennial Safe. The architect of the Capitol had discovered the safe in 1971, rusting under the steps of the East Portico. A wealthy Civil War widow had collected artifacts of the capital's life in 1876, to be opened on July 4, 1976, "by the Chief Magistrate of the United States."

The president had opened the inner door three days too soon, because of his overburdened schedule.

He held up the photograph of a woman who turned out to be Mrs. Rutherford B. Hayes. He also extracted a parchment scroll autographed by every member of the Forty-fourth Congress, a Tiffany inkstand only lightly tarnished, a directory of eighty thousand government workers, a pen engraved in gold with the name Henry Wadsworth Longfellow, a book on temperance, two identification cards that Supreme Court pages had evidently slipped in, and more.

None of it disintegrated in the Bicentennial air, as archivists had feared, though historians appraised the contents as useless. The collection was nearly as odd as the time capsules of cultural icons being everywhere preserved for the Tricentennial. One in Los Angeles contained a Barbie doll, beer cans, false eyelashes, a skateboard, a TV dinner, a pet rock, and all seven reels of *Jaws*.

"Something about the United States of America," Ford said, "is so mighty and so inspiring that it cannot be locked up in a safe."

Lindy had traveled around the country since 1974, as the House Democrats' representative on the American Revolution Bicentennial Administration's board, to help communities plan celebrations of their own. Later she advocated that the leftover funds from the Bicentennial be spent to create Constitution Gardens, a scattering of maples and willows along the Reflecting Pool. At certain angles, the thick hilt of the Washington Monument or the dome of the Capitol peered between the trees.

Lindy's sweetness of manner, her inoffensiveness, was more than charm; it was a political asset of consequence. The Democratic Party had decided in 1972 that women must fill half the delegates' seats at future party conventions and alternate with men as the presiding officer. For the 1976 convention in New York, Bob Strauss, the party's chairman, was to select the first woman ever to serve as the permanent chairman of a major party's quadrennial gathering. He passed over two fiery congresswomen, the black orator Barbara Jordan of

Texas—who delivered the keynote address—and the floppy-hatted Bella Abzug of New York City, adept at gaveling down unruly politicos in her hometown. Neither would do as the nightly face of the clamorous party.

But Lindy would.

"I assume I'll command with a strict gavel," she said. "I have the strong back and strong stomach of most political wives."

The day the choice became known, a House page told Lindy of a phone call for her in the Democratic cloakroom.

"Hi, honey," said President Ford. "Are you going to pick a good one for me?"

Tommy Corcoran, the old lobbyist, escorted her to New York, as he had been doing around the capital, while deflecting the rumors of a possible wedding.

In the smoothest Democratic convention in sixteen years, Lindy presided over the nomination of the nation's next president, the first from the Deep South in more than a century.

Nine

CARTER

On a Friday evening after the 1976 elections, Sterling Tucker invited Julius Hobson into his office. The voters had elected one new member to the City Council, and the chairman was planning its next biennium. He was under pressure to give the chairmanship of the education committee, with its substantial jurisdiction and staff, to somebody else.

Too ill to do much work, Julius had fallen quiet at council meetings. He followed the essence of legislation but not the details.

"Why don't you let me relieve you of the responsibility of having a committee?" the council chairman said.

Julius sat in his wheelchair and started to cry.

"That's about all I have left," he managed at last. He enjoyed the work, and he liked the responsibility of a chairmanship.

The doctors had just told him, he added, that the cancer had returned. The poisons that had checked the multiple myeloma for more than five years had caused leukemia. He had been given six months to live.

Julius was fifty-seven years old, though even Tina believed that he was fifty-four.

Sterling Tucker, a pensive and well-meaning man, promised to reconsider. He did not wait until Monday. He phoned Julius at home on Saturday afternoon to say that the committee would still be his.

Julius went public with his fate a few weeks later.

"The reason I didn't tell the papers this time," he informed the reporter from the *Post*, "is because the doctors only gave me six months to live last time, and I thought people might be bored." He had just returned home from the hospital because the doctors decided that a radical chemotherapy, offering a one in ten chance, was not necessary yet. "I'm under no illusions. I've lived a good life—I've lived long enough, anyway."

"Julius is facing his last battle"—this, from Tina. "We've spent a month shutting the door and crying, but now he plans to continue his work."

At the council's opening session of 1977, two days earlier, Julius had introduced nine bills on subjects ranging from a state fair to statehood. He complained that politics had become so important in the council that it might drive him away. He would leave council meetings muttering about his colleagues' posturing.

He had accomplished more as an outsider, he told Hobby, than as an elected official. He disliked being on the inside. It was not enough that a proposal was right. It also needed seven votes.

As the weeks passed, Julius grew uneasy with the change of tone toward a dying man. "I don't have any enemies now," he complained. "I can't find anybody that's willing to attack Julius Hobson."

He felt tortured in too many ways. One Sunday morning he telephoned Carol from the hospital. They had not spoken for months. "You know," he said, "since I left home, I haven't found a single solitary person to trust. And if I could find somebody to push me up that hill to Redeemer"—he meant the Church of the Redeemer, where Carol and Hobby were members—"I'd come to church with you."

On Tuesday morning, March 22, the council scampered through an agenda even fuller than usual. Among the twenty-seven topics were the closing of numerous alleyways, final approval of the Outdoor Sidewalk Café Act and the Consumer Goods Repair Board Act, first readings of the Residential Parking Tax Exemption Act and Dr.

King's Birthday Act, and resolutions on declaring Soccer Week and on—this was Julius's doing—extending a D.C. program of guaranteed student loans.

"Mr. Chairman," Julius said as his bill came up, "I regretfully ask that this be withdrawn at this point for further clarification."

"Without objections," said Sterling Tucker, "we will . . ."

Marion Barry asked about the clarification—"On what, Mr. Chairman?"

Barry had been inches from dying just thirteen days earlier, when bands of terrorists called the Hanafi Muslims seized the B'nai B'rith headquarters at Seventeenth and Rhode Island, a mosque on Massachusetts Avenue, and the District Building. Barry had returned to the District Building from a Kiwanis luncheon when he emerged from the elevator on the fifth floor and was shot two inches above his heart, a flesh wound.

"On the bill, man," Julius broke in. "We haven't been able to come up with how many students." He had never liked Barry. The guy was always late and lacked all discretion with women—"You just can't trust him," Julius would tell Tina.

Barry reported numerous phone calls to his office about students forced to leave college for lack of tuition. "The longer we wait," he said, "the more students are out in the cold."

That afternoon, Hobby stopped by Julius's fifth-floor office. The small room seemed dark, though the morning's rain had cleared up, and the top of his big wooden desk was uncharacteristically clear. Julius was calm but short on energy, and Hobby understood. Three weeks earlier, he had donated platelets—he was the only family member whose blood type matched Julius's—and for twenty-four hours he had felt the exhaustion his father knew all the time.

Their relationship had improved in the past couple of years, since they had begun to deal with each other on what Hobby saw as more of an equal footing. They talked for fifteen or twenty minutes. The conversation was unlike any they had ever held. Julius talked about his life. He acknowledged that he had made some mistakes, that he had neglected his family, that Carol was a good person who had often been right.

"I hope your mother understands that I really meant well," he said, "that I didn't mean you-all any harm."

He told his son to live life to the fullest, to be honest with himself, and not to run for reelection to the school board, though he seemed to suggest that Hobby might seek Julius's seat on the council, once he was gone.

"Yeah, Dad—sure, fine," a puzzled Hobby replied.

It was not until the following day that he understood.

After Hobby left, Julius's assistant drove him to GW's outpatient clinic for a routine checkup, and then home.

That night, Tina's younger son, Eric, showed up from the army, without leave. "I just have to come home," he had said by telephone from boot camp. Her sons regarded Julius as a hero—they had marched beside him in antiwar protests—though the marriage had probably been more painful for them than they had let on.

Jean went to see her father at Waterside Towers. Whenever she visited him, he spent every minute with her. Even in his council chambers, he included her in meetings or wherever he went. Jean had always taken pride, maybe too much, in being Julius Hobson's daughter.

Once she had burst into his council office, shouting, "Daddy, Daddy, can I have some money to get some snacks?"

"Jean, you're being rude."

"But they're getting ready to close."

As Julius gave her the money he said, "And this is Jesse Jackson."

"Hello," she said, and took off. In the corridor she braked and ran back in.

"I thought you wanted something to snack on," her father said.

"That's Jesse Jackson!" she screamed. The activist-minister was becoming famous for his preacherly style of politics.

This time Jean had not wanted to visit her father. She had asked Hobby to go along, but he was at work, as an editorial assistant at an educational think tank at Howard. She stayed three hours. Julius had been injected with morphine, and he was crying.

Just as a bus was delivering Jean to her home, the telephone rang. It was her father.

The national Mall was a wilderness early in the twentieth century, as pictured
here from the vantage point of the Washington Monument. Later, it was restored
to L'Enfant's original conception of an open vista west of the Capitol.
(*The Historical Society of Washington, D.C., City Museum*)

RIGHT. Stylish nineteen year-old Gwendolyn Cafritz returned from her honeymoon aboard the S.S. *Ile de France* in 1929 on an immigrant's visa issued in her native Hungary. (*Courtesy of U.S. Citizenship and Immigration Services, Washington, D.C.*)

BELOW: "Morris names all children, horses, dogs, and apartment houses," Gwen mused in 1938, seated next to Caesar, the family's Great Dane. (*Courtesy of Calvin Cafritz*)

LEFT: In the backyard of their mansion on Foxhall Road, Gwen spent a rare moment with her three young sons—(left to right) Calvin, Carter, and Conrad. *(Courtesy of Calvin Cafritz)*

BELOW: Employees gave Morris Cafritz a poster in 1954 that illustrated his early business ventures in a coal yard, saloon, and bowling alleys. The Argyle Golf Course was another name for the Columbia Golf Club, where he built his early homes and started to build a fortune in real estate. *(Courtesy of Calvin Cafritz)*

Commemorating 32 Years of Progress
Morris Cafritz

THIS IS HOW HALE BOGGS, Jones program candidate for Congress in the Second Congressional District, relaxes after a hard day of campaigning. In her daddy's arms is 13-month-old BARBARA BOGGS, who is the only dictator he ever tolerated.

WILLKIE SPEEDED ANSWER TO ICKES

Left Much Unsaid to Reach Public at Same Time as Attack

BY HAROLD BRAYMAN
(New Orleans States Staff Correspondent)
Rushville, Ind., Aug. 21.—Because of the eagerness of Wendell L. Willkie, ex-Democrat, who is now the Republican nominee for president, to answer Secretary of Interior Ickes promptly he responded publicly on only a few of the points made by Mr. Ickes in the reply of the Roosevelt cabinet member to the Elwood acceptance speech.

Mr. Willkie follows the policy, whenever he plans to answer anything, to get his answer in the same editions which carry the original story, if possible. That

'Mr. Boggs Goes to Washington' Is Hope of Hale and His 'Boss'

Young Leader Who Aspires to Congressional Honor Has Already Made His Mark as an Able, Courageous Champion of People's Rights

BY DAVE M'GUIRE
"He's a young man who's going places—we need more like him."

That's what Sam Jones said about Hale Boggs during the last gubernatorial campaign when the latter was leading citizens' groups in the fight for good government. That was before Sam Jones was governor of Louisiana and before Hale Boggs was the Jones program candidate for Congress in the Second Congressional district.

It's an interesting and typically American story, the life of this 27-year-old Orleanian whose voice was the mouthpiece of indignant and outraged young Louisiana

oped an interest and facility in writing.

Unable to go to college any other way, Hale won an honor scholarship to Tulane university and entered as a freshman in 1931 with $35 in cash.

"I didn't waste much time getting a job," he recalls today. "I just didn't eat if I wasn't working. At Tulane, I peddled chewing gum, magazines, dug ditches on the lakefront during the summer and in my junior year obtained the job of campus correspondent for the New Orleans States. In this way I managed to get through and am proud that I

ers in the Young Men's Business Club movement for tax reform in Louisiana. That was in 1939, before the scandals rampant in the former state administrations broke.

After public exposure through the press of the wholesale crookery existing in the operation of Louisiana's state government in June, 1939, Hale Boggs met with a group of young men as determined as himself to do something about it—to contribute their share in obtaining decent government.

Out of their spontaneous gathering came The People's League of Louisiana, dedicated to cleaning up the mess of political corruption which by that time was smelling throughout the United States.

What happened is history.

Led People's League

Judge George P. Platt had just dismissed two members of the Orleans parish grand jury from that body because they tried to read to him a petition of charges against District Attorney Charles A. Byrne, whom they said was impeding and obstructing their investigations.

With the sanctity and integrity of the grand jury as their goal, the People's League plunged into that fight in defense of the grand jurors.

Petitions were circulated for Byrne's recall. Special committees began working on the case, beginning other investigations, following up new clues and rumors and leads.

Hale Boggs, now chairman of the People's League, called a public mass meeting to be held outside the district attorney's office. And several thousand turned out that hot, sweating July morning to hear young Boggs call for a peaceful revolution to end forever the shameful conditions that existed here and elsewhere in Louisiana.

Charlie Byrne's resignation at the height of the open hearing forced by the People's League was the first major setback suffered by the still powerful state administration.

And if you don't think it took courage for Hale Boggs and others who spoke at that July, 1939, mass meeting for good and honest government, then just consider where they would be today in their legal livelihood had the state machine been victorious and in control of the courts before which they would have had to practice.

It took courage of a high order to stick one's neck out before the "overthrow." Today it's easy to say you were against them and didn't believe in this or that dictator custom. But only those who had the courage of their convictions said it publicly and openly before February 20.

The People's League did its share in other crusades and drives of the "Great Cleanup," and through it all Hale Boggs, chairman of the group, was on the job. With a score of other young fellows who were willing to work for a better day, he let his own private affairs go to work for the cause—a cause that at times appeared a lost one.

Active in Jones Campaign

After Sam Jones announced for governor last September, Hale Boggs, acting as an individual and not as chairman of the People's League, began actively campaigning for Jones and the anti-administration ticket. He worked in his ward and in his precinct; he and Lindy rang doorbells and

An article in the *New Orleans States* on August 21, 1940, during Hale Boggs's first campaign for the U.S. House of Representatives, was written by an old friend who then became his top congressional aide. (*Copyright The Times-Picayune Publishing Co. All rights reserved. Used with permission of* The Times-Picayune.)

ABOVE: Gwen Cafritz threw out the first pitch at an exhibition baseball game she organized in 1942 at Griffith Stadium, where servicemen and "government girls" filled alternate seats. With her is Clark Griffith, the owner of Washington's American League baseball club. (*Copyright* Washington Post, *reprinted by permission of the D.C. Public Library*)

LEFT: Educated in art history and fluent in five languages, Gwen Cafritz showed modern tastes and a continental flair. (*Copyright* Washington Post, *reprinted by permission of the D.C. Public Library*)

Julius Hobson proposed to Carol Andrews on their first date in 1947 and married her less than four months later.
(*Courtesy of Carol Joy Smith*)

ABOVE: Julius Hobson Jr., born in 1948, had an easier temperament than his father, and grew up to believe in compromise more than confrontation.
(*Courtesy of Carol Joy Smith*)

RIGHT: Young Hobby tried to emulate his father, who was once known as the best-dressed student at Tuskegee Institute.
(*Courtesy of Carol Joy Smith*)

The three Boggs children, pictured in 1947, practically grew up in the Capitol, where Cokie (left) celebrated her seventh birthday in the Speaker's Dining Room, and Tommy later ran the Speaker's private elevator. (*Courtesy of Hale Boggs Papers, Manuscripts Department, Tulane University*)

Lindy Boggs was becoming a political force in her own right, as when she invited Eleanor Roosevelt to speak to the Woman's National Democratic Club in 1958. (*Copyright* Washington Post, *reprinted by permission of the D.C. Public Library*)

As big-city Catholics and friends in Congress since 1947, Hale Boggs often had President Kennedy's ear. (*Courtesy of Hale Boggs Papers, Manuscripts Department, Tulane University*)

Julius Hobson applied the skills he learned as a statistical analyst for
the Social Security Administration, starting in 1959, to his activism in civil rights.
(*Copyright* Washington Post, *reprinted by permission of the D.C. Public Library*)

Policemen called him "Mr. Hobson" because he blamed the system
instead of individuals for social injustices and treated cops with respect.
(*Copyright* Washington Post, *reprinted by permission of the D.C. Public Library*)

LEFT: Gwen Cafritz, in the mid-1950s' flush of her social success, was a stunning woman and a regular on the best-dressed lists. (*Courtesy of Calvin Cafritz*)

BELOW: Gwen Cafritz reached her peak as a Washington hostess the night she entertained the Duke of Windsor and the Baltimore-born Duchess at a dinner and dance in 1962. (*Copyright* Washington Post, *reprinted by permission of the D.C. Public Library*)

RIGHT: Gwen and Morris Cafritz were opposites who fit well as a couple. (*Copyright* Washington Post, *reprinted by permission of the D.C. Public Library*)

BELOW: After Morris Cafritz died in 1964, Gwen continued to entertain, though she dispensed with her beloved sit-down dinners for twenty-two. (*Copyright* Washington Post, *reprinted by permission of the D.C. Public Library*)

ABOVE: Morris Cafritz, as host to the Duchess of Windsor, found that his wife's social prominence benefited his real estate business. (*Copyright* Washington Post, *reprinted by permission of the D.C. Public Library*)

After college, Cokie Boggs interviewed family friends, among others, as the moderator on a local Sunday television show called *Meeting of the Minds.* (*Courtesy of Cokie Roberts*)

When Cokie married Steve Roberts in 1966 in her family's yard in Bethesda, President Johnson was among the more than 1,500 guests. (*Courtesy of Cokie Roberts*)

From the left, at the New Orleans Fairgrounds in 1967 stood Cokie Roberts; Tommy's wife, Barbara; Lindy; Tommy; Hale; Steve Roberts; and Barbara and Paul Sigmund. (*Courtesy of Cokie Roberts*)

When D.C. was awarded a nonvoting seat in Congress in 1971, candidate Julius Hobson of the Statehood Party finished third. *(Courtesy of Tina Hobson)*

On election night in 1969, when Julius Hobson lost his seat on the D.C. school board, Tina suddenly accepted his longstanding proposal of marriage. *(Copyright* Washington Post, *reprinted by permission of the D.C. Public Library)*

Julius Hobson's children felt uncomfortable with a white stepmother, but Tina's sons admired their stepfather and marched with him in antiwar demonstrations. *(Courtesy of Tina Hobson)*

RIGHT: Lindy Boggs involved herself in Washington's many charity functions, including a 1971 fashion show at the Congressional Club. (*Copyright* Washington Post, *reprinted by permission of the D.C. Public Library*)

ABOVE: Lindy shared her husband's social obligations and smoothed out his abrasive edges. More than most congressional couples, they were truly a team. (*Copyright* Washington Post, *reprinted by permission of the D.C. Public Library*)

RIGHT: As Hale Boggs grew ever-busier as he rose in the congressional leadership, gardening became his favorite relaxation. (*Copyright* Washington Post, *reprinted by permission of the D.C. Public Library*)

At a 1975 hearing, school board vice president Julius Hobson Jr. (second from the right) faced his wheelchair-bound father, the chairman of the City Council's education committee. Future mayor Marion Barry was three seats to the younger Hobson's right.
(*Copyright* Washington Post, *reprinted by permission of the D.C. Public Library*)

Even after he fell ill with a rare cancer, Julius Hobson Sr. won a seat on D.C.'s first elected City Council in modern times and served as a gadfly until he died in 1977.
(*Copyright* Washington Post, *reprinted by permission of the D.C. Public Library*)

Julius Hobson's second wife, Tina, eulogized her outspoken husband at a memorial service at All Souls Church.
(*Copyright* Washington Post, *reprinted by permission of the D.C. Public Library*)

As head of his parents' foundation, Calvin Cafritz donated $1 million in 1997 toward the second coming of D.C.'s Jewish Community Center in honor of his father who had originally raised funds for the building. *(Brenda Schrier)*

Despite their differences in race and religion, Conrad Cafritz and his wife, Peggy, shared political interests and an intellectual bond. *(Courtesy of Peggy Cooper Cafritz)*

Peggy and Conrad Cafritz raised two sons, Cooper (left) and Zachary, but the couple divorced in 1998. *(Courtesy of Peggy Cooper Cafritz)*

As a legislative assistant to Senator Charles Robb, Democrat of Virginia, Julius Hobson Jr. offered conservative advice on budget issues and on confirming Clarence Thomas to the Supreme Court. (Roanoke Times)

The Hobson family (from left: Jean, Diane Lewis, Julius Jr., and Carol) gathered for the wedding of Julius Jr.'s daughter Faye in 2000. (Courtesy of Carol Joy Smith)

When he swore in Lindy Boggs as the ambassador to the Vatican in 1997, with two children and a grandson looking on, Vice President Al Gore noted she had known him since before he was born. *(Reuters)*

Tommy Boggs, in his spacious office overlooking Rock Creek Park, is generally regarded as the leading lobbyist in Washington. *(Richard A. Bloom)*

"I thought you were coming to visit me," he said.

Her mother blamed the morphine. Jean rode back to Southwest.

The next morning Julius suffered terrible pain in his abdomen.

"Eric, help me take him to the hospital," Tina said.

Julius had survived many such episodes before. But by the time Hobby got to GW hospital, his father had fallen unconscious. His breathing was labored.

Fifteen minutes later his body heaved, and then at last it was still. The clock stood at twenty-five minutes past noon.

Ten minutes later, with Julius's body still in its bed, Bardyl Tirana arrived. No one had phoned him.

"I just had a feeling that Julius was in the hospital," he said.

David Eaton showed up. The All Souls pastor thought Julius looked serene—too serene.

"Something must be wrong," he said, "because Julius has never been that peaceful."

"He just died," Tina replied.

Hobby went to the District Building, to tell Sterling Tucker and Walter Washington. He entered Mayor Washington's outer office and said, "I need to see the mayor right now."

"He's busy."

"You tell him I need to see him right now."

"I'm real busy, Julius," the mayor said; "what do you need?"

"I had good feelings about him," Walter Washington said years later, in remembering Julius Hobson, "though he didn't always return the favor." The two of them had come to recognize, "at least toward the end"—this was Hobby's recounting—that "there's one guy who's pushing and one who comes behind. Walter was the guy who came behind. He made a lot of things possible."

The word of Julius's death swiftly spread.

A memorial service on Sunday afternoon drew nine hundred mourners to All Souls Church. Julius had asked to be cremated, and his ashes rested in a box on a table in front, beneath the vaulted ceiling and the unadorned white walls, above a larger-than-life portrait of Julius in midharangue. Mention of Jesus hardly passed anyone's lips. The twenty-four-page program included a letter of condolence from

President Jimmy Carter, who had met Julius at a dinner at Bardyl Tirana's early in his outsider's presidential campaign.

"Julius Hobson's life is proof," the president wrote, "that one person can change the world he lives in."

The city's Establishment arrived in force, starting with Walter Washington and his wife. Sterling Tucker delivered a eulogy.

"While Julius may now be asleep," he said, "I somehow know he is sleeping mad." Tina spoke, and Hobby, and Tina's older son, and Julius's mother, who was eighty.

"Great men live," said Irma, ever a teacher, "so that there may be greater men."

Her listeners forgot that it was improper to stand and applaud in church.

Then Julius himself spoke, in a tape recording from a television documentary aired in 1972. "If there's a Maker, and I meet him," came the familiar twang, "and he's got any sense of justice and got any time, I'd like to talk to him."

The service ended with the congregation singing "When the Saints Go Marching In."

Afterward, Marion Barry arrived at the reception at Bardyl Tirana's house. Tina met him at the door.

"I can't stay long," he began.

He delivered a political speech to the mourners and then he left.

Tina arranged for Julius's ashes to be interred beside her son's, after a traditional service at her Episcopal church in Georgetown. Julius had told her how unwelcome he felt in this neighborhood, where he had once threatened to deliver rats. Now she would give him a home there.

Hobby and Jean had assented, but on the day of the interment they drove all over Georgetown and never found the church. Their mother suspected they did not want to.

Hobby had already announced, in newspaper interviews the day after his father's death, that he wished to fill the vacant seat on the council. The twenty-three members of the Statehood Party's central committee would select an interim successor. Julius had let it be known that he wanted Tina to replace him, though only "during the emotion of his illness," Hobby argued. "My father always wanted me to follow in his footsteps." His Afro had shrunk and his face was filling out. "I feel I have an obligation as his son. I know people are going to say, 'His father hasn't been dead twenty-four hours and look at him.' But he never felt that even though somebody passed, you would stop everything."

Two days after the memorial service, Tina announced that she would seek her husband's council seat, and Hobby announced his withdrawal. "It's very personal" was all he would say. Years later he explained that he had started to wonder why, other than financially, he would like the council any better than the school board. "Other parts you don't like about being an elected official," he reasoned, "you'll get in spades."

Tina would not commit herself to competing in the special election planned for July, which gave the central committee members pause in the course of their four-hour meeting at statehood activist Hilda Mason's house, out Sixteenth Street. Tina Hobson directed conservation programs at the Federal Energy Administration and was preparing to enter the new Department of Energy, proposed by the nuclear engineer in the White House. Why appoint someone for the interim who would not use it as an opportunity to keep the seat? Nor, in their minds, had Tina paid her dues. She was Julius's widow, but she had not spent years working for statehood.

There was something else, in the mostly black gathering, that was rarely put into words.

At last someone did, questioning the political appeal of a white candidate in a predominantly black city.

"That was the point when I got up and called a cab," Tina told a reporter later that night. Before leaving, she turned to a black friend and said, "Julius wouldn't put up with that c-r-a-p."

Hilda Mason was appointed. In July, at the polls, she narrowly defeated Barbara Sizemore.

In 1977, after eleven years away, Steve and Cokie Roberts moved back to Washington. From New York, Steve had been posted to Los

Angeles and then to Greece, as the bureau chief for the *Times*. Bangkok was to have been next. But he had tired of constantly traveling, of missing his children's lives, and he had always wanted to work in Washington.

Cokie was terrified. She liked the life of a foreign correspondent's wife, as a thirty-three-year-old mother of two. Going home, she feared, "was like being buried alive." She worried that Lindy might disapprove of watching her raise children in two religions, even though Cokie took them to mass every Sunday.

"This also was the only city in the world where she was Hale and Lindy Boggs's daughter," said Steve, "which had a lot of advantages but a lot of disadvantages." Would she be known as herself or as a daughter? If she succeeded, would it be obvious—to her, among others—that she had done it on her own?

Lindy invited them to stay with her on Bradley Boulevard. Lindy's mother had moved in with her after Hale disappeared, but she had died not long after. Lindy gave up her bedroom to Cokie and Steve and shared the four-poster bed in Cokie's girlhood room with her granddaughter, Becca. Lee moved into Tommy's old attic room. Lindy loved hearing children and laughter.

When Steve and Cokie went house hunting, the prices staggered them. Real estate had surged in eleven years, especially in the close-in suburbs, as the government's ever-expanding reach, its spreading presence in the nation's life, had drawn countless lawyers and lobbyists, bureaucrats and politicos, journalists and Beltway bandits to the capital and nearby. No longer could a *New York Times* reporter's salary support a house inside the Capital Beltway. Newcomers to the newspaper's Washington bureau all lived farther out.

Steve and Cokie thought about doing the same, except that the house on Bradley Boulevard was so clearly a good idea, from all sides. Lindy traveled to New Orleans almost every weekend. "It was immediately obvious to everybody," Steve said, "that it made more sense to sell us the house and move downtown to an apartment, where she could be much more accessible to the Hill and not have to worry about taking care of this big establishment out in the suburbs, which she didn't use very much."

She gave them a generous deal on the house, $235,000 for a comfortable three thousand square feet on a half-acre of land.

For Cokie and Steve, the advantages of buying the place on Bradley Boulevard were more than financial. They had dated in this house and married in its garden. The public schools nearby were good. Cokie considered the bathrooms and closets too small, but she had loved the house since she had first seen it that snowsuited day a quarter-century before.

"We cared very deeply about living in that house," Cokie said later, "and having that tradition carried on." Their children did, too. More than Cokie had realized, as they moved from place to place, Lee and Decca had regarded the porch-pillared house as their home.

They needed a second income for the mortgage. But for Cokie, finding a job was more than a matter of practicality. With the women's movement in full swing, even Cokie felt uncertain of her role. More than anywhere on earth, she believed, women in Washington who lacked a respectable job were not respected.

"The question of, 'What do you do, dear?'—if you don't have a fancy-sounding answer to that question, they're not very nice to you," Cokie said, meaning the people she might meet over dinner.

She had been interested in journalism since girlhood. In California she had coauthored with Steve an article on venereal disease for *The New York Times Magazine* and a homily on teenage pregnancy for *Seventeen*. At first she had done the research and interviewing and he had done the writing; later they both did. While in Greece she had freelanced for CBS News on the crisis in Cyprus and written articles for *The Nation*, *Commonweal*, and, on their return, a meaty if ponderous inquiry for *Atlantic Monthly* on the origins of Turkey's identity crisis. For a budding journalist, Steve was a mentor.

Still, the prospect of looking for a job scared her. At CBS, she said, "the bureau chief crisply told me that foreign stringer was one thing, Washington staffer quite another." With the other networks she got nowhere. She was crying herself to sleep.

The solution was Steve's. He introduced himself to Judith Miller, a new reporter at the next desk in the *Times* bureau, on L Street, and asked where she had worked.

National Public Radio, she said.

Steve replied, "What's that?"

Public radio had been an afterthought in the 1970 statute that created public television. *All Things Considered*, the radio network's flagship evening show of news and whimsy, went on the air the following year, broadcast from a basement studio on M Street. National Public Radio (NPR) could now reach 60 percent of the nation, mainly on FM stations, which a majority of new cars could tune in. Culturally, NPR was "a child of the '60s," as a chronicler grasped, which sought "to capture the energy and idealism of campus radio stations brimming with new voices and alternative ideas." A new form of radio was emerging, a throwback to the creativity of pretelevision days. Now that Frank Mankiewicz had taken charge, the onetime press secretary for Bobby Kennedy, the campaign manager for George McGovern, the veteran of Washington's political world was starting to make NPR financially and journalistically more serious—and increasingly noticed.

Judy Miller told Steve that her old job was open. "Call Nina Totenberg."

Steve carried Cokie's resume the short walk to NPR's offices on M Street, between Twentieth and Twenty-first, in an ugly brown building across from CBS's bunker of a Washington bureau. Nina met him on the sidewalk. Imposingly tall, with blunt features and an aggressive mind, the NPR reporter had been pushing the management to hire more women. In a news organization so young, paying salaries a third lower than elsewhere in broadcasting, women had an easier time. "You didn't have the old-boys' Establishment in place," Cokie explained later.

Nina mentioned Cokie to a colleague, Linda Wertheimer, who replied, "Is that Cokie Boggs?" They had not known each other at Wellesley, but everyone on campus was aware of the majority whip's daughter.

NPR kept Cokie on a weekly retainer for months, then hired her full-time in February 1978. She liked doing stories about schools—Lee was nine years old and Becca was seven—and the sorts of features that reflected the way she and millions of her listeners lived.

Cokie was reluctant, however, to cover Congress. "Not only was I back in my house," she fretted, "but I'd also be back in my second childhood home, the Capitol."

Yet as the 1978 election neared, Linda Wertheimer needed help covering the congressional campaigns. She suggested Cokie.

"And there it was," Cokie said later, "stuff I've known all my life, so it became silly *not* to do it."

She traveled and talked to voters, and she enjoyed it. (Their au pair had moved over from Greece.) She lent a hand on Capitol Hill and, after the election, joined Linda Wertheimer on the beat. Instinctively she understood how everything worked, and she knew people all over the Hill.

The House Speaker, for one: Carl Albert had retired, and Tip O'Neill, a family friend, had succeeded him. "I give you'se girls from NPR first shot at everything," he told them.

"I loved being on the Hill," Cokie said. "I loved it because I was good at it." As a girl she had been clumsy at sports, drawing, and singing. "I could do nothing kids were supposed to do," she said, "and suddenly, doing something as a grownup I was good at, of course you enjoy it."

Lindy's acceptance of Cokie's choices made everything easier. "I had left really as a kid and come back as a woman," Cokie remembered, "and my mother respected that."

Soon she was seen as something other than Cokie Boggs. She had truly gone home.

"Five years?" a guest exclaimed. "I can't believe it's been five years."

It had been, however. Gwen Cafritz had kept to her annual routine, of Florida in the wintertime and Spain or Monte Carlo in the summer. But she had stopped throwing parties. She had almost ceased seeing people, other than occasionally for a small dinner at home or at an embassy party or the Corcoran Ball.

But on this June evening in 1978, the quiet house on Foxhall Road came alive again. The guests on the terrace *ooh*ed and *ah*ed over the view from high ground. Many were habitués of Washington parties, and some were seldom seen except at Gwen's. Warren Burger looked the part of a chief justice, much as Warren Harding had mimicked a president. Barry Goldwater told a society reporter that he had been grateful to Gwen for twenty-six years.

"She was very kind to a fledgling Senator, who was really nobody at all, and we've been good friends ever since," the aging conservative said. "I've even square-danced with her, and I hate to square-dance."

Gwen was not dancing tonight. Minor surgery the week before left her sitting stiffly, her leg propped on a hassock, a pained look on her face. It was believed she had been ill, but nobody knew for sure. Her guests bowed slightly to greet her, at her level.

"Tonight I seem to be having trouble remembering names," she murmured.

Did she plan more parties?

"I hope not," she replied.

"Everyone at the party"—the next morning's *Post* mortem—"seemed to be having fun but the hostess."

The capital's social scene was deteriorating, even as Gwen's presence had faded. The old manners were dying; formality had collapsed, corroded by the indulgences of the 1960s. The wives of many high-powered men were high-powered themselves, holding demanding jobs that discouraged elaborate entertaining. For everyone, workdays had lengthened; cocktail parties that might once have started at five o'clock now did not begin until seven. The cost of cooks was more than most people could afford, and catered dinners lacked cachet.

The tone was set at the top. The peanut-farmer-turned-president had instructed the young Georgians he had taken to Washington to keep away from the capital's parties. "Black-tie dinners yielded to down-home barbecues, corn pone, and grits," a society raconteur wrote. Even Gwen might have thought twice about inviting a White House chief of staff who spewed amaretto down a blouse. *She* had been the vulgar one once.

She had grown short-tempered. Approaching Gwen was as dangerous as walking up to a rock star. Nobody was immune. If someone tried to light her cigarette, she would explode. Nobody knew what would set her off. She wanted to get into the car after her escort, from the curb side. She hated to be touched; summer and winter, she wore white gloves. Too vain to wear glasses, she was rude to people she could not see. A scotch or two before lunch fueled her reactions, though the decanter in the living room was kept full to the neck, for appearances' sake. She would snap at anyone who crossed her. "Bitch," she might snarl, or "bastard."

"I don't remember *you* being invited," she once said to a guest.

Only one of her escorts could tap her on the hand and calm her down.

She disparaged her sons to her friends for failing in marriage and accomplishing too little in business, and she referred to her late husband as a "little Jewish contractor," or words to that effect.

In fact, she no longer called herself a Jew. In 1971 she had told a reporter that she had attended synagogue with Morris twice a year, "but he never asked me to join his faith." She had begun to refer to herself as a Presbyterian. Her claim was startling though not without foundation. As a girl in anti-Semitic Budapest, her family had attended the Hungarian Reformed Church, a cousin of the Presbyterians.

In 1970, the onetime president of a synagogue's sisterhood volunteered a reaffirmation of Presbyterian faith and formally joined the National Presbyterian Church. The stark and stylish limestone edifice and tower out on Nebraska Avenue had supplanted, just a year earlier, the stone Romanesque church downtown on Connecticut Avenue.

"It's not just any Presbyterian church," Calvin pointed out—"it's the *National* Presbyterian Church. If you're going to do it, you want to go with the best."

In truth it was a local church that, located in the capital, had taken a national name. But Bill Rogers belonged, as had President Eisenhower, whose grandson had wed President Nixon's daughter in its sanctuary. Most Sundays found Gwen Cafritz in church.

"Mother, if you go on the Ways and Means Committee, you're wiping out my business."

Tommy Boggs pleaded with the gentlewoman from Louisiana, who had become a serious member of Congress, not merely a widow. "I don't care about appropriations," he said, alluding to the committee she was already on. "My clients care about taxes." A well-placed comma in the tax code could mean millions of dollars to a corporation. Trying to gain his mother's vote on Ways and Means would cause too much whispering and, for Lindy, a great deal of discomfort.

The Speaker had offered Lindy the loveliest of choices. When Otto Passman of Louisiana had lost his bid for a sixteenth term in the House in 1976, Louisiana's customary seat on the Appropriations Committee became Lindy's. Two years later, when Joe D. Waggonner retired, the Louisiana seat on Ways and Means he had inherited from Hale fell vacant. Hale had loved Ways and Means, with its grip on every American's financial well-being. Its role within the House as the Democrats' committee on committees had disappeared in the reforms that followed Watergate, but it still wielded the most power of any congressional committee.

Which did Lindy prefer?

Tommy's druthers aside, giving money away suited Lindy more than raising it. The Appropriations Committee was a collegial place, with a culture that valued accommodation and compromise. When it came to dollars and cents, unlike policy or right and wrong, any difference could be split.

"It was you-scratch-my-back-I'll-scratch-yours," Lindy said. "Every once in a while, you had to beg for something."

"Everybody came out a winner," her legislative director noted—"a perfect place for Lindy." The staff made her a footstool for her seat on the dais because her feet did not reach the floor.

More than most committees, Appropriations was an old boys' club, dominated by southerners and big-city machine Democrats.

As an old girl, one of three among the fifty-five committee members, and only the sixth ever, Lindy knew how to make her way with the boys. Jamie Whitten, the courtly Mississippian who became the chairman of Appropriations in 1979, had lived a couple of blocks away from the Boggses' house, on Stephenson Place.

"People ask me why Lindy Boggs can get anything she wants out of me," the chairman once said, "and I tell them, 'She's just like my wife, Rebecca. She makes me feel so *good* about it, whatever she wants.'"

That Lindy was cautious in what she wanted made her mission simpler. "I would never ask another member to do something I didn't think was right for him or her," she said. This restriction necessarily limited what she asked of them.

She joined two Appropriations subcommittees, on housing and on energy and water. Mainly she furthered the interests of her constituencies, whether for flood insurance or rent subsidies for the poor or housing for the elderly or money for exotic forms of energy. No one else, she boasted later, had ever eaten a hamburger cooked with electricity generated by the temperature difference between layers of seawater.

As the only Democratic woman on either subcommittee, Lindy wielded her influence in another way. Every year, when the head of any agency testified before her, she made a point of inquiring about progress in hiring and promoting women. Accordingly, Cabinet secretaries made sure to arrange for women to sit behind them. She directed money to women's shelters and rape-crisis centers, in the hope of reducing the need for abortions, and also made sure that money went to the space shuttle (a Louisiana plant manufactured the external tanks), the Smithsonian, and historic preservation.

Nobody got mad.

Some of what she wanted was personal. As Hubert Humphrey was dying of cancer, he asked friends each to take on one of his zillion projects. He told Lindy that he hoped the Smithsonian would acquire the Museum of African Art, located in a row house once occupied by Frederick Douglass on Capitol Hill, and move it to the Mall.

"Could I pass it off to you?" he said.

"Of course."

She introduced the legislation and saw it through to enactment.

She also made a project of Congressional Cemetery, even before she had a personal reason to do so.

The capital's oldest cemetery was situated by the Anacostia shore. It was the final resting place for veterans of the Revolutionary War and the wars that followed, and also for George Washington's secretary, Madison's vice president, Lincoln's valet, Mathew Brady, John Philip Sousa, Civil War generals, three librarians of Congress, ten mayors of Washington, and, more recently, J. Edgar Hoover. It was also the next-to-last resting place of many a nineteenth-century lawmaker who expired in a sweltering Washington summer and could not be shipped home unspoiled until fall. In place of each vacated grave was built a cenotaph, an empty tomb of three-quarters size, a cube on a pedestal, with a heavenward cupola. Row upon row of cenotaphs remembered the now-forgotten men who had seemed so important in their day. The cemetery had fallen into disrepair, and Lindy undertook its restoration as a Bicentennial project.

To show its gratitude to Lindy, the Congressional Cemetery suggested a cenotaph for Hale. None had been made for more than a century. Lindy asked that it also be made for Nick Begich, and she arranged to use the old stone staircases removed from the East Front of the Capitol (when it was extended in 1960) and left in Rock Creek Park.

In front of a calm clearing, at the edge of a checkerboard field of cenotaphs, a new one arose. Hale Boggs would be forever remembered an eavesdrop away from J. Edgar Hoover's thin tombstone. At last Lindy had a place to leave flowers for her husband on All Saints' Day.

Later, Tommy and Cokie bought cemetery plots for their own families beside Hale. Lindy, however, planned to be buried back home in Louisiana, beside her two-day-old son.

Tommy and Cokie had become Washingtonians. Lindy never would.

Pershing had lived there, as had William Howard Taft after he was president and before he became chief justice. No apartment building in Washington gloried in such ornamental detail. On the exterior at 2029 Connecticut Avenue, less than two blocks north of the old Temple Heights lot, salamanders and loving cups and snippets of shields and flowery vines engraved the terra-cotta that framed the lower windows and the elaborately porched entrances. The twenty-three apartments on seven floors, many as spacious as a sizable house, featured parquet floors, intricate plasterwork, and Corinthian columns. Yet they were sixty-one years old, with antique appliances and a frayed grandeur.

How could Conrad Cafritz resist?

He had inherited his father's ambition but shared his mother's sensibility. Morris's sense of architectural taste was blunt or nonexistent; not a single building of his was bound to be remembered. Conrad, however, had style. Of the three sons, he was probably the most like Gwen, in her wit and her spleen. He had inherited her dark looks, her acerbic sense of humor, her love of gossip, her sarcasm. He was considered the smartest of the three—Yale had followed Saint Albans—but also the hardest to get along with. Stories abounded of Conrad's chewing on his tie in business negotiations, ordering someone else's secretary to hang up on an important phone call, or oscillating between "mumbling" (in a journalist's description) and "a manic monologue." He spoke softly so that others would strain to listen or faster than anyone could follow.

Rare was the youngest child who became the repository of a family's continuing hopes, but Conrad saw himself as the son who should live up to his father's achievements.

He had worked for his father from age twenty-three and had ventured out on his own around 1974, as the inheritance from his father became his. For a dozen years, he and Carter, the middle son, had worked together on real estate. Carter was more affable than Conrad and had his own sharp sense of humor. As a teenager he had sent Gwen a Mother's Day gift of a Mickey Spillane mystery—as a speed reader, she could finish two detective novels in a night—and the *Kinsey Report on the Sexual Activities of the Human Female*. He enjoyed skin diving and electronics and betrayed less of a gnawing need for success. He despised publicity. In real estate, Carter let his younger brother, at least publicly, take the lead.

They operated secretively, through limited partnerships. Conrad became the public face for a seventy-two-unit apartment house of moderate rents on an undesirable stretch of Sixteenth Street, not far from their father's first construction. Next were the moderately priced, single-family homes in the Virginia exurbs of Prince William County, on land Morris had presciently purchased in 1960.

More than anything, they rode the decade's wave of condominium conversions. At a time of rising costs and rocketing interest rates, the city's rent controls drove landlords into a funk. It was profitable to convert a four-hundred-dollar-a-month apartment into a ninety-nine-thousand-dollar sale. The rental market lost hundreds of apartments month by month, from gritty buildings to the tasteful opulence of 2029 Connecticut Avenue.

This was hard on tenants forced to buy or move. In the three buildings Conrad converted along Connecticut Avenue, all went smoothly. But in two others nearby, on Van Ness, the tenants rebelled when Conrad notified them that his firm would be acquiring the buildings and turning them into cooperatives; they moved to buy the buildings themselves. He also encountered resistance in Foggy Bottom, when he tried to convert a nine-story apartment house on Twenty-fifth Street into a residential hotel for visiting consultants or business executives. The refusal by some tenants to move out ("I'm bound and determined to stay in The Bottom") reached the newspapers.

"Many people benefit from condominium conversion," Conrad argued in a *Post* op-ed, as the pressure mounted on politicians to favor the tenants over the developers and impose a moratorium. "New capital investment effectively recycles these properties for another 10 to 20 years."

Success in real estate required not only financial wherewithal, sound judgment, an architectural fluency, and a pleasure in playing rough, but political connections. What else, after all, was the teetering balance of competing interests—between tenant and developer, black and white, neighbor and neighbor—than the business of politics?

Conrad and Peggy loved playing politics. Peggy had always been politically involved. She had handed out pamphlets for Adlai Stevenson, "and my dad always told me, 'Giving isn't giving unless it hurts.'" For Conrad, having money to donate to candidates and causes made sure his voice was heard when he wished. Politics was fun as well as important and offered a means of socializing.

"He'll go to the opening of an envelope," said Peggy. "He's very gregarious . . . and I don't think he likes to be alone."

As the city contemplated its second mayoral election, in 1978, Conrad and Peggy had a candidate. Walter Washington, running for reelection, represented the city's Old Guard—the black ministers, the civil rights establishment, the labor unions. Sterling Tucker was considered his leading opponent, even the front-runner, as the favorite of the middle classes, black and white. They admired his businesslike, buttoned-down demeanor.

Neither was hip or stylish. But the third major candidate was. Though Marion Barry had given up his dashikis for business suits, his reputation as a street activist scared the staid of every race. He was an insurgent from the South, as Julius Hobson had been, unnerving to the city's Establishment, black and white. Barry, much as Julius had, found his core support among white liberals and angry young blacks, but he was more adaptable, adept at multiple faces. Having persuaded Sterling Tucker to appoint him as chairman of the council's finance committee, he used the position to court the city's business leaders, who by nature understood that to get something they must give in return.

For any developer in pursuit of political access, "the importance of being important is of far more concern than theory, program, policy, or philosophy," an observer of the city's business and politics explained.

With the *Post*'s endorsement, Barry's plurality in white neighborhoods—in Ward Three and on Capitol Hill—produced a narrow, stunning victory.

Conrad merited a license plate numbered 120, six lower than the one awarded to John Sirica, his father's old friend, who, as a federal judge, had assured an inquiry into the scandal that started at the Watergate. A rumor that reached "The Ear" column in *The Evening Star* that Conrad "will head the future D.C. housing finance agency" never panned out. Peggy fared better. She was named to the mayor-elect's transition team and then, at thirty-three years old, to the chairmanship of the D.C. Commission on the Arts and Humanities.

Her plan was to abolish the commission and convert it into a mayoral Office of Cultural Affairs. In this she failed. But the grants to artists and organizations almost doubled, furnishing the mayor with klieg-lighted press conferences, and then nearly doubled again. Complaints of Peggy's "field marshal brusqueness" turned into respect.

When the new mayor became a father, he and his third wife named Peggy Christopher's godmother. "It was a very spur-of-the-moment thing," she said later. "I was never close to them on a personal basis."

Her prominence in D.C. drew attention around Washington. She had been considered a dark-horse candidate for the chairmanship of the National Endowment of the Arts. ("Dark—YES! Horse—No!" she wrote to The Evening Star.) When President Carter gave his first state dinner for an African leader, Peggy took Conrad.

The opportunities were more than social or political. In 1979, she joined a group of black professionals to purchase radio station WOL, whose DJs had popularized D.C. as "Chocolate City." The next year she applied to the Federal Communications Commission to operate channel fourteen, in a group that included a self-assured black politico, Ron Brown, who was the deputy campaign manager for Ted Kennedy's audacious challenge to the president's renomination.

Mixing business and politics naturally produced complications. "I have never had a conversation with Marion Barry about condominiums or rent control," Peggy responded to the inevitable accusations. "Never!"

Tommy Boggs knew that his client had nary a chance at the Federal Trade Commission (FTC). The do-gooding regulatory agency was contemplating a ban on commercials for sugary foods that would prevent them from being aired on television shows meant for children. On behalf of Mars Inc., the maker of M&Ms and Milky Ways, he needed to block it.

He had known the president's—the then-governor's—closest aides since the 1972 campaign, when Tommy was Ed Muskie's man in Georgia. He was buddies now with Hamilton Jordan, the president's good ol' boy chief of staff. But he also understood that a White

House that was worried about a liberal challenge for renomination from the last Kennedy brother would not interfere with the independent FTC, even if it could.

Once upon a time, the art of lobbying meant taking a lawmaker to the racetrack and plying him with liquor or worse. Clark Clifford had worked his magic in a phone call. Tommy was more systematic. Washington, after all, had changed. The Watergate scandal had prompted the election to Congress of scads of new Democrats who undermined the seniority system, enacted government-in-the-sunshine laws, and constructed a campaign finance system that reduced the power of the few. No longer did a handful of like-minded men run the government. The pressure points, for a lobbyist, had multiplied.

The capital had long hosted only two varieties of law firms—the big ones, which did everything, and the small specialty firms. "The new type of Washington firm," Tommy explained to a business magazine's reporter, "looks at the problem and decides how to attack it," whether by litigation or legislation or an administrative remedy—or something less direct.

Surely an editorial in the *Washington Post* would help in thwarting the FTC. Few readers bothered with newspaper editorials, but the right ones, the political insiders who conversed with legislators day to day, did. The *Post*'s liberal reputation, though it exceeded the facts, would lend a sort of Nixon-to-China power to a denunciation of a liberal commission's act. The *Post*'s business interests aligned with those of Tommy's client, for the newspaper's four television stations in other cities stood to lose revenue if the FTC exiled Tony the Tiger from Saturday morning cartoons. But Tommy also understood the quandary in trying to persuade the self-important newspaper to use its editorial page to promote its financial self-interest—"in the sense that they consider themselves holier-than-thou," he said.

He sent material supporting his client's case over to Meg Greenfield, the editorial page editor. Later he said he could not remember whether he had also phoned her or not. He could not have imagined a better result. The editorial sounded like Meg Greenfield, colloquial yet morally severe. Its headline—"The FTC as National Nanny"—became the tagline for the opponents' campaign. "The proposal, in reality, is designed to protect children from the weaknesses of their parents—and the parents from the wailing insistence of their children," the editorial noted, never disclosing the *Post*'s corporate interest. "It is not a proper role of government."

An editorial alone could not undo the FTC. No court would hear a challenge until the commission acted, and Congress could not block a regulation yet to be promulgated. No one had thought before of going to Congress on a regulatory issue. This was Tommy's moment of insight. Legislating is not permitted on an appropriations bill, but "you can say thou shalt not spend," he explained. For the first time, Congress passed an appropriations rider that barred an agency from spending money to approve a regulation.

"Sort of started a trend," Tommy said years later with a laugh.

As power dispersed within the government, as within an ever-more-open society, the checks and balances of the founding fathers had, in effect, metastasized. Everywhere, deference was dying. The discipline of political parties was fading as the power of committee barons shrank. First Vietnam, then Watergate, had ruined the credibility of politicians. As the news media magnified the personalities in power, familiarity bred contempt. A president who walked in the inaugural parade and carried his own garment bag seemed smaller than life.

Increasingly, a capital once ruled by giants was subject to the tethers of Lilliputians. Year by year, it was becoming harder to accomplish anything in Washington, and easier to stand in the way.

This trend made Tommy's task harder when Chrysler Corporation came calling. The oil shock that followed the 1979 revolution in Iran ruined the market for gas-guzzling cars and left the weakest of the Big Three automakers sliding toward bankruptcy and, not surprisingly, looking to Washington for rescue. When a Chrysler vice president flew into the capital to hire a lobbyist, he wanted the best. The prominence of Chrysler's marine division in the Boating Industry Association led him to Tommy Boggs.

Tommy invited the Chrysler vice president and the company's

chairman, John Riccardo, for the weekend to his farmhouse on Maryland's Eastern Shore, where the marshland and water reminded him of Louisiana. Tommy and the men from Chrysler talked for hours about the company's problems and its prospects in Washington. The lobbyist's genial demeanor and his easy confidence that he understood Washington's customs and hidden byways were comforting to businessmen, for whom the capital was exotic terrain.

Tommy acquired a client.

The strategic insight to cast the proposed Chrysler bailout as an issue of jobs was supplied by Doug Fraser, the United Auto Workers president. Tommy's thought was to mobilize the company's four thousand suppliers—of steel, rubber, windshields, brakes—and almost as many Chrysler dealers as the primary lobbying force, to lean on lawmakers from every corner of the nation. The automaker hired Timmons and Company, a lobbying firm run by congressional liaisons for the previous two presidents, to approach the Republicans on Capitol Hill, while Tommy concentrated on the Democrats. A dozen lawyers at Patton, Boggs & Blow labored full-time.

Tommy also courted the administration on behalf of a bailout—"He conned them, convinced them," according to Tom Korologos, a principal at Timmons. Tommy had performed favors for the White House, lobbying on his own time for the Panama Canal and SALT II treaties and (ironically, given his lobbying for clients' tax breaks) serving on President Carter's Citizens' Tax Reform Committee. He highlighted the political dangers to the president's reelection of Chrysler layoffs in Michigan and Missouri, and he discerned in his meeting with a skeptical Treasury secretary a subtle shift in position, still opposed to a bailout based on manipulating tax rules but not necessarily opposed to a loan guarantee.

One of the conditions was John Riccardo's resignation, as an act of contrition for Chrysler's tailspin. Tommy was escorting his successor, Lee Iacocca, on his first lobbying visit to the Capitol when, suddenly, a floor below the Rotunda, the new chairman collapsed.

When he regained consciousness, Tommy said to him, "Can you walk?"

"I can walk."

The Capitol physician's office was fifty yards away. "The Capitol physician was at lunch," Tommy recounted, "so we got a decent doctor," who diagnosed a problem with the inner ear.

Just before Christmas, when Congress passed the largest loan guarantee in American history, Patton Boggs's reputation was made.

Ten

REAGAN

The Monday morning after the most conservative president in more than a half-century took office, the cocky young aide-de-camp to the new energy secretary summoned Tina Hobson out of a meeting.

Short, wiry Rock Reiser had left South Carolina with the unlikely secretary, an oral surgeon who had found himself governor and now the head of a young department the new president had promised to abolish. Outside the secretary's seventh-floor office, in the long, squat Forrestal Building on Independence Avenue, Rock Reiser confronted Tina, the director of the Office of Consumer Affairs.

The secretary was upset, he told her, about a meeting her office had cosponsored over the weekend in Des Moines, and a Republican senator had complained about a similar session scheduled for Denver. Tina explained about the series of ten regional meetings (the result of a demonstration in front of Forrestal) intended to solicit the views of poor people about energy.

"Things are going to change around here," Rock Reiser said. He instructed her to terminate the grant "immediately, if not sooner."

She asked whether the Department of Energy (DOE) might send a representative to the meeting in Denver. He suggested sending an "operative" instead.

"What is an operative?" she said.

"These are public meetings, aren't they?"

"Yes."

"Well, you know, just send somebody with a down jacket and jeans." Then he changed his mind—a flannel shirt. A down jacket was too fancy.

"You mean you want to send an unidentified DOE person?" She asked him three times, to make certain.

As a member of the Senior Executive Service, which President Carter had begun for the government's top-ranked civil servants, Tina knew how to fight back. She phoned the friendly deputy director of the department's recently disbanded transition team, who phoned an energy administrator in South Carolina, who phoned Rock Reiser. A conference call later, the order was withdrawn.

Tina already had a reputation within the bureaucracy for being prickly. Even with the Democrats in power, she and her staff had threatened to quit if proposed budget cuts went through. She had made enemies.

Four days after a newsletter published an account of her squabble with Rock Reiser, Tina Hobson got the word. She was to be "detailed"—that is, temporarily transferred—to the position of deputy director in an office about to be abolished, a rare stratagem by which a bureaucrat might be cast out of government.

Tina's friends found a sympathetic ear in Pat Schroeder, the languorous liberal from Colorado, the chairwoman of the House subcommittee on civil service. A hearing was scheduled within days—"my own personal hearing up on the Hill," Tina said.

"The Department of Energy's shoddy treatment of Tina Hobson," the congresswoman began, "reveals apparent violations of four laws." A bureaucrat of Tina's rank could not be moved unwillingly within an administration's first 120 days.

The hearing started at ten in the morning. By ten thirty the department caved in. Two weeks later Rock Reiser resigned.

Then after 120 days, Tina was transferred again and, two years later, was subjected to a "reduction-in-force"—that is, fired—as part of the president's stubborn, doomed effort to shrink the government.

She was forced out six months before she was to reach twenty years of government service, with its promise of a full pension.

She filed a lawsuit and settled for six months' service and legal fees.

"She has her own kind of radicalism," Julius had said of her, "which is not the same as mine."

Julius's first wife was having no easier a time. Carol now worked in the two-year-old Department of Education, also targeted for extinction. She was the executive director of a presidential commission on higher education for blacks, which developed statistics that showed black enrollment increased as the government spent more on student aid. For an administration intent on starving domestic spending, this was the wrong conclusion, and Carol was told to credit other factors whenever she addressed educators. Higher-ups reviewed her speeches, but in answering questions she could say whatever she thought.

For this she was chastised.

"Carol, you've got to remember who pays your check," a colleague told her.

"My check is from the federal government."

When the commission calculated that the government spent more on blacks in prison than in schools, she was told that its data would no longer be published. She used the Freedom of Information Act to deliver the statistics to sympathizers who requested them.

This was how Carol was labeled a troublemaker and moved to a job in which she had nothing to do.

So she found something. She had already served as the branch chief for surveys of elementary and secondary schools and had supervised education programs for minority groups and women. On her own she collected information on programs, governmental and otherwise, that could help minorities and women pay for college, which she photocopied and sent to anyone who asked.

"So after a while," Carol recounted, "they decided to publish it, and it became a best-seller."

Her go-between with the assistant secretary put her in charge of three programs to help poor and minority children pay for college. She kept track of $179 million in annual spending using a pocket calculator she had purchased herself. The stress she felt only increased.

On a trip to Santa Fe in the fall of 1985, she entered a meeting and, once seated, passed out. In the ambulance, the paramedics were unable to measure a blood pressure. "Almost like I had gone into a coma," she said later.

A man from the regional office followed her to the hospital.

"Carol, I wouldn't have a job that made me sick," he said.

She returned to Washington and retired, just short of her forty-year mark.

Lindy Boggs had found it hard to leave Bradley Boulevard, with its quarter-century of memories and Hale's clothes still hanging in the closet. But it was obvious she had to—Cokie dearly loved her mother but wanted a house of her own—and "I knew she wanted to," said Tommy's sweet but businesslike wife, Barbara, who had stepped in. She knew a friend of a friend who lived in the magnificent old building at 2029 Connecticut Avenue, where the condominiums were spacious enough for Lindy's treasures.

Conrad Cafritz had preserved the meticulous detail inside each apartment, including the ornate crown molding and the call box in the kitchen for bells to summon the servants. He had left the kitchens and the bathrooms alone, as too expensive to renovate, and had sold the condominiums as is, for between $150,000 and $240,000.

George McGovern and his wife had just purchased an apartment on the top floor, at the rear, when Lindy approached him. The senator from South Dakota had served in the House with Hale, and Lindy considered him a dear friend. She had been making telephone calls for his presidential campaign when Hale had tried to phone her from Anchorage.

Lindy had never asked them for a favor before.

"George, I want it that badly," she said. "Why don't you see if the large front room is available?" Lindy suggested that the huge apartment facing Connecticut Avenue, where Arthur Krock of the *New York Times* had lived for four decades, would be a better place for the McGoverns to entertain their grandchildren.

"I just couldn't say no," McGovern recounted. "We could adjust."

The McGoverns sold the apartment to Lindy for what they had paid. Lindy's memory was that the McGoverns preferred the front apartment.

Within two or three years after the building's conversion was complete, the ceilings in several apartments collapsed. Lindy and the McGoverns were spared. But when complaints to the developer produced no response, the condominium association took Conrad to court in February 1981, asking for three million dollars.

The owners had found Conrad difficult to deal with, but the lawsuit was settled before it went to trial. Conrad and his investors assumed the owners' legal fees and paid to fix the collapsed ceilings and to test the others for signs of sagging.

Lindy never really liked the apartment. But it sufficed. Even the smaller, two-bedroom apartment, with a generous foyer and high ceilings, was spacious enough for entertaining. She had room for her Oriental rugs, a vast dining table, antique furniture, her awards. The baby grand piano, which had once belonged to the late Justice Hugo Black, held photographs of her family and every president since FDR.

The piano was a gift from Tommy Corcoran. Lindy had dated John Warner, who had run the Bicentennial Commission, before he took up with Elizabeth Taylor, and she dated old friends in New Orleans, but she and Tommy Corcoran had grown especially close. At day's end, the canny accordion-playing leprechaun would go to her office in Longworth and patiently wait for her—"like a stage-door Johnny," said one of her aides—as she signed letters, returned phone calls, and dressed to go out.

Did she ever consider remarrying? "Occasionally," she said. "Not really." Tommy Corcoran died in December 1981.

Another beau, Herman Kohlmeyer, a bon vivant and stockbroker in New Orleans, flew to Washington early in the new presidency with a political request. He called Lindy out of a congressional hearing and made his case, as other businessmen had, that she vote with President Reagan to cut taxes and domestic spending. As a southern Democrat she was considered a swing vote.

Lindy listened and replied, "No, I'm not going to do that." To Lindy, the government's social programs mattered, so that women could avoid abortions and minorities might lift themselves up. Speaker Tip O'Neill, the Republican president's chief adversary, sent Lindy a pin that denoted 187, the number of Democrats who voted no. She showed what columnist George Will described as "austere disapproval" for the Gramm-Rudman mechanism that authorized across-the-board budget cuts, because by overriding the discretion of lawmakers it undermined democracy.

She found herself torn over the issue of a nuclear freeze. She believed in a strong military, and defense contractors dotted her congressional district. And yet when the nuns would go to lobby Lindy, to ask her how she could possibly support the Trident missile, what could she say? "It's very hard to say 'no' to a nun," said an aide, "especially nuns of the order that taught her when she was a girl." She voted their way.

Lindy had become an admired senior member of the Appropriations Committee, shrewd enough to play the angles; sometimes the Democratic majority had to wheedle and beg to gain her vote. She was widely respected within the House, so much so that when Congress celebrated the bicentennial of the Constitution, at a session in Philadelphia, Lindy was chosen unanimously by her colleagues to preside in George Washington's Rising Sun chair. Her feet did not reach the floor.

"Hey, Mamma, you've got the best scam going," her daughter Barbara told her. "Everything is bound to be two hundred years old sometime."

The newspaper photographs of the Capitol used as the backdrop were blown up so big that when the cameras rolled, the dots started to swim—the moiré effect, in television jargon. Viewers found it distracting, but the meager budget of public television meant that months would pass before Paul Duke, the host of *The Lawmakers*, could wear patterned ties again.

The Walter Cronkite of public television was anything but flamboyant, with his receding gray hair, plain eyeglasses, and wry smile. He finished his lengthy report, one night in June 1981, on the congressional tug-of-war over the president's push to slash taxes. Then he conversed with his correspondent, Cokie Roberts.

"I think, frankly, that that push can win," she said. "There are plenty of people in Congress who will do anything the President says right now." Her voice had a lazy lilt, as if she sidled up to her insights, yet something steely lay beneath.

"One of the things that a lot of Democrats don't understand right now," said Paul Duke, "is why the White House is so rigid on the big tax cut."

"The White House just insisted on this third year," Cokie replied, "and a lot of people are saying now that they insisted because they want to write into law a deficit that's so large that Congress will be forced to cut all of the social programs in the years to come."

She wore hoop earrings and had cut her hair short. Hired experts had advised it. Short hair meant fewer bad-hair days, and it dramatized Cokie's blue-gray, almond-shaped eyes. Cokie had raised no objection. Her shoulder-length brown hair "was always pretty horrible," she recalled. "Getting rid of it was okay."

The point of "all that looks stuff on television," as she characterized it later, was that viewers not be distracted.

The weekly half-hour show had been on the air for six months, from a warehouse in Arlington. The Greater Washington Educational Television Association had founded WETA twenty years before, broadcast originally from a classroom at Arlington's Yorktown High School. Channel twenty-six hoped to make itself a flagship station for public television, covering the capital, though at the D.C. Arts and Humanities Commission, Peggy Cooper objected to its location outside the city.

The idea behind *The Lawmakers* was to make Congress understandable, even entertaining. Any president ruled the airways and monopolized the public's mind, and especially this one, so attentive to the visual image, schooled in the movie business and then in TV. Yet the nation's legislature was a richer, messier, often sillier story— democracy on display, in all its exuberance and pettiness—one that the commercial networks mostly ignored. The Thursday night show, after Congress's workweek ended, examined in depth what the lawmakers had done or left undone. It might devote seven or eight minutes to a congressional debate that on NBC, where Paul Duke had worked, would merit a minute and a half.

WETA had tested the show the previous year using Paul Duke alone, but it needed something. The producer, Linda Winslow, was watching *Bill Moyers' Journal* on public television one night when Cokie appeared to report on the 1980 congressional elections. She was well-spoken and knowledgeable. The producer did not know whose daughter she was. A phone call to the news director at NPR found a radio network eager to dabble in television, for morale's sake.

Might WETA be interested in borrowing Linda Wertheimer, too? Yes.

For Cokie, going on *The Lawmakers* while continuing to report for NPR meant covering Congress full-time. She was intrigued: This was television, the medium of the age. Radio and television offered different ways to tell a story—both of them more compelling, she believed, than print.

Thus she returned to the other village of her childhood. The lady in the Senate carryout still cooked what Cokie judged the city's best barbecue. She rediscovered the sense of family among old-timers on the Hill—Sally, the funny Irish lady who ran the House restaurant, and John, the old black fellow in the post office, "people who can tell you stories about the institutions of Washington that are just different than you'd get from reading the paper."

Walter Little, her coconspirator in repairing the cake at her parents' first garden party, called to her from outside the door at Ways and Means, "Baby—I mean, Miss Baby." When Cokie learned which lawmakers had secreted themselves inside the room to decide the fate of the president's tax bill, she deduced the topic under discussion and scooped her competitors. Nobody could figure out how she knew.

Cokie was coached on reading scripts for television, on narrating, on using a TelePrompTer. She was considered a skilled writer and storyteller, in her distinctively nasal yet melodic alto. The show interspersed its magazine-style reports with conversations between the show's correspondents, leisurely interviews with lawmakers, and segments of actual debate. When the House voted on the president's re-molded budget on a Thursday night, the ten o'clock show carried it live. The critics liked *The Lawmakers* ("Congress—A Whale of a Show," said the *New York Times*) and teachers used it to explain how the government works. Two hundred stations aired it, and attention-hungry lawmakers lined up for interviews.

The financing of public television was perennially shaky, however. The defense contractors Lockheed and LTV, corporate sponsors for *The Lawmakers*, announced near the end of 1983 that they would continue to donate, but no more than $250,000 and $150,000, respectively; that left the show one million dollars short. The program limped into the following June, then expired.

Linda Winslow had already moved to the *McNeill-Lehrer News-Hour*, also on PBS, and Cokie followed, to cover Congress. This required little more reporting than she was already doing for NPR.

But she was frustrated at stepping back from the news—analyzing it, not chasing it. In the midst of a lengthy interview with Bob Dole, the Senate majority leader, he disclosed that he now favored a treaty on the International Monetary Fund.

She phoned an editor at *McNeill-Lehrer*. "This is news—you can break the story."

"It's not what the wires are saying."

"I actually didn't have a little Bob Dole doll there that I manipulated and had him say it. You can look at the tape and see him say it yourself."

The scoop was declined, and so she broadcast the story on NPR. She understood that *McNeill-Lehrer* was not the place for her.

NPR was. She had become fast friends with Linda Wertheimer and Nina Totenberg—the Troika, they were dubbed. The Robertses and the Wertheimers (Fred was the president of Common Cause) started going to dinner every Saturday at the casual and inexpensive Pines of Rome, in Bethesda, and then to a movie.

Cokie also loved NPR's audience. "It's an audience that listens," she said. "It's an influential audience, but also a young audience."

And it was growing. NPR's audience doubled over the decade, to more than seven million. (Eventually, more people listened to the radio network's *Morning Edition* than watched the three commercial TV networks' morning news shows combined.) The more Americans who relied on NPR for their news, the more straightforward and no-nonsense it needed to be.

This was one camp's argument, at any rate, in the culture war that raged within NPR. The outcome was probably inevitable. As the network's popularity grew, along with its need for corporate donors, its affinity for alternative radio faded. The liberal radio network came within minutes of going off the air in 1983, as a conservative admin-istration whacked at federal subsidies in the budget.

Cokie's loyalty was clear. She was a daughter of the Establish-ment, not a rebel. "I did not go to Woodstock, and I'm the right age," she explained later. "I felt very strongly, and continue to feel very strongly, that NPR should not be the Woodstock Network."

NPR was heavy with office politics, and the Troika successfully lobbied the management to name Linda Wertheimer as a cohost of *All Things Considered*, after Lynn Neary had been told that the job was hers. The three formidable young women were accomplished at the inside game—and no wonder. They were married, respectively, to the leader of a quarter-million middle-class reformers, a former sena-tor, and a *New York Times* reporter who owned a pile of Harvard sweatshirts.

For the first time in their married life Steve Roberts realized, with reluctance, that Cokie's job was comparable to his. The first time her career took precedence was in 1979, after the nuclear accident at Three Mile Island. Cokie rushed off to Pennsylvania, and when Steve's editor asked him to go, he refused—so that his children would not have both parents away and conceivably at risk.

Their careers were melding. They coauthored an article in *The New York Times Magazine* about the 1980 election, Cokie shouting over the phone from the West Coast about cutting the story that Steve had in galleys at home. Now that they both covered Congress, they commuted together and often pooled what they knew.

"Actually our bosses got two for the price of one," Cokie said.

They made it to most of the children's events, and they insisted—"out of the best of intentions," said Cokie—on dinner together as a family every night. Night after night, as their workday grew ever longer, Cokie and Steve would phone from the Hill, then phone again, while their children waited at home, much as Cokie and her siblings had once waited.

Shortly after the 1980 election, which had been a disaster for the Democrats at both ends of Pennsylvania Avenue, Ted Kennedy had telephoned Tommy Boggs. Someone on the senator's staff needed a job. Ron Brown had been promised the position of chief counsel for Kennedy's Judiciary Committee, as yet another racial first for the socially polished thirty-nine-year-old. But the Republicans' shocking seizure of the Senate, for the first time since 1954, had left him stranded.

Ron Brown had the shrewdness, self-confidence, and Rolodex of a successful lawyer-lobbyist. He and Tommy hit it off. Both had been raised in a household that served as the center of their world—in Brown's case, as the manager's son in Harlem's fanciest hotel, a home away from home for black entertainers, writers, gangsters, and politicians.

"We were brought up in public," Tommy said later, "both with exposure to all sorts of people . . . both schooled in raising money for Democrats before we could even count."

Both men had had a strong father they saw as a role model, and both were gregarious and complicated, with parts of themselves held in reserve. They had similar tastes—"copying each other as we made some money," Tommy said, "with Gucci loafers, sports cars, Hartman luggage. It would make me mad that he always looked better with his new toys than I did!"

Ron Brown became the law firm's thirty-seventh partner and the first of a minority race. (The first woman had become a partner the year before.) Brown found himself working twelve or fourteen hours a day, trying to line up new clients, the only real route to wealth at Patton Boggs. Luckily, Tommy threw business his way. Too busy to return to Tokyo to represent a consortium of Japanese electronics manufacturers (in the VCR battle between Betamax and VHS), he sent Ron Brown in his place, despite a warning of Japanese racial intolerance.

"You'd better not go and screw this up," Tommy told him, disclosing the client's sizable fees.

Upon his return, Ron Brown reported, "I've doubled the payment for you."

Jim Patton, as socially liberal as a Republican could be, "liked people who looked different, acted different, different religions, different beliefs, different lifestyles," said a partner. Yet another sort of diversity was needed now. To deal with the Senate and an unashamedly ideological administration, the firm needed a *real* Republican, beyond Patton and a tax wizard from the Nixon-Ford days.

It found one in Frank Donatelli, a fast-talking partisan Republican who had served as the Midwest regional director of the president's campaign. He stayed two years at Patton Boggs before he joined the administration; then he returned to the firm and again to the White House, as the political director—"the quintessential case of the revolving door," he acknowledged. Other Republicans arrived—an influential senator's chief tax aide, a defeated senator. An attempt to hire Howard Baker when he stepped down as the Senate's Republican leader failed.

The firm had already outgrown its quarters on Seventeenth Street. It had considered locations near Dupont Circle and on Pennsylvania Avenue but acceded to Jim Patton's will. His modernistic home, with the abstract art and the floor-to-ceiling windows, was in Great Falls, along the Potomac to the west. This made an easier commute into the capital's West End, a dreary and decayed neighborhood, just east of Georgetown, home to garages, a printing plant, a Chinese laundry, an ancient warehouse, an ironworks, an abandoned Sealtest dairy, and the last row houses at low rents within walking distance of the new downtown. The dairy was razed and in its place rose a handsome irregularly shaped office building of ten floors, counting the penthouse; its exterior of horizontal ribbons resembled the new downtown, using brick and glass that nodded toward Georgetown. Patton, Boggs & Blow had taken two floors in 1978.

Patton Boggs was among the first of the city's law firms to look for larger quarters. From 1970 to 1980, the number of lawyers in Washington had doubled to nearly forty thousand, and twenty new federal agencies had come to life, as the pages published of new regulations quadrupled. Over the following decade, nine of the city's ten biggest law firms moved, most of them leaving the new downtown for the old-and-now-resurrected downtown.

Jim Patton believed in growth. The firm refused to represent the governments of South Africa, Libya, or Syria or purveyors of pornography. But otherwise, only conflicts of interest barred the door. Ron Brown represented Haiti's dictator, "Baby Doc" Duvalier, who wanted more foreign aid. When friends teased him at parties about working for a butcher, he would laugh and reply, "Hey, he pays the bills." The firm represented the governments of Zaire and Guatamala and the sheikh of Abu Dhabi. At a crab feast at Tommy's weekend retreat on the Eastern Shore, guests were startled to see Tongsun Park, the villain of the "Koreagate" congressional bribery scandal.

Soon Patton essentially stopped practicing law and started running the firm full-time. To protect his own interests or his vision for the firm, the former CIA man could manipulate the firm's diverse personalities, play partners against one another, to make the organization work. The major decisions were not made by the partners or even by the management committee, but in discussions among Jim Patton, Tommy Boggs, and Tim May—the three of them formed a private investment club—and sometimes others sitting in, in Patton's office or over long lunches at one of his favorite restaurants.

Tommy, like Patton, was gracious in his dealings within the firm, openhearted in times of personal tragedy. But he could also be hardboiled and unsentimental. His partners found him as aggressive in protecting his own interests inside the firm as he was for his clients on the Hill. Once, when inaccurate data produced a mistake in the proportions of partners' shares, everyone who had benefited reimbursed the few thousand dollars to the partners who had lost, except Tommy, who argued that the shares had been voted.

The culture of the firm was one of sharp elbows and conspicuous consumption. Guided by his wife, an abstract painter, Jim Patton began to buy modern art that lined every corridor in the new offices with vivid colors and unapologetic shapes—so many pieces that Tim May took the chairmanship of the firm's art committee "to prevent Patton from spending us into the poorhouse." Patton smoked thick cigars and drove a tan Rolls Royce Corniche convertible (which he let partners use). A few years earlier, a Patton Boggs lobbyist had sold his Cadillac limousine because his partners thought it ostentatious, but by 1981 the firm had procured one of its own, along with three Rolls Royces and a Bentley. Tommy owned one of the earliest car phones. The partners took their wives to get togethers in Acapulco, Barbados, and Saint Croix.

Anything for money—this was becoming the firm's reputation, like that of the capital itself. Jimmy Carter, the purposefully modest president, had given way to Ronald Reagan, a denizen of Hollywood whose wife favored furs and designer dresses. A city that had once been genteel and shabby had burst into affluence. Wealth was no longer embarrassing. Flashy new restaurants opened, and limousine services boomed. By 1986, Washington, D.C., and its suburbs ranked as the wealthiest metropolitan area in the nation. As the city's mayor pumped money and city jobs into the black neighborhoods, the earnings of lawyers and top journalists and consultants of all descriptions soared.

By 1985, Tommy's annual salary, the firm's highest, surpassed one million dollars. A survey of lawmakers, congressional aides, and lobbyists judged Tommy the city's best lobbyist—and its most overrated.

After a respite caused by the 1982–83 economic recession and an antiregulatory administration, the firm's growth resumed. Its eighty lawyers became nearly twice as many in Washington by decade's end, plus another three dozen elsewhere. Patton, Boggs & Blow opened branch offices in Baltimore, in Greensboro, North Carolina, then in Denver and Dallas and Moscow and, briefly, Miami and Warsaw. In Washington, the epic battle over tax reform, culminating in 1986, proved a bonanza for every lobbyist whose client feared losing a beloved tax break. Patton Boggs organized two coalitions of companies with conflicting views. Tommy went to a diet doctor, to prevent his expanding waistline from ballooning as a result of all the receptions he was expected to attend.

Not everyone at Patton Boggs approved of the firm's direction. George Blow, the patrician Virginian, preferred the old, vanishing world of the law, in which an attorney was satisfied with prosperity and community stature, and litigators refrained from filing motions at five o'clock on Friday for the pleasure of making their adversaries work all weekend. "'Gentlemanly' is one word"—Blow tried later to describe what had been lost—"'elitist' is another." He had become an outsider, a man mired in the past at a forward-looking firm.

Gradually the dissenters left—one driven away by a dispute over the compensation formula, another by a question of ethics.

Lobbying, strictly defined, accounted for perhaps a tenth of the firm's revenue, but that failed to account for the time spent preparing strategy or writing legislation or organizing the grass roots. Tommy had become the outside face of the firm, as Jim Patton had imagined. Lobbyists had learned to turn the capital's political gridlock— between chambers of Congress, between branches of government, among competing interests—to their advantage. Within the legal profession, the contempt for the practice of lobbying was fading. Even Covington & Burling, among other old-line firms, had lowered itself to join in. Lobbying had become, if not quite a laudatory pursuit, an accepted means of doing democracy's business.

This was how the lobbyists cloaked their own pursuit of happiness, as fulfilling the First Amendment's guarantee of the people's right "to petition the Government for a redress of grievances." And to an extent, it was true, though the hundreds of dollars an hour that lawyer-lobbyists charged clients for redressing their grievances left this precious right more within the grasp of some Americans than of others.

"All interests are special," Tommy avowed, even if some were treated as more special than the rest.

Washington was awash in money, even after the Watergate scandal scared Congress into tightening the financing of campaigns. That had made matters worse, in a way—"dumbest thing they ever did," Tommy judged. Before, when political contributors could donate whatever they liked, a member of Congress could approach a committee chairman or the speaker or a political benefactor and quickly raise enough money to run. But restricting donors to one thousand dollars apiece (while the cost of television advertising climbed) turned lawmakers into retail salesmen for themselves. They had less time for legislating but greater political independence.

"Their relationship to the leadership evaporated," Tommy explained, "when they started to have to raise their own money, build their own constituencies, go out and hustle."

This gave lobbyists another means of making themselves useful to politically dyspeptic lawmakers who were increasingly pressed for money and time. Tommy's own congressional bid had taught him how many painful hours raising campaign funds took, so he set out to make himself indispensable to politicians he intended to lobby. He rented an elegant gray-brick town house with impossibly tall bay windows a block and a half from the House office buildings, to hold fund-raising events for members of Congress. Tommy was "a pioneer and probably *the* pioneer," as Tom Korologos recalled, in perfecting the technique of setting up political action committees, or PACs, mechanisms for corporate executives and trade association members to donate in concert, to maximize their impact. He organized his clients into fund-raising machines, none more enthusiastically than the trial lawyers. Wealthy and accustomed to politics, they quickly built one of the electoral system's mightiest PACs. Tommy had junior partners operate a political clearinghouse of sorts, matching members of Congress to prospective donors by using a computer program that combed the list of contributors to lawmakers who had similar voting records.

Tommy found he was attending three fund-raisers a night, for soirees of scotch, jumbo shrimp, and PAC donations. Consequently, his phone calls were returned and, when a client's interest required it, he gained entrée into a lawmaker's private office.

Two days before Christmas in 1981, a Wednesday, Conrad Cafritz and Peggy Cooper stood side by side in David Eaton's study at All Souls Church.

Before they met, Peggy could not have imagined marrying a white man. "But life happens," she said later, "and usually for the good."

The gossip columnists had trumpeted the couple's enduringly unmarried status. It was rare for people in the public eye in Washington to flout convention so, to live together openly without the benefit of clergy. This was not Hollywood or New York. Washington was for grown-ups, the place where young people went to end their adolescence. Anyone who chose to live or work—or remain—in Washington could be fairly assumed to play by the rules, to accept the principles and practices of the world as is.

Peggy had feared meeting Conrad's mother, anxious about being deemed too dark. "I was not sure how she was going to react to me," Peggy said. "However, when I was taken over to meet Gwendolyn Cafritz, she knew everything that I'd done, she was extremely complimentary, she was extremely nice. And there were times when we would see her out socially, and she'd speak to me but she wouldn't speak to Conrad."

After living together for eight years, Peggy and Conrad decided to have children. Conrad had five already, two from his marriage to Jennifer and three he had adopted from *her* earlier marriage. Peggy desperately wanted children of her own, and at last he had agreed.

Peggy had cared for two foster children already, the first while she was in law school. When she returned one day to her apartment in Adams Morgan, a cop was manhandling a wild colt of a nine-year-old.

"I thought that I was William Kunstler or whoever," Peggy recalled.

She asked what was going on. The officer was arresting the boy for loitering.

"Excuse me," she said. "He's with me."

She took him inside. Arthur had been living on the streets and could not read; she persuaded a friend to become his foster parent. She had once hoped to send him to Harvard but settled for his success in staying out of jail. A second foster child lived with her; others would follow.

Because Peggy was Catholic and Conrad was Jewish, they agreed on a Unitarian minister. David Eaton was more than a man of the cloth. He liked to read poetry, Hindu treatises, Buddhist writings, and modern sociology several hours a week in front of the fireplace in his study. His sideburns had silvered since the tall, lanky, Washington-born pastor had become an activist for civil rights, close to Dr. King and Stokely Carmichael. With his booming voice and dramatic gestures, he was named the first black pastor at All Souls and turned its tradition of social activism into a meeting place for radicals (though some of his parishioners suspected he was more concerned about David Eaton than about anything else). Just a month before, he had won election to the city's school board.

He conducted a simple ceremony. Peggy and Conrad recited the traditional vows. They had eloped; no one in either family attended.

They had signed a prenuptial agreement two years earlier and had already amended it twice. Almost three years later, Peggy gave birth to a son.

The day that David Eaton conducted the Cafritz wedding, a jury awarded him $81,062.50 in damages, and Tina Hobson and a half-dozen others that much or more.

The trial had drawn few spectators to the huge old Washington courtroom, to scrape through the political nastiness of a decade before—the FBI's snooping, the bogus leaflets, the dirty tricks, all these efforts by the legally constituted authorities to disrupt the antiwar and civil rights groups. Already it seemed so long ago. *COINTEL-PRO* had been one of the FBI's less pronounceable shorthands, for *counterintelligence program*, aimed at threats not foreign but domestic. Eight local activists had filed a lawsuit in 1976 for more than two million dollars, alleging violations of their constitutional rights, against Washington's police chief, his underlings, and five FBI agents.

Hobson v. Wilson had originally led with Julius Hobson's name, and now with Tina's.

All six jurors were black. Five well-dressed FBI men shared the defense table with their expensive attorneys, on the taxpayers' tab. The seven surviving plaintiffs took turns sitting beside the tiny woman from the American Civil Liberties Union, while the others stayed behind the rail. The testimony echoed with a tremulous past—Vietnam Moratorium, the New Mobe (short for "Mobilization"), Mayday, the Nixon counterinaugural, the Three Sisters

Bridge. The defense lawyers tried to show that no protests had been delayed or undone as a result.

The jury's awards totaled $711,937.50. "Too bad he can't be in court—he'd love it." Tina was speaking of her late husband. "I feel that it's a marvelous victory to have confirmed what I knew all along—that it was the police and the FBI that were violating the law, and not Julius Hobson."

Later a panel of appeals court judges—Antonin Scalia, Kenneth Starr, and Harry Edwards—upheld the verdict but reduced the damages. The recompense for Tina's lost rights amounted to $11,100.

Years later Tina recalled her "absolute amazement that our system of justice would present an all-black jury of modest people and a ninety-pound lawyer and go up against the juggernaut—they looked like it—and ever hope to win." She also remembered that Julius had told her before he died that, if they won, somebody else would need to file such a lawsuit yet again in ten or twenty years.

Julius's stature had grown since his death. No longer was he remembered only as a rabble-rouser. When the city government and a band of banks rehabilitated eighty-two boarded-up apartments at New York Avenue and First Street NE, lending down payments to needy buyers, the complex was named the Julius Hobson Condominiums. A middle school in Southeast was named for him in 1982. Mayor Barry spoke at the dedication, along with David Eaton, now the president of the school board, and several schoolchildren. A twelve-year-old said he was fascinated most by the threats to release the rats in Georgetown. Another boy was amazed that Julius Hobson had run for vice president. Said a thirteen-year-old, "He wasn't a prejudiced man."

Tina's eyes filled with tears.

Hobby had seen the shift in middle-class opinion firsthand. When his older daughter was floundering in school, he pleaded with her teachers to flunk her.

"I just don't know if I can give Julius Hobson's granddaughter an F," one replied.

"Why not? She earned it. If you don't do it now, I'm going to pay for it later."

Which he did.

After eight and a half years of working for Howard University, the last four and a half as its lobbyist on Capitol Hill, Hobby could not bear it anymore. Howard received more money from the federal government than any university except Johns Hopkins, in Baltimore, but he thought it was gliding on its reputation. It was too sure of itself, as the self-lauded "capstone" of black higher education, to see that with white universities open to black students, the "talented tenth" that W. E. B. Du Bois had counted on was trickling away.

Hobby knew, however, that he liked lobbying, that he had found his occupational niche. It made him part of the game, without dealing with voters or begging for their support. He also knew that to be hired as a lobbyist, he needed experience on the Hill, and that his best chance lay with a black member of Congress or with D.C.'s nonvoting delegate.

This was half the reason Hobby wanted to become Walter Fauntroy's administrative assistant. After Fauntroy's top aide quit to become Marion Barry's staff director, the seventh-term D.C. delegate asked a panel of prominent Democrats to winnow the candidates. They recommended two, a local minister with a Harvard law degree and Julius Hobson Jr.

Fauntroy never acknowledged how delicious a prospect it was to hire the son of his onetime tormentor, to have him on *his* payroll, in his employ.

"A closing of the books," as Hobby imagined it, "a sort of making amends." For Hobby, it was a matter "of making the truce and signing the treaty," while showing the world—and possibly himself—that he was not his father.

This was the other half of why he fancied his new job.

One afternoon, Fauntroy had gone to the National Education Association at Sixteenth and M, to plan the twentieth anniversary of the 1963 March on Washington, when four activists for gay rights entered his suite of offices in Rayburn and seated themselves on the reception room floor. They vowed not to leave until they were promised a speaker of their own at the march.

Hobby phoned Fauntroy.

"Walter, I've got four gay-rights people sitting in the office. What do you want me to do?"

"Well, I'm too busy—you handle it." As a Baptist preacher, Fauntroy was unsympathetic to the rights of homosexuals.

"I've tried to tell them to come down there. None of the planning is happening here."

"I'm too busy—you handle it."

"You want me to handle it the way I should handle it?"

"Yeah."

"Fine."

He called in the Capitol police and told the protesters to expect arrests if they remained after the office closed at six thirty.

They thought he was kidding.

At six-thirty, he had them arrested. They stayed in jail overnight, their leader sharing a cell with an accused murderer.

The next morning Hobby kept hearing that his father would have been one of those arrested.

"I'm not my father," he replied.

Hobby enjoyed his first year with Fauntroy. As the national director of the twentieth anniversary march, which drew as many demonstrators as the original one, Fauntroy agreed at the last minute to let a gay-rights advocate speak. He had become a supporter of D.C. statehood, once the prospect of a constitutional amendment collapsed, and he pushed to expand home rule. Hobby kept Fauntroy on the right side of the ethics rules—"you need a no-saying son of a bitch," he had said in his job interview—and lined up speaking engagements when the D.C. delegate ran short of cash.

But no politician likes to be told no, and Hobby by nature was loath to display the unquestioning loyalty that political leaders demanded.

"That was another benefit of being the son of a civil rights leader," Hobby said later, "because I'd seen enough people throw themselves down on a sword and other people trample over them and keep going and nobody remembers."

Hobby had started to grind his teeth in his sleep, and by 1984 he was wearing a night guard.

That was the year of another cause, the search for a black presidential candidate. Walter Fauntroy had himself in mind, but others did not, and soon he cast his lot with Jesse Jackson, whose career also rested on past proximity to Martin Luther King. Fauntroy's early endorsement gave him influence in the quixotic campaign, which took center ring in the nation's black politics. He wanted his own man on the inside and lent Hobby as the deputy campaign manager for field operations.

Hobby's father had disliked Jesse Jackson as a preacher of empty promises. When the Chicago minister would seat himself on a couch in the District Building and describe the great changes he foresaw in the city's high schools, Julius would say, "And how long are you going to be here?"

The son, too, preferred the cause to the candidate. Hobby had been working at the campaign headquarters for six weeks when Jesse Jackson showed up one day and announced: "I don't want this to be a regular campaign. I'm turning this into a crusade."

He turned to Hobby and said, "Julius, I'm taking you out of those three-piece suits and giving you a pair of overalls, and we're going to crusade around the country."

Hobby decided to leave.

Fauntroy could not simply fire the namesake of his nemesis. He phoned Hobby at home and said, "This is not working."

"Yeah, I know."

Hobby became the staff director of the District of Columbia Committee's fiscal affairs and health subcommittee, which Fauntroy chaired, and looked for a job.

Conrad Cafritz's tactic, as one of the five competing developers, was to call a news conference at the National Press Club. The dark musty rooms, with the clacking wire machines and the oversized nude above the fireplace, occupied the top floor of the National Press Building on Fourteenth Street, where Newspaper Row had stood. The object of Conrad's pleading was almost within sight, a mile to the south.

The ten-acre Portal site, the last undeveloped parcel in the renewed Southwest, stood at the foot of the Fourteenth Street bridge, where the highway from Virginia became a city street. The panoramic view of the Potomac took in the stubby skyscrapers of Rosslyn around to the Jefferson Memorial and the planes arriving at National Airport across the river to the south. Yet the site was isolated from the city by formidable federal buildings and a welter of rushing roads. Railroad tracks crossed the site, supplying the coal-shaking machines that shared the scruffy tract with parking lots and weeds. The hope was to create a glittering entrance into the capital from the South, and a lode of tax revenue.

Conrad's bid for the Redevelopment Land Agency's favor stressed the cultural flourishes of his proposal—the 250-seat theater, the gallery for black and local artists—more than its corpulent office buildings.

"Emerging groups need a small theater like this with rehearsal space and all the things that small arts groups have never had before," he told the reporters, sounding much as his wife would.

Four of the five development plans envisioned a cultural presence (Conrad had taken on the Cultural Alliance as a limited partner) along with plenty of office space and at least 25 percent in black-owned equity, as the mayor had decreed. Architecturally, Conrad's proposal was the most traditional of the five, as massive as the Bureau of Engraving and Printing annex just to the north.

"Handsome it might be," the *Post*'s architectural critic wrote, "but it is also tired, repetitive, dull, off-putting and quintessentially safe."

Conrad joined the 102-member campaign finance committee for the mayor's reelection. Less than two weeks later the redevelopment board awarded the Portal site to a group led by Ted Lerner, who had turned Tysons Corner from a dusty Virginia crossroads into a hub of upscale commerce.

When Lerner and the agency failed to agree on a price for the land, the bidding reopened. Conrad tried again.

An ambitious developer had reason to imagine the best. Washington was booming, despite a nationwide recession and the president's freeze on federal hiring. The city's private sector had surpassed government employment, with the surge of lawyers, lobbyists, and trade associations. Rents had rocketed; scarcely a street downtown lay beyond a building crane's range.

Surely there was money to be made at the Portal site. But more than profit was at stake: "I think Conrad wanted that for an ego thing," his brother Carter surmised.

The second round was down to two bidders. Conrad offered nine federal-style buildings ("simple and quiet," his architects alleged) and a 370-room Holiday Inn. He also presented another investor, Mortimer Zuckerman, a Boston developer who had recently acquired the Washington-based newsmagazine *U.S. News & World Report*. Herb Miller headed the competing group. The charming, aggressive, politically astute developer had recently turned a Georgetown car barn into a sophisticated mall called Georgetown Park and was building Washington Harbour, a complex of offices and condominiums on Georgetown's rundown waterfront. He trumped Conrad's plans with a 600-room Radisson Hotel, an architecture with curves and arches, a waterfront park, and multiple connections to the mayor's cronies.

"I have lots of thoughts," Conrad murmured to a reporter as the board spurned him, three to two, "but no comments."

He did not give up. "Conrad likes to get his way," Peggy said, "and when he doesn't, he's like a toddler. Once he gets an idea in his head about something, even incontrovertible evidence to the contrary could not convince him that he should perhaps consider something else."

He filed a complaint with the city's ethics board because an investor in Herb Miller's group had recommended a member of the Redevelopment Land Agency for a job. When the city found no conflict of interest, Conrad hired his own investigator, one sure to intimidate. Terry Lenzner, both a lawyer and a private eye, had starred on the Senate Watergate Committee staff and then in the uncovering of $1.5 billion in cost overruns on the Alaska pipeline.

Conrad succeeded in delaying the project but not in wresting it away.

"I think he's probably better off he didn't get it," Carter said later.

Despite the setbacks, Conrad kept expanding. He acquired an apartment house on Capitol Hill that became his fifth all-suite hotel for corporate travelers. Then he bought a sixth, in Foggy Bottom. He renovated a hotel near the Pentagon and joined Carter in buying half of a local company that managed eighty-one rental properties and residential communities.

In the late spring of 1986, Conrad and a partner showed a glint of the boldness his father had made plain in Petworth. They bought more than a thousand apartments, three-fourths of the rundown rental housing in the poorest section of Alexandria, just south of Arlington. Their plan was to renovate them, then lease them at higher rents to (as an Alexandria newspaper put it) a "Yuppie clientele." More than three thousand tenants of the neighborhood, known as "Little Salvador," might be displaced.

Two hundred tenants held hands in the hot sun on a Sunday afternoon and sang, "We Shall Not Be Moved."

The protests continued for months. Mitch Snyder, whose hunger strikes for the homeless in D.C. had forced even President Reagan to promise five million dollars for a shelter during his reelection campaign—Martin Sheen had portrayed him in a made-for-TV movie the year before—led a takeover of the Alexandria City Council. "Snyder's appearance dramatized the plight of the tenants," *The Alexandria Packet* said, "but, at the same time, signaled it as a lost cause." No grounds existed for blocking the developers. A lawsuit accusing them of racial discrimination (because the tenants to be forced out were mainly Hispanic or black) prompted a settlement, with relocation payments and apartments set aside for the poor.

All the while, Conrad kept away from the press. There was nothing chic about forcing poor immigrants, which his father and grandfather had been, from their homes.

Yet if he hoped to match his father, the most ambitious son had yet to make his mark.

Conrad was almost fifty years old, late in 1988, when he learned the glorious news: Washington Harbour, on the Georgetown waterfront, was for sale. Herb Miller had flopped. Conrad's rival for the Portal site had leased most of the office space and shops at Washington Harbour, sold most of the condominiums, and even found a restaurateur willing to risk a thousand-seat spread, facing out on the river and the back side of Theodore Roosevelt Island. The shore had once been home to lumberyards, a coal company, and an ice company, and later a place for the city to store its snowplows.

Geographical features, however, had proved the venture's undoing. The two long blocks south from M Street, passing beneath the Whitehurst Freeway, discouraged pedestrians from making the trek. Steep rents and high operating costs cast the mammoth restaurant into bankruptcy and the retailers into the red. The owners ousted Herb Miller and looked for a buyer.

Washington Harbour was bound to appeal to Conrad. It was architecturally exuberant, eccentric, unrestrained—close to his father's early haunts and in his mother's brash style. The jumble of archways, turrets, domes, battlements, and pointless pillars, all in poured concrete, the tinted windows of unpredictable shape, the vast pool with pulsating jets—it invoked almost every architectural motif, to convey a city in miniature. "Complexity at times bordering on chaos," an architect raved.

A "wonderfully wacky" theme park, said another—"and the theme, of course, is Ronald Reaganworld."

Conrad exulted over this jewel in his crown. "We believe it is— if not today, within a relatively short time—one of the best addresses in Washington," he told the press. "It has a relationship with the river which will never again probably be duplicated in Washington, D.C."

Morris Cafritz had ducked for cover just before the boom collapsed in 1929; his youngest and cockiest son kept getting in deeper.

For the first time, Hobby accompanied his new boss, Mayor Marion Barry, to Capitol Hill. They stepped along a corridor in Rayburn, with security guards and Capitol policemen in tow, on their way to a congressman's office to plead for the survival of Antioch School of Law, on Sixteenth Street, whose students provided legal aid to the city's poor.

A pretty young woman was walking toward them. Hobby kept talking. Three steps later, he realized he was talking to himself.

The security had halted as the mayor chatted with the woman passing by.

Hobby had spent eleven months searching for a job. The Pharmaceutical Manufacturers of America said he lacked Senate experience, then hired someone who had none. At last a close friend joined the mayor's staff and said, "Why not over here?"

So Hobby signed on as the city's lobbyist.

In the best of times, the D.C. government had precious little influence in Congress, on behalf of a citizenry that lacked the instrument of power that politicians respected most—a vote. And for Marion Barry, this was not the best of times. He had coasted to a second term, less as a reformer pursuing a people's justice than as a power broker who secured his political standing by cozying up to business and creating city jobs. Since then, accusations related to cocaine use and women had swirled around him, even as the city's finances sagged.

Hobby understood that most of his job was to discourage members of Congress from taking a legislative swipe at D.C. or making a crack about the city to a reporter or on the floor. He distributed tickets to the mayor's box for the Redskins. He purchased a pager and made sure he learned of any disturbance overnight at the city's Lorton prison, located in northern Virginia, so that he could phone Stan Parris, the local Republican congressman, before the calls from prison guards tempted him to bash D.C. When the House minority leader's wife received a ticket for the radar detector in her car, Hobby arranged to have it quashed.

He did the same for all members of Congress. The Constitution made them "privileged from Arrest" (except for treason, a felony, or breach of the peace) and thus immune from traffic tickets while on official business—and with a lawmaker, who could tell? A conservative Republican had his car towed twice in an afternoon from near a bar a few blocks from the Capitol, and twice Hobby got it back, without a peep in the press. When Les Aspin, the disorganized chairman of the House Armed Services Committee, left his dog in his car on a downtown street during morning rush hour while he addressed a think tank, his chief of staff confided to Hobby that the towed vehicle also contained classified papers; word of the incident never leaked to the future president, who named Aspin as the secretary of defense.

Hobby instituted a system for fixing tickets, so that both chambers' sergeants-at-arms collected them and certified each malefactor's business as official.

"It was a way of doing favors," Hobby explained.

Only to an extent did these favors succeed. "Everybody hated the District," Hobby said, "because the District was synonymous with Marion." Subsidies for abortions, a residency requirement for city jobs, a ban on discrimination in insuring homosexuals—hostile majorities in Congress could not resist smiting these. When Congress formally christened Sixteenth Street near the Soviet Embassy as Andrei Sakharov Place, Hobby arranged to have the new signs installed at three in the morning, to frustrate news photographers.

"We've become the U.S. Department of the District of Columbia," Hobby grumbled.

To nudge the city's budget through Congress with a minimum of meddling, Hobby tried to lash it to other fragments of the federal budget, to see it all passed in a last-minute rush. But when Reagan delivered his State of the Union address in 1988, he stacked up forty-three pounds of paper—the omnibus appropriations bill he had recently signed—and vowed never again.

"I'm fucked now," Hobby told his wife. "I cannot win any fights when we fly alone."

Then something worse happened: He began to attract publicity. He pleaded with the *Legal Times* reporter not to write a profile.

"You do that," he said, "it's going to cause me a problem."

The reporter went ahead (the headline, "The Hardest Lobbying Job in the Capital?"). The *Washington Times* profiled him two months later.

Hobby feared he would be targeted as a publicity hound, and he was. Soon he got word that the mayor had hired someone who professed to know how to handle the Hill.

"It's starting," Hobby said.

He began to look for a job.

The day after he landed one, on an incoming senator's staff, the mayor almost walked into a cocaine bust. The *Post* got a tip, the prosecutors pursued, and Marion Barry's tumble began.

"Such déjà vu," sighed a guest—and it was. Eight years had passed since Gwen Cafritz's previous reception, and the hostess took pains on a June evening in 1986 to re-create it, down to the band, the Belgian damask napkins, the whole poached salmon and the roast beef piled high, the engraved invitations ("Mrs. Gwendolyn D. Cafritz at Home from six until eight o'clock"), the guest list, and even the old man who was induced out of retirement for an evening to announce the guests. And the caterer. Gwen had first planned the party for Mother's Day, but Ridgewells could not fit her in. The city's most prominent caterer could not find its old records (a conglomerate had acquired the company two years before), but Gwen still had them.

She was seventy-six now, pale, in delicate health—"not her old self," said Carter. "She was trying to put together something from the past." That was the party's purpose, insofar as it had one.

She had suffered from breast cancer and at first refused to let the surgeons at Georgetown treat her at all. They phoned Calvin, and he went over the options with her. A mastectomy and the removal of lymph nodes produced a quasi recovery.

Gwen asked Carter and his warmhearted second wife, Lisa, to cohost the party. All three sons attended, a rarity. In a purple satin gown, Gwen sat in a yellow armchair and greeted her guests. The regulars showed up—Bill Rogers, the Warren Burgers, Barry Goldwater, three hundred more. Oatsie Charles, the socialite, had exhumed her white gloves.

"This was the place twenty years ago." Alejandro Orfila, the venerable Argentine diplomat, reminisced on the back terrace in the lingering light. "She used to give magnificent balls, magnificent dinners. The parties were out of this world."

How long ago it seemed. Four-fifths of the business at Ridgewells was now corporate. Hopes that the storytelling president and his clothes-conscious wife would revive the capital's high society had faded all too quickly. Nancy and her friends came to be seen by Georgetown socialites as shallow and nouveau riche.

Society was dying, and for reasons beyond the White House. The world had changed. The women worked, for one thing, and the men resisted a weeknight dinner party if they had scheduled a "power breakfast" the next morning. The journalists could no longer be counted on to keep the conversations out of print, and manners—not always, but too often—were a thing of the past. It was harder than ever to know whom to invite. The people who ran the country had grown too numerous to fit into a drawing room or even a yard.

"The Washington hostess is dead," Sally Quinn of the *Post* declared in 1987. The executive editor's wife had become the capital's reigning social chronicler. "Democracy has killed her off—and it has rendered those members of her circle, the small power elite that once ruled the country, obsolete as well."

Not long after her last party, while visiting Spain with Encarna, her devoted servant, Gwen broke her hip.

Then her cancer recurred. Visitors were told to call before visiting, to make sure she felt well and had time to put on makeup and fix her hair. She insisted on going to the living room to see even her sons. She stopped drinking, cold turkey, convinced that alcohol was harming her health.

On the next-to-last morning of November 1988, Gwen was in bed at home, in considerable pain, attended by nurses. The week before, she had missed her first meeting of the Cafritz Foundation board.

Calvin arrived and summoned the doctor, who rushed over. Gwen had lost consciousness.

The doctor emerged from her bedroom.

"Sorry to tell you," he said to Calvin, "your mother has passed on."

Gawler's handled the arrangements, as it had for Morris and President Kennedy and countless senators and justices.

Gwen would have savored the funeral at National Presbyterian Church. Only standing room remained in the sanctuary, which seated a thousand. The white modern pillars with clean curving lines, the creamy marble altar—these suited her taste. The pipe organ played Bach.

J. Carter Brown, the eminent director of the National Gallery of Art, a twenty-year member of the Cafritz Foundation's advisory board, eulogized "the smartness of Gwen Cafritz" and "her gnomic intuitive sense of what it was that needed doing." He alluded to the foundation's medical and educational grants and the "rifle shots that have made so much difference"—a chandelier for the White House, the Henry Moore sculpture outside the East Building of the National Gallery, a barge for the old C&O Canal through Georgetown, the bronze doors at the National Cathedral.

Then Warren Burger, the former chief justice, climbed to the altar. "This is a time to celebrate a great life," he began. "Gwen liked celebrations." He had known her well for two decades, but only in working with her in organizing the Supreme Court Historical Society had he really begun "to feel that I knew her, knew the person behind that glamorous, dramatic figure that photographed so well." She understood the importance of the historical society better than some of its organizers, he recounted, because anyone who had grown up in Central Europe did not need books to know how precious was freedom. "I don't think she had any concern about the law as such," the retired jurist marveled, "but the symbol of the law and of our system was this—and is this—city of Washington, the capital."

The Presbyterian funeral concluded with *Yigdal*, the closing hymn in a Jewish service.

Morris had been buried in Washington Hebrew Congregation's cemetery in Anacostia. Gwen had kept paying the synagogue's dues, but after she joined National Presbyterian, she wanted to stop. If she did, she was told, she could not be buried by her husband.

"I don't want to be buried there," she had replied.

Instead, she had chosen a nondenominational Christian cemetery near Rockville. In a lovely glade, beneath a modest metal plate in the grass, surrounded by strangers, Gwendolyn Cafritz was laid to rest.

"Let them rest in peace," Conrad said of his parents after years had passed. They never had much of it while they were living.

Eleven

BUSH

Peggy and Conrad Cafritz were dogged Democrats, but they had thrown a party at the previous Inauguration, so why not for this one? Peggy had worked with President-elect George H. W. Bush on the board of trustees of the Eisenhower Fellowships, which arranged exchanges of promising young leaders from foreign lands, and she had met his youngest son, Marvin, more than once.

She and Conrad decided to honor the president-elect's five children the afternoon before the Inauguration. It was something Gwen would have done. Conrad had just the place for it now.

Marvin Bush, slender and genial, the family's best tennis player, stood before the five hundred guests at the extravagant bankrupted restaurant in Washington Harbour.

"We said, 'Conrad, we're going to have a party—we need a space,'" he recounted. "So he planned it and bought the whole building."

Four of the five honorees showed up, all but the eldest, George W., the blueblooded family's party animal. Uncles, aunts, and cousins wore the prized *Bush Family* buttons. They mingled with the capital's A-list—Katharine Graham of the *Post*, R. W. "Johnny" Apple

of the *New York Times*, the CIA's William Webster, the Swedish and
Italian ambassadors, Stan Parris, CBS's Lesley Stahl, Oatsie Charles,
Bill Rogers, and oh yes, the Gatling Brothers, the country crooners
beloved of the transplanted Texan entering the White House.

Compared to the usual Inaugural bash, Conrad boasted to a reporter, "this is going to be a little more upscale."

Social stalwarts in the capital were impressed. "That's the definition of a real Washingtonian," said Philip Merrill, the publisher of
Washingtonian, the glossy monthly, nodding toward his hosts, "someone who can throw a fund-raiser for Jesse Jackson and then have a
party for the Bushes."

The previous spring's fund-raiser for Jesse Jackson had put
$70,000 into the improbable presidential candidate's coffers. He was
stumping D.C. in hopes of running up 70 percent of the votes in
the Democratic primary, to narrow the 172,000-vote gap that the
front-runner, Michael Dukakis, the Massachusetts governor, had
built up in all of the primaries and caucuses thus far. It was less a
fund-raiser, Peggy had said, than a "celebration of his candidacy," al-
beit one to which admission cost $250 to $1,000 for popcorn and
soft ice cream in the backyard.

She and Conrad had bought Stuart Symington's house on winding Chain Bridge Road, a half-mile west of Foxhall, then razed it and
built their own. The airy, rambling house with gray shingles, steep
roofs, and a wraparound porch resembled Peggy's family beach house
on Mobile Bay, as well as the seaside mansions of East Hampton,
where they now summered. The several hundred black professionals
and white liberals who paid homage to Jesse Jackson had spilled out
onto the lawn on the unseasonably chilly afternoon.

"When I become President," the candidate had promised, "I will
shift the direction of the wind."

The guests cheered. Many stayed late to pose their children by
his side, for posterity.

"I have this great house," Peggy explained later. "I think I should
be pretty generous about its use."

She and Conrad showed themselves as Gwen's true successors,
in an altered political age. The passing of Gwen Cafritz "signaled the

fading of the era in Washington society when the wealthy set the social style with lavish parties in private homes," or so the *New York
Times* proclaimed. Nowadays the parties usually had a point, besides
the self-serving, whether it was charitable or expressly political. Yet
the grander purpose remained, as Gwen had pretentiously put it, "to
serve civilization."

This Gwen kept trying to do, even from the grave. She had bequeathed the mansion on Foxhall Road not to her sons but, by her expressed wish, to the State Department, as a residence for the
secretary of state or as another Blair House, to house foreign dignitaries. That a former secretary of state, Bill Rogers, had been her legal confidant and an executor of her will was no coincidence. George
Shultz, the outgoing secretary, had spent years searching for just
such a residence, suitable for diplomacy and entertaining.

Except that Jesse Helms objected. The cranky conservative senator from North Carolina had squabbled with Shultz over receiving a
privilege that no other Cabinet officer had. Even with Shultz gone,
Helms refused to relent.

In the will she had signed in 1969, Gwen had left her home to
Calvin and two-thirds of her estate to her sons. But her relationships
with them had unraveled, especially since they had challenged a provision in Morris's will that had left a quarter of his estate in a marital
trust. She had settled the dispute by promising them a quarter of the
marital trust, but at the cost of her erratic goodwill. Her subsequent
wills endowed almost everything to the foundation.

"I make no other provision in this will for the benefit of my children," she decreed, "as their financial needs are adequately provided
for." She left them only family mementos, to be divided (if they could
not agree among themselves) by the executors.

The coolness in her phrasing was not inadvertent. Gwen's last
will "was designed to have her sons fight each other," a son of her sister later informed the probate judge. "This was to be her payback, in
revenge for what her sons had done to her. . . . She was very mad
about this." She had instructed him again and again, said the nephew,
that if the wrangling over her will lasted less than five years, he
should step in and "stir up the legal soup."

One last time, Gwendolyn Cafritz got her way.

Not quite seven months after her death, her two younger sons went to court. They contested the three-fourths of the marital trust (worth eighty-four million dollars, in total) that the sons had not been promised already. The legal basis was the provision in Morris's will that gave Gwen discretion to pass her inheritance along "to such person or persons" as she might wish. The foundation, they argued, was not a person.

In their lawsuit, Conrad and Carter accused William Rogers and Martin Atlas, the executors (along with Riggs) of Gwen's estate, of having "exerted undue influence" over a sick woman who "lacked a sound and disposing mind," on behalf of a foundation they helped to run. These were unlikely villains, an amiable corporate lawyer who had been too cautious a secretary of state to keep Kissinger tamed and a tax lawyer with an aversion to risk. The brothers hired a team of lawyers, led by Lloyd Cutler, who had been President Carter's counsel and reigned as one of the capital's last remaining superlawyers.

Lending the lawsuit a Shakespearean cast—and splashing it across the front page—Conrad and Carter also named Calvin as a defendant. This would be brothers against brother, in D.C. Superior Court.

Was this simply greed at work? Or a reflection of Conrad's financial fears? Or a wellspring of personal pique, the deep disaffection bequeathed by a mother who withheld love?

Calvin had his own theory, which he explained later in a letter to the directors of his family's foundation: "It has been patently clear from the beginning that the whole thrust of the lawsuit was to obtain seats on the Board of the Foundation for Conrad and Carter." The prospect plainly horrified him. "Just as my father wanted to leave a legacy that could benefit the city and the people that he loved and about which he was concerned, I would like to see the structure that he established to preserve the legacy, to continue. I have serious reservations about whether my brothers share that desire."

Gwen's will had directed that Calvin serve on the foundation's board but made no mention of his brothers. "I thought my mother's wishes ought to be upheld," Calvin said.

Morris's generosity to the city he loved was now tearing his family apart.

"If we had grown up in a warm, nurturing family, then we would have been the next generation to carry on Morris's line," Carter would later lament. "The three of us together do not equal Morris Cafritz."

"What is your definition of womanizing, Sam?"

John Tower, dapper and combative, had already unveiled a no-drinking pledge this Sunday morning in February 1989 on ABC's *This Week with David Brinkley*, in a last-ditch tactic to gain Senate confirmation as the secretary of defense.

"Well, it's not mine," Sam Donaldson replied. "The accusations are made against you—"

The former senator flung his arm toward the only woman on the show, seated before a wall-sized map of the world.

"Cokie, do you have a definition of the term?"

"I think most women know it when they see it, Senator."

Cokie Roberts smiled, glanced across toward Sam, and changed the subject. Her short-cropped, swept-back hairdo gave her a no-nonsense look. With her crisp cheekbones and easy composure, there was something sensible and down-to-earth about her. Cokie's what-you-see-is-what-you-get nonchalance was bound to wear well.

When the interview turned to charges about the senator-turned-consultant's $760,000 in defense contractors' fees, Tower defended himself.

"That's not an exorbitant . . ." He pointed at Cokie. "Cokie, you ask your brother if that's an exorbitant amount for experienced consultants in this town. I think he would tell you that it is certainly not exorbitant."

She smiled uncomfortably and was silent. Thirty seconds later, she thought to reply, "I am not my brother's bookkeeper."

But the moment had passed.

Live television still scared Cokie, but she was faster on her feet than when she had started. The first time she had joined the journalists' roundtable that concluded Brinkley's hour-long show, fourteen months earlier, she tried again and again to break into the conversational melee. As a woman, she knew, "you can't be too aggressive, because people will think you're a jerk."

Then she had succeeded.

"That treaty could be a problem for Dole there"—the Iowa presidential caucuses, pitting Bob Dole against George Bush, were a month away—"because the people who turn out in Iowa at caucuses are peace people, in both parties."

"In *both* parties?" George Will, haughty as an Oxford don, was disbelieving.

"In both parties in Iowa," she assured him.

The columnist nodded.

"I did better by the end," Cokie said afterward.

After she started on *McNeill-Lehrer,* Cokie had appeared from time to time on *Agronsky and Company,* Hodding Carter's *Capitol Journal,* and other public affairs shows aired at hours when most sensible citizens communed with God or with one another. Sam Donaldson had seen her—they knew each other only to say hello—and thought of her for the roundtable, which needed a woman.

"I can't express any views," she said when someone from ABC phoned. Then she realized how to finesse it, by offering an analysis of political reality in place of opinion.

Roone Arledge had taken the pizzazz he had put into televised sports to reinvent the sleepy format on Sunday morning. He doubled the length and brandished the hour-long show to lure David Brinkley from NBC. The newsman with the quavery voice and acerbic insights had been the towering presence in television journalism since Cronkite's retirement. His repartée with Sam Donaldson and George Will offered a crackling chemistry.

Women had joined the roundtable before but none had succeeded. "It is hard to find—not a woman, but it's hard to find anybody to do this kind of thing," Brinkley said, "because the program is all ad-lib. There's no script, there's no TelePrompTer, there's no nothing. You go in there essentially naked. All you have is what you have in your head and you are asked to talk about the gross national product and the collapse of the Soviet Union and so on."

Until recently, he said, casting about for an explanation, "most women were not much involved in public affairs."

But Cokie had been, from the womb. A roundtable discussion resembled the dinner conversation of her childhood, where she had learned to hold her own.

"Throughout our lives at home," she said, "we talked and analyzed and synthesized."

Not everyone at ABC was aware of her pedigree. Chatting with Brinkley and George Will one Sunday before a show, she mentioned that her son would be staying with fraternity brothers at her mother's house on Bourbon Street.

"Oh, just like Lindy Boggs's house," was the reply.

"*That's* my mother's house."

Soon she was a regular at the roundtable, the first woman on the show accepted by Sam and George. ABC talked to her about a job.

"I was really repeating myself at NPR," she recounted. "At some point when you've covered your thirteenth budget, you don't want to do that anymore."

Television intrigued her, as a different way to tell a story from radio, yet she had no desire to write minute-long pieces on Congress for ABC's evening news. The network hired her as a special correspondent, with duties on the Brinkley show, the evening news, and *Nightline*, another of ABC's defining features.

She stayed on part-time at NPR. "ABC was nice about it," she said.

At forty-four years old, Cokie was ready for a change. Her son was in college and her daughter was about to leave. Her appeal depended not on being glamorous, but on being a woman of substance, of a certain age.

Gwen Cafritz had hated the opera. Yet she would sit through Wagner's Ring Cycle when the Kennedy Center staged a production, and her foundation conferred as much as $400,000 in a year upon the Opera Society of Washington. Once it had donated another $2,500 so that the city's schoolchildren might witness opera free.

Despite her drinking and her snappishness, Gwen had taken the foundation seriously. Gwen told the newspapers that she was at the office by eight every morning, though she actually showed up at 1825 K once a week after lunch. Packets with one-page, double-spaced summaries of the grant requests were sent to the house, and she read them. Mrs. C., as the staff called her, was conscientious about preparing for meetings. She would sit silently, then ask a penetrating question. As always, she knew what she wanted, and she usually got it.

Morris had bestowed his grandest gifts on Jewish charities and the Community Chest; Gwen had focused on high culture and the established purveyors of the arts—the ballet, the symphony, the Corcoran, WETA, the Smithsonian, the National Gallery of Art, the Phillips Collection, even the opera, with dollops for homeless shelters, soup kitchens, hospices, recordings for the blind.

Now Calvin was the foundation's chairman. With his mop of dark hair, he was a shy and gentle man, short and deliberate. He was indecisive by temperament, but he was sure of the direction he wanted the foundation to take.

His native city was in pain. Crack cocaine had ravaged street corners and families. Even the mayor was alleged to have smoked it. Blocks of sturdy row houses with landscaped yards that looked gracious and tranquil in the daylight became killing fields at night. The nation's capital had become the murder capital; the record for homicides set in 1988 was broken by Halloween of 1989. President Bush's nearest neighbors slept on park benches and heating grates.

Calvin spoke later of "really a conscious decision, to change the focus." Of the foundation's four categories of beneficence—arts, community services, education, and health—he wanted to fund them equally. This meant considerably more in social services. He continued his father's generosity, as Gwen had, to the Metropolitan Police Boys (and now Girls) Clubs of Greater Washington. Money also went, in Calvin's first year in charge, to install an elevator in a residence for poor people with AIDS, to finance a rape crisis center's outreach to Hispanics and the deaf, to subsidize the Central American Refugee Center, to provide a permanent home for five homeless women, to hire two counselors at the Duke Ellington School, to under-write the executive director's salary at Habitat for Humanity, to pub-licize a suicide hotline, to collect surplus food for the hungry, and to do more.

A foundation that had occupied the cultural stratosphere was, by sad necessity, moving into the street.

Late on an autumn afternoon, the limousines rolled up to Fourteenth and G, and the directors of the National Bank of Washington negoti-ated the bustling corner and hurried upstairs. The squat gray fortress with Greek pillars housed the city's oldest bank. Promptly at five, the emergency meeting of the executive committee began. The ma-hogany and soft leather failed to calm the dozen directors, Tommy Boggs included.

The emergency was the outbreak of civil war. Six days earlier, the bank's odd trio of dissenting directors, a slick black local lawyer and two Arabs bankrolled by a Saudi prince, had filed an amended Schedule 13D with the Securities and Exchange Commission, de-manding that the bank's chairman, Luther Hodges Jr., resign.

The era of gentlemanly banking in Washington had ended.

The august history of the National Bank of Washington (NBW), just nine years younger than the city itself, was inseparable from the capital's own. After the British burned Washington, the House de-cided by nine votes to keep the capital where it was, but the Senate agreed only after the banks in D.C. promised to lend $500,000 for re-building the city. Presidents Madison and Monroe had been deposi-tors, as had Webster and Clay and Francis Scott Key and (in the amount of forty dollars, for two days in 1834) Davy Crockett. More recently, Yitzhak Rabin's wife's account at NBW, in violation of Is-raeli currency laws, had prompted his departure as prime minister.

By the time Tommy joined the board, in 1980, the United Mine Workers owned three-fourths of the city's fourth largest financial in-stitution, as the union's principal investment. More than ever, as a bank director, Tommy straddled the capital's natural divisions. "In those days," he said later, "you had the real estate community, the banking community in Washington, and the legal community in Washington, and then you had political Washington—lobbyists, Congressmen. And one of the advantages of growing up here is that I was in both of those worlds."

Forced by federal regulators skittish about the union's tradition of corruption, the bank was looking for a new president. Tommy had not been alone in suggesting Luther Hodges Jr. The son of President Kennedy's secretary of commerce had been a *deputy* secretary of commerce for President Carter, a friend of Jim Patton's from North Carolina; Tommy had raised money for his 1978 Senate campaign. Hodges, much like Tommy, was a cigar-chomping southerner with a strong face and a hearty manner. He had run a small bank as a banker-politician admired more for his skill with a drink in his hand than with a ledger.

Soon Hodges succeeded at NBW in getting rid of problem loans and reviving the bank's beleaguered image.

He wanted more than that, however. The stuffy world of banking was fast becoming a racier and riskier place, in which fortunes could be made overnight. Hodges's scheme was to assemble investors to buy the bank from the Mine Workers, revive it, and "position it as sort of a national brand"—this was Tommy's explanation—"because it was *here*." Then they would wait for a deep pocket who wanted a Washington presence—maybe a foreign bank or investors with designs on a money-center bank for pursuing international business—to buy them out.

"It was a good plan," Tommy said.

Tommy put in a half-million dollars; other directors invested more. Hodges required all of them to have a stake, though credit was easy to find. Bob Washington, a black lawyer with impeccable connections, a tennis partner of Hodges, owned a million-dollar house on Foxhall Road and enjoyed lighting up an expensive cigar in the no-smoking section at Duke Zeibert's. He put up $20,000 of his own and borrowed $980,000 from Citibank. Ron Brown invested, and Brent Scowcroft (though he left the board upon becoming the president's national security adviser) and developer William Cafritz, Morris's nephew, among others. Saudi investors put up the most, for a quarter of the stock.

Soon there were charges of mismanagement, insider loans, a balance sheet in disrepair. Until 1988, not a single director had ever voted against a single loan, unsecured or otherwise. Loans went to the capital's notables on their signatures alone—to Bob Washington's own law firm, to businesses run by directors' friends, even to Senator Gary Hart's presidential campaign. A golden parachute in Luther Hodges's contract promised three times his $400,000 salary if he were ousted or if control of the bank changed hands.

"Remember, these directors were selected because they were a certain type," an officer explained—"well-connected socially and politically, wealthy, well-educated."

The executive committee argued among itself for three hours. The dissidents tried to raise their criticisms of the management, but the eight directors who defended Hodges refused to let them. Many were his friends or depended upon his favor in their business. By votes of eight to three—Hodges abstained—the directors declared their confidence in him and created a four-man committee to "review" the dissidents' indiscretion in making their displeasure public, with Tommy Boggs as the chairman.

That was in October 1988. One morning the following February, Tommy found himself in a conference room at Covington & Burling, at Twelfth and Pennsylvania, on the wrong end of a deposition.

"They could be doing a better job," Tommy testified, "but any management or any corporation could do a better job."

"But you still believe the adjective 'excellent' is one that is apt for this particular management?"

"I do."

He also recounted what had happened a few minutes after the emergency meeting the previous fall, when Luther Hodges chatted with four or five directors and told them of the overture from the dissidents. "I found that somewhat disheartening," Tommy testified, that the dissidents "were offering him greenmail to get him out, screw the rest of the shareholders. . . . It seems to me I recall the figure of three million dollars."

"Was it your understanding," one of the lawyers asked, "that this offer to purchase his shares was contingent upon him also resigning?"

"That's the way he characterized it."

The charges and countercharges flew—of negligence, gross negligence, breaches of fiduciary duty, of supposedly Saudi money that secretly arrived from the Libyans, of an "unlawful, surreptitious scheme" to seize control of the bank. The lawsuits and countersuits, before they were exhausted, consumed thousands upon thousands of pages. "In banking, as in love, timing seems to be everything"—so began *Memorandum of Points and Authorities in Support of Washington Defendants' Motion to Dismiss Counts I, II, & VII.* Later emerged such masterpieces of legal reasoning as *Motion for Enlargement of Time to Respond to Boggs's Motion to Dismiss or, Alternatively, for Summary Judgment,* and *First Amended Verified Counterclaims of Robert B. Washington Jr., Washington Investors Limited Partnershp, and RBW Investment Limited Partnership V,* and many more. The parties engaged in back-and-forths on the bank's adoption of the "equity flipin–flipover" poison pill, on the cunningly created blind trust, on the Special Fund that allegedly lent Luther Hodges one million dollars at below-market rates.

Any of these proceedings could satisfy a tuition payment at Saint Albans School.

Who was right? Was anyone? Beyond the protagonists, did anyone care? A decent citizen contemplating such a spectacle of legalisms and greed could only shudder.

Nobody could have enjoyed this anymore except the lawyers. As the bank's legal bills mounted, Luther Hodges agreed at last to a settlement. He would find a buyer for the bank by the end of 1989 or resign.

Five bidders stepped forward. Japanese businessmen, represented by Tongsun Park, reportedly submitted the highest bid, but they withdrew after Delegate Walter Fauntroy threatened regulatory scrutiny of a foreign takeover. None of the bids sufficed.

The bank stayed solvent for six months after Hodges left. But in the wake of the unsteady management, the unionized workforce, and the shaky foreign loans, Washington's real estate boom of the egotistical eighties collapsed. Too much had been built, and in a glutted market the prices dived.

Washington as recession-proof? This was bunk.

The National Bank of Washington lost eighty-six million dollars on its real estate loans in the first half of 1990 alone. By summer it failed to repay loans from other banks. On the first of August, the federal regulators seized control.

For the first time since the Depression, a major bank in the capital had failed.

This generated another round of lawsuits. The Federal Deposit Insurance Corporation (FDIC) insisted that NBW's officers and directors pick up some of the $300 million that the bank's collapse cost the taxpayers.

Eighteen months and twenty-four hundred boxes of investigative documents later, the FDIC filed suit against ten directors and a loan officer, alleging gross negligence, breach of fiduciary duty, and more. The claims against Thomas Hale Boggs Jr. numbered a dozen.

"It will be a big mess," Tommy prophesied to the *Post*.

He and the other defendants conducted what the *Washington Times* called "a surprisingly scrappy legal defense." Despite all the accusations, Tommy contended, "FDIC does not allege (nor could it)" that he had engaged in any self-dealing or shown any personal gain. Why had he been charged, he asked, while "prominent and identically situated" Republicans, such as Brent Scowcroft, had escaped?

Tommy and his fellow defendants drew the right judge. Royce Lamberth was known for his antipathy to the government. He accused the FDIC of "a selective recital of the facts" and assailed the agency's weak case, in dismissing all charges against nine of the eleven defendants, everyone but Luther Hodges Jr. and Bob Washington.

"The failure of NBW is a loss for this city, its customers, and the taxpayers," Judge Lamberth declared. In the defendants' countersuit for frivolous prosecution, the judge levied a hefty fine against the FDIC. "After two years," he pronounced from the bench, "the court expected more."

Tommy Boggs lost his half-million dollars. The defendants spent one million dollars or more on lawyers. The corpse of the city's oldest bank was sold for a paltry thirty-three million dollars to a savvy Texan, Joe Albritton, who had already acquired Riggs Bank.

The limestone fortress at Fourteenth and G was put up for auction; because it was a designated historic landmark, the name of the dead bank remained lettered across the top, just below the roofline.

Luther Hodges Jr. defended the loans issued to Conrad Cafritz on his signature, followed by the loans to cover the interest. Conrad owed NBW an estimated sixty million dollars.

"When someone comes from a prominent, respected family, like the Cafritz family," the deposed banker explained, "it seems logical to assume that he will pay his debts eventually."

Conrad was considered to have a knack for turning money-losing properties into gold, and he had curried connections to financiers in Europe and the Pacific Rim. He had continued to invest, without discernible strategy. He bought a racetrack in Laurel, Maryland, to develop as an office and industrial park, and a huge Holiday Inn in Crystal City, near National Airport. He planned an office building and a hotel across the Potomac from Georgetown, in Rosslyn, where D.C.'s continuing limit on building heights had inspired a steel-and-glass canyon. He reportedly held interests in at least a hundred properties—hotels, office buildings, apartment buildings, shopping centers, industrial parks—in and around D.C. and beyond.

He was advised to slow down his deal making. "Lots of people warned Conrad, including me," Peggy said, "and he wouldn't listen."

The rents on downtown offices plunged from thirty-four to twenty dollars a square foot from 1989 to 1992, as land prices shriveled by half. The developers who stuck to their business plans scraped by.

"The people who get in trouble are the deal junkies," a real estate executive said. "You make a deal for the sake of doing a deal and pretty soon you lose sight of your business plan. All of a sudden somebody stops the turntable and things fall off."

By the spring of 1990, Conrad was running short of cash, and he asked his bankers for extra time to repay his loans. Every major lender in D.C. had a stake in what a banker described—unimaginatively if understandably—as Conrad's "house of cards."

Other developers were stunned.

"If Cafritz can't raise money, who can?" sighed a market re-searcher for a local real estate firm.

"Mr. Cafritz is just a microcosm of what's happening in the real estate market nationwide," said a man in a position to know.

In June there was another jolt. A new restaurant was about to open at Washington Harbour, and a couple of major tenants had moved in. But top-flight retailers had stayed away. Nothing could be done about the distance downhill from M Street. At the Fantasyland on the Potomac, the absence of street traffic discouraged retailers, and the absence of retailers discouraged street traffic.

It emerged that Japanese investors had put up most of the $200 million paid for Washington Harbour. Conrad managed the project, served as its public face, and reportedly owned a $31 million stake.

Suddenly he sold it. His jewel was gone.

"Raising cash is important," he said. He delivered a three-volume presentation to each of his seventy-one lenders on three continents, proposing a three-year plan to work out his loans and prevent bankruptcy.

After Labor Day, as Conrad and Peggy returned to Washington, a front-page headline in the *Post*, just above the fold, announced: "Conrad Cafritz Owes $1.1 Billion."

"Well, that's interesting," Peggy said. "Gee, Conrad, I didn't know we had a billion dollars."

In sorrowful fact, they had quite a bit less. Conrad figured he could sell his properties for only $754.5 million, on which he had borrowed $1.1 billion, including $500 million on his personal guar-antee. He was nervous about being forced into personal bankruptcy.

Peggy found it surreal to be a billion—a *billion*—dollars in debt. She wanted to help, at least a little bit, and she knew how.

Did he appreciate it? "Of course not," she said later. "Most men have short memories, but most women are very good at reminding them."

Her prenuptial agreement with Conrad, amended twice more since their wedding, was now valued at $30 million. Peggy gave it up for a sum of $760,000, in the event of a divorce, plus an annual payment of $250,000, even while they were married. To assure her yearly dowry, Conrad transferred his $7 million stake in his father's marital trust to Peggy.

Conrad's creditors screamed, suspecting an attempt to conceal assets. "A patent sham," the FDIC alleged, having sued Conrad for $18.6 million in delinquent loans to the National Bank of Washington. The agency had made him the test case of a year-old law designed to simplify seizure of the assets of borrowers who default on loans to failed banks, such as by undoing the sort of transfer Conrad had made to his wife.

When a judge ordered him to pay, Conrad settled.

He still had to face dozens of unhappy lenders. Any setback, he knew, could tip him into personal bankruptcy. If one lender forced him into court, the others might do the same, to protect their interests.

Yet Conrad also had an advantage in the enormity of his debt. Borrow a little money, the bank owns you—so went a saying in real estate—borrow a lot, you own the bank. The longer a bank held off, the more it would likely get back in the end. Rushing to collect meant collecting less, and publicity about bad loans could depress a bank's own stock and bonds.

When his creditors rejected his first proposal, he approached them one by one. His largest lender, a Finnish bank, agreed to stretch out the repayment of the eighty-eight million dollars he owed and to lend him millions more, mainly to build warehouses near Annapolis.

His luck did not hold. The Ohio teachers' pension fund foreclosed on a half-dozen of Conrad's warehouses and suburban strip malls, and Perpetual Savings Bank lost patience and pursued Conrad personally in court.

And yet—

Peggy's explanation later was "smarts, luck, and cooperation"—from the lenders—and shrewd lawyers. Creditor by creditor—Citicorp, First Chicago, a Japanese bank, the Texas teachers' pension fund, the frightened local banks—Conrad signed out-of-court settlements with thirty lenders by year's end. He collected his properties into a pool and promised to pay off the creditors over time. To prevent lenders from seizing individual projects, which were structured as separate corporations—as his father's had been—he cast some of them into bankruptcy. But never himself.

Conrad on a high wire was at his best.

Jim Jones was closer to Tommy Boggs than Ron Brown was. They had been the best of friends in law school, and Jones had even been "of counsel" to Patton, Boggs & Blow for a year after leaving the White House, before he won election to the House.

When it came to the Democratic National Committee (DNC) chairmanship, however, this counted for naught.

Tommy had encouraged Ron Brown to work as Jesse Jackson's convention manager in 1988, in the hope that forging political peace among Democrats (as Brown succeeded in doing) would strengthen the firm's relations with Congress and bolster its business. As the two law partners sat at a bar in an Atlanta hotel the night the Democrats nominated the bloodless Michael Dukakis for the presidency, Tommy raised the question of the DNC chairmanship.

"You should think about running," Tommy said to Brown. The 404 members of the party's national committee elected the chairman.

He already had, for months, maybe for years.

"I don't want to be chairman to a Democratic president," Brown replied. In the polls, Dukakis stood seventeen percentage points ahead of the surefire Republican nominee.

"Ron, we're not going to have a Democratic president."

Tommy and the firm went all-out to make Brown the party chairman. To house his eight-week campaign, the firm provided a three-room suite, rent-free, and hosted a fund-raiser that attracted contributions from two dozen of the sixty partners.

No campaign for party chairman had ever cost so much. Brown raised $300,000 to hire a staff, set up a computer system for tracking delegates, charter airplanes, rent hotel suites, deliver videos to every voting member—the paraphernalia of a modern political campaign.

He was considered a long shot for the job, against Michigan's nuts-and-bolts state chairman, Richard Wiener, and against Jim

Jones, who consoled the conservative Democrats of the South and West. The fear was that Brown was a stalking horse for Jesse Jackson or Ted Kennedy—that he would make the party's image too liberal.

But for Tommy, this was business. He was spending so much time on his partner's campaign (and on a Louisianan's bid to run the Senate Democrats' campaign committee) that he told another politically active Washington lawyer, "I don't have time for clients anymore."

Another partner at Patton, Boggs & Blow helped to secure the crucial endorsement. As a liberal congressman from Michigan, Jim O'Hara had been close to Big Labor. (Hale had defeated him for majority leader in 1971.) Now he took Ron Brown before the political directors of the AFL-CIO's unions, and a week later they made up their mind.

When Jim Jones became the last of his opponents to withdraw, Ron Brown achieved yet another racial first, as the only person of color ever to head a major political party in the Western world.

Brown also announced that as the party's chairman, he would remain at the firm. The entangling of politics and lobbying was complete.

Tommy and his partners had become ever more deeply involved in the capital's political routine. In the race for Senate majority leader, Tommy raised money for Daniel Inouye, beloved by the National Cable Television Association, a Patton, Boggs client. He hosted sixty-five lobbyists at breakfast in support of Al Gore Jr., who was running for reelection to the Senate and possibly for president again in 1992. When Jim Wright, the House Speaker, faced losing his job because of penny-ante ethics, Tommy defended him before an audience of lobbyists ("If we know somebody is honest, we ought to say so") and lent the speaker's lawyer a forum to state his client's case.

This was more than a son's doing a favor for an admirer of his father. Tommy understood that going to the rescue of a politician in trouble was an act long remembered, not only by the miscreant but also by any officeholder who could imagine being in the miscreant's place—that is, all of them.

Tommy also put his money where his mouth was. As the 1990 elections approached, he and his wife donated $40,000 to congressional candidates and political committees, then another $45,000 over the next two years. He could afford this, now that he was earning $1.6 million a year. *Forbes* had named him the best-paid Washington corporate lawyer in 1989.

Washington's superlawyers, as a 1971 book had dubbed them, were nearing extinction. Tommy Corcoran and Edward Bennett Williams were dead. Lloyd Cutler and Bob Strauss had entered their seventies. Clark Clifford had slipped into disgrace, as the chairman of a northern Virginia bank in which BCCI, the Arab bank that veiled a worldwide Ponzi scheme, had secretly acquired control.

After Clifford's firm was forced out as BCCI's official counsel, Patton, Boggs took its place.

Who was following in the superlawyers' footsteps? Lawyers had become specialists, now that power in the capital had become too dispersed for generalists to prevail. Few lawyers in Washington bounced between the government and private practice anymore, though this was the likeliest path to rising higher in stature than pursuing either endeavor alone. Hardly anyone remained above the fray anymore, probably because the combat paid so well. The notion of disinterestedness, a transcending of the parochial interest in order to pursue the greater good, had grown quaint. The greater good was someone else's job.

The lobbyists were the generalists now, the closest thing to superlawyers. Tommy regarded even specialized lawyers as fungible but lobbyists as unique, each offering a particular set of relationships and opportunities for access.

"Now what we do is in vogue," Tommy said. Law students were flocking to the capital to become lobbyists. These are, he said, "the kids who in an earlier time came to Washington to work for Jack Kennedy."

In the fall of 1992, as the Senate prepared to vote on ending a filibuster blocking a bill that the trial lawyers opposed, Tommy stood in the Democratic cloakroom. Senators waved and nodded to him, as if he were a colleague, and sidled over to chat. To rival lobbyists he boasted that he had lined up a surprise supporter, and he had. It was Daniel Inouye.

The trial lawyers triumphed by a margin of two votes.

Hobby wanted to work for Chuck Robb in part because of their similar circumstances. The onetime marine guard at the White House would never have been elected governor of Virginia, much less become a senator-elect, had he not been President Johnson's son-in-law—"which always means you've got to prove something," Julius Hobson Jr. said. He understood this all too well.

Hobby had another reason for his interest. He had been elected to the school board and then worked for the city's congressional delegate and its mayor—but then what? He had reached a dead end. D.C. politics was intense because the opportunities were few. Hobby wanted to cross from local politics over to the national side of Washington.

"If I didn't step out of it then," he said later, "I would never have been able to."

After returning to Howard to finish his bachelor's degree, he had earned a master's in legislative affairs from George Washington University. To complete his training as a lobbyist, he needed to check off one last box on his résumé—Senate experience.

"I'm going to have a checkmark in every box that I need to have a checkmark in," he vowed, "in order to advance."

The incoming senator with a pedigree by marriage received hundreds, even thousands, of applications for fewer than two dozen jobs on his Washington staff. Hobby used his only political connection in Virginia, someone two years ahead of him at Howard who had become a law partner of Chuck Robb's. The senator-elect also knew of Hobby's father by reputation.

"Having a brand name does help," Robb acknowledged later, as *he* well knew.

The opening on his staff was for a legislative assistant on issues of budget and finance. This suited Hobby.

"What I was trying to do," he explained, was "move out of a black perspective."

The subject appealed to him. "Budget politics," he had said while in Fauntroy's employ—"that's where power lies."

Robb was no liberal on budget questions. The deficit-disfigured federal budget offended the former marine's sense of order—and, he noted, "Lynda says I'm cheap." On the Budget Committee, the new senator resisted domestic spending and wanted to limit the "entitlement" programs for the aged and poor, which grew without anyone's say-so.

Hobby was considered a conservative on Robb's staff, and not only on budget issues. He argued in favor of fighting the Persian Gulf War and confirming Clarence Thomas, a black conservative, for Thurgood Marshall's Supreme Court seat.

"If we are as black Americans to become a part of the country," he told his white colleagues, "we ought to be entitled to our mediocre pieces of shit just like you are."

Hobby's surprising position "was certainly a factor," the senator said later, when he ultimately, painfully, voted *aye*.

Seven staff members shared a single room, allowing Hobby a wingspan's worth of working space. Everyone knew everyone's business. Hobby's daughters, who were then in high school, phoned at four o'clock every afternoon, to tell him where they were.

At age forty, Hobby was the oldest of Robb's aides except for the chief of staff, and he knew more about the culture and procedures of Capitol Hill than any of them. Colleagues approached him for advice not only on professional quandaries but also on personal ones.

For the youngest aides, who considered him the token black, "just by demonstrating that I was knowledgeable about issues and about process, I brought them around to respect me, and in turn to look at blacks differently," he said. "You can't change people's attitudes by running right at them. Sometimes you have to go at 'em at an angle."

Robb, himself a man of careful demeanor, never saw Hobby agitated or emotional. He was impeccably dressed and mannerly. When he walked to lunch with a woman on the staff, he took the side near the street.

"He must have a wonderful mother," a colleague sighed to herself.

Hobby genuinely liked Robb, even if true loyalty remained beyond reach, and he enjoyed the job. He wangled a floor pass to watch

Nelson Mandela address a joint session of Congress. He served as eyes and ears on D.C. politics for Robb, whose home stood just across the Potomac, in McLean.

But right away, Hobby saw that the new senator was an inattentive politician.

"He didn't have the heart and drive to be senator," Hobby said later. "All he ever wanted to be was governor." His longtime aides still addressed him as "Governor." When Hobby asked about the new senator's thank-you trip around the state, he was told that none was needed, for Robb had drawn 71 percent of the vote and had six years ahead.

"Six years can go by really fast," Hobby said.

Trouble arrived for Robb within two years and never departed. At last he called a press conference to defend himself against the accusations of having a nude massage and of attending parties at which cocaine was snorted. When he strenuously denied that he had used illegal drugs, Hobby found him convincing. When Robb was asked about extramarital sex, he replied that he had always loved his wife.

Hobby cursed to himself.

Robb's stern views on the budget prompted his fellow Democrats to oust him from the Budget Committee, which picked up three-fourths of Hobby's salary. Robb's office assumed the difference, but with no raises in prospect.

Hobby had intended to stay the full six years, but with both daughters in college, he left after four.

On a hot summer's day in 1990, Lindy Boggs bestowed smiles and kisses as she made her way through an emotional crowd, in the stately brick building on the Tulane campus that bore her name.

"We are standing in one example of my efforts to help equip our local colleges and universities to educate our young people to compete in the twenty-first century," she said, in the Lindy Claiborne Boggs Center for Energy and Biotechnology, a fruit of her years on the Appropriations Committee.

Now in her eighteenth year in Congress, Lindy had become a

venerable member of the House, with no shortage of supplicants or ways to gratify the voters back home. She was a founder of the congressional Shipyard Coalition and had delivered federal dollars to dredge the Mississippi River and to improve the port of New Orleans. She worked behind the scenes. That no major legislation carried her name was regarded by friends as a secret of her success.

On this bittersweet occasion, Lindy spoke of her own "small role in opening doors for blacks and women," of "my part in helping get the Head-Start program off the ground," of "my role in making the preservation of our national buildings and neighborhoods a national policy," and of the way Hale had urged the countries of Western Europe to join together after the war—"an idea that may well be a reality in the next two years."

Lindy had arrived on this campus fifty-nine years earlier. "Half a century is a very long time in the life of an individual," she said, "though it is but a fleeting moment in the history of nations."

And now, she announced, she was retiring. She never said why. She did not need to.

Lindy had struggled, as Hale had, to strike a political balance. But their circumstances differed. Hale strained to satisfy the racially minded voters to his political right while keeping the nationally minded Democrats content. After successive bouts of redistricting, the majority of Lindy's constituency was black, the only such district in the nation represented by a white member of Congress (after Peter Rodino of New Jersey retired in 1988); she also wanted to keep her southern colleagues happy and to vote her Catholic conscience. When an aide urged her to mail a summary of the surgeon general's report on AIDS to her district's voters, many of them homosexuals, she objected, "Honey, I just can't put out anything with my signature on it that says 'condoms,'" though she was willing to send a copy to anyone who asked.

She had survived a formidable challenge in 1984 from a black ex-judge, with the help of Ron Brown's campaigning, and had won easily the next two times. But there was at least a tacit understanding that blacks now wanted the seat for themselves. She faced two black opponents so far in the coming primary, promising the hardest race of her career. She was ahead in the polls, but Lindy felt uneasy about trying to thwart black ambitions that she regarded as legitimate.

She had agonized over her decision for months. The determining factor had no relation to politics or race but to what she alluded to afterward as "family obligations that are obviously a joy to meet."

Lindy had once hoped to be part of the first mother-daughter duo in the history of Congress, with the only working politician among Lindy's three children. Barbara Sigmund had started at the bottom, as a Princeton borough council member, then as a county freeholder, the board's president, then mayor of Princeton. She had a knack for politics—she *was* her father's daughter—though she resembled her mother in her distaste for making people mad at her.

"I sometimes feel she has had a tiny bit of longing to be with all of us," Lindy had said in 1982, during Barbara's U.S. Senate campaign—"that she felt maybe a little bit left out."

It was then that the melanoma had been discovered behind Barbara's left eye. Less than two hours after leaving the hospital, the one-eyed candidate showed up at a fund-raiser in a red silk dress and a heart-shaped eye patch.

"You're a sight for a sore eye," she had said with her raucous laugh. Still, she lost.

As Barbara ran for governor in 1989, and lost, the cancer recurred. This time it was behind the right eye and elsewhere, and nobody thought it could be cured. When chemotherapy failed, she tried an experimental drug and regular transfusions from loving donors.

She wrote poems, unsentimental and unsubtle but wry, with titles like "And Now, the Right Eye Too" and "Ode to My Cancer-Ridden Body," which began

> *Hey, old buddy,*
> *When did you decide*
> *That you and I aren't*
> *Best friends any more?*

From wherever ABC had sent her to cover the 1990 midterm elections, Cokie would rush to Barbara's bedside for another stint as (in another poem) her "private duty sister." Cokie's daughter, Becca, was at Princeton University and became her aunt's favorite nurse. Lynda Robb's daughter, also at Princeton, phoned home and asked, "Mother, do you think it will be all right if I give her a purple nightgown from Victoria's Secret?"

Lindy spent her workweek in Washington—"on automatic pilot"—and traveled to Princeton by train every weekend.

All three children tried to dissuade her from retiring, but Lindy had always known her own mind. "She feels strongly that for everything there is a season," Barbara said.

Twelve weeks after Lindy's announcement, four days after the Democratic primary she had passed up, three months before her tenure in Congress was to end, her eldest child died. Barbara died in her own bed, asleep, at age fifty-one.

Afterward, Lindy made coffee. Her veil never slipped. Cokie never even saw her cry.

George Bush, famous for his courtesies, sent a handwritten note. The women in Congress returned from campaigning to share a private mass with Lindy, in the Congresswomen's Reading Room in the Capitol, soon to be named in her honor.

After a half century in Washington, Lindy moved back to New Orleans. At first she missed being in Congress. Had she stayed, however, she would have been miserable, for her gracious and accommodating culture was becoming extinct.

Twelve

CLINTON

Tommy Boggs had thrown in with the candidate early. In the fall of 1991, just before a debate among the Democratic presidential aspirants at the Kennedy Center, one of his law partners took him to a small room at the Mayflower Hotel, where potential donors were meeting with the prematurely gray-haired governor of Arkansas.

"The most masterful politician I've ever seen," Tommy judged him later—"including Lyndon Johnson, including Sam Rayburn."

The respect was mutual.

They were bound to hit it off. Both of them were broad-beamed, smooth-talking southern Democrats with a northern edge, practical men who believed in winning. "Two of the world's great networkers," said a man who worked with both. They had known each other a little for years, through Democratic Party councils. The two had kept in touch during the Arkansan's four and a half terms as governor.

Tommy became Bill Clinton's main fund-raiser in Washington, and the trial lawyers the leading contributors to his presidential campaign. And Tommy was not the only Boggs to help. Lindy hosted a fund-raiser for him at her Bourbon Street house the day after the candidate and his wife, Hillary, appeared on *60 Minutes* (after the

Redskins' victory in Super Bowl XXVI) to defend his marital and political honor against the word of Gennifer Flowers. Soon he would
become the first president of his generation, whose idealism had
somehow transmuted into self-indulgence and greed.

"Patton, Boggs & Blow: Ready to Cash In on Clinton," the cover
of *National Journal*, featuring a photograph of Tommy, heralded a
month before the election.

The benefits stood to be more than financial. Ron Brown had
imagined himself a secretary of state and was torn about the offer to
be the secretary of commerce. Tommy urged him to remain at the
law firm for the money he could make, but Brown could not bear to
think of a photograph of the new Cabinet that lacked his face. He
and sixteen other lawyers left Patton, Boggs & Blow to join the first
Democratic administration in a dozen years.

By spring, *Washingtonian* named Tommy as the capital's top
lobbyist—with his law partner in the Cabinet, "he can't service everyone seeking his advice"—and, by fall, with his wife, as a habitué of
society's A-list.

Tommy and the firm profited by their connections, less by dra-
gooning the administration than by thwarting it. An opportunity arose
with Hillary's plan to restructure the nation's health care system,
which accounted for a seventh of the world's mightiest economy. The
proposed restrictions on jury awards and lawyers' fees in cases of
medical malpractice resembled the changes that Tommy and the trial
lawyers had stymied for twenty years.

Tommy visited Ira Magaziner, the architect of Hillary's proposal,
an awkward intellectual with a penchant for grandiose schemes. His
earliest one, while an undergraduate, had transformed Brown University's curriculum into the most desirable in the Ivy League, but
every attempt since had failed the leap into reality. In an airy corner
office in the Old Executive Office Building, permanent Washington
clashed with meritocratic Washington, to a draw. Tommy persuaded
Magaziner to quash the proposed limit in the size of malpractice
awards, but nothing else.

The battlefield shifted to the House of Representatives, Tommy's
second home. He leaned on Dan Rostenkowski at Ways and Means

to give up jurisdiction over malpractice to Judiciary, chaired by Jack Brooks, an old friend who frequented the duck-hunting retreat that Tommy had bought a few years before. The Eastern Shore preserve served up enough dead ducks to make his weekend getaway a favorite of shotgun-toting members of Congress.

When the Judiciary Committee met to draft a bill, a front-row seat had been reserved for Tommy Boggs. An amendment included innocuous-looking language that nullified the limits that numerous states had already imposed on lawyers' malpractice fees.

"We didn't think it would pass," Tommy recounted, "but thought it would cause some mischief."

He had miscounted the votes.

This was not what killed the president's grand rearrangement, despite the *Washington Monthly*'s judgment by headline, "Tommy Boggs and the death of health care reform." The "Harry and Louise" television ads fed a fear of change in a public that was largely content with the status quo. The 1,342-page Rube Goldberg construction collapsed of its own overambitiousness in a political system that was built for gradualism.

Tommy's apostasy produced no recriminations at the White House. And it did not preclude an invitation to watch the election results in 1994 with the president and his wife, upstairs in the residence.

It was a sad night at the White House. Tommy had hosted a "meet and greet" to raise money for the only member of the president's family on the ballot, Hillary's brother Hugh, a Senate candidate in Florida. That night they watched him get trounced, by more than two to one. An inkling of worse had occurred in the late afternoon, when the president's chief of staff, Leon Panetta, and his political strategist, George Stephanopoulos, examined the early exit polls and feared that not only the Senate might go Republican but also the House.

As the election returns trickled in after eight o'clock, the first couple and a few guests sat in the austere oak-paneled study beside the Lincoln Bedroom and watched the capital turn upside down. The president stayed calm, almost resigned, amid the shock. Before nine,

Panetta ventured onto the White House lawn and told CNN's viewers that voters were sending the same message as in 1992—they wanted change, even faster.

"What you said is exactly right," the president said to Panetta upon his return.

"It's total bullshit," Tommy told the president. "We lost because of you."

In forty-eight years, he said, the Democrats had never lost the House. "People are confused about what you are, whether you're a New Democrat, an old Democrat, a liberal Democrat," Tommy said, "and confused about what the Democratic Party stands for right now."

Two months earlier, Tommy had bought a table at a fund-raiser for Newt Gingrich, the persistent and provocative Georgia Republican who was soon to occupy Sam Rayburn's chair as Speaker of the House. "Tommy Boggs doesn't waste his money," said a spokesman for the incoming Speaker.

The president telephoned Tommy three or four times over the next couple of days. Why did Tommy think as he did? What could the president do about it?

"If you criticized the President, he would sort of pursue you," Tommy recalled.

Those were the only substantive political conversations the two men ever held.

Hobby had never found a job before except by knowing someone, certainly never through answering a want ad. When he saw the notice in *Roll Call*, the gossipy tabloid that covered Capitol Hill, he submitted his résumé to the American Medical Association (AMA) and forgot about it. He was surprised to be called for an interview. He was even more surprised, in March 1993, to be hired.

Right after he accepted, the Commerce and Treasury Departments called with offers.

"You're going to work for the AMA?" Doctors' incomes had lent the organization a Republican tint.

"Yes."

"You don't want to work for the President?"

"No."

Having seen enough of politicians, he preferred the private sector, for its salary and stability. No longer was it government jobs that necessarily offered blacks in the capital more of both.

"I needed to go somewhere where I could still be in the game," Hobby explained. The allure of the AMA was not the subject but "the fight. It's waking up every morning and knowing I'm going out in the trenches and I'm going to lock and load and I'm going to shoot at somebody, or somebody's shooting at me. It's fun. It's really, really a lot of fun."

The AMA's offices in Washington occupied two floors in a utilitarian building at L and Vermont. He commuted the half hour each way, first in a 1984 Nissan Maxima and later in a 1996 silver Mustang, a V-8 with dual exhaust and eight speakers—"pure me"—listening to jazz.

After he had remarried and gained custody of his daughters, they moved into Upper Northwest for the city's best high school. Hobby did not mind living mainly among whites, in a modest brick colonial on McKinley Street, though "we hardly knew anybody on the block," he said, "because nobody spoke."

Hobby's second wife, Diane Lewis, had grown up mostly in the Bronx, living in apartments, attending predominantly white schools. He had met her while he was on the school board and she was a law student at Georgetown conducting legal research for the board. She was a self-possessed, open-faced woman who was of West Indian ancestry and thus had escaped (as Stokely Carmichael had) the deficits in pride and leadership so common among descendants of slaves. She had become a management consultant, often on the road, helping minority-owned businesses wean themselves from relying on federal contracts. When the girls left for college, they wanted to move.

"I buy the houses," she said; "Julius buys the cars."

She picked out two places, a house off Sixteenth Street and a three-bedroom condominium on two floors at McLean Gardens, out Wisconsin Avenue. Evalyn Walsh McLean had already moved into

Georgetown when the government acquired the acreage three weeks after Pearl Harbor. In place of the French villa where President Harding had played poker, with its eighteen-hole golf course, the fountains, statues, and stables, forty-one three-story brick buildings housed war workers. They had gone condo in the 1970s after neighborhood opponents stymied the construction of fifteen-story buildings—"another Crystal City"—in their stead.

Hobby chose McLean Gardens. Ever since his father had made him trim and rake as a boy, he had hated mowing the lawn.

This reduced his stress, but everything else increased it.

The AMA's Washington office had never employed a black professional before. When an in-house lawyer sent an officewide e-mail questioning Hobby's use of the word "rescission"—budget jargon for a retraction in spending—he could not let the challenge stand. He coldly quoted the budgetary statute and the definition from *Congressional Quarterly*'s *American Congressional Dictionary,* in reply to everyone.

"Those are ways you establish yourself," he said later. "I knew that somebody would say, 'Why is he here?'

"'Oh, they must need some diversity.'"

The formidable organization was expanding its lobbying staff from six to eight, plus the director, to cope with the administration's immodest—and to doctors, frightening—health care plan. For decades the AMA had fended off what it portrayed as "socialized medicine," but now the doctors feared capitalism at least as much, as the insurance companies rushed into "managed care." The organization had declined in power, shunned by doctors schooled in the 1960s, but it still wielded clout. It boasted one of the ten largest PACs and had Marcus Welbys in every congressional district—at the grass roots, as the political professionals liked to say. Shortly after Hobby started, a thousand physicians flocked to Washington for briefings on health care reform, and half stayed on to lobby.

Before the administration's plan died a merciful death, its very complexity and the specialization in the medical world pitted doctor against doctor. Hobby had already been grinding his teeth at night. At the AMA, he began to have high blood pressure, allergies, and tendinitis.

One steamy afternoon in the summer of 1994, he was ushering members of the Medical Association of Georgia into Congress-woman Cynthia McKinney's office. Her office was cold, but Hobby could not stop sweating. A doctor who had survived a heart attack ordered him to a nurses' station, and his own doctor prescribed nitroglycerin tablets.

Eight days later, while at home, Hobby felt a tightness coursing down his arm. Stupidly he insisted on driving himself to Washington Hospital Center, where his father had conducted a lie-in. He stayed two and a half days no heart attack, but a muscle spasm in the aorta, caused by stress.

"I am never, never going to do that again," he promised himself.

The Republican takeover of Congress in 1994, which Hobby had predicted, worked to his advantage. The Georgia delegation had recently become part of his purview because Senator Sam Nunn was close to Robb and he had known John Lewis, the black congressman, through Carol's church. The delegation included Newt Gingrich, the new Speaker, whose promotion meant one, in effect, for Hobby, too.

When skeptics wondered about the wisdom of assigning a black lobbyist to handle the conservative Republican leadership, the director of the AMA's Washington office, Lee Stillwell, held firm.

"When he put out for me, I put out for him," Hobby said later. "That's as close as I will get to loyalty."

When he accompanied doctors from Texas in to see Tom DeLay, the ardently partisan House majority whip from near Houston, Hobby let them do the talking. Afterward, the exterminator-turned-congressman phoned Lee Stillwell and said that, henceforth, he would welcome only Republican lobbyists into his office. Hobby had no choice but to comply.

"I should not be the issue," he said.

Hobby changed his registration from Democrat to independent, and not only for show. Ideologically, he had been leaving the Great Society behind. "You could put up all the programs you wanted," he observed, "but if the individual didn't decide to achieve, want to do better, it wasn't going to happen."

"You can't typecast him, philosophically or by race," Lee Stillwell said.

As a black lobbyist, Hobby lacked for mentors. So he read the insiders' weeklies (*Congressional Quarterly* and *National Journal*) cover to cover as well as lawmakers' biographies and every book he could find about Congress, all to penetrate the subtleties of the legislative process.

"Process kills policy," he learned, often by making sure the policy never gets to a vote.

His interest in the subject of lobbying grew. A friend was working as an administrator and professor at George Washington University's Graduate School of Political Management, which considered itself the oldest school of practical politics in the country. Its founders conceived of politics as no longer simply a matter of personal contacts, but as a profession, more or less, with tested principles and proven best practices. The exercise of democracy need not be haphazard.

Hobby taught a class each semester in his friend's course on public administration, and in another friend's at the University of the District of Columbia. His letter to the dean at GW led to a class of his own, on lobbying.

His one-night-a-week course required students to create a lobbying strategy—which lawmakers to target, how to influence each. He loved noticing which students understood the material and which ones were lost. Students could phone him anytime between seven in the morning and eleven at night, except during Redskins games. He rarely gave As.

"If teaching paid what the AMA paid," he said, "I'd teach full-time."

He was forty-five years old before his salary breasted $100,000. It might have happened a decade earlier, he figured, had he been white.

General Colin Powell sat near a television in a corner at the Cafritz house on Chain Bridge Road and rooted for *Apollo 13*. It was not to be, though as a military man he could not have been very disappointed to see the Oscar for Best Picture of 1995 go to *Braveheart*.

It was flattering just to have been invited. Was he not the *former* chairman of the joint chiefs of staff? Obviously *George* magazine considered him to have star power.

And *George* should know, with its celebrity founder and editor in chief, John F. Kennedy Jr. The new bimonthly was attempting to inaugurate the sort of Oscar night party that burnished *Vanity Fair*'s image in Los Angeles and *Entertainment Tonight*'s in New York. After years of casting about for a suitable life pursuit, the slain president's son had recently founded a glossy magazine that covered politics as entertainment, thereby completing a transformation in political style that his father had begun. Between advertisements for Mercedes and Versace Couture, the magazine ran interviews with politico-actor Warren Beatty and basketball bad boy Charles Barkley, profiles of Bob Woodward and Newt Gingrich's lesbian half-sister, and a recipe for sour apple pie (to celebrate George Washington's 264th birthday) from "America's First Lady of Homemaking," Martha Stewart.

This was the New York–based magazine's first party in the capital, which was ostensibly its reason to exist. A friend of Peggy's had asked her to cohost it with Buffy Cafritz, a Republican hostess married to Conrad's first cousin. There was a glamour to Peggy, with her graying brush-cut hair and her long dangling earrings. She had met John Jr. a couple of times and knew his sister, Caroline, through friends they had in common during summers in East Hampton.

Washington's glitterati had attended. George Stephanopoulos, his hair tousled and his red "power" tie loosened, chatted before *George*'s camera with Colin Powell and Vernon Jordan, the president's immaculately dressed First Friend. Ron Brown schmoozed. Jane Alexander, the actress in charge of the politically dicey National Endowment of the Arts, retreated into a bedroom to watch the show—and won the Oscar pool.

The truest celebrity was John Kennedy Jr., born five weeks after the last of the Kennedy-Nixon debates that launched the television age, the man judged by *People* as the "Sexiest Man Alive," who physically resembled his father but had accomplished so much less. When his girlfriend spirited him into a room and shut the door, lips flapped.

"It was great fun," Peggy said.

This was the new salon of Washington, political celebrities watching television, thinking of Hollywood. Almost anyone could join, of any race, of either gender, of any don't-ask-don't-tell sexual orientation, as long as the wrinkles were few—in clothes or conversation—and the meritocracy meshed with social grace. Yet for the most part, Washington remained socially segregated, and by more than race.

"Most people in Washington at a certain level, they have a group," Peggy explained—"the political pundits and the journalism community, and then you have the arts people, and then you have the megabucks people, and you have a Jewish group. . . . Except for large events, there's not a lot of cross-fertilization."

Other than Peggy herself. She belonged to overlapping political circles—Marion Barry's and Jesse Jackson's, the Bushes and Kennedys—and to the arts world. She was black and the wife of a Jew.

Her marriage, however, was unraveling. Neither she nor Conrad was easy to live with. Peggy suggested in her petition for divorce that Conrad had infected her with genital herpes in 1983 and claimed that he had withheld sex since the fall of 1984; admitted to several extramarital affairs, including one with the lawyer he hired to negotiate their latest postnup; and "referred to their relationship as a 'European-style' marriage, with each being free to have sexual relations with others as they desire, despite Mrs. Cafritz's wishes to the contrary." He had resisted having children, tried to dissuade her from trying in vitro fertilization—these were Peggy's accusations—and after Zachary was born in 1984 and they had adopted Cooper in 1991, he had discouraged her efforts to teach their racially mixed sons about their black heritage. Oh, and he "used his control of the family's financial resources," she alleged, "to control and demean" her.

News of their split arrived in the gossip columns before it reached the courthouse.

"I have asked Conrad for a divorce," Peggy announced to the *Post*.

"We have made no final decision," Conrad replied.

A popular disc jockey known as the Greaseman repeated specifics from her filing to his radio audience of teenage males.

Conrad denied the juicy allegations—"a vile and personal attack . . . penned to attract media attention"—and struck back. "Mr. Cafritz affirmatively avers that Mrs. Cafritz had traumatic experiences prior to the parties' relationship that affected her ability to have a normal conjugal relationship," and that her family had a history of depression. Her father's suicide, her rape in Paris—the tone deteriorated.

In the fall of 1997, at their older son's therapist's urging, they agreed to separate. The following summer, after sixteen years of marriage, they were divorced.

But even as Conrad's marriage fell apart, the Cafritz family had started to mend. Shortly before Peggy filed for divorce, Conrad and his brothers had settled their eight-year-long lawsuit over Gwen's will. Conrad and Carter each received $7.4 million in property (and Calvin almost as much) beyond the $7 million Gwen had agreed to years before. The younger brothers also got $5.3 million apiece to start a foundation, except that it could not be called a foundation, to preclude confusion with the one that Calvin ran. They used *Charitable Trust* instead. Another $8 million or more went to the lawyers.

Relations between the brothers remained raw.

Conrad and Carter took one of their father's last office buildings, at Eighteenth and I Streets, stripped it to the shell, and renovated a "C" building into an "A" building. By selling it to a Nevada pension fund, they turned their inheritance into cash.

Calvin went to work on the building next door.

Carter started a business that leased high-speed Internet lines. As an industry open to new ideas, even bad ones, he said, "it's the exact opposite of the real estate business."

Tommy Boggs was driving to the office on a spring morning in 1996 when he heard a sketchy report on the radio. A military plane on a U.S. trade mission had crashed into a mountainside in Croatia. Ron Brown was aboard.

From his office he phoned the deputy secretary of the army, a former partner at Patton, Boggs, who said he did not know much more. Tommy was driven back out to Ron and Alma's brick town house by Rock Creek Park, near the northern tip of D.C., not far from his own home. Four or five people had arrived before him, much as the mourners had shown up at Bradley Boulevard twenty-four years before.

President Clinton had already phoned Alma personally—"I want you to hear it from me first"—and he went to the house with his wife, who seemed to be choking back tears; her sunglasses evoked Jackie Kennedy's. Ted Kennedy visited, and Vernon Jordan, Mayor Barry and his wife, basketball buddies, neighbors, family members, Lindy Boggs.

The funeral at the National Cathedral "was the only place I have been in maybe thirty-five years where it was truly, truly integrated"—this, from Cokie. Tommy had gone along on Air Force One when Clinton flew to Delaware to greet the thirty-three caskets.

Tommy played hearts with the president on Air Force One on the way back from Louisiana for a fund-raising event and sat in his box to watch the second inaugural parade, as a reward for the $600,000 he had raised in "soft" money during the campaign (besides the $100,000 he had persuaded MCI, a client, to kick in). Being seen chatting with the president could only be useful to Tommy, even if they had nothing to say.

Conspicuous closeness to power attracted clients, often defensively. A corporate director of federal affairs who hired Tommy as a lobbyist was protected against rebukes from headquarters—who could complain if the company lost with the best? Putting Patton, Boggs on retainer also kept the firm out of opponents' clutches, and lobbying clients drew in other business to satisfy the retainer. Tommy took to describing the firm's lobbying as "a loss leader that brings clients into the store."

He was already the firm's face to the world, and now its overlord. Jim Patton told his partners in 1995 that he intended to pass along his clients and phase himself out. Tommy became the managing partner the following spring, though for only two years, while he trained a successor.

The firm had changed its name yet again. George Blow was leaving, too. Patton, Boggs & Blow—a Dickensian name, in George Will's mind—gave up its comma, its ampersand, and its final flourish.

Clean and crisp it sounded: *Patton Boggs*.

———

The ceremony was billed as a groundbreaking, a misnomer. The ground had been broken seventy years before, and the renovation—a resurrection, really—was a few months under way. The true purpose, at Sixteenth and Q, on a sunny morning in the waning winter of 1995, was to raise more money.

Calvin Cafritz and Katharine Graham (who had never learned from her father that he was a Jew) and the *Post*'s Jewish president, Alan Spoon, climbed to the top of the worn steps that faced the Avenue of the Presidents. Each held a taut rope, and with simultaneous yanks, three banners unfurled from above:

DC   COMING

JCC   HOME   1996!

Twenty-six years had passed since the Jewish Community Center had closed downtown and moved out to Rockville, a year after the riots, as crime saturated the neighborhood and most of the city's Jews and other whites hastened to the suburbs. The city acquired the building as a home for Federal City College, which was consolidated into the University of the District of Columbia in 1977 and left for larger quarters uptown. The abandoned temple became a refuge for addicts and prostitutes.

During the 1980s, Jews migrated back into D.C., the young singles near Dupont Circle and on Capitol Hill, the young families in Upper Northwest, the elders who had kept their Victorians in Cleveland Park. Soon a new JCC opened, in a rented town house near Dupont Circle, and a search started for an enduring home. A committee looked at two dozen sites before coming around to one they had known before.

Reconstructing a building with an existing, unforgiving shell cost more than starting from level ground. Vandals had stripped the copper pipes from the old JCC, and city workmen had left a mess in removing the asbestos. Only the high-ceilinged lobby on Sixteenth Street looked much the same. The twin giant nameplates—*NELSON CAFRITZ AUDITORIUM, ANNA CAFRITZ AUDITORIUM*—remained, in drab brown, over the doorways.

Morris had paid for the auditorium in 1926 and for eight years was the JCC's president. He turned a pool and a gymnasium into a health club and moved his pool manager from the Ambassador to run it. The walk-in steam bath had a half-dozen chairs in which lawyers and doctors and businessmen, Gentiles and Jews, swapped gossip and told tales. A bookie would take a bet in front of a judge, or an ambitious young fellow spurned by the banks might find financing for a real estate deal. Later an addition was built with squash courts, a library, and a teenagers' canteen, the anonymous half-million-dollar donors were eventually revealed as Eugene and Agnes Meyer, the owners of the *Washington Post*.

Their daughter, Katharine Graham, honored their beneficence with an identical pledge. Calvin Cafritz was asked for a gift twice as large. The foundation had been cool to Jewish causes while Gwen was in charge. Calvin felt differently.

"My father had been instrumental in building the building," he said simply.

When he learned of the plans for a program in social service and another in theater and the arts, "I felt that represented both the major interests of the foundation."

So the Morris and Gwendolyn Cafritz Foundation donated one million dollars, half to each program. Offered a naming opportunity, Calvin passed up a room or a wing and asked instead to name the two centers, and not for the foundation but for his father alone.

Between the restored nameplates of Morris's parents, a sign in the Sixteenth Street lobby would read:

MORRIS CAFRITZ
CENTER FOR THE ARTS

Morris's eldest son wore a crooked and boyish expression as he shared the steps for a photograph with Katharine Graham and four dozen donors. Then they headed to a luncheon at the *Post*, at Fifteenth and L, to be lectured on the project's financial shortfall.

Speakers offered personal remembrances of the original JCC, to nostalgic smiles. Calvin followed a stately Mrs. Graham to the podium.

"The Jewish Community Center meant a great deal to my father," he said. "The Cafritz Foundation grant will preserve my father's legacy and our family name in the renovated building."

Someone who had given $25,000 pledged $1.5 million.

When the new JCC opened two Januarys later, past presidents quoted from President Coolidge's original dedication speech. Yet something fundamental had changed since 1925. The JCC had originally made Americans of immigrant Jews. Now it was intended, as an administrator in Rockville had pointed out, "to help 'Judaize' Americans."

David Brinkley was seventy-six and looked it. In the past year, his laconic style had begun to seem tired; his wry skepticism, merely cranky. On Election Night 1996, having already announced his retirement, he described the reelected president to a national audience as "a bore." It took an on-air apology to lure the president onto the last edition of *This Week with David Brinkley*.

Already the newsman's fifteen-year grip on the Sunday morning ratings had slipped. *Meet the Press*, with Tim Russert as its inquisitorial host, had caught up and, more often than not, was pulling ahead. Roone Arledge wanted the show "freshened up." A lot depended on Brinkley's successor—or successors.

Cokie's star at ABC had been rising—and Roone Arledge loved stars. Her blunt but unthreatening manner and her throaty laugh were easy to take. She was the network's first woman with a high-visibility news beat. When Sam Donaldson skipped the 1992 Republican convention in Houston, she took his place in the booth with George Will, to analyze each day's events. If Sam was a terrier scratching for news, and George Will elucidated the context of history and philosophy, Cokie deciphered the dynamics of politics—why politicians behaved as they did.

Politics, she liked to say, was the family business.

Sam and Cokie had cohosted while Brinkley was on vacation. Neither alone seemed right. They lacked Brinkley's courtliness, his gravitas. Was it their lesser ages (sixty-two and fifty-two, respectively) or the lesser age in which they lived?

Together, however, they made a match. Sam was the brash out-sider, who pestered politicians into coming clean. Cokie was calmer, feminine yet no-nonsense, as self-assured as television required, the one who understood events from the inside. She believed in the insti-tutions, in the essential goodness, of the capital. Still a girl of the 1950s who had never absorbed the cynicism of the 1960s, she thought that "public service" meant exactly that. When rumors had washed over Washington in 1989 that Tom Foley, the House speaker-in-waiting, had a homosexual past, she tried but failed to keep the story off the air. When she interviewed her mother on ABC's *Prime Time Live* in 1994, she appeared not only as a journalist but also as the daughter of a political family.

This Week, the show was called, *with*—well, with nobody yet, ex-cept that Brinkley delivered a commentary at the end.

"It took some shaking down—frankly, more than we expected," Cokie said later. She and Sam conducted interviews together, then separately. Both of them joined the staff of ABC's evening news, to draw more of a following. David Brinkley ended his homilies, con-cluding a fifty-four-year broadcasting career.

"All's well that ends well," he finished his final commentary, in September 1997. "My time here now ends extremely well."

That lasted six weeks, until Brinkley returned to the show—in an advertisement. Archer Daniels Midland Company had sponsored *This Week* from the first, and its chairman had helped Brinkley pur-chase a condo in a Florida hotel at a bargain price (along with Tip O'Neill, Bob Strauss, Howard Baker, and the Doles).

"I will still speak straight and true," the longtime newsman said—only this time about the wonders of agribusiness.

Cokie issued a statement on the show's behalf, "to congratulate David Brinkley on his new role" and to point out that he had left ABC News.

The reaction was unforgiving. After two weeks, ABC pulled the ads.

This had to make Sam and Cokie squirm. They had become more than purveyors of the news—they were stars. Television magni-fied everything, in the familiarity it bestowed upon anyone invited into bedrooms and dens at an intimate hour. Both were in demand as speakers. Sam Donaldson charged as much as thirty thousand dollars for a speech (sometimes with a limousine), besides the two million dollars or so a year he reportedly earned from ABC and the ninety-seven thousand dollars the government paid him for growing wool and mohair on his New Mexico ranch. How could he lambaste a congressional junket to Florida sponsored by an insurance group that had recently paid him for a speech?

"Fairly or unfairly," the *Post*'s media critic concluded, "he has become a symbol of the journalistic plutocracy."

Cokie was close behind. She was paid less for a speech—typically, $20,000—and yet she supposedly earned as much as $300,000 in a year this way, beyond the $500,000 or more that ABC was believed to be paying her, plus her salary from NPR. She spoke to the mortgage bankers, the chain drugstores, the restaurateurs, the AAA, the Junior League of Greater Fort Lauderdale (for $35,000). Reportedly for $45,000, a Chicago bank hired Cokie and her husband for three joint appearances over a weekend. She spoke to the trade association for health maintenance organizations (HMOs), which opposed the president's proposals to overhaul the nation's health care system, then she donated the money to a medical center named for her late sister.

Should anyone mind?

Press critics did—Jim Warren, for one. When the new bureau chief for the *Chicago Tribune* arrived in the capital, his willful naïveté made him the latest in the surge of outsiders who climb the capital's battlements and eventually, with rare exceptions, either assimilate or leave. He styled himself something of an anthropologist, assailing the culture of the capital as mercenary and incestuous, thereby stoking the outrage of readers at home and getting his newspaper, widely unread in the capital, noticed. "Cokie Watch," a periodic feature in his Sunday column, followed "a doyenne of Washington's mediatocracy" and "the irrepressible moonlighting of a journalistic cash machine."

"A reprehensible individual," Steve Roberts flung back—"on a crusade to make his own reputation by tearing down others."

Jabs kept coming from paladins of journalistic purity—in the *Post* ("Cokie and Steve Inc."), in *Mediaweek* ("High Priestess of Insiders"), in *The New Yorker*.

"We were both stung by it," said Steve. "No one has ever, ever, ever been able to point to a specific incident and say, 'Here's a story you wrote that was influenced by the money you took,' or 'Here's something you said on television that was influenced by the money you took,' because it never happened."

"You show up, you entertain, you go away," Cokie said. "They're looking for celebrity value."

But by 1995, ABC had changed its rules to ban paid speeches to trade associations or for-profit businesses, reportedly over protests from Cokie and Sam and Brinkley and several of their colleagues.

Edward R. Murrow had hawked Colombian coffee in *Life*, but until well along in the age of television, only occasional journalists had passed as celebrities. The more Cokie appeared on television, the more she was stopped on the street. It became known that she would shop at Safeway after mass on Sunday, after the show.

"Are you Cokie Roberts?" people would say, as if they were not quite sure. With Sam Donaldson, they were sure.

She did not like it, but she tried not to complain. "Even people who stop you, they're polite," she said. Once, as she was grousing to Steve, he accused her of being ungrateful, "and just somewhere out of the depths of my stomach, this atavistic thing came out, and I said, 'Y'know, I couldn't walk down Canal Street with my father without being stopped every three feet.'" She had not realized before the source of her distress.

Day to day, she and Steve did not live a celebrity life. Most nights meant dinner at home. Cokie phoned for the air-conditioning repairman, and they did little hobnobbing with senators and such (other than Floyd Haskell, who had been a one-term senator from Colorado before he married Nina Totenberg). Steve lovingly tended Hale's garden. He took the soil to Beltsville to have the pH measured; the azaleas Hale had planted grew huge.

"I'm the most normal person I know," Cokie told the *Post*, mystified as to Jim Warren's motives. "I live in the house I grew up in. On the weekends we're puttering around the kitchen, arranging flowers and seeing good friends and having our kids over for dinner."

Yet they also marketed themselves as celebrities. In 1994 they launched a weekly newspaper column, syndicated to about twenty newspapers, including the *New York Daily News* and dailies in New Orleans, Dallas, Denver, Baltimore, and San Jose. Its topics were to include the political and the personal, from their "perspective as journalists, Washington insiders"—this, from their promotional brochure—"and also parents and working professionals." Sometimes these perspectives blended, as in branding term limits "the single worst idea in recent American politics." The notion that politics is inherently corrupting, they wrote, "is flat-out wrong, even dangerous."

Lindy's memoir, *Washington Through a Purple Veil*, published in 1994, was too gracious ("I was honored . . . a lovely reception . . . . my good friend") to be compelling. Her editor pushed Cokie to write a book of her own. Narrative nonfiction was giving way on best-seller lists to memoirs and books by celebrity authors, but Cokie kept saying, "I'm fifty years old—please God, I'm not over yet—and I don't have a book."

Was there nothing she had spoken or written about that she cared enough to expound at book length?

Then she realized that there was, in the speeches she had delivered to young women on campuses about the continuity and unfolding tasks of women's lives.

She wrote *We Are Our Mothers' Daughters* while juggling her jobs and both children's weddings the summer of 1997. "So much of the work that I do is collaborative," she said. "It was nice to do something by myself." The small, slim, smooth-reading book mixed tales of her own life, her mother's, and her late sister's with those of accomplished women past and present. The feel-good volume, with her picture on the cover, her name looming over the title, reached the summit of the *New York Times* best-seller list.

It was followed by an even more personal book. The joint venture of Cokie and Steve, *From This Day Forward* centered on their marriage, documenting their interfaith family and their cooperative-but-competitive careers, interspersed with stories of marriages from American history. Timed for Valentine's Day, it also scaled the best-seller lists for six or seven weeks.

"Washington's power couple," they were dubbed when they appeared on *Larry King Live*.

Walter Lippmann had been an insider's insider, as had Arthur Krock and Philip Graham and Drew Pearson and James Reston, Steve's mentor. So now it was Howard Fineman, *Newsweek's* political correspondent, urging the president to send Chelsea to Sidwell Friends, where *his* daughter went, or Cokie serving as emcee for the retiring House minority leader, Bob Michel, "a very dear friend."

"I think that I probably have a bias toward Congress that other reporters don't have," she said. "It's nice to have some countervailing voice. . . . It's important to have both."

But these competing approaches to life in the capital would soon prove fateful for Steve.

He had left the *New York Times* a few years earlier, in 1989, in part because of the newspaper's arrogant unwillingness to allow its reporters to appear regularly on television. He had done everything he could realistically expect to do at the *Times*—writing a column was not in the cards—and he feared that becoming an editor and losing his byline, his visibility, just as Cokie was becoming known, "would be risky for our relationship." He liked being recognized in airports. When *U.S. News & World Report* offered him a senior writer's post, he accepted.

He was a commentator, an analyst, one of the newsmagazine's most visible people—"they specifically hired me for that," he said. *U.S. News* perennially trailed *Time* and *Newsweek* in circulation and clout, but because it was the only one based in Washington, Steve could write about whatever he wanted. He produced cover stories on wage stagnation, the religious Right, antismokers, Rush Limbaugh, Colin Powell. He appeared regularly on *Washington Week in Review* and showed up on CNN, *Meet the Press*, C-SPAN—both on cable and on broadcast TV. The management at *U.S. News* encouraged him to give speeches to advertisers or anyone else, to promote the magazine.

In the bland modern offices of *U.S. News* in the refurbished West End, Steve was happy.

Then the developer Mort Zuckerman, the owner of *U.S. News*, hired a new top editor. Jim Fallows was a Puritan about the practice of journalism. He was a thoughtful and earnest journalist—sanctimonious, said some—who had quit as President Carter's chief speechwriter and (as his critics delighted in pointing out) promptly condemned his former boss in the *Atlantic Monthly* for conducting "The Passionless Presidency."

For Steve Roberts, the choice could not have been worse. Fallows had just published a book that berated journalists in the capital—and Cokie and Steve in particular—for practicing celebrity journalism, for encouraging a "star-oriented" news culture that put entertainment and conflict ahead of substance. "Fallows has attacked the Church of the Insider," was *Mediaweek*'s summation.

An insurgent now had power.

Even before Fallows started, Steve was fired.

Within two years, however, Fallows himself was axed. Even Jim Warren had wound up on television, as a regular on CNN's *The Capital Gang*.

"My own personal relationship with Lindy Boggs," said Al Gore, "goes back to, really, the time when I was born."

Before the packed auditorium in the Old Executive Office Building, the famously wooden vice president burst into laughter and added, "Before that, actually."

The senior senator from Louisiana, John Breaux, had prompted the president to think of nominating eighty-one-year-old Lindy as the ambassador to the Vatican. The president's personnel director phoned Tommy to ask whether his mother would accept, should an offer be made. The lobbyist noted that he represented a chain of nursing homes and said, "She's taking the job."

The job suited Lindy. The Vatican was a diplomatic listening post, and Lindy was a listener. She also spoke "fluent Catholic," as Breaux put it, and she was a safe choice for an administration that had suffered too many nomination slugfests. With her antiabortion views and her soothing demeanor, and of course her decades around Capitol Hill, Lindy was sure to gain the Republican-run Senate's consent.

She wore a purple dress to her confirmation hearing before Foreign Relations. The proceedings would have killed a diabetic. Breaux said that introducing Lindy "makes me feel like I've been assigned to come here and present Mother Teresa." The committee's senior Democrat, Joe Biden, had known Lindy since he was a senator-elect. When an auto accident killed Biden's wife and daughter just weeks after Hale's disappearance, Lindy traveled to Delaware to help organize his incoming staff.

The chairman, Jesse Helms, had not planned to attend, but he stopped by late and gave Lindy a kiss. He had still been a Democrat when Hale spoke at Jefferson-Jackson Day dinners in North Carolina years before, and as a Republican senator he had traveled with Lindy on congressional delegations.

"There may be somewhere in this broad land a potential nominee who would have greater acceptance of respect from this committee than this dear lady," he said, "but I can't think of them."

"Oh, thank you, Mr. Chairman," Lindy replied.

"Top of that, Cokie Roberts is your daughter and we like her too." A former television commentator himself, Helms admired Cokie's skill before a camera.

As a Baptist from a Baptist-dominated state, Helms had never voted to confirm an ambassador to the Holy See.

"You may as well pack," he told her.

Lindy asked the vice president to administer the oath. Their families had been friends for fifty-six years, united in part by their common travails as southern moderates. More than two hundred people looked on, including George McGovern, the Shrivers, Tip O'Neill's widow, lawmakers galore, and five cardinals—the ones who ruled dioceses, not Appropriations subcommittees.

The vice president told them of a photograph he treasured, of him at four years old, in Lindy's arms, after he had become cranky during a congressional trip to Switzerland.

"And here we are all these years later, I'm the vice president swearing Mrs. Boggs in," he said. "It's a lovely story about how Washington works."

On *This Week with Sam Donaldson and Cokie Roberts*, as the show was eventually called, Cokie likened her role to another she had known.

"I have children," she said—"it's good experience for a lot of things."

She had to step between Sam Donaldson and George Will, and then between another ideologically matched set, of George Stephanopoulos and Bill Kristol, the new regulars on the roundtable, to make sure that everyone's views were heard.

One Sunday in January 1998, Bill Kristol started to mention a report overnight on the World Wide Web that *Newsweek*'s editors had killed a story about an affair between the president and a White House intern.

George Stephanopoulos cut him off.

"And Bill, where did it come from? The *Drudge Report*. You know, we've all seen how discredited . . ."

They fought for control of the conversation. Sam Donaldson won.

"I'm not an apologist for *Newsweek*," Sam said, "but if their editors decided they didn't have it cold enough to go with, I don't think that we can here."

Cokie changed the subject.

Twelve days later, in the Diplomatic Reception Room at the White House, where FDR had delivered his fireside chats, Tommy Boggs attended Lanny Davis's going-away party. Lanny was a Patton Boggs partner who had already scheduled his return to the firm after a two-year stint as the president's spokesman on scandals, just as the most consequential one erupted.

Bill Clinton pulled Tommy Boggs over to the side to ask his advice. How bad was it? Could he prevail?

The president's advisers believed he was history. But Tommy thought he could survive Monica Lewinsky. He told Clinton that Abe Fortas should never have resigned from the Supreme Court in 1969, after it was learned he had accepted a twenty-thousand-dollar fee from a financier's foundation. Usually, Tommy said, Washington gets over these things.

This was just what a besieged president wanted to hear.

As had his two twentieth-century predecessors who gained the White House while still in their forties, Clinton had a recklessness about him, one that fit the nation's unearned prosperity, the decade's air of abandon. His talents could hardly be disentangled from his oversized flaws. Philandering in presidents could correlate with a capacity to manipulate with grace—women, politicians, the public. How else might he have escaped a broken home in a backward state and catapulted into the meritocracy and then into the presidency, at the forefront of the largest generation in the nation's history?

Surely more than ever, anyone could grow up to be president.

When the president's adultery veered into impeachment, Tommy heard from the White House. Every morning at ten o'clock, he joined in a conference call to discuss tactics with a score of Democratic lobbyists, spin doctors, and old Washington hands.

Then the president did whatever he liked.

In December a solemn and bitter House of Representatives, for the first time in 130 years, voted to impeach the president, narrowly approving two articles of impeachment and rejecting two others. That evening, Tommy was reluctant to attend the White House Christmas party, but he and his wife, Barbara, passed through the receiving line.

"Pretty good vote, don't you think?" the president said.

Tommy was surprised at his optimism.

The following spring, after the Senate had acquitted him, Clinton went to Tommy's house in Chevy Chase for a Democratic fund-raising dinner. Barbara disapproved, because a presidential motorcade late in the rush hour along Connecticut Avenue disrupted the neighborhood.

The sunshine-colored house, just beyond the District line, had been built in 1896 as a three-story summer place, rambling and cheery—Irish Gothic, it was called—though Tommy and Barbara were only the third owners. (One of Gwen Cafritz's lawyers lived next door, and the cable television host Chris Matthews and his wife, a local newscaster, lived down the street.) The house was roomy enough for the donors who hoped against hope to restore the House to Democratic hands.

A priest from Georgetown University delivered a prayer, and the president wondered aloud, "How did the conversation go when Tommy Boggs asked you to come and pray over all these politicians, lobbyists, and fund-raisers?" He imagined the priest's reply: "Well, if I can pray over you, Tom, I can pray over anybody."

Clinton recalled his encounter with Hale a week before he disappeared and mentioned Lindy's current role, as "maybe the only person on the earth who could convince the Pope that I am worth dealing with."

The wealthy Democrats laughed.

"So I love the Boggs family."

Tommy had acquired a startling physical resemblance to his father, even in his unconscious mannerisms, such as rocking back and forth on the podium while delivering a speech. On Tommy's fifty-eighth birthday, Cokie had noticed a particular sadness in her older brother. Cokie disliked birthdays, and Tommy was worse. Then she remembered that their father had died at fifty-eight.

Only Cokie understood. The two were close.

"You're going to make it to fifty-nine," she said to Tommy. "I promise you."

He knew what she meant.

Julius Hobson Jr. returned to the AMA's offices from Capitol Hill one day in December 1998 and the other lobbyists congratulated him.

"For what?" he said.

He had been named the acting director of congressional affairs.

Hobby had joined the AMA for the salary and the benefits—as a place to retire from—and of course for the love of the game. He had never intended to become more than a staff lobbyist—the director was just a year older than he was.

But the director realized that a vice presidency was beyond his reach, and Hobby was seen as having the right personality and skills to lead a staff. The following April, Hobby's position became permanent.

At last, he had moved beyond race.

Or had he? Once, he arrived at a meeting on Capitol Hill and the conversation stopped, until a senator said, "Hi, Julius."

"I just don't give a shit," Hobby said later. "I'm the AMA—you either talk to me or not."

He carried a self-conscious toughness about him, which he also directed at his staff. Soon after he became the director, he called the AMA's lobbyists into a conference room and shut the door. In a stodgy organization that had long been known for lack of new blood, nearly the entire lobbying staff had turned over since Hobby's arrival five years before.

"Let me tell you something," he began. "I promised my family and myself that I would never go to the emergency room with a heart problem again as long as I can control it. You people drive me crazy, and if I think there's a problem I'll get rid of every one of you sons-of-bitches before I go back."

Over the next two years, all but one of them left. The alcoholic went first, after Hobby stacked empty boxes outside his door and gave him three minutes to resign or be fired. As for the others, Hobby had lost confidence in the information they passed along.

In replacing them, Hobby openly discriminated. He preferred women as lobbyists, because "they don't have the testosterone problem" and yet were more aggressive than men. They would introduce themselves to a male legislator and, instead of needing to make their presence felt, immediately start stating their case.

"Also, I will only hire first-born, last-born, or somebody from a large family," he said—that is, pathfinders or battlers for attention. He sought combative, self-centered lobbyists, "because that's what it takes to do the job."

He structured his staff as a team of horses pulling a wagon or an infantry squad—"this one is a machine gunner, this one's a sharpshooter, this one's aggressive, this one's consistent and steady."

He had spent years reading military history, as a way to relax. He also found it enlightening. In his course at GW on advanced lobbying strategies, the first reading assignment was Sun Tzu's ancient text, *The Art of War*. Military strategy helped him think through a lobbying problem. In pushing for a patients' bill of rights, which insurance companies and HMOs opposed, "they have more money than we will ever be able to put on the table, they have more individual lobbyists to walk around on Capitol Hill," Hobby reasoned. "What do I have they don't have? Grass roots—doctors in every congressional district. And I also have every American citizen— everybody is a patient. I have to use that broad base to overcome the money."

He understood that the preparation for battle mattered more than the combat itself, and that midcourse adjustments could win the day. He studied the strategy of Joe Gibbs, the Redskins coach who had won three Super Bowls, buttressed by an ability to modify his game plan at half-time.

When the Republican speaker took the patients' bill of rights to the Senate floor, Hobby was thrilled to defeat him on four straight roll-call votes. Yet he found these triumphs vaguely deflating, for the game was over. And ultimately the bill never passed, though he cared less about the outcome than the game itself. In this, he was not his father's son.

He had new opportunities to prove it. One morning without warning in the spring of 2000 hundreds of protesters from a disability-rights group took over the wide sidewalk along Vermont Avenue and invaded the AMA's offices upstairs. The twelfth floor was wall-to-wall wheelchairs.

As the senior manager on the premises, Hobby insisted on no arrests—"no film at eleven." This time he would wait out the protesters. Soon he would be known around the office as the Negotiator.

For six hours the incapacitated held their ground, demanding that the AMA endorse a Senate bill that would create alternatives to keeping the disabled in nursing homes. Hobby had the AMA's chef send down water to relieve the demonstrators' thirst—knowing that nature would take its course. At four o'clock they left, carrying a memorandum of understanding that promised a meeting to review the group's legislative wishes. Julius Hobson Jr. signed for the AMA.

Julius Hobson Sr., were he still alive, might have signed for the protesters.

———

Hillary Clinton looked resplendent in blue, which matched the sky behind her, in an open-sided tent on the Mall on this windy spring day in 1999. Despite all the talk that she would run for the Senate from New York, in tandem with her husband's departure from the White House, she was doing what presidents' wives traditionally did. On behalf of a grateful nation, she accepted the Sculpture Garden beside the National Gallery of Art as a gift from the Morris and Gwendolyn Cafritz Foundation.

"The vision for a garden on this spot," she said, "was developed two centuries ago, with the original plans for the city of Washington." L'Enfant had foreseen a landscaped park with "copious water" for precisely this site, between Seventh and Ninth Streets.

But he could never have imagined a typewriter eraser nearly twenty feet tall or a bronze hare perched on a rock or Calder's red sheet-metal horse. The six acres of whimsy, across Constitution Avenue from the National Archives, where the Center Market had once stood, contained seventeen pieces of sculpture, an ice-skating pond, and paths that curved among a profusion of native American trees and shrubs, in every shade of green. It resembled the Mall as it had been at the century's beginning, when young Morris Cafritz loped through.

Now his eldest son sat beside the first lady's empty chair, as she spoke.

"This is truly the manifestation of the generosity of the American spirit," she said. "For three decades this foundation has set the standard for philanthropy in Washington, D.C."

The project had languished for at least that long. After Gwen had pledged the statuary as part of Lady Bird's beautification, the federal contribution vanished, a victim of the costly Vietnam War, until the foundation became involved again.

"This is a city that is really on its way back," Hillary Clinton said, "in every respect."

Calvin followed the first lady to the podium. He did not care for public speaking, though it had grown easier over the years. He had written out his remarks.

"Both of my parents loved Washington," he said, "and wanted the foundation to reflect their dedication to the metropolitan area. Both were excited by new ideas."

The foundation had given the project more than ten million dollars, to build the garden and to acquire eight of the sculptures. The extraordinary gift marked the fiftieth anniversary of the foundation, and just about a century since its founder had ridden past.

Tommy Boggs had invested in The Palm when, at George Bush's urging, it opened a restaurant in Washington in 1972. Bush had been the ambassador to the United Nations at the time and wanted the New York restaurant to open a branch in the capital. Epic steaks, chest-hair martinis, the wall-mounted caricatures of loyal customers and politicians (George Bush in a loincloth on a Republican elephant's back) gave a macho bonhomie to Nineteenth Street, in the third block north of K.

This was Tommy's style. "Boy toys?" said his wife. "Yeah, he likes his Range Rover and his Mercedes, his hunting lodge. He likes his big old boat."

The atmosphere suited the capital, too—blustery, backslapping, meat-and-potatoes, the continuation of politics by gastronomic means. The Palm had hosted Chuck Colson's going-away party the day before he went to prison for his Watergate transgressions. Twenty-two years later Monica Lewinsky celebrated her twenty-third birthday at The Palm, when few beyond the president knew her name.

"Kind of like a 'Cheers' for Washington's elite," the *Washington Times* noticed.

Washington had never been known for fine dining. It was an eating-in, not an eating-out, city. Even into the 1960s, the better households employed servants, and middle-class families could afford restaurants only on occasion. Culinary quality was confined to the best hotels and the rare old favorite. (Harvey's had served presidents from Lincoln to Carter.) The Kennedys had inspired a wave of French restaurants and upscale saloons, such as Clyde's in Georgetown. The ascendance of lawyers and lobbyists with clients to impress, the rising incomes of permanent Washington, fueled a surge of white-tablecloth restaurants in the 1970s and 1980s. "Power lunches," "power dining"—the self-mockery mingled with pride.

Duke Zeibert had made the culinary style famous in the restaurant he had opened in 1950 at Connecticut and L and named after himself. Gruff and jaunty, a bristly moustache on his fleshy face, with his defiantly open collar and his long mane of gray hair, Duke was discerning in his judgment of political status; by assigning a table for lunch he could make or ruin a customer's day. Surly waiters served unsubtle food to the notables there to hobnob and be seen—J. Edgar Hoover and Bob Strauss and John Sirica and Tip O'Neill and Art Buchwald and Ben Bradlee and the Redskins' owners, Jack Kent Cooke and superlawyer Edward Bennett Williams, and the coach, Joe Gibbs.

"Great to see you, Larry," David Brinkley had greeted his interviewer one night on *Larry King Live*. "I usually see you at Duke Zeibert's at lunch."

"Yes."

"I'm happy to see that you do work at night."

Even Clinton—"making his peace with Old Washington," said the *Post*—had broken bread one evening at Duke's with the Senate minority leader, Bob Dole, in a meeting of the bulls that was hosted (and promoted to the press) by Bob Strauss.

Duke Zeibert's had closed, twice, and by 1997 its proprietor was dead. Haley Barbour approached Tommy with an idea. He was an affable bear of a Mississippian, a former Republican Party chairman (and later a governor of Mississippi) and a lobbyist of ample proportion, politically and physically. When a lobbyist took a client to lunch, the client paid for the meal *and* for the lobbyist's time—"sort of a sweetheart deal," as one of Tommy's law partners pointed out. How much sweeter if the lobbyist also owned the restaurant.

Haley went first to Tommy Boggs, as a prominent Democrat and decade-old friend, to go in with him on what a co-owner described as "a Washington-ambianced restaurant." After Haley lined up experienced restaurateurs to run the place, Tommy said yes.

They agreed to put in $150,000 apiece and looked for smaller investors. Within four days, they were oversubscribed, and reduced their own shares by a third. The sixty-some investors included the playground kings of permanent Washington, the likes of Terry McAuliffe, the president's top fund-raiser and new best friend; Boyden Gray, George H. W. Bush's White House counsel and aspiring superlawyer; congressman-turned-lobbyist Tom Downey, the vice president's crony; Ted Leonsis and three of the other high-tech titans in suburban Virginia who were displacing the city's real estate magnates as sources of civic support; a Republican pollster; and the Senate's sergeant-at-arms. They chose a location just off Pennsylvania Avenue, halfway between the Capitol and the White House, four blocks from Haley's office. Now that Pennsylvania Avenue had been closed in front of the White House, after the terrorist bombing in Oklahoma City, driving to the restaurants to the west took too long.

Tommy proposed to call the restaurant Fat Boys. Both he and Haley had begun to resemble the Falstaffian power brokers, jowly and stout, in the old Thomas Nast cartoons. Instead, the restaurateurs named it the Caucus Room, a title that Tommy said "sort of symbolizes what it's trying to be"—a gathering place for swapping information, cutting deals, raising money, being seen.

The restaurant strived for a certain dignity, with mahogany walls and brass fixtures and a tasteful blue carpet reminiscent of the House of Representatives. The décor, subdued and serious, alternated wine racks with black-and-white photographs of presidents—Teddy Roosevelt with John Muir, Woodrow Wilson making peace, FDR in a wheelchair, an exhausted LBJ, Nixon and Elvis, George Bush and his eldest son with a Texas Rangers ballplayer between them. The *New York Times* and *Newsweek* covered the opening.

Tommy imagined even a higher purpose for the Caucus Room than caucusing. He saw it as a place to salve the capital's partisan wounds, over drinks.

"This town has been kind of a mean town the last few years," he said. "We're not mean people. We like being with each other. It is an attempt to sort of make it a happier place."

This was not so different from Gwen Cafritz's ambition, to foster a sense of an "us" in the capital, which necessitated a "them." Only this time it was meant to turn a profit.

"Your father would turn over in his grave if he knew." A black minister was shouting from the audience.

Julius Hobson Jr. resisted telling him that his father had been cremated.

For less than two months, Hobby had been the chairman of the city's Health and Hospitals Public Benefit Corporation, the quasi-governmental board that oversaw D.C. General Hospital. It was like being back on the school board. The hospital board had met all morning in private, in August 2000, to sift through the awful alternatives. Afternoon ushered in the public, including the hospital workers who faced losing their jobs and the neighborhood activists aghast at the continuing decline of the only hospital that assured medical care for the city's poor. They crowded into the stuffy auditorium in D.C. General's basement to make their feelings known.

Originally known as "The Poor House," the hospital had treated the city's indigent since 1806. During the Civil War, already located on the Anacostia River shore, it expanded as a barracks hospital for Union troops. Later it became known for beds in hallways, cockroaches in the kitchen, tubercular nurses, food stolen from the patients. It took its current name in 1953, in a vain attempt to escape its past.

The aging brick complex sprawled next to the city jail and the morgue, and by law it could turn away no D.C. resident. The city government picked up more and more of the hospital's mounting costs, just as the city's finances collapsed. Congress insisted that the subsidies to D.C. General cease. Once the largest public hospital between Philadelphia and New Orleans, D.C. General had already seen its capacity of a thousand beds halved, then halved again, and still it could not live within its means.

Home rule had ushered in a mayor who pandered for votes by creating city jobs and catering to constituents. In the booming 1980s the city's revenue could support such democratic beneficence, but the slump in real estate and taxes (with a mayor distracted by his personal demons) plunged the undisciplined city into financial crisis. So

Congress created a financial control board, appointed by the president, with the authority to overrule the mayor and the City Council—a suspension, really, of home rule. Only after four consecutive years of a balanced budget could the control board relinquish control. By 2000 all that stood in its way was D.C. General.

The City Council chairwoman, Linda Cropp, whose husband was Hobby's best friend, had named the onetime school board member, the AMA's top lobbyist, to the hospital board near the end of 1996. As its members dropped off the unpaid, time-consuming, and ever-more-stressful board, Hobby became its vice-chairman and then the chairman, in charge of the public hospital's fate.

"I just thought it was a form of community service," he said.

He made it his task to convince the others that, after years of blustery threats, D.C. General might truly disappear. "You've never been in a situation," he told them, "where the Mayor, the control board, and the Congress were ready to do this, and you can't count on the City Council to save you."

In executive session, they agonized and agreed at last to lay off 550 of the hospital's 2,000 workers, turning D.C. General into little more than an emergency room. Unhappily this is what the hospital did best, repairing stabbings and gunshots in its top-notch trauma center. The twelve board members had convened at eight in the morning, but not until midafternoon were they ready to face the public.

The narrow stage in the hospital's basement auditorium concealed a board member at both wings. The worn carpet and bare plaster walls lent the auditorium an institutional feel. Hobby had never seen it so full. Maybe three hundred people filled the blue-cushioned seats and jammed the aisles, which sloped down toward the front. They buzzed with hostility.

Hobby's colleagues wanted to summon protectors in uniform. But he had learned something from the war over Barbara Sizemore—not to provoke just the reaction they hoped to avert.

"It's not about intimidation," he told them. "There will be no arrests in here."

When the meeting started, he said to the audience, "I'll stay here as long as anybody wants to talk to us." Curses and insults and scriptural pleadings were flung to the front. "What you do to the least of God's children will be rendered unto you!" For three and a half hours the board members listened to emotional appeals. No minds were changed, on stage or in the audience.

Black men in D.C. had a shorter life expectancy than any group of Americans except the male Oglala Sioux, and losing D.C. General was bound to devastate the medical care in the poorest and sickest quadrant of the city. Yet this paled beside the fact that the hospital was losing more than two million dollars a month.

"We are forced to live within the amount that has been budgeted," Hobby tried to explain to the angry audience, "and that left us virtually no option."

The board adopted its proposal to eviscerate D.C. General in order to save it—to dismiss a quarter of the staff and reduce the hospital to a place where patients would be treated no longer than a day, then sent elsewhere. The meeting ended around six o'clock, and Hobby stayed and answered questions for almost an hour and a half.

Then the City Council stepped in, hoping to restore the dilapidated hospital to a modern facility and affiliate it with Howard's own medical complex. Hobby liked the idea, but it would cost far more than the city could afford or Congress would allow.

The mayor had another idea. Tony Williams had succeeded the redeemed-then-rejected Marion Barry after serving as his chief financial officer. With his trademark bow tie and his accountant's soul, his degrees from Yale and Harvard, he was a white voter's ideal of a black politician—the unBarry. His lack of a political touch was part of his appeal. His plan would leave D.C. General with an emergency room and outpatient care—nothing else—and otherwise rely on a network of clinics and referrals to private hospitals, at taxpayers' expense.

The stalemate that took hold between the rival restructurings posed the worst danger of all. "We'll be out of money by the end of next month," Hobby warned during the fall of 2000.

He knew that doom for the public hospital was only a matter of when. So he vowed, in the meantime, to "shame and embarrass everybody I can," to ask hard questions, to point out the flaws. When Mayor Williams suggested transferring D.C. General's trauma unit to Greater Southeast, formerly Cafritz Memorial, Hobby noted that this would require an arduous round of accreditation. He wondered in public about the identity of the one-time ex officio member of the hospital board who had never attended a meeting while D.C. General's finances were sinking. His name was Tony Williams.

Hobby had precious little faith left in home rule, which his father had made a crusade. Already the son had proposed placing the city into a receiver's hands, suspending elections for three to five years, and hiring a city manager. Residents would prefer a city government that works, he argued in the *Post*, "to one whose only virtue is that its citizens put it in place."

The nation's capital, he implied, had grown incapable of democracy.

The financial control board ended the impasse over D.C. General by siding with the mayor. When the mission of providing medical care to the city's poor and uninsured was put out for bid, the victor was Greater Southeast.

D.C. General soon closed, leaving the eastern half of the city without an emergency room that could meet the dreaded demand. Soon it was clear that people were dying as a result.

Hobby had given up more than half of his vacation time for two years and was tired of hearing the telephone ring at all hours.

"More draining than the school board," he said. Hobby doubted he would try public service again, "because that just about wiped me out."

Late in the summer of 2000, Peggy Cooper Cafritz dined with friends at a sidewalk table outside Kinkead's, a seafood restaurant along Pennsylvania Avenue near George Washington University. Her friends, all educators, conversed about the agony of black schoolchildren in D.C. and whether it was inevitable.

A few weeks earlier, when the mayor's chief of staff had phoned to inquire whether she might be interested in running for president of the school board, Peggy had answered, "No." She was raising two sons after her divorce.

Over the seafood, Peggy changed her mind. "I decided that night," she said later, "that I would put my money where my mouth was and do it." She thought that nobody else who could turn the schools around was likely to run.

The president was to be directly elected instead of chosen by the board, according to the reorganization that Mayor Williams had narrowly persuaded the public to adopt—as if the structure of authority were the problem with D.C. schools. The hybrid board was to consist of four appointed members and five elected ones, including the president. The mayor had been expected to support a former city councilman for the post, but his political advisers warned of creating a rival for his own reelection.

The mayor's wife became Peggy's campaign treasurer and his aides took leave to work on her behalf, though at Peggy's request the mayor refrained from a public endorsement until a week before the election, so that he would seem less like a puppeteer.

Anxiety was rising among black Washingtonians, as Chocolate City had grown milkier. African Americans (in the term Jesse Jackson had popularized) had been moving out to the suburbs, mainly to Prince George's County, while Central Americans, Asians, and gentrifying whites were moving in. The city's voters had astonished themselves in 1998 by electing a majority of whites to the City Council.

Peggy's opponents were a black preacher who was the president of the outgoing board and a PTA activist who assured audiences that he was part Native American. Peggy replaced her all-text yard signs with ones that included her photograph.

"I've run into so many people on the street who say, 'Oh, we thought you were white,'" she explained. Her dark skin and her white name and neighborhood gave her a certain appeal in a city so divided by race.

On the stump her tone was blunt. "All I ask you to do, ladies and gentlemen, is get copies of the test scores," she said at a candidates' forum. "These guys do not understand the problem is acute." Her promises were ambitious indeed. She called for "a Marshall Plan" to fix and replace dilapidated school buildings and an effort to recruit teachers "who are masters of the subjects they teach" and to pay them whatever the market demanded. She sought autonomy for individual schools.

"We have cracked the code at Ellington," she said. "Please give me the chance to employ what we have learned across the city."

Voters liked Peggy's intention to shake things up. She also had the money to get her point across on radio. With the election still days away, she had spent $119,445 on her campaign, to the incumbent's $7,232. She was intent on winning in black neighborhoods—85 percent of D.C. public school students were black—as well as in white ones.

And she did, except east of the Anacostia River. She won decisively citywide, drawing 53 percent of the votes, to the incumbent's 37 percent.

"People want reform quickly," she declared. "We all know that one thing that came out of the election is a mandate for change."

The new Board of Education, including the mayor's four nonpolitical appointees, went on a two-day retreat, in the hope of averting resentments between the elected and the appointed members. Instead a different division began to emerge—between Peggy and the other members.

Soon word spread that Peggy's colleagues on the board found her autocratic and hard to work with, that they had tired of learning about her plans in the newspaper. The impulsive frankness that had attracted Peggy votes in November caused her quite a lot of trouble. When she told the editorial board at the *Post* that probably half the city's teachers were unqualified or incompetent, the teachers' union exploded. As a power struggle developed between the school board and the mayor over control of the schools, matters only seemed to get worse.

What hubris there was, in any event, in believing that a clever restructuring, an assertion of authority, a reordering of priorities could fix the crumbling buildings, the shortage of textbooks, the broken homes, the drugs and the gangs, the babies who bore babies, yet another generation of children who saw no future for themselves. If the Board of Education could fix all that ailed the city's public schools, why would it have waited until now?

A reporter from the *Kansas City Star* phoned Cokie Roberts to interview her about widows in Congress. The article was about Jean Carnahan, whose husband, Missouri's governor, had perished in a plane crash too late to be removed from the Senate ballot. The widow was in the throes of deciding whether to accept an appointment to the Senate in the unimaginable event that, come Election Day, her husband triumphed from the grave.

The reporter wanted to know how Mrs. Carnahan could be expected to handle the burden of politics with so fresh a loss.

"I think it would be the best thing possible for Jean Carnahan," Cokie replied. Lindy had found that furthering Hale's legacy helped her through her grief. "Every day," Cokie said, "you're doing it for yourself as well as for the one you've lost."

Jean Carnahan read the article on page thirteen and started to think of her dilemma differently. Afterward she said her decision to accept was inspired in part by Cokie's remarks.

This also won Cokie a "get," an exclusive interview. On the Sunday before the election, Mrs. Carnahan appeared with Cokie on *This Week*. Her own father's death and posthumous election, her mother's election in his place—"That's one of the reasons you wanted to talk to me," Cokie began.

"Yes, that's right," the widow of two weeks replied.

Jean Carnahan's restraint and dignity in her grief made the interview all the more affecting.

She recounted that she had been sitting at her computer one night when a security man entered and knelt before her, took her hand, and delivered the news—"and it just seemed like the light of my life went out." She gave Cokie the smallest of shrugs.

"We shared," she said, "not just a lifetime, but the ideals and the values and the visions that he had, and I felt that those things were just too important to let die."

Cokie, too, was restrained. Had they been on *Good Morning America* instead of a news show, she would have asked how Mrs. Carnahan could survive losing an election after losing her husband and her son, the plane's pilot.

"I just felt that was unfair to poor John Ashcroft," Cokie said later, referring to the Republican incumbent whose interview followed.

Jean Carnahan entered the Senate without regrets.

Inside the mansion on Foxhall Road, time had stood still. Gwen Cafritz had been dead for a dozen years, Morris for three dozen, yet the blond furniture, the risqué murals, the volumes of Hemingway on the library shelf: nothing had changed—except that the house seemed so dated now, in its architecture, its décor, its sensibility. The foundation had resisted adding it to the National Register of Historic Places, for fear of lowering the selling price.

Once the lawsuit over Gwen's will was resolved, the time came to dispose of the house.

Calvin Cafritz had a fiduciary duty to obtain top dollar. Earlier in the year Christie's had auctioned off the Degas for $1.8 million and the Dalí for $1.3 million. A 1953 gown of Gwen's had gone for sixteen thousand dollars, the top lot. Eugene Schoen's furniture of exotic woods and industrial plastics sold in lots of varying size, starting in the fall of 2000.

The house itself had first gone on the market in 1996 for $9.95 million, twice the assessed value. Years passed, with no takers.

Yet there was interest. A local developer, a friend of Calvin's, craved the ten-acre plot that backed up against a park, with its breathless view of the city. He intended to raze the mansion and build thirty-five or forty houses, a gated community. Such had been the fate of the Rockefeller estate, farther north along Foxhall Road. As a developer himself, Calvin understood that this was the most profitable use of the property.

"Perfectly decent," Calvin said, "but a gated community?" Not in his childhood home, his parents' refuge.

He wanted to sell instead to the Field School. Founded in 1972, the heyday of progressivism in education, the private school believed in self-expression and one-on-one teaching. Calvin was smitten with the school, with the self-confidence it instilled in its students. The student body had squeezed into two carriage houses, with only a side yard as a playground, on Wyoming Avenue, off Connecticut. He took the director out to Foxhall Road.

"It seems to me," he said, "this is something that really ought to be yours."

So he waited two years until they could raise the money. The $9.3 million sale was closed ten days before 2000 expired and, officially, a century ended.

Gwen's bedroom would become the library and media center; Morris's, the middle school lounge. Calvin knew that his parents would have been pleased.

The school gave Calvin six months to move everything from the house. A week before the groundbreaking on a second building and the renovation of the first, nightgowns still lay across Gwen's bed and makeup remained in her dressing room. Morris's rooms held his favorite softball bat and the softball he had pitched in the real estate league, along with pajamas from Garfinckel's and pads for scoring gin rummy.

Calvin Cafritz was nearly seventy now, though with his dark lush hair and his gawky grin he looked at least a decade younger. He still seemed boyish, and also the old man he was becoming all of his life.

He had auctioned off his father's construction company, razed the Ambassador Hotel, laid both of his parents to rest. Now he sold the fairyland he had first loved as a boy. Of all the endings he had faced, he thought of this one as the crowning event.

It was Phil Graham, the Florida-reared publisher of the *Washington Post,* who had described the capital as a sleepy southern town. And it had been.

"It was a sleepy southern town when I arrived," Lindy Boggs said many years later, "and now it's a transient metropolis."

She was transient, if returning home after fifty years of living in Washington counted as impermanence. When her time at the Vatican expired as President Clinton left office, her children pleaded with her to return to Washington to live.

"I guess it's peculiar that I don't want to make it my permanent home," she said, "but I don't."

From Rome she flew directly to New Orleans.

This was fitting, for Lindy no longer belonged in the city that Washington had become.

The tone in the capital had become ornerier as the decades passed. "They didn't send us here to bicker," President George H. W. Bush had said in his inaugural address, in 1989, before the bickering deepened into trench warfare. Legislators of unlike mind rarely socialized anymore. Civility had yielded to partisan antipathy and self-segregation. How could Lindy Boggs feel at home in the Washington of Tom DeLay?

Physically, the capital had grown only more enchanting. Its sequins of white were set in ribbons of green. Even the most dangerous neighborhoods looked inviting in daylight. The air was clean, the sky wide open, the sightlines unimpeded. L'Enfant, the McMillan Commission, and Lady Bird Johnson had succeeded beautifully in their self-imposed tasks.

In many ways, however, Washington had grown ever uglier. Architecturally, for one: The personable and eccentric buildings of bygone days, with cupolas and towers and even a windmill on the roof, had surrendered to boxy bulk. In 1938, Frank Lloyd Wright had railed to federal architects at the Mayflower Hotel that governmental "buildings are not built to serve the people, but to satisfy a kind of grandomania." Might he have been picturing the Rayburn House Office Building or the Kennedy Center or the Air and Space Museum or the Madison Building of the Library of Congress?

Except that now the nongovernmental buildings, too, were every bit as ungainly. Look no farther than the canyon of K Street. The gracious mansions of the past had given way to office buildings that were hard, cold cubes.

It was the fact of them, more than their soulless style, that had changed the capital—the rise of permanent Washington. Politicians, Lord knows, still behaved as politicians, with their erratic mix of egotism and high-mindedness that was little more than a magnification, after all, of human nature. But the apparatus that had grown up around them, representing in disproportionate degrees the people and interests that Washington governed, had transformed the way the capital worked.

Lindy's surviving children had become stalwarts—indeed, emblems—of permanent Washington. After failing to follow in his father's elective footsteps, Tommy happily pursued a profession that was far more lucrative (beyond two million dollars a year) and did not depend on the unforgiving whims of public opinion. The law firm, too, had insulated itself from the vagaries of democracy. Roughly half of the in-house partisans at Patton Boggs were now Republicans.

"The firm is a microcosm of Washington," Ben Ginsberg, who was one of them, said. Ginsberg put the firm at the center of political events after the election of 2000, when he headed the legal team that delivered Florida—and the White House—to George W. Bush. A half-dozen others from Patton Boggs helped.

And thus the presidency itself was drawn into the maw of the law and of Washington lawyers.

"My old man really wanted me to go to an established law firm—so I'm there," Tommy recounted with obvious pride. Patton Boggs had filled every floor at 2550 M Street with so many partners that they no longer all knew one another. (His youngest child, Douglas, was soon one of them.) The firm opened an office in Tysons Corner, to pursue high-tech business, and Tommy was thinking of expanding again into New York. He believed that the nation's law firms were eventually going to consolidate into a handful of giants, as accounting firms had, and he meant to make Patton Boggs mighty enough to be among them, or at least to dictate the terms of its demise.

His sister was having a harder time. Cokie Roberts had grown tired of the weekly grind at *This Week*, as the show's ratings continued to slide. ABC managers put considerable pressure on Sam and Cokie, but to do what? "That was always my question," Cokie said.

She took her first opportunity to announce that she would leave the show when her contract expired.

"I want a life," she explained.

This proved harder than she might have imagined. Three months before her departure, to assume unspecified duties at ABC, Cokie was diagnosed with breast cancer. In a mildly public manner, she endured treatment—she wore a wig on her last shows—and was declared cancer-free.

Steve was now a professor at GW's School of Media and Public Affairs, filling an endowed chair named for Morris Cafritz's first cousin and earliest partner, J. B. Shapiro, and his brother, Maurice. He loved teaching—"I've redefined my standards of professional success"—and the professorship gave him a base from which to continue his writing and broadcasting.

Cokie and Steve had gathered an extended family around them

in the Maryland suburbs. Tommy lived five minutes away, and two of his children and *their* spouses and children lived nearby. Steve's brother, a lobbyist, had married a woman from New Orleans who had worked with Cokie at NPR. "And then there's the cousins who grew up six blocks from me in New Orleans and their children—we're all each other's godparents," Cokie said. "When we have just the real close family, just siblings and their children, it's twenty people."

Seated in her kitchen in Bethesda, in the house her family had occupied for a half century, Cokie sighed. "This is home, this is definitely home."

Permanent Washington, it was true, had fostered a sense of community among the lanes of lawyers in Chevy Chase, the consultants in Potomac, the journalists in Arlington, the trade association executives in McLean, the regulars of the revolving door all over the city. But surely it was also responsible for so much of the capital's ugliness.

Consider the ubiquity of lobbyists, an estimated twenty thousand of them, in their well-tailored suits. Tommy was charging close to seven hundred dollars an hour. If the public was aroused about an issue, lobbyists wielded little influence on the outcome. But if the voters had no interest or knowledge, and that was most of the time, the lobbyists' behind-the-scenes maneuvering could rob the public blind. They thrived on the money in politics—extricating it, raising it, earning more of it than any mortal needed.

Nearly as unsavory to the sensibilities beyond the Beltway was the burgeoning business of journalism. Gone was the courtly world of the three nightly news shows and the gentlemen of the press devoted to the greater good. Instead, journalists yelled at one another in television studios to bolster their speaking fees, and they covered Washington as if it were sports, as contests between winners and fools. Style trumped substance in pursuit of ratings, and attitude reigned. News blurred into entertainment; journalists envied celebrities and became celebrities themselves.

In politics, image and sound bites predominated; realists knew that reality kowtowed to perception. Earlier generations had wrestled over Lend-Lease and school desegregation and, yes, the preservation of civilization. Modern politicians worried about positioning TV cam-

eras, exploiting an opponent's gaffe in a thirty-second attack ad, raising enough money for the next campaign.

Always, money. At times it seemed as if Washington cared, almost to the point of obsession, about money. The public arena embraced battles over budget deficits and money-draining essentials.
But the preoccupation went beyond programs and principles. PAC
contributions, billable hours, bankruptcies, ratings wars, speaking
fees, six- and seven-figure salaries—the story of Washington had
grown tawdry indeed.

No wonder that running against Washington had recently become the surest route to political success, for Jimmy Carter, Ronald
Reagan, Bill Clinton, and even George W. Bush, the first son of a
president to become a president since John Quincy Adams. Americans had grown to enjoy denigrating their capital.

And yet there was something beautiful in all of this ugliness, arising from the source of it. The civility of the past was possible because
a small circle of people—with rare exceptions, white men of compat-
ible backgrounds and unexceptional views—prevailed in a hierarchical world. But the era when twenty-five men ruled Washington was
gone for good. The city had opened up, allowing lobbyists their livelihood. The Vietnam War and the Watergate scandal, and the distrust
toward the government that they had inspired, had ushered into
Washington the sorts of changes under way all over the civilized
world. Authority was on the defensive; power was dispersing.

Throughout the society, power was becoming dispersed. What
else, after all, was the history of the twentieth century but a chroni-
cle of group after group of excluded Americans—Jews, women,
blacks, gays—painfully claiming a place for themselves inside?

Outsiders becoming insiders—this was the nation's story, and
Washington's as well. Julius Hobson intruded into places he did not
belong, in life and even in death, both in the wider society and among
his own race. He picketed and threatened and insulted and provoked,
so that his son might someday become the top lobbyist at the AMA, a
block from K Street—out of the ghetto. Julius's first wife, Carol, was
still living on Queens Chapel Terrace, a block from the Maryland
line, even as young white couples were moving back into Brookland.

Entering her eighties, she had stopped worrying about matters that she could not control and had never been happier in her life. Julius's second wife, Tina, had moved out to Front Royal, Virginia, into a house in the woods (twelve miles from Pat Saltonstall, unbeknown to both). Hobby became a grandfather, and Jean remarried. This family, outsiders no longer, was living the American dream.

Even in D.C., with its enduring limits on self-rule, the financial control board had dissolved at last. Democracy was growing ever deeper. Everywhere, the politicians stood terrified of public opinion and the next election, perhaps to a fault, to the exclusion of principle. Yet what else did the profusion of pollsters and image-*meisters* and sound-bite artists mean—their catering to the shallowest, to the most human in human nature—except that the opinions of the citizenry counted more than anything?

Instruments of democracy were lodged in permanent Washington. Julius Hobson had credited the press for the success of civil rights in the capital. When Gwen Cafritz was barred from society's doors, Cissy Patterson of the *Times-Herald* yanked her through. As Perle Mesta did, Gwen used the attentions of the press to plot her way into the capital's social establishment.

This was the genius of liberty—it provided cracks in the barriers that insurgents could slip through.

Or if the decision maker one needed to persuade had not been a classmate at Saint Albans, Tommy Boggs was available for hire. In an arena where pretty much everyone could play, money had become the medium of common exchange, the engine of persuasion, the measure of desire. Morris Cafritz marshaled his advertising dollars and his connections at the bank on his wife's behalf. Their sons used their father's fortune to assure themselves influence—political, cultural, economic—in the life of the city. It was money that enabled the vulgar to join the ranks of the refined, constantly nourishing a nation and renewing it, so that it could become whatever history required it to be. Maybe democracy looked its ugliest when it was most alive.

The ugliness and beauty of the nation's capital were nothing more, it seemed clear, than a mirror of what the nation had become. When the twentieth century dawned, Washington had been the provincial capital of a newly imperial power. In the course of what Henry Luce called the American Century, the capital lost much of whatever local character it had. As the twenty-first century arrived, Washington was no longer sleepy or southern. It had become a compendium of the American character, the nation's true capital.

Notes

All interviews cited were with the author unless otherwise noted. All cited FBI files were received from the Federal Bureau of Investigation in Washington, D.C., under Freedom of Information Act requests.

Chapter One: THEODORE ROOSEVELT TO HOOVER

1   **Kafitz:** The family used several spellings after its arrival in the United States. Its original name was apparently Chaifetz, the *ch* pronounced as the Hebrew gutteral *k* (the violinist Jascha Heifetz is thought to be a sixth cousin). The 1899 city directory in Washington, D.C., lists a Nosen Keiftz; the 1900 federal census spells the family as Kafets; the 1900 city directory has Nochen Cafitz, the 1901 version, Nelson Cafitz. Kafitz is the name Morris's father used in a deed of trust dated October 15, 1902, and again in his naturalization papers signed June 8, 1905. The family arrived in the United States in 1898, according to census records, or in 1894, according to the naturalization papers of Morris's father.

1   **at four thirty:** Leslie Milk, "Master Builders," *Washingtonian*, October 1996, 68ff. The morning routine was also described by Calvin Cafritz, his eldest son, in interviews.

1   **at age fourteen:** According to D.C. public school records, he was last registered for the 1901–2 school year, at the Corcoran School. According to the 1900 census, he was born in March 1887, but Calvin Cafritz said his father "always insisted" his birthday was in September.

2 **the five children:** Sarah (b. 1884), Morris (b. 1887), Carrie (b. 1890), Edward (b. 1893), and William (b. 1896), according to 1900 and 1910 census data.

2 **twenty-some blocks north:** The 1899 city directory, for which information was presumably collected in 1898, lists a grocer named Nosen Keiftz at 240 Wilson NW, now V Street, near Howard University.

2 **Glick Alley:** The 1900 city directory puts the Cafitz family at 1722 Glick Court NW, an alleyway located in the same square block as Glick Alley. According to the 1904 Sanborn map, however, the house numbers on Glick Court ranged from 1700 to 1708, and on Glick Alley from 1707 to 1744.

2 **into his eighties:** According to a family member who asked not to be named.

2 **the most common:** Hasia R. Diner, *Fifty Years of Jewish Self-Governance: The Jewish Community Council of Greater Washington, 1938–1988* (Washington, D.C.: The Council, 1989), 23.

2 **little money or know-how:** Paul Tuchman, "A History of Jewish Washington," *Federation News*, September–October 1978.

2 **lacked indoor plumbing:** Carter Cafritz, Morris and Gwen's middle son, in interviews.

2 **a half-day's ride:** George Washington wrote in his diary for April 16, 1789, that he left Mount Vernon at 10:00 A.M. on his way to New York City for his inauguration, and he arrived at the Potomac across from Georgetown at 2:00 P.M., then waited for a ferry. I am indebted to Ellen Clark and to Mary Thompson, the historian at Mount Vernon, for this information.

3 **as a residence for:** C. H. Forbes-Lindsay, *Washington: The City and the Seat of Government* (Philadelphia: The John C. Winston Co., 1908), 295.

3 **had become an industrial suburb:** Kathryn Schneider Smith, *Port Town to Urban Neighborhood: The Georgetown Waterfront of Washington, D.C. 1800–1920* (Washington, D.C.: The Center for Washington Area Studies of the George Washington University, 1989), 18–29.

3 **Morris liked to race:** Carter Cafritz interviews.

3 **"When they say noon":** Mrs. John A. Logan, *Thirty Years in Washington, or Life and Scenes in Our National Capital* (Hartford, Conn.: A. D. Worthington & Co., 1901), 526.

3 **Tidewater accents:** Tom and Marguerite Kelly, in an interview.

4 **original Diplomatic Row:** Lawrence Sullivan, *All About Washington: An Intimate Guide* (New York: John Day Co., 1932), 108.

4 **Its architect committed suicide:** Alfred B. Mullett took his own life in 1890, according to Christopher Weeks, *AIA Guide to the Architecture of Washington, D.C.* (Baltimore: Johns Hopkins University Press, 1994), 142.

5 **just before nine:** "Morning Hour When the Streets of Washington Put on Their Liveliest Aspect, Thronged With Government Clerks Who Are Really in a Rush." *Washington Times*, March 1, 1903, 1, Section II.

6 **William Henry Harrison:** According to John Clagett Proctor, "In Old Center Market," *The Sunday Star,* September 9, 1951, C-2.

6 **"mammies" and maids:** Verbatim from Logan, *Thirty Years in Washington,* 525.

7 **aimless gravel paths:** "The mall as it stands to-day is an anomaly, little used, and extremely inconvenient to pedestrians, though offering rare opportunities to the footpad and to other criminals. Its paths are aimless, and even those who argue that it is to represent a great forest will hardly aver that the trails of a forest never get anywhere," an unidentified editorialist wrote in "The Treatment of the Mall," *Washington Life,* February 6, 1904, 6.

7 **Virginia had demanded back:** "The retrocession of Alexandria to Virginian jurisdiction allowed the lucrative Alexandria slave-trading activity to continue to operate after the Compromise of 1850 abolished slave-trading in the District of Columbia effective January 1, 1851. Had Alexandria remained part of the District of Columbia Alexandria's slave-trading operations would have had to move to a less advantageous central location. Alexandria's location and port facilities made the City an important link in the slave-trade with New Orleans and Mississippi River ports," the historian Nelson F. Rimensnyder wrote in a report on the 1846 retrocession of Alexandria in *The Planning, Development, Government and Institutions of the Nation's Capital, 1808–1978: A History of the Committee on the District of Columbia, U.S. House of Representatives* (Washington, D.C.: Government Printing Office, 1978), 191.

7 **could smell the fish market:** From ten or fifteen blocks away, according to James Banks, a former D.C. housing official and community leader, in an interview.

8 **"District (not exceeding":** U.S. Constitution, art. 1, sec. 8.

9 **twelve hundred acres of woodland:** Kenneth R. Bowling, *The Creation of Washington, D.C.: The Idea and Location of the American Capital* (Fairfax, Va.: George Mason University Press, 1991), 213.

9 **Critics of a Potomac:** D. H. Forbes-Lindsay, *Washington: The City and the Seat of Government* (Philadelphia: John C. Winston Co., 1908), 31, 305.

10 **"as to leave room":** A 1789 letter quoted in H. Paul Caemmerer, *The Life of Pierre Charles L'Enfant* (Washington, D.C.: National Republic Publishing Co., 1950), 128–29.

10 **Cabinet officers who complained:** Bob Arnebeck, *Through a Fiery Trial: Building Washington 1790–1800* (Lanham, Md.: Madison Books, 1991), 53.

10 **The thickets and moors:** James Sterling Young, *The Washington Community 1800–1828* (New York: Columbia University Press, 1966), 74.

10 **restrict the height of buildings:** Explained in Elizabeth S. Kite, *L'Enfant and Washington, 1791–1792* (Baltimore: Johns Hopkins Press, 1929), 20, in the introduction by J. J. Jusserand, former French ambassador to the United States.

10 **"here will be no waste":** Jefferson's August 18, 1791, letter to L'Enfant, quoted in Caemmerer, *The Life of Pierre Charles L'Enfant,* 156.

10   **roughly reflecting its location:** According to Pamela Scott, "'This Vast
      Empire': The Iconography of the Mall, 1791–1848," in *The Mall in Washing-
      ton, 1791–1991,* ed. Richard Longstreth (Washington, D.C.: National
      Gallery of Art, 1991), 37.

11   **make it sound more German:** Calvin Cafritz interviews.

11   **on Eighth Street:** At 920 Eighth Street SE, which was torn down for the
      Southeast Freeway.

11   **Old-Timers Bar:** This is the name on a drawing of the saloon in a collage
      celebrating Morris Cafritz's career, a present from his employees, now in
      Calvin Cafritz's possession.

11   **on P Street:** The 1906–8 city directories locate the grocery at 2610 P Street
      NW, which was also where he and his father (and presumably the rest of his
      family) lived.

11   **"My father liked":** Milk, "Master Builders."

12   **take patrons, free of charge:** Carter Cafritz interviews.

12   **Nats' first baseman:** Chick Gandil, who was later banished from organized
      baseball in the 1919 Chicago Black Sox scandal.

12   **"There is something satisfying":** "Women Becoming Devotees of Bowl-
      ing," *Post,* March 21, 1915.

12   **"I know it would be":** "Bowling with Rod Thomas," *Star,* October 14, 1954.

12   **on G Street:** At 916–918 G Street NW.

13   **picked up his pin-setters:** Carter Cafritz interviews.

13   **facility, for the ladies:** Calvin Cafritz interviews.

13   **he owned four:** Carter Cafritz interviews.

13   **"What's on your mind?":** Rod Thomas, *Star,* October 14, 1954.

13   **solicited Morris's advice:** Carter Cafritz interviews.

14   **"Washington is":** Harrison Rhodes, "War-Time Washington," *Harper's
      Monthly* magazine, March 1918, Vol. CXXXVI, No. DCCCXIV, 465.

15   **"the end of Washington":** Leo Bernstein, in a 1980 interview for the Jew-
      ish Historical Society of Greater Washington.

15   **B. F. Saul:** According to B. F. Saul II, his grandson, in an interview.

15   **International Building:** At 1319 F Street NW.

15   **shoes with elevated heels:** Carter Cafritz interviews. He said his father
      was "maybe five-five," and Calvin Cafritz thought he was about five-nine.
      Newspaper accounts put him at five-seven or a half inch more.

15   **He believed that it was important:** Calvin Cafritz interviews.

16   **woods and undulating meadows:** "Columbia Golf Club," *Washington
      Life,* October 24, 1903, 5.

16   **was appealing:** Calvin Cafritz interviews.

16   **"Out there":** Rod Thomas, *Star,* October 14, 1954.

16   **He bought three coal-fired:** Calvin Cafritz interviews.

16   **single-family houses cost:** A Bureau of Labor Statistics survey in 1928 es-
      timated the average cost at $8,543 in Washington and $5,165 in fourteen

U.S. cities with at least a half-million people, according to "Apartments Represent Gigantic Industry Here," *Star*, August 30, 1930, C-1.

17 **"city of cliff dwellers":** Ibid. Commissioner Ethelbert Stewart had made his observation a year or two earlier.

17 **seven apartment houses:** At Spring Road and Sixteenth Street NW.

17 **approaching 90 percent:** Cafritz sold them in 1926 for about $1.5 million, a $700,000 profit, according to James E. Roper, "Court Upholds Cafritz Firm in $371, 659 U.S. Tax Fight," *Star*, October 8, 1952.

17 **the new nation's prime meridian:** Robert Shackleton, *The Book of Washington* (Philadelphia: Penn Publishing Co., 1922), 250.

17 **As wide as Pennsylvania Avenue:** John Fondersmith, development review specialist at the D.C. Office of Planning, in an interview.

18 **community of fourteen thousand:** The estimate was Calvin Coolidge's, in addressing the JCC's cornerstone ceremony on May 3, 1925.

18 **squat building:** Diner, *Fifty Years of Jewish Self-Governance*, 26.

18 **Morris organized:** Recollection of Elizabeth Kahn, "Washington Jews: An Oral History, Part 2," *The Record* (Washington, D.C.: Jewish Historical Society of Greater Washington, November 1984), 38.

19 **"Hebraic mortar":** "Address by President Calvin Coolidge at Laying of Cornerstone of the Jewish Community Center Building, Washington, D.C., Sunday, May 3, 1925," published by the Jewish Welfare Board of New York City. The historian was W.E.H. Lecky.

20 **he had known in high school:** Fred Pelzman, a nephew of Ivy Pelzman, in an interview.

20 **"I met the girl":** Shirley Leva, a niece of Ivy Pelzman, in an interview before her death in 2002.

20 **Fra Angelico:** Sheila Hines, the long-term assistant secretary of the Morris and Gwendolyn Cafritz Foundation, in an interview.

20 **scapegoat:** Raphael Patai, *The Jews of Hungary: History, Culture, Psychology* (Detroit: Wayne State University, 1996), 501.

21 **Gwen remembered a lawless:** Carter Cafritz interviews.

21 **Hungarian Reformed Church:** Calvin Cafritz interviews.

21 **coined the term *antigen*:** According to "Emlekezes Dr. Detre Laszlora (1874–1939), az antigen nevadojara," a remembrance of Dr. Detre, by Dr. Karasszon Denes, published in *Orvosi hetilap*, a Hungarian medical journal, May 20, 1990, 1089–90, and translated through the generous efforts of Stephen Allen, the regional legal adviser at the U.S. Agency for International Development's office in Budapest.

21 **"recognition it deserves":** Harry Eagle, *The Laboratory Diagnosis of Syphilis: The Theory, Technic, and Clinical Interpretation of the Wassermann and Flocculation Tests with Serum and Spinal Fluid* (St. Louis: C.V. Mosby Co., 1937), 23.

21 **an expert bridge player:** Betty Warner, a niece of Dr. Detre's, in an interview.

21 **"I fell first in love":** Virginia Irwin, "Who's 'Hostess with the Mostest?'" *St. Louis Post-Dispatch*, August 22, 1954, 1G.

21 **Tall and rangy:** Shirley Leva interview.

21 **the family's stories:** Carter Cafritz interviews. He was told this story by an aunt and said, "I think it's probably true, yeah."

22 **Morris's first date:** Betty Beale, "Mrs. Cafritz: People Remember Uninhibited 'Gwendolynisms,'" *Star*, November 28, 1954.

22 **Morris stopped by:** Calvin Cafritz interviews.

22 **tempos, smokestacks, and trees:** Keith Melder, *City of Magnificent Intentions: A History of Washington, District of Columbia* (Washington, D.C.: Intac Inc., 1997), 372.

22 **and loved it:** Gwen Dobson, "Luncheon With . . . Gwen Cafritz," *Star*, 5 March 1971, C-1.

22 **They were affectionate:** Carter Cafritz interviews.

23 **by moving the Sabbath:** Fred Pelzman interview.

23 **"My race is *Hebrew*":** Petition for Citizenship #8354, filed in the Supreme Court of Washington, D.C., on March 11, 1931, by Gwendolyn Cafritz. She dated her arrival from August 20, 1929, when she returned from her honeymoon.

23 **this was a step down:** Carter Cafritz interviews.

23 **as their permanent home:** Gerson Nordlinger, a friend of the Cafritz family, in an interview.

23 **she mounted her horse:** Account is from "Mrs. Gwendolyn Cafritz Hurt in Fall from Horse," *Star*, January 15, 1930, A-2.

24 **her personality had changed:** Calvin Cafritz interviews.

Chapter Two: ROOSEVELT

25 **"It matched my skinny frame":** Carol Joy (Hobson) Smith, in interviews.

26 **stylish, light-skinned:** Gwen Acsadi, a close friend of Carol Joy Smith's, in an interview.

26 **colored Connecticut Avenue:** Constance McLaughlin Green, *The Secret City: A History of Race Relations in the Nation's Capital* (Princeton, N.J.: Princeton University Press, 1967), 179.

26 **sleep on a blanket:** Carol Joy (Hobson) Smith interviews.

27 **From its beginning:** "As early as 1810, 10 percent of the city consisted of free blacks; by 1850 the figure had increased to nearly 20 percent," Sam Smith wrote in *Captive Capital: Colonial Life in Modern Washington* (Bloomington: Indiana University Press, 1974), 114.

27 **ninety thousand:** E. Franklin Frazier, *Black Bourgeoisie* (New York: The Free Press, 1957), 164.

27 **president's wife was horrified:** Green, *The Secret City*, 172–73.

27   **except behind a screen:** Mary Church Terrell, *A Colored Woman in a White World* (Washington, D.C.: Ransdell Inc., 1940).

28   **"Not my daughter":** Carol Joy (Hobson) Smith interviews.

28   **"I came from a community":** Ibid.

29   **by the 1920s:** Seventh Street NW succeeded Pennsylvania Avenue as the city's main commercial thoroughfare until about 1910, and F Street had replaced it by the 1920s, according to the historian and author James Goode, in an interview.

29   **"My daughter is graduating":** Carol Joy (Hobson) Smith interviews.

29   **"I was so glad":** Ibid.

29   **a provocative profit:** Morris Cafritz bought back the Corcoran Courts apartment house for $410,000 in 1935 and sold it for $651,000 in 1938, according to Roper, "Court Upholds Cafritz." The State Department headquarters was later built on the site.

30   **"the very air":** Frederick Lewis Allen, *Since Yesterday: The 1930s in America, September 3, 1929–September 3, 1939* (New York: Harper & Row, 1939), 111.

30   **hemmed in by white merchants:** Diane Grant, "Who We Are," *Washingtonian*, September 1995, 46ff.

30   **One winter's evening:** "Capital Rated High," *Star*, 9 January 1932, B-2.

30   **as a birthday present:** James M. Goode, *Best Addresses* (Washington, D.C.: Smithsonian Institution Press, 1988), 351.

31   **eighty-five apartment houses:** Ibid., 353.

31   **the largest low-cost housing:** "$3,000,000 Housing Project Under Way in Southeast," *Star*, October 26, 1940, B-4.

31   **He would tell the lowest bidder:** Carter Cafritz interviews.

31   **Or he would refuse to pay:** Abe Pollin, the majority owner of the Washington Wizards, the National Basketball Association team, in an interview.

31   **One day, at the site:** Ibid.

31   **fired his own brother-in-law:** Liane Atlas, widow of Martin Atlas, in an interview.

32   **morning of the bar exam:** John J. Sirica, *To Set the Record Straight: The Break-in, the Tapes, the Conspirators, the Pardon* (New York: W. W. Norton Co., 1979), 26.

32   **won three times:** Calvin Cafritz interviews.

32   **"You can't pretend":** Dobson, "Luncheon with . . . Gwen Cafritz."

32   **"Every day was different":** Calvin Cafritz interviews.

32   **rotted trees and overgrown:** "The History of Franklin Square," *Washington Business Journal* advertising supplement, February 18, 1991, 12.

32   **"Morris names all children":** Beale, "Uninhibited 'Gwendolynisms.'"

33   **"any Negro":** Robert K. Walsh, "The Covenants Issue," *Star*, October 6, 1947, A-6.

33   **"of the Semitic race":** William Chapman, "'Restricted' Community Yields to Rebellious Mother," *Post*, June 21, 1960, B1.

33   **"To suddenly find myself":** Calvin Cafritz interviews.

33   **almost three dozen rooms:** Counts of the number of rooms at 2301 Foxhall Road have ranged from twenty-five to fifty-eight. Kirstine Larsen, the facilities manager at the Field School, which bought the house in 2000, said she counted thirty to thirty-five rooms.

35   **fifty-five thousand dollars:** According to the building permit filed on October 17, 1936. A permit for the elevator was filed on July 6, 1937. By that time the name of the street had been changed to Foxhall Road.

35   **unaware of the tears:** A transcript of her remarks to a congressional breakfast in her honor, September 14, 1990.

36   **the tanned young men:** Verbatim from Thomas L. Stokes, "It Was Just a Parade . . . 'Til the Tanks Came," *Washington Daily News*, January 21, 1941, 2.

36   **frightening:** "To one who has witnessed 10 Inaugural parades, this one was stark and frightening," Fraser Edwards reported in "Military Might Awes Throng," *Washington Times-Herald*, January 21, 1941. "Not only were the engines of death and destruction awesome, but the very speed of the procession left a vague feeling of weakness, a lack of ability to combat such mighty monsters. The crowd seemed to sense the same thing."

36   **"That was the worst":** Lindy Boggs, in interviews.

36   **"May you be":** Her January 2, 1941, telegram to Hale Boggs, at the Carroll Arms Hotel, from a scrapbook in the T. Hale Boggs Papers, Manuscripts Department, Special Collections, Tulane University Library.

36   **almost six feet:** According to the Personnel Placement Questionnaire he filled out for the War Department in 1942, he measured five feet eleven and one-half inches and 190 pounds, in the Boggs Papers.

37   **"I'm going to marry you":** Lindy Boggs with Katherine Hatch, *Washington Through a Purple Veil: Memoirs of a Southern Woman* (New York: Harcourt Brace, 1994), 43.

37   **"Who is that weird boy?":** Lindy Boggs interviews.

37   ***Thomas* was an afterthought:** On his birth certificate, found in the Boggs Papers, *Thomas* is written above and to the left of the newborn's name. "You have to have a saint's name, in the Catholic Church, and of course his uncle was Thomas Hale and his grandfather was Thomas Patrick Hale," Lindy Boggs explained in an interview.

37   **literary and aesthetic:** Ibid.

37   **to beat the rent:** Cokie Roberts, in interviews.

37   **to catch mullet:** Gary Hymel, Hale Boggs's longtime administrative assistant, in interviews. Lindy Boggs commented, "That was a little overstated."

37   **"the usual boy jobs":** In a supplemental statement he filed with his War Department questionnaire.

37   **"a high class boy":** Written by A. K. Day, the manager of Day Drug Company, dated June 29, 1930, in the Boggs Papers.

37   **as many as a thousand:** Garry Boulard, *The Big Lie: Hale Boggs, Lucille May Grace, and Leander Perez in 1951* (Gretna, La.: Pelican Publishing Co., 2001), 85.

37   **"splendidly intelligent essay":** *Times-Picayune* (New Orleans), in undated clippings from the Boggs Papers.

38   **reading William Blackstone:** Rosemary James and Philip Moreton, "The Majority leader—a short history of a controversial man," *New Orleans* magazine, July 1971, 24ff.

38   **the second time:** Undated *New Orleans States* and *Item-Tribune* clippings, in the Boggs Papers. He wrote to the War Department in 1942 that it was the first time.

38   **"and that was the beginning":** Mrs. Joseph E. Casey, the first vice president of the Woman's National Democratic Club, "Profile of Mrs. Hale Boggs," *W.N.D.C. News,* Summer 1958, 2.

39   **"I'm just going to sit":** Boggs, *Purple Veil,* 18.

39   **"To be or not":** Lindy Boggs interviews.

39   **the first white settler:** Steven V. Roberts, in interviews.

39   **In every generation since:** Boggs, *Purple Veil,* vii.

39   **the Constitution decreed:** Steven V. Roberts interviews. The Constitution also grants Congress the authority to seat its own members, and it seated him after a 1797 by-election, he remains the youngest member of Congress in history.

40   **They had taken Teddy Roosevelt:** Lindy Boggs interviews.

40   **another Margaret Bourke-White:** Myra MacPherson, "Lindy Boggs. Heir to the House," *Post,* March 4, 1973, K1.

40   **Hale placed an apple:** Lindy Boggs interviews.

40   **"write very soon":** July 10, 1935, note, Boggs Papers.

40   **Lindy never knew:** Lindy Boggs interviews.

40   **something of a radical:** According to Vic Gold, who became known as "another" Hale Boggs when he wrote a column in the *Hullabaloo* a half-generation later, in an interview.

40   **His editorials:** Patrick J. Maney, "Hale Boggs: The Southerner as National Democrat," in *Masters of the House: Congressional Leadership over Two Centuries,* ed. Roger H. Davidson, Susan Webb Hammond, and Raymond W. Smock (New York: Westview Press, 1998), 225.

41   **unanimously chose Hale:** Morris Ardoin, "A Sense of Optimism and Youthful Exuberance: Recollections on the People's League," in *Tulane Lawyer,* Summer 1992, 14–15.

41   **more committees than members:** According to Marian Mayer Berkett, a member, in Elizabeth Mullener, "Illustrious Law School Class Comes Together for Reunion," *Times-Picayune,* March 7, 2002, B–1.

41   **the youngest Democrat:** Rep. William G. Stratton, a Republican from Illinois, was eleven days younger.

41   **"I'll have plenty":** Associated Press, December 24, 1940, Boggs Papers.

41   **audition:** Paul F. Healy, *Cissy: The Biography of Eleanor M. "Cissy" Patterson* (Garden City, N.Y.: Doubleday & Co., 1966), 316. Healy writes that this took place in 1938, but he also writes that the *Times-Herald* "soon" featured her as a "Beauty of the Week," and that did not happen until 1940.

42   **"She heard me speak":** Beale, "Uninhibited 'Gwendolynisms.'"

42   **"Cissy saw":** Alice Albright Hoge, *Cissy Patterson* (New York: Random House, 1966), 142.

42   ***Times-Herald:*** The *Times* and the *Herald* merged on February 1, 1939. Before the merger she was the editor and publisher of the *Herald*.

42   **the Hope diamond:** When Pierre Cartier left it in her custody over a weekend in 1911, "at some time during that night I began to want the thing," Eva lyn Walsh McLean wrote in her 1936 autobiography with Boyden Sparkes, *Father Struck It Rich* (Ouray, Colo.: Bear Creek Publishing Co., 1981), 201.

42   **Friends of Cissy's thought:** "Many of Cissy's horrified friends asked why she was promoting a Hungarian Jewess as the capital's leading social hostess. Why not? asked Cissy. . . . For Cissy this was part of the fun of power," Ralph G. Martin wrote in *Cissy: The Extraordinary Life of Eleanor Medill Patterson* (New York: Simon & Schuster, 1979), 435–36.

43   **silk tea gown:** David Brinkley, *Washington Goes to War* (New York: Ballantine Books, 1988), 163.

43   **"She's an exotic type":** "Beauty of the week . . . No. 7: Mrs. Morris Cafritz," *Times-Herald*, February 12, 1940, 10.

43   **"always so smart":** "Peter Carter Says," *Times-Herald*, June 29, 1942, 10.

43   **Lindy Boggs steered:** Lindy Boggs interviews.

44   **"Lindy," he said:** Ibid.

44   **New York to watch a play:** Lindy Boggs, in remarks on the House floor as a new member of Congress from Louisiana, April 18, 1973, *Congressional Record*, 93rd Congress, 1st sess., 13191.

44   **everything deep-fried:** Brinkley, *Washington Goes to War*, 21.

45   **"Don't worry, dear":** Lindy Boggs interviews.

45   **Crossover was uncommon:** "Washington was a deceptively complicated place," Joseph W. Alsop, with Adam Platt, wrote in *"I've Seen the Best of It": Memoirs* (New York: W. W. Norton & Co., 1992), 81, "for the town was endlessly divided by a series of tall, unseen barriers. The most important of these was the barrier that separated white Washington from black Washington. . . . On the professional side, too, the small world of newspapermen I entered [in the late 1930s] was only one Washington among many. The Senate Washington, which I also inhabited when I first arrived in town as a reporter, was paralleled by congressional Washington; and there was an army Washington, navy Washington, and business Washington."

45   **a warm community:** Tom Kelly, a longtime newspaperman with the *Daily News*, in an interview.

45   **more than in any American city:** W. M. Kiplinger, *Washington Is Like That* (New York: Harper & Brothers Publishers, 1942), 8.

46   **"Almost immediately":** Lindy Boggs interviews.

46   **and so forth:** Thursdays for the Senate, and Fridays for the diplomatic corps.

47   **"Oh, sure, honey":** Boggs, *Purple Veil*, 3.

47   **"I'm Mrs. Boggs":** Ibid.

47   **When Tommy cut his first tooth:** Anecdote from Lindy Boggs interviews; Boggs, *Purple Veil*, 77–78; Cokie Roberts interview with Lindy Boggs on ABC's *Prime Time Live*, December 1, 1994; and a congressional breakfast in her honor, September 14, 1990.

47   **"Impressed with our views":** Lindy Boggs interviews; Boggs, *Purple Veil*, 77; her eulogy to Hebert on the House floor, January 22, 1980, *Congressional Record*, 96th Congress, 2nd sess., 236.

48   **"Sincerely your friend":** Rayburn's note, dated February 15, 1941, is in the Hale Boggs collection at Tulane.

48   **a rare gesture:** H. G. Dulaney, a former aide to Rayburn and the longtime director of the Sam Rayburn Library in Bonham, Texas, in an interview.

48   **"I am a member":** In the House of Representatives, August 12, 1941, *Congressional Record*, 77th Congress, 1st sess., 7039.

48   **named for the legislators:** According to Brinkley, *Washington Goes to War*, 270. Robert W. Merry, "Board of Education," *Roll Call*, Vol. 32, No. 13, October 9, 1986, 3, attributes the name to "the leaders' use of the sessions to educate themselves on behind-the-scenes activities in the House."

48   **Occasionally the Speaker asked:** D. B. Hardeman and Donald C. Bacon, *Rayburn: A Biography* (Austin: Texas Monthly Press, 1987), 303.

48   **he went often:** Lindy Boggs interviews.

48   **"more or less adopted me":** "I was 26 when I came to Congress. Mr. Rayburn had no family, no son, no children, and he more or less adopted me," Boggs said in James and Moreton, "The Majority Leader," 44.

49   **disappointing football season:** The Redskins finished 6–5 in 1941. They had won the National Football League's East division in 1940 with a 9–2 record, though the Chicago Bears dealt them the worst defeat in league history, 73–0, in the championship game.

49   **team policy forbade:** Thomas R. Henry, "Capital Retains Outward Calm Despite Shock of War News," *Star*, December 8, 1941, A-6.

49   **Generals and admirals:** Brinkley, *Washington Goes to War*, 87.

49   **reception at Mrs. Edward Stotesbury's:** Katharine Elson, "That Atomic Cloud Is Silver Lined," *Post*, May 3, 1957.

50   **"He means Manila":** Lindy Boggs interviews.

50   **"Those people are just":** Ibid.

50   **They wondered whether bombs:** According to Lindy Boggs, quoted in Diana Pinckley, "Politics with Pearls," *Tulanian*, Fall 1992, 11–17.

50   **turned into a wartime capital:** Verbatim from "Washington Quickly Turned Into a Wartime Capital," *Star*, December 8, 1941, B-19.

50   **"A sense of hurry":** James B. Reston, "Capital Swings into War Stride; Throngs Cheer for the President," *New York Times*, December 9, 1941, 5.

51   **"A Young Man's Challenge":** *Times-Picayune*, September 6, 1942, 10.

51   **"I was not surprised":** Lindy Boggs interviews.

51   **probably enter the navy:** "Boggs Concedes Election to Mahoney; Will
      Enter Congress Race Again in '44," *Times-Picayune*, September 11,
      1942.

51   **shimmering silver gown:** Maggie Wimsatt, a longtime friend and associate
      of Gwen Cafritz's, in an interview.

52   **"We could get an answer":** Note from "PLF," Prudence L. Frece in the
      White House Office of Social Correspondence, to "Miss [Malina] Thomp-
      son," Mrs. Roosevelt's secretary, before a meeting was scheduled for April
      22, 1942, from the Franklin D. Roosevelt Library.

52   **"the most colossal job":** Vincent X. Flaherty, "Straight from the Shoulder,"
      Times-Herald, June 7, 1942, 1-B.

53   **only twelve thousand:** Dave Reque, "Tickets Printed for Service Tilt,"
      Daily News, June 22, 1942. The article reported that only fifteen thousand
      tickets had even been printed.

53   **a past president:** At Washington Hebrew Congregation, in 1934–35, ac-
      cording to Lois England of the synagogue, in an interview.

53   **"Old Washington was":** Quoted in Marjorie Williams, "The Legacy of
      Gwendolyn Cafritz," *Post* magazine, February 25, 1990, 16–21, 32–37.

53   **"How can you do":** Fred Pelzman, in an interview. His late mother, Helen
      Pelzman, was the lunch partner.

53   **made her mad as hell:** Verbatim from Carter Cafritz interviews.

53   ***Times-Herald* society columnist:** Gene Tierney had recently eloped with
      the fashion designer Oleg Cassini, whose younger brother Igor's column was
      called "These Charming People."

53   **"like something from *Vogue*":** Marie McNair, "Gay Farewell Party Given
      for Officers of Third Cavalry," *Times-Herald*, February 16, 1942.

54   **grimy gray cement-and-asbestos:** Brinkley, *Washington Goes to War*, 119.

54   **"My mama didn't send me":** Carol Joy (Hobson) Smith interviews.

54   **"I quit":** Ibid.

54   **"So for one year":** Ibid.

55   **"have a fur coat?":** Ibid.

55   **"How many of you":** Ibid.

55   **Professor Frazier:** Gwen Acsadi interviews. She was a graduate student at
      Howard at the time.

56   **"a deep-seated inferiority complex":** Frazier, *Black Bourgeoisie,* 27.

56   **"Europeans don't bathe":** Carol Joy (Hobson) Smith interviews.

56   **he demanded more:** Gwen Acsadi interview.

56   **first colored president:** In 1948.

56   **too technical a case:** *The Hunter Co. Inc. v. Joseph L. McHugh, Commis-
      sioner of Conservation of the State of Louisiana*, argued October 18–19,
      1943, and decided on November 8.

57   **administrative, legal, or:** His October 1942 application, in the Boggs Papers.

57   **Stephenson Place:** The address was 2911 Stephenson Place NW.

57   **"I am extremely anxious":** An October 28, 1943, letter from Hale Boggs to Telfair Knight, in the Boggs Papers.

57   **"And please, God":** Boggs, *Purple Veil*, 96.

58   **it came out "Cokie":** Ibid., 97.

58   **"It's a good thing":** Lindy Boggs's letter to Hale, January 11, 1944, in the Boggs Papers.

58   **"as round as he is tall":** Letter of March 13, 1944, Boggs Papers.

58   **her left eye:** She suffered a severe attack of false glaucoma in 1942 and again in 1945. A letter of March 3, 1942, quotes her doctor as saying, "My experience is that [similar cases] go under cataract formation with ultimate loss of vision & even the loss of the eye itself."

58   **said she'd eaten herself:** Letter from Lindy to Hale, January 28, 1944, Boggs Papers.

58   **"Am busier than":** Letter of March 13, 1944, Boggs Papers. The period was missing in the original.

58   **for an embryonic bureaucracy:** "For eighteen months we have been treated like an orphan child insofar as space is concerned," a War Shipping Administration official wrote to the budget director, quoted in Brinkley, *Washington Goes to War*, 120.

58   **"represent us":** A handwritten memo, marked "Confidential," from Telfair Knight to Ensign Hale Boggs, dated February 11, 1944, Boggs Papers.

58   **"At your rate":** Letter from Archie Boggs, dated January 25, 1945, Boggs Papers.

59   **"practically announced":** Lindy's letter to Hale, March 13, 1944, Boggs Papers.

59   **"I will not leave":** Paul Wooton, *Times-Picayune*, "Boggs to Forego Congress Race," July 24, 1944.

59   **William Robertson Boggs:** Hale Boggs's father was a first cousin of Senator Willis Robertson of Virginia. This made Hale a second cousin to the televangelist Pat Robertson.

59   **"so I was wondering":** A handwritten letter signed "Love, Daddy," dated July 24, 1944, in the Boggs Papers.

59   **"Oh my Lord":** Lindy Boggs interviews.

Chapter Three: TRUMAN

61   **"Do you see that man":** Carol Joy (Hobson) Smith interviews.

61   **"Excellent carriage":** Ibid.

62   **"I have a paper":** Ibid.

62 **Julius eventually told his daughter:** Jean Marie Hobson, Julius Hobson's daughter, in an interview.

63 **"He questioned everything":** Marvine Bradford, Julius Hobson's first cousin, in an interview.

63 **"Your everyday living":** Ibid.

63 **"I got almost as black":** John Mathews, "Julius W. Hobson: The Gadfly for District's Negro Majority," *Star*, April 16, 1967.

63 **"Scratch any black":** Quoted in a booklet distributed at a November 14, 1972, testimonial for Julius Hobson.

63 **"Why have I failed":** Written while he was training in California, from Jean Hobson's private collection.

64 **Florence and Rome:** An undated letter from Julius to his mother, found in her effects after her death and generously shared by Julius's daughter, Jean Hobson.

64 **despised the army:** Phil Hilts, "Julius Hobson: 'I'm Damn Angry on Issues,'" *Daily News*, March 15, 1971, 7.

64 **Sharing bathrooms:** Tina Hobson, Julius's second wife, in interviews.

64 **same blood and plasma:** Ibid.

64 **"very meager indeed":** Letter from Carl Wittke, dean of arts and sciences at Oberlin, dated May 9, 1946, in Jean Hobson's private collection.

64 **"I hated whites":** Mathews, "Julius W. Hobson: The Gadfly."

64 **"the promised land":** Quoted in "Julius Hobson: Local Legend," *Cause* magazine, March 1978, 21–28.

64 **"It just seemed like":** Carol Joy (Hobson) Smith interviews.

65 **"Mother piggy bank":** Sheila Hines, the longtime assistant secretary at the Morris and Gwendolyn Cafritz Foundation, in an interview.

65 **Morris was called out:** Calvin Cafritz interviews. In another version of the story, both developers were at the directors' meeting and were called away.

65 **drawn Morris into Riggs:** Jerome Silverman, the son of a plastering contractor who dealt with Morris Cafritz, in an interview.

65 **Morris had first tried to buy it:** Larry Van Dyne, "The Making of Washington," *The Washingtonian*, November 1987, Vol. 23, No. 2, 254.

66 **presented a check:** In an October 11, 1957, interview with George Kennedy, "The Rambler . . . Visits Project with Morris Cafritz," *The Evening Star*, A-27, Morris Cafritz said, "We gave them a check for $1 million and probably had to make some arrangements about it the next morning, but there was no danger that it would be returned to the title company."

66 **"another Radio City":** "Developer Hopes to Create a Temple Heights 'Radio City,'" *Star*, December 11, 1945, B-1.

66 **"It took a sense of adventure":** Calvin Cafritz interviews.

66 **"Well, I can see":** Ibid.

66 **Conrad, sat with him in the mornings:** Peggy Cooper Cafritz, Conrad's second wife, in interviews.

67   **a good father:** Verbatim from Erv Ornstein, a nephew of Morris Cafritz, in an interview.

67   **"sort of an affection":** Carter Cafritz interviews.

67   **"It was not the kind":** Calvin Cafritz interviews.

67   **"My best child":** "'Smartest' Cafritz Boy to Get Equal Trust Share, Court Says," *Post*, May 14, 1947.

67   **"She damaged all":** Peggy Cooper Cafritz interviews.

67   **they were confused:** Carter Cafritz interviews.

68   **"but the important thing":** Calvin Cafritz interviews.

68   **"Dad wanted me":** S. Oliver Goodman, "Son, 33, to Head Cafritz Complex," *Post*, June 25, 1964.

68   **to require timekeeping:** Jerome Silverman interview.

69   **$1.5 million:** John B. Willmann, "Footprints at Pentagon City," *Post*, December 3 1977, D1. According to Robert J. Lewis, "2 D.C. Men Contract to Purchase 200 Acres Adjoining Pentagon," *Star*, April 11, 1946, the price tag "was reported to be approximately $1 million."

69   **J was considered:** Bob Arnebeck, *Washington Post Magazine*, September 7, 1986, W23, in launching "J Street," a column of miscellany.

69   **demand was rising:** Robert J. Lewis, "Ground-Breaking Slated Today for 10-Story Cafritz Building," *Star*, April 16, 1949, B-1.

70   **"As we took the curves":** Robert J. Lewis, "Cafritz Building to have 27 levels and Half-Mile 'Inside Highway,'" *Star*, August 12, 1950, B-1.

70   **"I can't afford the rent":** Quoted in "Cafritz, 77, Dies at Bank Convention," *Post*, June 12, 1964, A1.

71   **"a swivel-chaired officer":** Quoted in Gary Boulard, *The Big Lie: Hale Boggs, Lucille May Grace and Leander Perez in 1951* (Gretna, La.: Pelican Publishing Co., 2001), 95.

71   **"another milestone":** "Primary Victors Express Thanks," *Times-Picayune*, September 11, 1946.

71   **"and nearly died myself":** Lindy Boggs interviews.

71   **"That's my family":** Carol Joy (Hobson) Smith interviews.

72   **Julius W. Hobson IV:** When he ordered a birth certificate in order to join the tennis team. The middle name is Wilson.

72   **"Nobody loves you like":** Ibid.

72   **"Well, Carol's busy":** Carol Joy (Hobson) Smith interviews.

72   **laying out her clothes:** Ibid.

72   **low-heeled shoes:** Gwen Acsadi interview.

72   **"I saw your lights":** Carol Joy (Hobson) Smith interviews.

72   **"Did you have a":** Ibid.

73   **"He had all these deep":** Ibid.

73   **a form and a context:** Roscoe Nix, the head of the NAACP in Montgomery County, Maryland, and a former classmate of Hobson's at Howard, in an interview. The visiting professor, Otto Nathan, was later convicted of contempt of Congress for refusing to answer questions before the House

Un-American Activities Committee, then saw his conviction overturned. He also became the executor of Albert Einstein's estate.

73   **"Did I hate whites":** "Julius Hobson: A Goad for Change," *Post*, July 2, 1972, B1.

73   **a path-breaking book:** Edward E. Lewis, *Methods of Statistical Analysis in Economics and Business* (Boston: Houghton Mifflin Co., 1953).

74   **"your big M.A.":** Carol Joy (Hobson) Smith interviews.

74   **"you need to drop out":** Ibid.

74   **"Some things aren't forgivable":** Ibid.

74   **Legislative Reference Service:** Later called the Congressional Research Service.

74   **only two black professionals:** Carol Joy (Hobson) Smith interviews.

74   **"an accomplishment for a black":** *Post*, "A Goad for Change."

75   **twenty-three thousand inquiries:** Apparently as of 1949, according to Charles A. Goodrum, *The Library of Congress* (New York: Praeger Publishers, 1974), 142.

75   **speak until spoken to:** Verbatim from Charles A. Goodrum, who sat across the aisle from Hobson at LRS, in an interview.

75   **"His feelings were very":** Carol Joy (Hobson) Smith interviews.

75   **"Gwendolyn Cafritz Makes Her Bid":** *Life*, August 1, 1949, 81–86.

76   **four vice presidents:** Thomas Marshall, who was Woodrow Wilson's vice president; Calvin Coolidge, who served Warren Harding and succeeded him; and Charles Curtis, who was Herbert Hoover's VP; besides Harry Truman.

76   **a Broadway musical:** *Call Me Madam* premiered on October 12, 1950, and ran for 644 performances.

76   **No ambassador had ever known:** So judged "Swearing In of Mrs. Mesta Turned into a Gala Occasion," *Star*, July 8, 1949, 1.

76   **"party-for-the-party-giver":** Mary Van Rensselaer Thayer, "There Were Stars Among the Standees to Felicitate Madame Minister Mesta," *Post*, July 9, 1949, 3B.

77   **"I used to see him":** Andrew Tully, "The Story of Gwen Cafritz," first of three articles, *Daily News*, December 7–9, 1959.

77   **"Now that you're":** "Life Among the Party-Givers," *Time*, July 11, 1949, 16.

77   **between the world wars:** Sarah Booth Conroy, "The Cafritz Largesse," *Post*, November 30, 1988.

77   **an air of mystery:** Julia Sparkman Shepard, a longtime friend of Gwen Cafritz, in an interview.

77   **"My real ambition":** Evelyn Peyton Gordon, "Gwen Cafritz . . . Washington Hostess," *Washington Daily News*, July 18, 1949, 14–15.

78   **"I always invite Senators":** Jack Anderson, "Gwen Reveals Some Secrets," *Post*, September 11, 1957.

78   **had invited himself:** Clark Clifford with Richard Holbrooke, *Counsel to the President: A Memoir* (New York: Random House, 1991), 254.

79 **"The moon has"**: "Cafritz Party a Prelude to Anniversary Today," *Post*, July 11, 1949, 4B.

79 **into dawn**: Achsah Dorsey Smith, "Society Wined and Dined at Cafritz Lawn Party," *Times-Herald*, July 10, 1949, Society section, 2.

80 **Christmas velvet**: She "probably" wore that and the white gloves, she said in Paul Hendrickson, "Robert Rules," June 20, 1993, *Washington Post Magazine*, W8.

81 **everyone's opinion was considered valid**: Cokie Roberts interviews.

81 **"Daddy, what's a tuxedo?"**: Lindy Boggs interviews and Boggs, *Purple Veil*, 106.

81 **"the pooh-bahs"**: Cokie Roberts interviews.

81 **"some of my best times"**: Lady Bird Johnson, *A White House Diary* (New York: Holt, Rinehart & Winston, 1970), 597.

82 **"not too impressive"**: Oral history interview with Hale Boggs for the John F. Kennedy Library, Boston, Mass., conducted May 10, 1964, by Charles T. Morrissey.

82 **hit it off**: Lindy Boggs interviews.

82 **"He was the kind of fellow"**: Oral history, JFK Library.

82 **"he would kid with you"**: Cokie Roberts interviews.

82 **from her stroller**: Lindy Boggs interviews.

82 **"a little bitty girl"**: Cokie Roberts interviews.

82 **"I'd better be the one"**: According to Lindy Boggs, quoted in Celia W. Dugger, "The Challenge and Clout; Lobbying with Tom Boggs," *Post*, September 25, 1979, C1.

82 **It was not a household**: Thomas H. Boggs Jr., in interviews.

82 **"she didn't know I"**: Cokie Roberts interviews.

83 **They tried to eat dinner**: Lindy Boggs interviews.

83 **two or three times a week**: Thomas H. Boggs Jr. and Cokie Roberts interviews.

83 **"We had a total"**: Cokie Roberts interviews.

83 **"There was nothing warm"**: Ibid.

83 **"I don't know who"**: Ibid.

83 **"Emma was terrific"**: Thomas H. Boggs Jr. interviews.

83 **congressional stipend**: According to House records for 1970, she earned $12,609.96 as a clerk; for earlier years payroll records no longer exist.

83 **accusations of nepotism**: Bruce Eggler, "The Life and Career of Hale Boggs: The Early Years," *States-Item*, January 4, 1973.

83 **"Everybody loves Lindy"**: Jan Schoonmaker, a page for Hale Boggs and then legislative director for Rep. Lindy Boggs, in an interview.

84 **he returned with Lindy**: The three of them then formed the state's delegation, though Lindy had not been elected as a delegate, according to Lindy Boggs interviews.

84 **the American Student Union**: "Boggs did more than offer the ASU moral

support. He helped organize the Tulane chapter and was put in charge of a committee to support a student activities building, one that could be used to promote increased student activism," according to Boulard; *The Big Lie*, 133.

84   **"He understood"**: Cokie Roberts interviews.

84   **missed learning long division**: Ibid.

84   **"Darling, this is what"**: Ibid.

84   **"Do it again"**: Ibid.

85   **"a much more private"**: Ibid.

85   **Tommy found this fun**: Thomas H. Boggs Jr. interviews.

85   **moved out to Bethesda**: In 1919, according to William S. Abell, *Fifty Years at Garrett Park, 1919–1969: A History of the New Georgetown Preparatory School* (privately published by Georgetown Preparatory School, 1970).

85   **fresh grown Louisiana okra**: Letter from Dave McGuire, Hale Boggs's former secretary, dated July 17, 1945, to Jack Lester of the New Orleans *Item*, from the Boggs Papers.

85   **"Mean old daddy"**: Lindy Boggs interviews.

85   **farmland was becoming subdivisions**: Margaret Marshall Coleman, *Montgomery County: A Pictorial History* (Norfolk, Va.: Donning Company/ Publishers, 1990), 196.

86   **"It looked like Tara"**: Carolanne Griffith Roberts, "Strong Women of Capitol Hill," *Southern Living*, May 1996, 149, in a profile of Cokie and her mother.

86   **"I want to live in this house"**: This account is from Boggs, *Purple Veil*, 136–37.

86   **for $52,500**: The real estate transaction, filed with Montgomery County, Maryland, on March 11, 1952, showed $57.75 in state tax. The tax rate at the time was $1.10 for each $1,000 of the sales price.

Chapter Four: EISENHOWER

87   **"This is Adlai Stevenson"**: Boggs, *Purple Veil*, 134.

88   **"Oh, sit down, charming"**: Quoted in George Dixon's "Washington Scene" column "Adlai's Coat-Tail Rider," *Post*, September 5, 1956.

88   **walked for hours**: Robert Caro, *Master of the Senate: The Years of Lyndon Johnson*, Vol. 3 (New York: Alfred A. Knopf, 2002), 157.

88   **"God, what I"**: Ibid.

88   **their "buddy"**: Lindy Boggs and Thomas H. Boggs Jr. interviews.

88   **"You've got to come"**: Boggs, *Purple Veil*, 141.

89   **enjoyed tormenting her**: Cokie Roberts interviews. "My brother, older by three years, was never terribly nice to me. He was fulfilling his role."

89   **"a nice chicken"**: Ibid.

89   **a poodle skirt:** Ibid.

89   **"I was undone":** Ibid.

90   **satin-upholstered walls:** James M. Goode, *Capital Losses: A Cultural History of Washington's Destroyed Buildings* (Washington, D.C.: Smithsonian Books, 2003), 152–54.

91   **"Washington's busy builders":** Photo caption. *Star*, December 20, 1952, B-1.

91   **As early as 1929:** Calvin Cafritz interviews.

91   **bay windows:** Robert Shackleton, *The Book of Washington* (Philadelphia: Penn Publishing Co., 1922), 141.

91   **"A street can't be":** Stanford's 1886 statement was quoted in "Historic Old Residence Will Be Razed for Office Building," *Star*, January 31, 1923.

92   **hired an architect:** Edwin Weihe, who had worked for Charlie Tompkins.

92   **limit was 130 feet:** Buildings as tall as 160 feet are permitted on Pennsylvania Avenue.

92   **the national monuments predominant:** Verbatim from John Fondersmith interview.

92   **Its developer had spurned Morris's:** Calvin Cafritz interviews. John McShain was the developer of 1001 Connecticut Avenue NW, which was also designed by Edwin Weihe.

92   **ice cubes spilled:** Jennifer Harper, "K Street: Boulevard of Power," *Washington Times*, January 9, 2000, C1.

92   **Continental Building:** 1012 Fourteenth St. NW.

93   **of the sixteen office buildings:** Francis P. Douglas, "District Lists 16 New Buildings in Downtown," *Star*, March 12, 1953, A-25.

93   **Julius Hobson often complained:** FBI file No. WFO 140-25531, on Julius Hobson, in a report dated December 20, 1967.

93   **"very, very blessed":** Carol Joy (Hobson) Smith interviews.

93   **"the nicest man":** Ibid.

94   **"Get him the bike":** Ibid.

94   **"I see you wrote":** Ibid.

95   **In September 1953:** "He Was a Fighter . . . and He Battled to the End," *Star*, March 24, 1977, D-5.

95   **The principal had once testified:** Carol Joy (Hobson) Smith interviews.

95   **"A close scrutiny":** Quoted in the minutes of the D.C. Board of Education meeting, December 16, 1953, located in Charles Sumner School Museum and Archives.

96   **"model":** President Eisenhower said this to the D.C. commissioner Samuel Spencer after a White House bill-signing ceremony, according to Jeanne Rogers, "Recreation Board Scraps Segregation as City Acts for Integration of Schools," *Post*, May 19, 1954, A1.

96   **"My boy washes":** Quoted in testimonial booklet for Julius Hobson, November 14, 1972.

96   **"No, it wasn't a windfall"**: Transcript of the Senate Banking and Currency Committee's continuing hearings on a Federal Housing Administration investigation, 83rd Congress, 2nd sess., August 3, 1954, 999.

97   **"I don't like the idea"**: Warren Unna, "Feelings of Cafritz Ruffled by Ingrates," *Star*, August 20, 1954.

97   **"But isn't it true"**: Transcript, pp. 996–97. The committee's counsel was William Simon.

97   **interest of the Federal Bureau of Investigation:** The FBI's file on Morris Cafritz amounted to nine pages released.

98   **"Now first, sir"**: The show of December 17, 1952.

99   **to spend more:** The committee proposed to raise the limits on campaign spending by national political parties from three million to ten million dollars a year, and "substantially" to raise the limits on expenditures for Senate candidates from twenty-five thousand dollars and for House candidates from five thousand dollars.

99   **"a smashing victory"**: Inserted into the *Congressional Record*, 85th Congress, 2nd sess., June 4, 1958, A5641, by Rep. Frank E. Smith, a Mississippi Democrat. The House vote was 317 to 98.

99   **was a Catholic too:** Gary Hymel interviews.

100   **shortest man in Congress:** According to Larry L. King, "The Road to Power in Congress," *Harper's Magazine*, June 1971, 42.

100   **expert in the parliamentary rules:** According to Keith White, an Oklahoman who is the executive editor of *CongressDaily*, in an interview.

100   **and even less for Hale:** Patrick J. Maney, in *Masters of the House: Congressional Leadership over Two Centuries*, eds. Roger H. Davidson, Susan Webb Hammond, and Raymond W. Smock (Boulder, Colo.: Westview Press, 1998), 226.

100   **confront predicaments:** Gary Hymel interviews.

100   **"the fantastic dreams"**: Rep. William Jennings Bryan Dorn, Democrat of South Carolina, in the *Congressional Record*, 84th Congress, 1st sess., February 18, 1955, 1767.

100   **"I hear people using"**: Ibid., 1768.

100   **"He destroyed that fellow's"**: Jim Wright, Democrat of Texas, Speaker of the House from 1987 to 1989, in an interview.

100   **"sharp-eyed"**: Drew Pearson, "Excess Profits Tax Irks Witness," *Post*, June 8, 1953, 25.

101   **"Your constant support"**: Hoover's June 26, 1950, letter was published in the *Congressional Record*, 81st Congress, 2nd sess., on June 29, A4794.

101   **"What would be the mileage"**: Cokie Roberts interviews.

102   **tearfully explained:** Ibid.

102   **"You see, Ed"**: Aired on Friday, September 30, 1955, at 10:30 P.M. eastern standard time.

103   **a six-page script:** Carter Cafritz interviews.

103   **"If you give them"**: Tully, "Story of Gwen Cafritz," first article.

104   **She started the fad**: Andrew F. Tully, "Washington's Third Party—The Cocktail Party," *Collier's*, January 3, 1953, 60–61.

104   **ladies retired to the drawing room**: "Dinner at Gwen's," *Star*, March 26, 1970.

104   **"abominations of the devil"**: Susan Naulty, an archivist at the Richard M. Nixon Library, in an interview.

104   **Lyndon Johnson**: Caro, *Master of the Senate*, 414.

104   **watching a Tyrone Power movie**: Calvin Cafritz interviews.

104   **"simply shouted Paris"**: Betty Beale, "Italian Dinner Highlights; Weekend Full of Parties," *Star*, June 24, 1956.

104   **"where everybody is prominent"**: The retiring Swedish ambassador, Erik Boheman, quoted in Betty Beale, "Sluggers and Socialites to Spar for Spotlight," *Star*, June 4, 1958, B-4.

104   **"If you have enough pretty women"**: Anderson, "Gwen Reveals Some Secrets."

104   **"when they're out"**: Maggie Wimsatt interview.

104   **"Fulbright and Saltonstall"**: "Capital Hostess," *Pathfinder*, December 14, 1949, 40. She referred to Senators J. William Fulbright, an Arkansas Democrat, and Leverett Saltonstall, a Massachusetts Republican.

105   **"I'm bipartisan"**: An interview with the television correspondent Mike Wallace, published in the *New York Post* and republished as "Gwen Tosses Parties to Save the West," *Washington Post*, April 27, 1958.

105   **"I carry my intellectual"**: Betty Beale, "Democrats, Including Talloo, to Take Over Washington," *Star*, October 8, 1958, B-2.

105   **Barry Goldwater reminisced**: Joseph McLellan, "Back at Gwen Cafritz': An Elegant Echo," *Post*, June 15, 1978, B1.

105   **softened the city**: Verbatim from Roy Pfautch, a public affairs consultant in Washington, D.C., in an interview.

105   **Between the salad and the dessert**: Irwin, "Who's Hostess with the Mostest?'"

105   **At the hospital**: He recounted being hospitalized in a *Post* interview, "Hobson: Illness Just Bad Luck," July 5, 1972. Carol's recollection is that he was hospitalized during their marriage only for a double hernia.

106   **a factory**: Intelligent Machines Research Corp., 1101 Lee Highway, Arlington, Virginia, from 1952 to 1954, according to a December 20, 1967, memorandum in FBI file No. WFO 140-25531.

106   **"between the ages of 35 and 50"**: Letter from Julius Hobson to his mother, dated January 30, 1955, in Jean Hobson's private collection.

106   **"a messianic itch"**: Tina Hobson interviews.

107   **"was a devoted father"**: Carol Joy (Hobson) Smith interviews.

107   **"I was an only child"**: Ibid.

107   **"nobody's vice president"**: The Reverend Jefferson Rogers, in an interview.

107   **commended Julius:** "Civic Federation Hits City Heads," *Star*, November 23, 1957, B-12.

107   **"The large department stores":** "The Quest for Jobs: Median family income per capita—$2050 for whites, $1000 for Negroes—reflects unequal job opportunities in D.C.," in the May 1958 edition of an unidentified publication, in Jean Hobson's private collection.

107   **"each organization theoretically":** *Post*, "A Goad for Change."

108   **"Progress cannot be left":** "NAACP Official Raps District Urban Renewal," *Afro-American*, January 23, 1960.

108   **"That's the way he conducted":** Carol Joy (Hobson) Smith interviews.

108   **"Julius, your schoolmate":** Ibid.

108   **"wearing last Easter's":** Undated letter, in Jean Hobson's private collection.

108   **a GS-9:** As a social insurance analyst in the Division of Program Analysis, at an annual salary of $6,135.

109   **"I am a bit afraid":** Undated letter, in Jean Hobson's private collection.

109   **without a day's delay:** Verbatim from Margaret S. Dickey, "Mrs. Cafritz No. 1 Hostess to Post Office Department," *Post*, November 5, 1951.

109   **"Gwendolynisms":** Beale, "Uninhibited 'Gwendolynisms.'"

109   **"Oh, there'll be millions":** Ibid.

109   **"if you're from Europe":** George Dixon, "A Santa Surprise, or Shock, for Women's Ad Club," *Post*, December 16, 1958, A15.

109   **"posterior of the afternoon":** Marie McNair, "'Fall Gal' Gwen Takes a Roasting," *Post*, October 14, 1958.

109   **"My dear, you look":** Tully, "The Story of Gwen Cafritz," third article.

109   **"Darling, I just couldn't":** Ibid.

109   **Neither had ever hosted:** Betty Beale, "Gwen Shows Up at Perle's Party," *Star*, March 5, 1957.

109   **The only parties that both:** According to C. David Heymann, *The Georgetown Ladies' Social Club: Power, Passion, and Politics in the Nation's Capital* (New York: Atria Books, 2003), 39.

109   **"This soft-shoe jostling":** Robert S. Allen and William V. Shannon, *The Truman Merry-Go-Round* (New York: Vanguard Press, 1950), excerpted in *Katharine Graham's Washington* (New York: Alfred A. Knopf, 2002), 160.

109   **"She's not a hostess":** Betty Beale's "Exclusively Yours" column, "Mesta–Cafritz Confrontation Followed by Reverberations," *Star*, March 10, 1957.

110   **beginning to cluster:** Verbatim from Perle Mesta with Robert Cahn, *Perle: My Story* (New York: McGraw-Hill Co. Inc., 1960), 216.

110   **"Isn't this what happens":** Beale, "Gwen Shows Up."

110   **the egg man:** Barbara Rathe, who was on Hale Boggs's staff from 1949 until his death, in an interview.

110   **the best southern cooking:** Cokie Roberts interviews.

110   **the sweet corn:** "New Majority Leader," *New York Times*, January 20, 1971, 14.

110   **his exercise and relaxation:** Lindy Boggs interviews.

111   **his hip pocket:** Barbara Rathe interview.

111   **temper, even with colleagues:** Rep. David Obey, Democrat of Wisconsin, in an interview.

111   **"eye contact, Hale?":** Former representative Dan Rostenkowski, Democrat of Illinois, in an interview.

111   **speculation had it:** Dixon, "Adlai's Coat-Tail Rider."

111   **"one of the better organizations":** Former senator George McGovern, Democrat of South Dakota, in an interview.

112   **More lawmakers had been moving:** Richard Baker, U.S. Senate historian, in an interview.

112   **"just too weird":** Cokie Roberts interviews.

112   **the campaign cash:** According to someone who was present when representatives of oil and gas interests passed campaign cash to Hale Boggs at a lunch in Washington, but who asked not to be identified.

113   **"We never had any money":** Cokie Roberts interviews.

113   **"Blind Tom" O'Brien, nicknamed:** Richard E. Cohen, *Rostenkowski: The Pursuit of Power and the End of the Old Politics* (Chicago: Ivan R. Dee, 1999), 35.

113   **"We invited everybody":** Lindy Boggs interviews.

113   **"I think we're going to":** Ibid.

114   **the rain always stayed away:** Until 1970.

114   **In the metropolitan area:** The population of metropolitan Washington, D.C., totaled 621,049 in 1930, 907,816 in 1940, 1,464,089 in 1940, and then 2,001,897 according to data provided to the author by an official at the Bureau of the Census, Washington, D.C.

114   **"the least of the threats":** William Press, executive vice president of the Washington Board of Trade, quoted in "New York World Fair Plans Dismissed Here," *Star*, August 10, 1959, B-1.

114   **"As a builder":** William A. Millen, "Cafritz Plans Hotel Regardless of Fair," *Star*, October 28, 1959, E-6.

114   **wealthiest active businessman:** Verbatim from Tully, "The Story of Gwen Cafritz," third article.

114   **money for the *Exodus*:** Abe Pollin interview. "He was the richest Jew, but not a leader of the Jewish community. I wouldn't say that was a knock against him, but the 15 or 18 or 20 who were there that night raising money for the *Exodus*, he wasn't there. They were the leaders of the Jewish community and my father was one of them."

114   **on scraps of paper:** Liane Atlas interview.

115   **"dreams for Pentagon City":** Jay Waldron, "$100 Million 'Pentagon City' Outlined by Builder Cafritz," *Northern Virginia Sun*, December 16, 1958, 1.

115 **cookie-cutter office buildings:** Carter Cafritz interviews.

115 **"There is more real wealth":** William A. Millen, "New Cafritz Building Marks K St. Growth," *Star*, June 24, 1958, A-16.

115 **"the main artery":** "Developer Seeks Zone Extension to 1800 Block of K," *Star*, October 18, 1963, A-8.

115 **Mr. Office Building:** Byron Black, who joined the Weihe Design Group in 1958, in an interview.

115 **"John," he said:** I have put quotation marks around John Hechinger's paraphrase, in an interview.

Chapter Five: KENNEDY

117 **"Tommy, I can't take":** Thomas H. Boggs Jr. interviews.

118 **"he loved Kennedy":** Ibid.

118 **party's chairman:** Paul Butler of Indiana.

118 **Hale's friends suspected:** "Articulate Congressman," *New York Times*, January 10, 1962.

119 **"The desirable thing":** Winzola McLendon, "Ball List, Like Topsy, Just Keeps on Growing," *Post*, December 25, 1960.

120 **a floor-length sheath:** "In Full Regalia for Tonight's Inaugural Balls," *Star*, January 20, 1961, B-1.

120 **"I liked the way":** Lindy Boggs interviews.

120 **Johnny Carson:** Julia Shepard interview.

120 **"a nice woman":** Lindy Boggs interviews. But she does not recall obtaining tickets to the inaugural ball for the Cafritzes.

121 **"storybook queen":** Betty Beale "There Was Dancing All Around: At the Mayflower," *Star*, January 21, 1961.

121 **parties that became Washington salons:** Sally Quinn, "The Party's Over," *Washington Post Magazine*, December 13, 1987, W24.

121 **"Jackie and the President":** Lindy Boggs interviews.

121 ***Washington, D.C.*:** The character of Irene Bloch in the novel (New York: Ballantine Books, 1967) was "suggested" by Gwen Cafritz, according to Gore Vidal, *Post Magazine*, February 25, 1990.

121 **"Cafritzes are Old Frontier":** Elspeth Rostow, a professor emeritus in American studies at the University of Texas (Austin), in an interview.

122 **"Socially, it isn't correct":** Tully, "The Story of Gwen Cafritz," third article.

122 **twenty dollars apiece:** Kirstine Larsen, *Tregaron: A Magical Place*, privately published in 2002, 71.

122 **"Negro Senator in the future":** Associated Press article "Dr. King to Play Georgia Senator," *Star*, October 20, 1961, A-8.

122   **the same twelve bars:** "Capitalites Play Themselves in Film," *Star*, C-4, September 22, 1961, by Betty Beale, who was also an extra.

122   **"a pique of":** "Dolly Climbs to Social Debacle," Maxine Cheshire in the *Post*, September 22, 1961, D9.

123   **tried to dance the twist:** Betty Beale, *Power At Play: A Memoir of Parties, Politicians and the Presidents in My Bedroom* (Washington, D.C.: Regnery Gateway, 1993), 70.

123   **light in his arms:** Gerson Nordlinger, in an interview.

123   **"I tried to explain":** "CORE's Picketing, Sit-ins Big Factor in Employment," *Afro-American*, April 25, 1964, B-8.

123   **D.C. chapter:** August Meier and Elliott Rudwick, *CORE: A Study in the Civil Rights Movement, 1942–1968* (Urbana: University of Illinois Press, 1975), 93, 121.

123   **"rare as a white crow":** "Top Achievement: Change in Hiring Practices," *Post*, July 4, 1972.

124   **"to determine as accurately":** Memorandum from Julius Hobson, president of the CORE chapter, dated March 28, 1961, from the Papers of Julius Hobson, Washingtoniana Division, D.C. Public Library.

124   **all but 5 of the 270:** Edward Peeks, "Hecht's Race Bars Hit: 'We Will Picket Store,'" *Afro-American*, May 6, 1961, 1.

124   **"CORE can't break any":** Spoken at a March 18, 1964, meeting of CORE, according to internal CORE documents, Julius Hobson papers, D.C. Public Library.

124   **"We intend to take them on":** Stephen S. Rosenfeld, "CORE Unit to Protest Job Bias," *Post*, July 22, 1961, C1.

124   **"easy targets":** "D.C. Heads Offer Help in Curbing Job Bias," *Star*, August 2, 1961, A-20.

125   **as few as a half-dozen:** Edward Peeks, then the *Afro-American* reporter who covered Washington CORE's activities, in an interview.

125   **suit coat and a tie:** William Duke, "The Rules for Sit-In Conduct," *Star*, December 3, 1961, F-3.

125   **"I had no troops":** *Post*, "Top Achievement."

125   **"The Deacon":** Roscoe Nix interview.

125   **four colored salesgirls:** Verbatim from Peeks, "Hecht's Race Bars."

126   **"more or less a father":** *Congressional Record*, 84th Congress, 1st sess., January 6, 1955, 129, on Rayburn's seventy-third birthday.

126   **"rugged honesty":** *Congressional Record*, 87th Congress, 2nd sess., January 18, 1962, 489. Rayburn died on November 16, 1961, after Congress had adjourned for the year.

126   **House floor, walking around:** Gary Hymel interviews.

126   **"a network of whips":** Dan Rostenkowski interview.

127   **"kind of an egocentric":** Ibid.

127   **"lubricated with sugar":** David Obey interview.

127   **Most of his colleagues:** Dan Rostenkowski interview.

127   **"When he was good":** Lindy Boggs interviews.

128   **with her father's influence:** Cokie Roberts interviews. "I'm sure she got it from Daddy, I assume."

128   **only place in Washington:** Paul Sigmund, Barbara's widower, in an interview.

128   **"simple joys of maidenhood":** Ibid.

128   **"I just don't get it":** Ibid.

129   **"The eggs are Boston-style":** As recalled by Hale Boggs, in his oral history interview for the John F. Kennedy Library, 18.

129   **"I finally got him":** "South's Democrats Urged to Back JFK," *Post*, April 7, 1963, A26. He spoke at a Jefferson-Jackson Day dinner sponsored by the Arlington County Democratic Committee at the Knights of Columbus Hall.

129   **"he came really because":** Kennedy Library oral history, 30.

129   **"If the time ever comes":** Ibid., 30–31.

129   **"Call Lawrence O'Brien":** "Harmony Invades Cuban Crisis . . . Possible Casualty . . . Fortunate Fish," *Post*, October 29, 1962, A2.

130   **"and the calmest man":** Kennedy Library oral history, 12.

130   **"I want to introduce":** Boggs, *Purple Veil*, 177.

130   **"I want to see":** This dialogue is according to Charles Cassell, a Washington architect who was a longtime civil rights associate of Julius Hobson's, as "sort of his lieutenant" at CORE, in an interview.

131   **"This worked very well":** "Hobson's Specialty: Successful Hoaxes," *Post*, July 4, 1972.

131   **More than eighty picket lines:** Hobson estimated the number at eighty-four from 1960 to 1964, according to "At the Shoreham Terrace," a column by Nicholas von Hoffman, *Post*, July 30, 1967.

132   **"Governor Ross Barnett of Mississippi":** "CORE Planning Continued Drive Against Utilities," *Star*, October 15, 1962, A-5.

132   **Frank Rich sought an apology:** Frank Rich Sr., in an interview.

132   **could want in a son:** Thanks to Dick Kirschten of *National Journal*.

133   **"a grave tactical error":** Letter from Rep. Charles Diggs, Democrat of Michigan, dated June 25, 1962, from the Julius Hobson Papers.

133   **"Sorry second-guessing":** Edward Peeks, "How CCJJ Fell Flat on Its Face," *Afro-American*, June 30, 1962, 4.

133   **"preachers whose only objective":** Quoted in "Renew America: Hobson the Great Gadfly," a documentary in the early 1970s by Marilyn Robinson at news channel 4.

133   **a higher standard of living:** Haynes Johnson, "Wealthy Elite Build Class Walls Within Their Own Race," fifth in the series "The Negro in America," *Star*, May 25, 1961, A-1.

133   **disturb the comfortable arrangements:** David Cohen, a former president of Common Cause, in an interview.

133 **"don't-rock-the-boat":** Sharon Pratt Kelly, mayor of Washington from 1991 to 1995, in an interview.

133 **"hated my father":** Julius Hobson Jr. interviews.

134 **"He is a peculiar":** Letter from Julius Hobson to his mother, dated February 3, 1959, Jean Hobson's private collection.

134 **"When you're growing up":** Julius Hobson Jr. interviews.

134 **"You've got a choice":** Stephen Klaidman, "Hobson's Illness 'Cured' Marriage," *Post*, August 31, 1975, A15.

134 **"You see Miss January?":** Carol Joy (Hobson) Smith interviews.

134 **"In my father's eyes":** Jean Hobson interview.

135 **Julius stayed home to paint:** Carol Joy (Hobson) Smith interviews.

136 **"it's personal, damn it":** Julius Hobson Jr. interviews.

136 **Negro leaders by surprise:** "A Greater Urgency on Rights," *Star*, June 2, 1963, D-1.

136 **very fine colored funeral homes:** "Funeral Home Refuses Body," *Star*, June 8, 1963, A-4.

136 **lines between white and Negro:** "The 1960 census figures showed Washington is less integrated in housing than it was in 1950," said Paul Rilling, executive director of D.C.'s Human Relations Council, quoted in "Segragated Schools Laid to Hong," *Star*, June 8, 1963, A-4. "Consequently, the schools are becoming more segregated in a de facto sense, as the Negro ghetto grows and as neighborhood segregation is perpetuated."

137 **bigger or more obvious:** Edward Peeks, in an interview.

137 **Negroes were barred:** "CORE Pickets Morris Cafritz Home," *Post*, March 6, 1963.

137 **"Morris Cafritz's Plantation":** *Afro-American*, June 1, 1963, 4.

137 **all-Negro building:** Parkway Plaza Apartments, at 1835 24th St. NE.

137 **"the shameful segregation policy":** Charles Tyler, "Cafritz Co. Does the 'Twist,' Turns Away White People," *Afro-American*, April 6, 1963, 1.

137 **"continuous sit-in":** "Cafritz Co. Picketed by CORE," *Post*, March 16, 1963.

137 **"completely unaware":** "CORE Starts 2 Additional 'Dwell–Ins,'" *Post*, August 17, 1963.

138 **"A slap in the face":** Charles Tyler, "CORE NAACP to Picket Cafritz Bldg. on PUC Move," *Afro-American*, May 11, 1963, 1.

138 **"biggest bigot in D.C.":** "Rep. Diggs Helps Picket Mr. Cafritz," *Afro-American*, May 18, 1963, 1.

138 **"If the Cafritz Company":** James A. Washington Jr., quoted in "2 P.U.C. Officials Refuse to Pass CORE Pickets," *Star*, May 13, 1963, A-1. Edgar Bernstein was the vice-chairman.

138 **"I have lived in":** Sam Eastman, "Cafritz Backs Housing Open to All Races," *Star*, July 1, 1963, A-3.

139 **"It was the first time":** Chris Harvey, "Like Father, Not Like Son: Hobson Jr. Has Own Style," *Washington Times*, October 31, 1988, B1.

140   **"he had a very beautiful"**: Carol Joy (Hobson) Smith interviews.

140   **the other cosponsoring groups:** Roy Wilkins of the NAACP, Whitney Young of the National Urban League, and James Forman of the Student Nonviolent Coordinating Committee, along with A. Philip Randolph, president of the Negro American Labor Council.

140   **"nothing but friendly persuasion"**: Quoted in Tom Kelly, "'. . . Not Even Harsh Language,'" *Daily News*, August 15, 1963.

140   **passed over for attention:** Carol Joy (Hobson) Smith interviews.

140   **unknown to the other organizers:** Walter Fauntroy, in an interview.

140   **"pertinent information"**: An August 31, 1964, FBI memorandum, 11, from F. J. Baumgardner, to W. C. Sullivan, in Julius Hobson's FBI file No. 157-3707 Section 1a.

141   **"a nice, clean-cut"**: Nicholas von Hoffman, "Picketers, Conferees Swap Jests," *Post*, June 2, 1966.

141   **"Well, until the first frost"**: Lindy Boggs interviews.

141   **"into a hornet's nest"**: Hale Boggs recalled he "may have said" that, in his oral history interview for the Kennedy Library.

141   **"Things always look"**: Hale Boggs, in December 5, 1963, remarks on the House floor, *Congressional Record*, 88th Congress, 1st sess., 23353.

142   **account was overdrawn:** Kennedy Library interview, 35.

142   **"The whole place"**: Ibid.

142   **"Nobody knew whether"**: Lindy Boggs interviews.

142   **Already McCormack was complaining:** Hale Boggs, in a November 22, 1963, statement, in a portion he evidently prepared but never delivered on the House floor, Boggs Papers.

142   **"the radicals and haters"**: Press statement issued on November 22, 1963, Boggs Papers.

142   **"crucified this man"**: According to Representative William Colmer, Democrat of Mississippi, in an October 27, 1978, Former Members of Congress Oral History, Library of Congress, quoted in Patrick J. Maney, in *Masters of the House: Congressional Leadership over Two Centuries*, eds. Roger H. Davidson, Susan Webb Hommand, and Raymond W. Smock (Boulder, Colo.: Westview Press, 1998), 235. Colmer quoted Boggs as having accused "the people who crucified . . ."

143   **"They wouldn't even let"**: Hale Boggs, in Kennedy Library interview, 34.

143   **"I am President"**: Ibid.

143   **"God bless you"**: Hale Boggs's November 22, 1963, statement.

143   **"Nothing's stopped"**: Julius Hobson Jr. interviews.

Chapter Six: JOHNSON

145 **"That's the nicest house":** Quoted in Katharine Graham, *Personal History* (New York: Alfred A. Knopf, 1997), 285.

145 **Johnsons' daughters:** Lynda Johnson Robb, in an interview.

146 **friends but also competitors:** Jim Jones interview.

146 **"you're on it":** Paul Sigmund interview. He was in the den, along with Cokie Roberts, when Hale Boggs was on the telephone, and he told them what President Johnson had said.

146 **"I can say on the highest":** *Congressional Record*, 88th Congress, 1st sess., November 29, 1963, 22954.

146 **"He's talking all":** From telephone conversations between Johnson and Fortas, at the Lyndon B. Johnson Library, quoted in Patrick J. Maney, in *Master of the House: Congressional Leadership over Two Centuries*, ed. Roger H. Davidson, Susan Webb Hammond, and Raymond W. Smock (Boulder, Colo.: Westview Press, 1998), 236.

146 **two Democrats:** The other one was Senator Richard Russell of Georgia.

146 **emotionally draining:** According to Lindy Boggs, quoted in Arlen Specter with Charles Robbins, *Passion for Truth: From Finding JFK's Single Bullet to Questioning Anita Hill to Impeaching Clinton* (New York: William Morrow, 2000), 47. Specter, now a Republican senator from Pennsylvania, served on the Warren Commission staff.

146 **"a sweet, feminine smile":** Hale Boggs's handwritten notes from the February 3, 1964, meeting, in his papers at Tulane.

147 **"It was like I killed Jack":** Lindy Boggs interviews.

147 **"pertinent questions":** Gerald Ford, in an interview.

147 **"we showed better judgment":** Ibid.

147 **panel's four working politicians:** The fourth was Senator John Sherman Cooper, Republican of Kentucky.

147 **Chief Justice Warren later told Lindy:** Boggs, *Purple Veil*, 182.

147 **Hale never doubted:** Lindy Boggs interviews.

147 **"on the rebound":** Paul Sigmund interview.

147 **"we do things in":** Ibid.

147 **"Everybody was there":** Ibid.

148 **"I'm awful glad":** "Miss Boggs Is Bride; Johnson at Reception," *Star*, January 26, 1964.

148 **"Emma," said Lindy:** Boggs, *Purple Veil*, 194.

148 **"the GNL":** Gwen Acsadi interview.

148 **"This is the first":** Transcript of *City Side*, broadcast on March 8, 1964, from the Julius Hobson Papers. The questioner was James Wright of WTOP News.

149 **"only when progress":** "11 Negro Leaders Hit School Boycott Plan," *Post*, March 11, 1964, 1.

149 **"Uncle Tommery":** On WMAL, March 11, 1964.

149 **"policies that seemed liberal":** Susan L. Jacoby, a *Washington Post* reporter, "National Monument to Failure," *Saturday Review*, November 18, 1967, 72.

149 **"heart":** Ray Boone, "Hobson's Resigning, He's 'Tired,'" *Afro-American*, March 28, 1964, 1.

150 **"suspend all boycott activities":** Walter Gold, "CORE Defers Decision on School Boycott," *Star*, March 25, 1964, B-1.

150 **"I'm tired":** Boone, "Hobson's Resigning."

150 **"agents of the Confederacy":** "Disruptive Force Seen As Threat to CORE," *Star*, April 18, 1964, A-10.

150 **"You can't run a revolution":** Ibid.

150 **"rudely cut off":** From a bill of particulars against Julius Hobson, labeled INTERNAL CORE BUSINESS: NOT TO BE RELEASED TO THE PRESS, from the Julius Hobson Papers.

151 **"I'm nonviolent":** *Post*, "A Goad for Change."

151 **"I frankly believe":** "Boycotts Endorsed," *Post*, November 30, 1964.

152 **won a five-dollar bet:** Mandell Ourisman, whose father was a close friend of Morris Cafritz's, in an interview.

152 **"get a pill":** "Morris Cafritz, Builder, Dead; Developed Properties in Capital," *New York Times*, June 13, 1964, 23.

152 **pain from his angina:** Carter Cafritz interviews.

152 **Morris had donated:** David Altschuler, ed., *The Jews of Washington, D.C.: A Communal History Anthology* (Chappaqua, N.Y.: The Jewish Historical Society of Greater Washington and Rossel Books, 1985), 37.

152 **"soared to eloquent heights":** "Morris Cafritz Tribute Paid by Gerstenfeld," *Post*, June 15, 1964.

152 **A senator:** Senator Clinton Anderson, Democrat of New Mexico; Justice Thomas C. Clark; Ambassadors Guillermo Sevilla-Sacasa of Nicaragua, Wilfried Platzer of Austria, and Hans Kristian Egen of Norway; and Metropolitan Police Chief Robert V. Murray.

152 **the three people:** Calvin Cafritz interviews.

153 **twenty-five miles:** From Old Georgetown Road near Rockville, to the extension of Pennsylvania Avenue in Prince George's County.

153 **eighty minutes a day:** Letters printed in the *Star*, August 23, 1964, A-10.

153 **Mike Causey:** "100 Years in Pictures," *Washingtonian*, December 1998, 87.

153 **"A huge wedding ring":** Rex Whitton, quoted in Lee Flor, "Ceremony in Maryland Opens Last of Beltway," *Star*, August 17, 1964, B-2.

154 **"by Negroes for Negroes":** Quoted in an undated *Post* article, apparently in July 1964, from the Julius Hobson Papers.

154 **fifteen or twenty people:** Charles Cassell interview.

154 **"paper tiger with teeth":** Mathews, "The Gadfly."

154 **"Maybe I shouldn't say":** "Hobson Assails D.C. Schools," *Post,* July 4, 1972.

154 **"thirteen or fourteen":** "'Rat Rally' Nets 100 Spectators But No Rodent," *Post,* August 23, 1964, 82.

155 **"I don't think Julius":** Roscoe Nix interview.

155 **"What he was doing":** Charles Cassell interview.

155 **"Pack your things":** Carol Joy (Hobson) Smith interviews.

156 **"important information":** An August 24, 1964, FBI memorandum, 1, from F. J. Baumgardner to W. C. Sullivan ("Subject: Julius Hobson, Confidential Source—Racial Matters"), in Hobson's FBI file No. 157-3707 Section 1.

156 **"Get in the car":** Carol Joy (Hobson) Smith interviews.

156 **another two hundred dollars:** Baumgardner FBI memo, 1.

156 **"a state of shock":** Quoted in Earl Wilson, "Parties to Go On for Gwen Cafritz," *Star,* July 31, 1964.

157 **"I guess it's not":** "Gwen Cafritz Rescued by Postmaster General," *Star,* November 22, 1964.

157 **"THE party of the year":** Ruth Dean, "Hoover Steals the Show," *Star,* November 21, 1964.

157 **rarely seen:** Betty Beale, *Power At Play: A Memoir of Parties, Politicians and the Presidents in My Bedroom* (Washington, D.C.: Regnery Gateway, 1993), 105.

157 **"she was terribly sad":** Calvin Cafritz interviews.

157 **Carol Channing until two fifteen:** Beale, *Power at Play,* 109.

158 **secured every door:** Carter Cafritz interviews.

158 **"Carter, don't":** From FBI file No. WFO 87-12836, on Gwendolyn Cafritz and the robbery, a report dated January 25, 1965, 6.

158 **be quiet or be killed:** "Mrs. Cafritz Is Robbed of Fortune in Jewels," *Star,* January 25, 1965, A-1.

158 **"White bitch":** FBI report, 6.

159 **"The cops":** Carter Cafritz interviews.

159 **$600,000:** Alfred E. Lewis, "Cafritz Loot Set at Close to $1 Million," *Post,* January 23, 1969. Estimates at the time put the loss at $400,000.

159– **"Mrs. Cafritz has been":** From a two-page letter to FBI director Hoover,
160 dated January 25, 1965, from Joseph D. Purvis, the special agent in charge, in FBI file No. 87-81099, Enclosure 3.

160 **"considerable doubt":** In a February 25, 1965, memorandum on the case to Hoover. Ibid.

160 **"Cafritz grab":** March 12, 1965, FBI memorandum, 8, file No. WFO 87-12386.

160 **she was imagining this:** James Cafritz, Edward's younger son, said in an interview that he had never heard of any such promise and surely would have if his father had thought this.

160 **intimidating but not standoffish:** Steven V. Roberts interviews.

161   **proposed a constitutional amendment:** "Boggs, Begich Disappearance: No Trace in 4 Days," *Congressional Quarterly Weekly Monitor*, October 21, 1972, 2775.

161   **hoped to lead it there:** Dan Rostenkowski interview.

161   **"You've got to do it":** Cokie Roberts interviews.

161   **"Look, don't push me":** Ibid.

162   **no discrimination:** Waggonner's remarks as printed in the *Congressional Record*, 89th Congress, 1st sess., July 9, 1965, 16221, seem to say the opposite: "I make no pretense that there has not been any discrimination in Louisiana or anywhere else." However, Edgar Poe, "Boggs Receives House Ovation," in the next day's *Times-Picayune*, 2, reported: "Rep. Waggonner maintained there was no need for such a law in Louisiana because, he said, there is no discrimination now practiced in the state. He said many Negroes are exercising their rights to register and vote." Boggs, whose remarks immediately followed Waggonner's, said, "I wish I could stand here . . . and say that there has not been discrimination, and agree with the gentleman from Louisiana." Apparently Waggonner had his controversial statement excised from the official transcript, not an unprecedented event.

162   **had nothing prepared:** Gary Hymel interviews.

162   **"Mr. Chairman":** *Congressional Record*, 89th Congress, 1st sess., July 9, 1965, 16221–22.

162   **word would go out:** Cokie Roberts interviews.

163   **Lindy had arrived:** Lindy Boggs interviews.

163   **"against the best interest":** Quoted in Ruth Jenkins, "Hobson Will Fight Case," *Afro-American*, July 24, 1965.

163   **Jean had been placed:** Jacoby, "Monument to Failure."

164   **"three Uncle Toms":** Gerald Grant, "School Board Parley Upset by ACT Trio," *Post*, July 20, 1965, A1.

164   **"I'm asking you like":** Jenkins, "Hobson Will Fight."

164   **"We were as surprised":** The Reverend E. Franklin Jackson, quoted in Grant, "School Board Parley," A3.

164   **"Mr. Hobson," they called him:** Julius Hobson Jr. interviews.

164   **"meet the chief of police":** Tina Hobson interviews.

165   **"only a smile":** "Hobson's Day in Court: Wasn't Me, Judge, It Was Them . . . ," *Afro-American*, July 31, 1965, 1.

165   **the word *beauty*:** Lady Bird Johnson, *A White House Diary* (New York: Holt, Rinehart & Winston, 1970), 235.

165   **the second meeting:** Ibid., 248.

165   **factions that favored:** Described in Jan Jarboe Russell, *Lady Bird: A Biography of Mrs. Johnson* (New York: Scribner, 1999), 277.

165   **the tulips in Washington:** Lindy Boggs interviews.

166   **"Every time Mother":** Lynda Johnson Robb interview.

166   **"the one I wanted":** "Cafritz Donations for Art Garden to Total $80,000," *Star*, May 9, 1965.

166 **"I'm through with my social":** Scottie Lanahan, "News to Me . . . Parties Are Past; Arts Are Future," *Post*, June 10, 1966.

166 **diamonds in the sunlight:** Donnie Radcliffe, "No Sameness About This," *Star*, May 5, 1968.

167 **in a circular pool:** The Calder stabile was moved later from the Fourteenth Street side of what is now called the National Museum of American History out toward the corner of Constitution.

167 **"I call it the Cafdolyn":** Meryle Secrest, "Cafdolyn or Gwenfritz?" *Post*, June 4, 1969, B4.

167 **"I had my old man":** Thomas H. Boggs Jr. interviews.

167 **"This is no secret":** "Boggs' Son Holds $9,986 Staff Job," Associated Press article in the *Star*, June 14, 1963. Tommy Boggs started working at the committee in 1961.

167 **eight thousand dollars a year:** The Report of the Secretary of the Senate for fiscal year 1962, in the U.S. Senate Library, put his salary at $666.36 a month, which amounts to $7,996.32.

167–
168 **two future senators and:** Senators Patrick Leahy, Democrat of Vermont, and John Durkin, Democrat of New Hampshire, and Representatives Steny Hoyer, Democrat of Maryland; Jim Jones, Democrat of Oklahoma; and Robert Baumann, Republican of Maryland. Tommy Boggs attended Georgetown Law Center 1961–65.

168 **"impressed with his dad":** Steny Hoyer, in an interview.

168 **"poor kid from Muskogee":** Jim Jones, in an interview.

168 **Jim Jones's law partner:** At Manatt Phelps & Phillips.

168 **his father's footnoted dissent:** Thomas H. Boggs Jr. interviews.

168 **force behind the hearings:** Timothy May, in an interview.

168 **"destroyed the shipping industry":** Thomas H. Boggs Jr. interviews.

168 **When a Harrisburg newspaper:** "President's Address Here Will Be Televised Statewide," *The Patriot*, September 9, 1964.

168 **"I'm supposed to announce":** Ibid.

169 **a lot of advance work:** Jim Jones interview.

169 **"It wasn't hard":** Thomas H. Boggs Jr. interviews.

169 **"because of my brilliance":** Ibid.

169 **"I had a ridiculous":** Quoted in Carl Bernstein, "King of the Hill," *Vanity Fair*, March 1998, 175ff.

169 **silken elegance:** Clifford's aura is described in Joseph C. Goulden, *The Superlawyers: The Small and Powerful World of the Great Washington Law Firms* (New York: Weybright & Talley, 1971).

169 **"he uses the Mayflower":** Jack Lait and Lee Mortimer, *Washington Confidential* (New York: Crown Publishers, 1951), 200.

170 **"I shouldn't tell you":** Thomas H. Boggs Jr. interview.

170 **"I felt more challenged":** Ibid.

170 **"I liked Jim Patton":** Ibid.

170 **"I'm not going to let":** Jim Patton, in an interview.

171   **"a stroke of genius":** Timothy May, in an interview.

171   **eighteen thousand dollars:** Thomas H. Boggs Jr. interviews. The law firm paid him eight thousand dollars, the committee ten thousand dollars.

171   **"It gave him a chance":** Jim Patton interview.

171   **"Who?":** Thomas H. Boggs Jr. interviews.

171   **stupidity:** "The best he could give me was heritage and opportunity, and here I was not taking advantage of 'opportunity,'" Tommy Boggs explained in Paul Taylor, "'One-Stop Shopping': A Law Firm Prospers in the New Marketplace of Influence," August 1, 1983, *Post*, A1. "He said I was stupid."

171   **"You testified yesterday":** From the July 19, 1966, transcript of *Hobson v. Hanson*, 269 F. Suppl. 401 (1967), Civil Action No. 82-66, filed in U.S. District Court for the District of Columbia, 370.

172   **He had approached:** Tina Hobson interviews.

173   **Nobody else had believed:** Ibid.

173   **"programmed retardation":** "Tobriner Assails Track System," *Post*, October 27, 1965.

173   **"the junk heap":** Ann Wood, "Sorority Honors New Envoy," *Star*, July 20, 1965.

173   **"It's a deliberate attempt":** "D.C. Schools Breed Racism, Panel Told," *Post*, September 14, 1965.

173   **the same statistical techniques:** John Stacks, "Hobson Spells Out Claim of School Segregation," *Star*, July 21, 1966, B1.

173   **"Hey, don't you think":** Patricia Saltonstall, in an interview.

174   **lead plaintiffs:** The formal name of the case was Julius W. Hobson, individually and on behalf of Jean Marie Hobson and Julius W. Hobson Jr.; all residing at 4801 Queens Chapel Terrace NE, D.C.; Samuel D. Graham, individually and on behalf of Barbara Jeane Graham and Karen Chandelle Graham; all residing at 1827 Massachusetts Ave., SE, D.C.; Mary Alice Brown, individually and on behalf of Charles Hudson Brown; both residing at 2412 20th St. D.C.; Pauline Smith, individually and on behalf of Maurice Hood; both residing at 1017 4th St. SE, D.C.; Willie Davis Jr., individually and on behalf of Ronald D. Davis, Reginald D. Davis and Myoshi J. Davis; all residing at 3931 14th St. NW, D.C.; James K. Ward, individually and on behalf of Chrycynthia Elain Ward; both residing at 1100 Trenton Pl. SE, D.C.; Joyce M. Makel, individually and on behalf of Michelle I. Makel; and Carolyn Hill Stewart, residing at 1303 Congress St. SE, D.C.

Plaintiffs,

against

Carl F. Hansen, Superintendent of Schools of the District of Columbia; The Board of Education of the District of Columbia; Wesley S. Williams, President of the Board of Education of the District of Columbia; Carl Smuck, Everett A. Hewlett, West A. Hamilton, Louise S. Steele, Euphemia L. Haynes, Gloria K. Roberts, Preston A. McLendon, and Irving B. Yochelson, members of the

Board of Education of the District of Columbia; Chief Judge Matthew F. McGuire; Senior Judges Joseph L. Jackson, Henry A. Schweinhaut, Charles S. McLaughlin and David A. Pine; and District Judges Alexander Holtzoff, Richmond B. Keech, Edward M. Curran, Burnita Shelton Matthews, Luther W. Youngdahl, Joseph C. McGarraghy, John J. Sirica, George L. Hart Jr., Leonard P. Walsh, William B. Jones, Spottswood W. Robinson III, Howard S. Corcoran, Oliver Gasch, William B. Bryant, all of the United Sates District Court for the District of Columbia; The Board of Elections of the District of Columbia; Charles H. Mayer (Chairman), Ernest Schein and Dr. Robert Earl Martin, members of the Board of Elections of the District of Columbia, Defendants.

174 **"Nobody else was going":** Patricia Saltonstall interview.

174 **"vanity on his part":** Carol Joy (Hobson) Smith interviews.

174 **"And is it your testimony":** Transcript of *Hobson v. Hansen*, 269 F. Suppl. 401 (1967), 380–82.

174 **most gratifying decision:** William M. Kunstler with Sheila Isenberg, *My Life as a Radical Lawyer* (New York: Birch Lane Press, 1994), 146.

175 **"really paved the way":** Steven V. Roberts interviews.

175 **they became sweethearts:** Boggs, *Purple Veil*, 201.

175 **"my sweetest child":** Lindy Boggs interviews.

175 **Steve would eat lunch:** Steven V. Roberts interviews.

176 **"Could we be married":** Boggs, *Purple Veil*, 206.

176 **"looking for an abortionist":** Cokie Roberts interviews.

176 **"This is getting silly":** Ibid.

177 **"All of the Democrats":** Ibid.

177 **"It doesn't get more humiliating":** Cokie Roberts and Steve Roberts, *From This Day Forward* (New York: William Morrow and Co., 2000), 27.

178 **"In my tradition":** According to a copy of Arthur Goldberg's notes, provided by Steven V. Roberts.

178 **"When you watch Lindy":** Steven V. Roberts interviews.

178 **he was distracting attention:** Dorothy McCardle, "Goldberg Also Sees 'Cokie' Boggs Become Steven Roberts' Bride," *Post*, September 11, 1966.

178 **Lawyers for the school board:** "Hobson v. Hansen," *The Reporter*, July 13, 1967, 20.

178 **183 pages:** *Post*, June 20, 1967. The opinion as published later in the *Federal Supplement*, 269 F. Supp. 401 (1967), ran 119 pages.

178 **"unconstitutionally deprived Negro":** *Hobson v. Hansen*, 269 F. Supp. 401 (1967), 401.

178 **"tendency of resegregating":** Ibid., 411.

179 **"separate but unequal":** Ibid., 495.

179 **"its unclear basis in precedent":** *Harvard Law Review*, 81, no. 7 (May 1968): 1523.

179 **contemplated a lawsuit:** Patricia Saltonstall interview.

180   **"he really liked white women":** Ibid.

180   **"There was no way":** Ibid.

180   **"to tell the truth?":** Ibid.

180   **pretty shaken up:** Ibid.

180   **"a white divorcée":** FBI memo dated November 5, 1969, in Julius Hobson's FBI file No. 157-3707.

180   **"a nice house":** Solveig Eggers, "Candidates' Wives Differ on Their Roles," *Daily News*, February 15, 1971, 16.

181   **"saint or a total sinner":** Letter dated September 21, 1967, from the Julius Hobson Papers.

181   **"I'll cook":** Tina Hobson interviews

181   **"live in the ghetto":** Mathews, "The Gadfly."

181   **"special barbecue sauce":** Tina Hobson interviews.

181   **"absolutely perfect gentleman":** Ibid.

182   **"You can take me seriously":** Ibid.

182   **"I wanted to stay home":** Julius Hobson Jr. interviews.

182   **way of life:** Jefferson Rogers interview.

182   **"We're talking about black men":** Quoted in William Raspberry, "Black Nationalism Seen by Hobson As Reaction to Nationalism of Whites," *Post*, June 22, 1966.

183   **a D.C. native:** Her name was Robin Gregory.

183   **"And she stopped subjecting":** "Tribute to the Queen," *The Hilltop*, October 21, 1966.

183   **Julius had complained:** Patricia Saltonstall interview.

183   **"Because if the police came":** Julius Hobson Jr. interviews.

183   **In a class of fifty:** "Julius Hobson, Local Legend," *Cause*, March 1978, 26.

184   **"ominous":** Betty Wolden, a reporter for NBC News, quoted in Ben W. Gilbert and the staff of the *Washington Post*, *Ten Blocks from the White House: Anatomy of the Washington Riots of 1968* (Washington, D.C.: Federick A. Praeger, 1968), 14.

184   **"Let's not get anyone":** Ibid., 18–19.

184   **"Burn, baby, burn!":** According to then-mayor Walter Washington, in an interview.

184   **"Goddamn, I've waited":** Attributed to Joseph Califano in Graham, *Personal History*, 405–6.

185   **"Oh, Mama":** Carol Joy (Hobson) Smith interviews.

185   **five Safeways:** Harry S. Jaffe and Tom Sherwood, *Dream City: Race, Power, and the Decline of Washington* (New York: Simon & Schuster, 1994), 79.

185   **"What are you doing here?":** Julius Hobson Jr. interviews.

185   **"Let's go pick up Jean":** Carol Joy (Hobson) Smith interviews.

185   **At Rich's Shoes:** Frank Rich Sr. interview.

185   **"I was so angry":** Carol Joy (Hobson) Smith interviews.

186   **"Where are my keys?":** Ibid.

186   **"Julius, do you want":** Tina Hobson interviews.

186   **Hale Boggs was nervous:** Gary Hymel interviews.

187   **He also understood:** Gary Hymel interviews: "I know he believed [in open housing] sincerely, but he also knew—we never discussed it, but it was obvious—that if he was going to go up in the leadership, that was a must vote. There was no doubt about that."

187   **He handpicked Hale:** According to Rowland Evans and Robert Novak, "LBJ's Intent to Dictate Platform Presages Open Battle with HHH," *Post*, July 17, 1968.

187   **known Hubert Humphrey:** Boggs, *Purple Veil*, 219.

187   **stopped off at Tommy's:** Thomas H. Boggs Jr. interviews.

187   **wig and a fluffy top-piece:** Lindy Boggs interviews.

188   **"Jack is Rose's son":** Cokie Roberts interviews.

188   **a stack of first editions:** Leon Billings, a platform committee staff member who accompanied Tommy Boggs to Albert's hotel room, in an interview.

188   **"carefully chosen portions":** Clark Clifford with Richard Holbrooke, *Counsel to the President: A Memoir* (New York: Random House, 1991), 564.

188   **"But that slave trade":** Gary Hymel interviews.

189   **Hale's staff found microphones:** Dan Rostenkowski interview.

189   **"highly respected Hale Boggs":** Jim Jones interview.

189   **Barbara screamed at:** Cokie Roberts interviews.

189   **"And much to our horror":** Ibid.

189   **"Do it again":** Roberts and Roberts, *From This Day Forward*, 98.

189   **"first national political assignment":** Steven V. Roberts interviews.

189   **"Bobby's campaign is like":** Quoted in Steven V. Roberts, "McCarthy Urges Leaders to Wait," *New York Times*, April 3, 1968, 1, 28.

190   **"All through that period":** Steven V. Roberts interviews.

190   **"A mistake on my part":** Ibid.

190   **"Why does Steve":** Ibid.

190   **"under such terrible pressure":** Paul Sigmund interview.

190   **burned a cross:** Lindy Boggs interviews and "Cross Is Burned at Boggs Home," Associated Press, *Post*, November 19, 1964.

190   **"so ugly to Hale":** Lindy Boggs interviews.

190   **Had the ad started:** Thomas H. Boggs Jr. interviews.

191   **drinking too much:** Cokie Roberts interviews.

191   **"The poor need somebody":** "Hobson Willing to Run for D.C. School Board," *Post*, September 10, 1967.

191   **would have no more power:** Jacoby, "Monument to Failure."

191   **uninspiring field of candidates:** "Hobson Set to Leave School Race," *Star*, August 19, 1968, B-1.

191   **"The school case gave":** Patricia Saltonstall interview.

191   **"I have no ambitions":** "Hobson to Run for New School Board," *Post*, August 25, 1968, C2.

192   **"law and order":** Sidney Lippman, "Hobson: 'Law and Order,'" *Daily News*, September 27, 1968, 14.

192   **"When I get on":** Ibid.

193   **Julius despised her:** Carol Joy (Hobson) Smith interviews.

193   **"in the same department":** Anita Allen, in an interview.

193   **"an invaluable gadfly":** "Election (III)—In the District," *Post* editorial, November 2, 1968, A18.

193   **Poor blacks and white liberals:** Bardyl Tirana, a political ally of Hobson's, in an interview.

193   **"I'm flabbergasted":** "Hobson Appears Only School Winner," *Star*, November 6, 1968, B-3.

193   **"Give me all":** Julius Hobson Jr. interviews.

194   **handed him eight dollars:** "Hobson's Son Robbed Near His Doorstep," *Post*, March 7, 1969.

194   **arranged by Gwen's assistant:** Sheila Hines, in an interview.

194   **"I am too old":** Dobson, "Luncheon with . . . Gwen."

194   **"Don't worry":** "Gwen Cafritz Robbed of $750,000 in Inaugural Repeat." *Star*, January 16, 1969, A-1.

194   **brandy and a pill:** Gwendolyn Cafritz's FBI file, No. WFO 87-16978, in a January 23, 1969, internal report.

195   ***Dear Gwen:*** Betty Beale, "A Personal Letter from Dick," *Star*, February 2, 1969, D-2.

Chapter Seven: NIXON

198   **odds-on favorite:** Herbert H. Denton, "School Board Elects Coates as President," *Post*, January 28, 1969, D1.

198   **"I wasn't going to win":** Anita Allen interview.

198   **"Shame on you":** Charles Cassell interview.

198   **"Somebody's not voting":** Anita Allen interview.

198   **Anita Allen moved:** Official minutes of the January 27, 1969, meeting, at the Summer School archives. No one objected to her motion.

199   **"The people declare":** Denton, "School Board Elects Coates."

199   **"Let Mr. Coates":** Sidney Lippman, "Rev. Coates Will Head School Board," *Daily News*, January 28, 1969, 5.

199   **"back in the brier patch":** Peter Milius, "Why Coates? Image . . . Unity," *Post*, January 29, 1969.

200   **"No, no, no":** Sidney Lippman, "Swahili, 'Black History' Ok'd After Stormy Session," *Daily News*, February 13, 1969.

200   **"a respectable word":** "Malcolm X Tribute Weighed," *Post*, March 25, 1969.

200   **"Jefferson Davis seems":** A passage from a textbook approved for use in D.C. schools, read aloud at the school board's February 19, 1969, meeting by

the board member Mattie Taylor, as reported the following day in John Mathews, "Passage in Textbook Assailed as Racist," *Star*.

200   **"I intend to be an agitator"**: Quoted in Susan Jacoby, "Julius Hobson: The Man behind the Mouth," in an unidentified magazine in the Julius Hobson Papers.

200   **"needless to say"**: "Black Lectures Concluded," *The Hoya*, April 24, 1969, 3.

201   **"have nothing to lose"**: According to coverage by Paul Hodge, "School Seizures Seen Way to Improve Them," *Post*, April 16, 1969, D3.

201   **"I would remind those boys"**: Herbert Denton, "Hobson the Activist Needs New Outlook," *Post*, April 19, 1969.

201   **"personally interested"**: A memorandum from Hoover to the FBI's Washington field office, dated May 7, 1969, in Julius Hobson's FBI file No. 140-35548 Section 4.

201   **Agitator Index:** According to a February 24, 1969, memorandum to Hoover (in FBI file No. 157-3707 Section 1) and a July 10, 1969, memo from W. V. Cleveland to Mr. Gale (FBI file No. 140-35548 Section 4), he was placed on the Agitator Index on February 28, 1968; on the Rabble Rouser Index on February 24, 1969; and on the Security Index on April 18, 1969, three days after his speech at Georgetown.

201   *Post* **reporter refused:** Internal FBI memorandum, April 25, 1969. The *Star* reporter was Winston Groom Jr.

202   **Saltonstall had ghostwritten:** Patricia Saltonstall interview.

202   **"no odious comparisons"**: William Raspberry, "Hobson on Black Struggle," *Post*, April 9, 1969.

202   **"If I thought Congressman Broyhill"**: In an interview on *Comment*, WWDC Radio, Silver Spring, Maryland, April 22, 1969.

202   **"Come to our autograph"**: Advertisement in the *Star*, A-2, April 22, 1969, for the party the following day at noon.

203   **"complexion . . . Florida"**: Quoted in an October 21, 1969, memo to FBI director Hoover, an account of the October 16 interview, in FBI file No. 58-6996 on Thomas Hale Boggs. The earlier interview took place on September 15, 1969.

203   **"Let's just go ahead"**: Ibid.

203   **five million dollars:** The original estimate to build the sixteen-hundred-car garage was $11.8 million. Frenkil attributed the overrun to a costlier means of bracing the walls.

203   **had specifically requested:** According to an internal FBI memorandum dated April 13, 1971, from R. D. Cotter to C. D. Brennan, in FBI file No. 94-37804, for Thomas Hale Boggs.

203   **at the Preakness:** Lindy Boggs interviews.

203   **a name-dropper:** FBI account of the October 16, 1969, interview.

203   **"It so happened"**: Lindy Boggs interviews.

204 **"with no patina"**: Ibid.

204 **$45,082.95:** April 13, 1971, FBI memo.

204 **Tommy examined the records:** Thomas H. Boggs Jr. interviews.

204 **on front pages:** See Robert M. Smith, "Judge Releases Secret Jury Data," *New York Times*, June 23, 1970, 1.

204 **"what embarrassment is":** Lindy Boggs interviews.

205 **"fifteen balls in the air":** Tina Hobson interviews.

205 **preferred the conservative *Star:*** Ibid.

205 **hire a new superintendent:** Bardyl Tirana interview.

206 **"Mr. Hobson and I":** Richard E. Prince, "Styles Contrast in Ward Two," *Post*, October 21, 1969.

206 **"before the television cameras":** Barry Kalb, "Free-Swinging Style Marks D.C. Race," *Star*, October 27, 1969.

206 **"the most exciting":** "The D.C. School Board Race," *Daily News* editorial, October 31, 1969, 24.

206 **"His knowledge of the details":** "A Chance to Improve the School Board," *Sunday Star* editorial, November 2, 1969.

206 **"his tendency to indulge":** "D.C. School Board Voters' Guide," *Post* editorial, October 31, 1969.

207 **FBI and CIA agents were spying:** Bardyl Tirana interview.

207 **saddened but not shocked:** Ibid.

207 **Julius had had no inkling:** Tina Hobson and Bardyl Tirana interviews.

207 **"I hadn't really decided":** Tina Hobson interviews.

207 **"I wish Mrs. Washington":** Robert F. Levey, "Hobson Foe Wins District School Race," *Post*, November 5, 1969, A1, 12.

208 **"crazy as a loon":** Thomas H. Boggs Jr. interviews.

208 **"The best way":** Jim Patton interviews.

208 **Less than fourteen months:** Tommy Boggs joined the law firm on April 12, 1966, and became a name partner on June 1, 1967.

208 **"Nothing came up":** Jim Patton interviews.

209 **showed up in person one October:** Thomas H. Boggs Jr. interviews. He said he had been "like the sixty-eighth lobbyist" in 1967 or 1968. He told Charles Lewis of the Center for Public Integrity in a 2003 interview that he had been "the sixty-first or sixty-second" lobbyist to register in September of 1967 or 1968. Lewis kindly provided a transcript to the author.

209 **shortened to *lobbyist:*** See James Deakin, *The Lobbyists* (Washington, D.C.: Public Affairs Press, 1966), 54, and Jeffrey H. Birnbaum, *The Lobbyists: How Influence Peddlers Get Their Way in Washington* (New York: Times Books, 1992), 9.

209 **"member of the Metropolitan Club":** George Blow, in an interview.

210 **"Washington was run by twenty-five people":** Thomas H. Boggs Jr. interviews.

210 **"intense self-importance":** Leon Billings interview.

210 **"all my Louisiana buddies":** Thomas H. Boggs Jr. interviews.

210 **"I would like to ask"**: Transcript of the February 9, 1971, House Agriculture Committee hearing on Extension of the Sugar Act, Serial 92-E, 92nd Congress, 1st sess., 304.

210 **"a son's respect"**: Taylor, "'One–Stop Shopping.'"

210 **"It's in the blood"**: Barbara Boggs, in an interview.

210 **"got better"**: Thomas H. Boggs Jr. interviews.

211 **"Voters in the Eighth"**: Stated on WRC-TV on October 4, 1970, according to Bob Woodward, "Gude and Boggs Running on Incumbent's Record," Montgomery County, Maryland, *Sentinel*, October 8, 1970, A1, 10.

211 **"I intend of course"**: Diane Brockett, "Allen Charges Conflict as Shriver Aids Boggs," *Star*, July 24, 1970.

211 **inexpensive black suits:** "Boggs, Gude in 8th District Find Few Issues to Debate," *Star*, November 4, 1970.

211 **JFK-like gestures:** Kirk Scharfenberg "Boggs Takes Analytical Style into Primary Election Race," *Post*, August 3, 1970.

211 **"swords into plowshares":** *Sentinel*, August 20, 1970, A14.

211 **Barbara wore a wig:** Barbara Boggs interview.

212 **"Ever hear of the Gude bill?":** Thomas H. Boggs Jr. interviews.

212 **"We had to disband":** Calvin Cafritz interviews.

213 **"I'd worked in different":** Ibid.

213 **Calvin's younger brothers:** S. Oliver Goodman, "Son, 33, to Head Cafritz Complex," *Post*, June 25, 1964.

214 **Carter's ex-wife:** Charlene Lawley married Carter Cafritz in May 1966, and they were divorced in August 1968.

214 **twelve capsules of heroin:** "Charlene Cafritz Is Indicted," *Post*, April 16, 1970, B2.

214 **found dead:** "Charline [*sic*] Cafritz Is Found Dead," *Star*, September 4, 1970.

214 **"'beatnik' types":** An internal FBI memorandum dated February 16, 1965, in Gwendolyn Cafritz's FBI files, No. 87-81099 Enclosure 5, 405.

214 **town house in Georgetown:** A photographic spread of the remodeling at 3038 Cambridge Place NW, "Remodeling for Today," by Abby Chapple (photograph by Robert Lautman), appeared in the *Star*'s *Sunday Magazine*, June 4, 1967, 18–19.

214 **"I'm forty years old":** William H. Jones, "Cafritz Quits Real Estate Firm; Differences with Mother Hinted," *Post*, December 21, 1971.

214 **"differences between mother":** Ibid.

214 **"My expectations":** Calvin Cafritz interviews.

215 **subdued surroundings of H-128:** Robert L. Peabody, *Leadership in Congress: Stability, Succession, and Change* (Boston: Little, Brown and Co., 1976), 189–90.

215 **four declared rivals:** The others were B. F. Sisk of California, James O'Hara of Michigan, and Wayne Hays of Ohio.

215 **"lethargy and arrogance":** Rowland Evans and Robert Novak, "McCormack

Aims to Thwart Liberals by Supporting Boggs, Rostenkowski," *Post*, July 20, 1970.

215   **"too liberal for"**: Richard L. Lyons, "House Caucus Day: They All Talk Like Winners," *Post*, January 19, 1971.

215   **"bizarre and erratic"**: From a memorandum, "The case against Boggs," in the Morris K. Udall Papers at the University of Arizona.

216   **"May I ask a question?"**: From a transcript of Hale Boggs's October 11, 1968, press conference, in the Udall Papers.

216   **"and there was *no way*"**: An unidentified member of Congress quoted in Larry L. King, "The Road to Power in Congress," *Harper's Magazine*, June 1971, 39ff.

216   **"babysitting, primarily"**: Thomas H. Boggs Jr. interviews.

216   **get a maybe:** Ibid.

216   **four garden parties:** "Battle Takes Shape for House Democratic Leadership," *Congressional Quarterly Weekly Monitor*, November 27, 1970, 2867.

216   **"I'm not status quo"**: From his postelection press conference, quoted in Andrew J. Glass, "Congress Report: House Democrats Back Establishment in Electing Boggs Floor Leader," *National Journal*, January 23, 1971, 188.

216   **"the big-city guys"**: Thomas H. Boggs Jr. interviews.

217   **"In the House"**: Quoted in King, "The Road to Power," 61.

217   **"taking candy from a baby"**: Michael Anders, "Fund-Raising, Hobson Style," *Star*, February 18, 1971.

217   **Norton Parker Chipman:** Jack Eisen, "D.C. Delegate—100 Years Ago," *Post*, March 23, 1971.

218   **"Little Lord Fauntroy"**: Richard E. Prince, "Hobson Jumps Into Delegate Contest," *Post*, January 15, 1971.

218   **ugly:** Julius Hobson Jr. interviews.

218   **"a man or a boy"**: "4 Delegate Hopefuls Air Views," *Post*, March 7, 1971.

218   **"I am not a politician"**: "D.C. Statehood Party: Julius Hobson," 30 January–1 February, *Quicksilver Times*, 1971, 3.

218   **"pure Baptist minister"**: Josephine F. Caplan, "The Year of the Nonvoting Delegate," *Sunday Star*, May 16, 1971, 4.

218   **"a chance of winning"**: Tina Hobson interviews.

219   **"I hope Washington"**: David R. Boldt, "Fauntroy Sweeps Delegate Race," *Post*, March 24, 1971, A1, 10.

219   **"the second time"**: "1 Man's View of D.C.'s Ills," *Post*, July 3, 1972.

219   **"four-and-a-half hours"**: From a tape of an Oval Office meeting with President Nixon, White House Chief of Staff Bob Haldeman, Attorney General John Mitchell, and Senator Bob Dole, from 4:02 to 4:50 P.M. on March 16, 1971, from the Nixon White House Tapes Conversation 468-16, casette 361, at the National Archives and Records Administration, College Park, Maryland.

220   **had hated Richard Nixon:** Thomas H. Boggs Jr. interviews.

220 **in loud comments:** Jerry terHorst, in an interview. He was later President Ford's press secretary.

220 **"That voice of his":** Stated apparently by Attorney General John Mitchell on the March 16, 1971, Nixon tape.

220 **a bagman:** Thomas H. Boggs Jr. interviews.

220 **"a loyalist":** March 16, 1971, Nixon tape.

220 **susceptible to drink:** James M. Tuholski, the author's late father-in-law, who knew Ed Mitchell when both lived in Evansville, Indiana, and had daughters who were friends.

220 **Hale threatened to give:** An unidentified informant's letter to FBI Director Hoover, dated April 12, 1971, in Boggs's FBI file No. 94-37804, Part 1 of 2.

220 **he was bleeding:** A guest at the dinner who was standing outside the men's room when Hale Boggs emerged but who asked to remain unidentified, in an interview.

220 **as "Jack Dempsey":** "Boggs Punched," UPI, *Post*, March 16, 1971.

220 **talk of the after-dinner parties:** Jerry terHorst interview.

221 **"Gestapo!":** According to April 7, 1971, memorandum from T. E. Bishop to Mr. Mohr, and April 9, 1971, memo to FBI Director Hoover, both in Boggs FBI file No. 94-37804, Part 1 of 2.

221 **"with electric silence":** "Battin' the Breeze," column by Ed Bandjough, editor and publisher of *The Gulf County Breeze* in Wewahitchka, Florida, April 18, 1971.

221 **"out on the beach":** Clark Hoyt, "Hale Boggs Accused of Disorder at Dinner," *Star*, May 21, 1971.

221 **"He was taking antibiotics":** Ibid.

221 **fistfight with a congressman:** Rep. Durwood G. Hall, a Missouri Republican, at an afternoon reception for Rep. Daniel Flood, a Pennsylvania Democrat. Rep. H. R. Gross, an Iowa Republican, reported the incident by phone to FBI Director Hoover, according to an April 7, 1971, memo from Hoover to Mr. Tolson and Mr. Bishop, Boggs FBI file No. 94-37804, Part 1 of 2.

221 **a senator's lapels:** Peter Dominick, a Colorado Republican.

221 **Albert canceled trips:** Jack Anderson, "McCormack Left a Power Vacuum," *Post*, March 10, 1972, D19.

221 **East Room at the White House:** Dan Rostenkowski interview

222 **"Doc, what the hell's":** Ibid.

222 **"Untouchable Hoover":** Ken W. Clawson, "Untouchable Hoover, FBI under Fire," *Post*, April 5, 1971, A1.

222 **"done this with":** Thomas H. Boggs Jr. interviews.

222 **"very non-specific":** Typed at the bottom of a copy of Hoover's January 17, 1950, reply to Boggs for his "thoughtful letter" of January 10, in the Boggs FBI file No. 94-37804, Part 1 of 2.

223 **"a political stunt":** Internal FBI memorandum from M. A. Jones to Mr. DeLoach, May 16, 1962, in Boggs file No. 94-37804, Part 1 of 2.

223   **reporters who questioned him:** Curt Gentry, *J. Edgar Hoover: The Man and the Secrets* (New York: W. W. Norton & Co., 1991), 678.

223   **"I apologize for my voice":** *Congressional Record*, 92nd Congress, 1st sess., April 5, 1971, 9470.

224   **"or if he was paranoid":** David Obey interview.

224   **Two of the Democrats':** Senators Edmund Muskie of Maine and George McGovern of South Dakota.

224   **"a bad smell":** Written on the FBI's clipping of Mary Anne Dolan, "A Great Win for the Fans," *Star*, April 6, 1971, B6, from Boggs's FBI file No. 94-37804, Part 2 of 2.

224   **"we should attack Boggs":** H. R. Haldeman, *The Haldeman Diaries: Inside the Nixon White House* (New York: Berkley Books, 1994), 267.

225   **"I charge categorically":** "FBI Spied on Him, Boggs Says," *Star*, April 6, 1971, A-1.

225   **"What's the matter with":** From a seven-minute telephone conversation, No. 42-9, cassette 410-9, on April 6, 1971, on the Nixon White House Tapes.

225   **"Facts?" Hale replied:** Cartha D. "Deke" DeLoach, *Hoover's FBI: The Inside Story by Hoover's Trusted Lieutenant* (Washington, D.C.: Regnery Publishing, 1995), 41. Thomas H. Boggs Jr. said in interviews that it did not sound like his father.

226   **(and later convicted):** Rep. John Dowdy's December 1971 convictions for bribery and conspiracy were overturned on appeal, but he spent six months in prison for perjury.

226   **"We have established":** *Congressional Record*, 92nd Congress, 1st sess., April 22, 1971, 11561–66.

226   **rambling and garbled:** David Obey interview.

226   **sat stonily:** Verbatim from Kevin P. Phillips, "Boggs Boomerang," *Post*, May 1, 1971.

226   **"full of contradictions":** Lindy Boggs interviews.

226   **"a huge difference":** Thomas H. Boggs Jr. interviews.

226   **still drank a lot:** Ibid.

227   **"Don't worry about this":** Tina Hobson interviews.

227   **said he would kill himself:** Carol Joy (Hobson) Smith interviews.

227   **"never been sick a day":** *Star*, October 25, 1971.

227   **"a fact of life":** William Raspberry, "Hobson Foe Unbeatable," *Post*, October 25, 1971.

227   **tried not to think:** Tina Hobson interviews.

227   **"the white superintendent":** "Julius Hobson: Local Legend," 22.

227   **"Death doesn't frighten me":** Raspberry, "Hobson Foe Unbeatable."

228   **"You don't sit around":** Tina Hobson interviews.

228   **"Your father talks black":** Klaidman, "Hobson's Illness 'Cured' Marriage," A16.

228   **"I think my option":** Tina Hobson interviews.

228 **"I can usually outwait him"**: Solveig Eggers, "Candidates' Wives Differ on Their Roles," *Daily News*, February 15, 1971, 16.

228 **"It's no reflection"**: Tina Hobson interviews.

228 **"Julius and I were partners"**: Ibid.

228 **"Frankly, after a while"**: Ibid.

228 **"It's hard for me"**: In an interview with Marilyn Robinson of channel 4, WRC-TV, broadcast not long before Hobson's death.

228 **More than anything:** *Post*, "A Goad for Change."

228 **"The most wonderful thing"**: David Braaten, "Julius Hobson Says He Has Fatal Disease," *Star*, October 25, 1971.

229 **"One of the frustrations"**: Raspberry, "Hobson Foe Unbeatable." *Post*, October 25, 1971.

229 **"I am writing to ask"**: A letter dated October 21, 1971, from the Hobson Papers.

229 **"is hardly a mass movement"**: Steven V. Roberts, "A Fourth Party Is Organized, But It's Not a Mass Movement," *New York Times*, November 29, 1971, 32.

230 **"Sir," he was asked:** Nicholas von Hoffman commentary "People's Party: From the Ground Up with Secondhand Goods," in the *Post*, August 2, 1972.

230 **"pasteurized colored boys"**: "NAACP Pasteurized, Black Aspirant Says," *Pittsburgh Post-Gazette*, February 4, 1972.

231 **"the liberated name"**: People's Party literature, in the Hobson collection.

231 **"the facts on our side"**: Thomas H. Boggs Jr. interviews.

232 **tactic for the Senate:** Tom C. Korologos, then a Senate lobbyist in the Nixon White House, in an interview.

232 **devil-may-care laugh:** David Obey interview.

232 **"almost everything"**: Judy Hennessee, "The Washington Legal Establishment," *Washingtonian*, August 1967, 40.

233 **"My kind of guy"**: Bill Foster, now retired and writing books about Texas history, in an interview.

233 **hunted and caroused:** Ibid.

233 **"Wonderful, irresponsible days"**: Ibid.

233 **"Jim, let's see"**: Timothy May interview.

234 **"attractive and democratic"**: Charles Verrill Jr., in an interview.

234 **"created a whole lot"**: Bill Foster interview.

234 **"lost its collegiality"**: Charles Verrill Jr. interview.

235 **lost six inches:** Tina Hobson interviews.

235 **"Call Dr. Spock"**: Ibid.

235 **"We can help him"**: Ibid. The doctor at Sloan-Kettering was named Timothy Gee.

236 **Civil Service Commission salary:** She earned $26,126 from 1969 to 1973 and $27,479 in 1973–74.

236 **"You white people"**: Klaidman, "Hobson's Illness," *Post*, August 31, 1975, A15.

236   **"We know he's sick":** Tina Hobson interviews.

236   **"What saved my life":** Ibid.

236   **"I think everything":** Ibid.

236   **"There's no way":** Julius Hobson Jr. interviews.

237   **In size and elegance:** Description from Jeff Dirksen, the space convention manager at the Marriott Wardman Park Hotel, in an interview.

237   **Seven members of Congress:** Senator George McGovern of South Dakota and Representatives Bella Abzug, Shirley Chisholm, and Charles Rangel of New York; John Conyers and Charles Diggs Jr. of Michigan; and Ron Dellums of California. All were Democrats.

237   **"colorless, tasteless":** "Activist Who Succeeded Given Tribute In Capital," *New York Times*, November 16, 1972.

237   **polite applause:** *Post*, November 15, 1972, D1, 3.

237   **"You are not at a funeral":** The Reverend William Wendt of Saint Stephen and Incarnation Church, quoted in Lillian Wiggins, "2,000 Honor Hobson for Crusading Deeds," *Afro-American*, November 18, 1972, 1.

238   **"To the casual ear":** William Raspberry, "Julius Hobson's Luck," *Post*, November 17, 1972.

238   **a wake:** Tina Hobson interviews.

238   **four-part interview:** July 2–5, 1972, conducted by columnist William Raspberry, editorial writer Robert Asher, reporter Irna Moore, assistant managing editor Harry Rosenfeld, and D.C. editor Barry Sussman.

238   **"Fauntroy is my brother":** Scharfenberg and Terrell, "'Never Expected It All.'"

238   **"don't like needles":** J.Y. Smith, "Hobson Tries Acupuncture for Pain, Calls It a 'Miracle,'" *Post*, December 14, 1972.

239   **"If I've ever lived":** Ibid.

239   **drove him to the airport:** Patrick J. Maney, in *Masters of the House: Congressional Leadership over Two Centuries*, eds. Roger H. Davidson, Susan Webb Hammond, and Raymond W. Smock (Boulder, Colo.: Westview Press, 1998), 224.

239   **stopped off for ice cream:** Thomas H. Boggs Jr. interviews.

240   **"There is no man":** *Congressional Record*, May 2, 1972, p. 15314.

240   **breakfast with the president:** On June 23, 1972, according to his schedule of engagements in the Boggs Papers.

240   **"the largest private party":** Ymelda Dixon, "Peppery Comments," *Star*, June 8, 1972, C-3.

240   **Before the English was translated:** According to an unofficial transcript of the discussions, which lasted from 12:48 to 3:10 A.M. on June 29, 1972, in Boggs Papers.

240   **"everything that went on":** Lindy Boggs interviews.

241   **"the Easter bunnies":** Ymelda Dixon, "To Honor an Old Soldier," *Star*, October 9, 1972, C-1.

241   **the last light:** David R. Legge, "Cafritz Axiom Revisited," *Post*, October 9, 1972, B3.

241   **"At my request":** Jim Patton interview.

241   **"it's my duty":** Ibid.

241   **"fostered by Sam":** Lindy Boggs interviews.

241   **had voted for Udall:** William "Fishbait" Miller as told to Frances Spatz Leighton, *Fishbait: The Memoirs of the Congressional Doorkeeper* (Englewood Cliffs, N.J.: Prentice-Hall, 1977), 225.

242   **Begich asked Congressman Jim Wright:** Jim Wright interview.

242   **Obey accepted:** David Obey interview.

242   **"Goddam it":** Dan Rostenkowski interview, quoting Boggs.

242   **batch of black-eyed peas:** Shirley Leva, Marx Leva's widow, in an interview before her death in 2002.

243   **to fifty dollars:** Bill Foster interview.

243   **twenty-five dollars a plate:** Allan Frank, "Boggs Brings in the Begich Money," *Anchorage Daily News*, October 16, 1972, 1.

243   **thirty or forty oilmen:** Bill Foster interview.

243   **booming voice commanded attention:** Allan Frank, "It was a pleasant Sunday . . . ," *Anchorage Daily News*, October 17, 1972, 2.

243   **"Not much":** From an audiotape of Hale Boggs's speech in Anchorage, October 15, 1972, in the Boggs Papers.

244   **as *Laugh-In* blared:** Jerry Oppenheimer, "A Long Night Here," *Star-News*, October 17, 1972, A1.

244   **"Oh, Carl":** Lindy Boggs interviews.

244   **"You probably haven't heard":** Thomas H. Boggs Jr. interviews.

245   **"sounds like a nightmare":** Oppenheimer, "A Long Night," A6.

245   **"Son of a bitch":** Ibid., and Hank Burchard, "Boggs' Office Seems Quiet Though Phones Still Ring," *Post*, October 18, 1972.

245   **"he was a happy man":** Thomas H. Boggs Jr. interviews.

245   **not really know why:** Julius Hobson Jr. interviews.

245   **"But I'm his son":** Richard Prince, "Community Ties Become Anacostia Board Race Issue," *Post*, October 29, 1973, C3.

246   **"We needed space":** Julius Hobson Jr. interviews.

246   **"Miss Anacostia":** Ibid.

246   **"really under the radar":** Julius Hobson Jr. interviews.

246   **"There's no question":** Prince, "Community Ties."

247   **Lady Bird Johnson phoned:** Lindy Boggs interviews.

247   **She had often been the go-between:** Jan Schoonmaker, longtime legislative director for Representative Lindy Boggs, in an interview.

247   **"I just sort of found":** Lindy Boggs interviews.

247   **"I wouldn't have run":** Boggs, *Purple Veil*, 267.

247   **She dyed her eyelashes:** MacPherson, "Heir to the House," K3.

248 **"isn't anybody like Shakespeare":** Tom Zito, "Shakespeare and a Little 'Water Music,'" *Post*, September 4, 1973, B1, 3.

248 **"Here in the world's":** Brendan Gill, *John F. Kennedy Center for the Performing Arts* (New York: Harry N. Abrams, 1981), 17.

249 **"on the painful side":** David Richards, "'Measure for Measure' Played Inch by Inch," *Star-News*, September 4, 1973, D-1.

249 **"sheer death":** Dorothy McCardle, "After the Play," *Post*, September 5, 1973, C1.

249 **"How many Pinkertons":** Dobson, "Luncheon with . . . Gwen," C-7.

249 **"I wouldn't dream":** Ibid.

249 **"an Oscar de la Renta":** McCardle, "After the Play," C3.

249 **"We could feel the audience":** Ibid.

Chapter Eight: FORD

251 **"maudlin farewell":** "Plain-Spoken Promises and a Level Gaze," William Greider's front-page commentary in the *Post*, August 10, 1974, A1.

251 **"excellent friends":** Gerald Ford interview.

252 **A constituent's letter:** Barbara Rathe interview. She was the executive secretary successively to Representatives Hale and Lindy Boggs.

252 **"be retyped":** Jan Schoonmaker interview.

252 **"Unlike a lot of freshmen":** An unidentified "longtime friend on the Hill," quoted in MacPherson, "Heir to the House."

253 **"You're so sweet":** Ibid.

253 **"being southern helped me":** Quoted in C. G. Roberts, "Strong Women of Capitol Hill."

253 **"Purple veil approach":** Lindy Boggs's remarks at a September 14, 1990, breakfast in her honor.

253 **"She makes you want":** Lynda Robb interview.

253 **constantly at his door:** According to former Representative Leon Panetta, Democrat of California, and later President Clinton's White House chief of staff, in an interview.

253 **"Charm-plus":** Former Representative Patricia Schroeder, Democrat of Colorado, in an interview.

253 **if Hale was the father:** According to Meredith Inderfurth, a former legislative assistant to Lindy Boggs, in an interview. Hale Boggs was one of three sponsors when federal flood insurance was first enacted in 1968.

254 **women were the equal of men:** Jan Schoonmaker interview.

254 **"Knowing the members":** Boggs, *Purple Veil,* 278.

255 **"He's a jerk":** Peggy Cooper Cafritz interviews.

255 **"love at first sight":** Ibid.

255   **separated from Jennifer:** Conrad and Jennifer Stats Cafritz separated "on or about July 1, 1973," according to their May 14, 1975, divorce decree in D.C. Superior Court.

255   **Donald Rumsfeld:** Peggy Cooper Cafritz interviews.

255   **"a basket case":** Ibid.

255   **"never a humble child":** Jack Mann, "Peggy Cooper and the Art of the Grant," *Potomac* magazine, *Post*, October 27, 1974, 14.

255   **curls to her waist:** Justin Blum, "A is for Activist: D.C. Schools President Peggy Cooper Cafritz Raises Her Hand," *Post*, May 21, 2002, C1–2.

255   **comfortable in a melon patch:** Don Shirley, "Bridging the D.C. Arts Divide; Peggy Cooper Aims to Abolish the Commission She Heads," *Post*, May 9, 1979, D1.

255   **"for each little goal":** Mann, "Art of the Grant," *Post*, October 27, 1974, 17.

256   **"I was acutely conscious":** Peggy Cooper Cafritz interviews.

256   **"In the course of my interview":** Ibid.

256   **"would like to belong":** Quoted in "Negroes Disavow Pickets," *University Hatchet*, Vol. 61, No. 3, the campus newspaper at GW, September 29, 1964, 1.

256   **"very, very active":** Peggy Cooper Cafritz interviews.

257   **"to zip":** Ibid.

257   **introduction to Martin Atlas:** Calvin Cafritz interviews.

257   **"the first truly color-blind":** J. Y. Smith, "Lily Guest, Arts Figure, Dies at 79," *Post*, March 25, 1990, D5.

257   **"Joe," Conrad replied:** Peggy Cooper Cafritz interviews.

258   **"Conrad was extremely kind":** Ibid.

258   **"Conrad was just mesmerized":** Carter Cafritz interviews.

258   **"There was no distinction":** Ruth Dean, "The Meteoric Career of Arts Activist Peggy Cooper," *Star*, March 24, 1980, C-1.

258   **"all these talented kids":** Peggy Cooper Cafritz interviews.

259   **"black people attaining autonomy":** Jacqueline Trescott, "Arts School Needs Support," *Star*, January 18, 1971.

260   **"I'm taking acupuncture":** Kirk Scharfenberg, "Hobson Flays Home Rule Bill," *Post*, October 18, 1973, C1, 6.

261   **"The way these damn fools":** Raul Ramirez, "Statehood Party Backs Hobson as Councilman," *Post*, March 4, 1974; C1.

261   **85 percent of the voters:** Exceeded only by Walter Washington and Walter Fauntroy, according to Jay Mathews, "Alexander vs. Washington: Middle-Road Voters May Be Key," the *Post*, August 18, 1974, H1, 3.

261   **"Only statehood":** "17 Candidates Seeking 4 At-Large Seats on City Council," *Post*, October 27, 1974, E3.

261   **"a radical council":** LaBarbara Bowman and Jay Mathews, "New D.C. Council Reunites Warriors of Activist Days," *Post*, November 6, 1974, A1.

262   **a mutual respect:** Sterling Tucker, in an interview with the author. Hobson, asked about his heroes in "A Goad for Change," replied: "There's a

man in this town I admire. You'll jump out of the window when I tell you I admire him. That's Sterling [Tucker] . . . one of the few men in town that I consider has an honest record of his own."

262 **"now they *are* the Establishment"**: Bowman and Mathews, "New D.C. Council."

262 **"Faggot!"**: Julius Hobson Jr. interviews.

262 **"You little nigger bitch"**: Gladys Porter, a demonstrator, was quoted in Martha M. Hamilton, "School Board Picks Judge, Sizemore Supporters Erupt," *Post*, 25 June 1975, C1.

262 **"all the damn names"**: Julius Hobson Jr. interviews.

263 **"found all kinds of crap"**: Julius Hobson Jr. interviews.

263 **Unspoken in both:** Diane Brockett, "The 20 Chaotic Months," *Star*, June 1, 1975, A-1.

263 **"I will never compromise"**: Julius Hobson Jr. interviews.

264 **"nutless, punk"**: Ibid.

264 **"That's my last tactic"**: Diane Brockett, "The Hobsons, Father and Son, Have Grip on D.C. Schools," *Star*, February 26, 1975, B-1, 4.

264 **"She's just destroyed"**: Ben A. Franklin, "Washington's School Chief Fights Dismissal by Board," *New York Times*, June 27, 1975, 38.

265 **severe aching:** John Mathews, "Sizemore Case Exacting an Emotional and Physical Toll on Board," *Star*, August 3, 1975, B-1.

265 **"Burst of Yawns"**: Diane Brockett and John Mahews, "Sizemore Hearings Start, with a Burst of Yawns," *Star*, August 2, 1975.

265 **carpets had grown worn:** "Ambassador Hotel to Close Doors," *Star*, March 4, 1975, C-6.

266 **"We want to change"**: "Hotel Gets New Management," *Star-News*, September 15, 1972.

266 **"a simple hotel"**: Claudia Levy, "Redoing the Ambassador," *Post*, April 8, 1973.

266 **"I got tired of fighting"**: Claudia Levy, "Ambassador Hotel May Close," *Post*, March 4, 1975.

266 **"Levitz or Marlow's"**: Patricia Camp, "Liquidating a Doomed Landmark, Piece by Piece," *Post*, August 8, 1978.

267 **"It was very sad"**: Calvin Cafritz interviews.

267 **He expected no objection:** Sterling Tucker interview.

267 **"If you do"**: LaBarbara Bowman, "Council Meetings to Begin with Moment of Silence," *Post*, January 7, 1975.

267 **"Why start out"**: Sterling Tucker interview.

267 **In their first six months:** Paul W. Valentine and LaBarbara Bowman, "6 Months on Job, City Council Shows Energy, Independence," *Post*, July 8, 1975, C1–2.

268 **Once, in a rainstorm:** Diane Brockett, "Hobson's Choice: A $60,000 Ramp to Aid Handicapped at City Hall," *Star*, April 13, 1976.

268   **law would eventually pass:** D.C. Law 3-76 was passed on April 22, 1980, and signed into law on May 4, 1980.

268   **"I appreciate your bringing":** From an April 16, 1973, letter to Dr. Stanley A. Boucree, president of the Robert T. Freeman Dental Society Inc. in Washington, in the Hobson Papers.

268   **council members liked him:** Sterling Tucker interview.

268   **"an unusual grip":** Brockett, "The Hobsons, Father and Son."

269   **"You don't know":** Julius Hobson Jr. interviews.

269   **"to make the compromises":** Ibid.

269   **"I cannot in good conscience":** From an audiotape of the January 23, 1976, hearing.

270   **"as servants and underlings":** Ibid., and Julius Hobson Jr.'s prepared statement.

270   **"Lindy!":** Judith Martin, "History in Capsule Form," *Post*, July 2, 1976, B1.

271   **a parchment scroll:** "Mrs. Deihm's Centennial Safe: Autographs, Photographs and a Book on Temperance," *Bicentennial Times*, November 1976, 398.

271   **a Barbie doll:** In a time capsule, at the Griffith Observatory in Los Angeles. "Time Capsules Identify 1976 Life Styles for 2076," *Bicentennial Times*, December 1976, 425.

271   **"Something about the United States":** Martin, "History in Capsule Form."

272   **"I assume I'll command":** "Some Key Faces on the Podium," *New York Times*, July 12, 1976.

272   **"I have the strong back":** Mary Russell, "Party's Permanent Chairman," *Post*, 12 July 1976.

272   **"Hi, honey":** Boggs, *Purple Veil*, 308.

272   **Tommy Corcoran:** Maxine Cheshire, "Another Governor Wallace," *Post*, July 13, 1976, B3.

Chapter Nine: CARTER

273   **Sterling Tucker invited Julius:** Sterling Tucker interview.

273   **followed the essence:** Ibid.

273   **"Why don't you let me":** Ibid.

274   **"people might be bored":** J. Y. Smith, "Doctors Give Hobson 6 Months to Live," *Post*, January 6, 1977.

274   **"Julius is facing":** Ibid.

274   **a state fair to statehood:** Almost verbatim from a *Post* editorial, "Julius W. Hobson Sr.," March 24, 1977.

274   **He had accomplished more:** Julius Hobson Jr. interviews.

274 **"I don't have any enemies"**: Cynthia Gorney, "Julius Hobson Sr., Activist, Dies Age 54," *Post*, March 24, 1977, A1.

274 **"since I left home"**: Carol Joy (Hobson) Smith interviews.

275 **"Mr. Chairman"**: From a transcript of the March 22, 1977, meeting.

275 **a flesh wound**: Harry S. Jaffe and Tom Sherwood, *Dream City: Race, Power, and the Decline of Washington, D.C.* (New York: Simon & Schuster, 1994), 111.

275 **"You just can't trust him"**: Tina Hobson interviews.

276 **"I hope your mother"**: Julius Hobson Jr. interviews.

276 **"I just have to"**: Tina Hobson interviews.

276 **"Daddy, Daddy"**: Jean Hobson interview.

277 **"I thought you were coming"**: Ibid.

277 **"Eric, help me:** Tina Hobson interviews.

277 **"I just had a feeling"**: Ibid.

277 **"Something must be wrong"**: Cynthia Gorney, "Eulogies Praise Raging Spirit of Julius Hobson," *Post*, March 28, 1977, C1.

277 **"I need to see"**: Julius Hobson Jr. interviews.

277 **"I had good feelings"**: Walter Washington interview.

277 **"at least toward the end"**: Julius Hobson Jr. interviews.

278 **had met Julius:** Bardyl Tirana interview.

278 **"Julius Hobson's life"**: A March 25, 1977, letter from Jimmy Carter to Tina Hobson.

278 **Her listeners forgot:** Gorney, "Eulogies Praise."

278 **"I can't stay long"**: Tina Hobson interviews.

278 **delivered a political speech:** Bardyl Tirana interview.

278– **"during the emotion"**: William Jobes, "Hilda Mason Gets Interim Post,"
279 *Star*, April 3, 1977, C-1.

279 **"My father always wanted"**: Jacqueline Bolder, "Five Consider Filling Hobson's Council Seat," *Star*, March 25, 1977, D-5.

279 **"an obligation as his son"**: Milton Coleman, "Julius Hobson Jr. Seeks Father's City Council Seat," *Post*, March 25, 1977.

279 **"It's very personal"**: Milton Coleman, "Hobson's Wife Declares Interest in His Council Seat," *Post*, March 30, 1977.

279 **"you'll get in spades"**: Julius Hobson Jr. interviews.

279 **"called a cab"**: Jobes, "Hilda Mason."

280 **"was like being buried alive"**: Roberts and Roberts, *From This Day Forward,* 169.

280 **"only city in the world"**: Steven V. Roberts interviews.

280 **"It was immediately obvious"**: Ibid.

281 **$235,000 for:** The deed, recorded on April 25, 1978, in Montgomery County, Maryland. The assessed value of the house rose to $1,046,040 by January 1, 2001.

281 **Cokie felt uncertain:** Steven V. Roberts interviews.

281 **"not very nice to you"**: Cokie Roberts interviews.

281   **on venereal disease:** Cokie Roberts and Steven V. Roberts, "The Venereal Disease Pandemic," *New York Times Magazine*, November 7, 1971, 62ff.

281   *Seventeen:* Cokie Roberts and Steven V. Roberts, "Having a Baby Is a Very Alone Thing," *Seventeen*, January 1973.

281   *Atlantic Monthly:* Cokie Roberts, "Turkey: The Reluctant Westerners," *Atlantic Monthly*, September 1977, 14–19.

281   **"the bureau chief crisply":** Roberts and Roberts, *From This Day Forward*, 220.

282   **"What's that?":** Steven V. Roberts interviews.

282   **60 percent:** "Where Aim Is for Innovation," *U.S. News & World Report*, January 16, 1978, 50.

282   **a majority of new cars:** Karl E. Meyer, "Now Hear This," *Saturday Review*, July 21, 1979, 42.

282   **"a child of the '60s":** Marc Fisher, "The Soul of a News Machine," *Washington Post Magazine*, October 22, 1989, W16.

282   **"Call Nina Totenberg.":** Steven V. Roberts interviews. He said he phoned her, though Totenberg, in Claudia Dreifus, "Cokie Roberts, Nina Totenberg and Linda Wertheimer," *New York Times Magazine*, January 2, 1994, 14, recalled that she phoned him.

282   **"the old-boys' Establishment":** Cokie Roberts interviews.

283   **"Not only was I back":** Roberts and Roberts, *From This Day Forward*, 227.

283   **"And there it was":** Judith Michaelson, "The Liberated Look at PBS," *Los Angeles Times*, December 17, 1987, Part 6, 1.

283   **"I give you'se girls":** Quoted by Cokie Roberts, in Dreifus, "Cokie Roberts, Nina Totenberg."

283   **"I loved being on the Hill":** Cokie Roberts interviews.

283   **"my mother respected that":** Ibid.

283   **"Five years?":** Quoted in Joseph McLellan, "Back at Gwen Cafritz': An Elegant Echo," *Post*, June 15, 1978, B1.

284   **"She was very kind":** Ibid.

284   **instructed the young Georgians:** Betty Beale, *Power at Play: A Memoir of Parties, Politicians and the Presidents in My Bedroom* (Washington, D.C.: Regnery Gateway, 1993), 249.

284   **"Black-tie dinners":** Quinn, "The Party's Over."

285   **decanter in the living room:** According to the butler, Michael Dowling, quoted in Williams, "The Legacy of Gwen Cafritz."

285   **one of her escorts:** Victor Shargai of W. J. Sloane.

285   **"but he never asked me":** Dobson, "Luncheon with . . . Gwen," *Star*, March 5, 1971, C-7.

285   **"the *National* Presbyterian Church":** Calvin Cafritz interviews.

285   **"Mother, if you go":** Thomas H. Boggs Jr. interviews.

286   **"It was you-scratch-my-back":** Lindy Boggs interviews.

286   **"a perfect place for Lindy":** Jan Schoonmaker interview.

286 **"People ask me why":** Lindy Boggs interviews.

287 **"I would never ask":** Jonathan P. Scott, "Rep. Lindy Boggs Looks Back on Half a Century of Lawmaking," States News Service, November 2, 1990.

287 **Cabinet secretaries made sure:** Jan Schoonmaker interview.

287 **historic preservation:** When Michael Lewis asked Lindy Boggs to name her political interests, "Having Her Say at the See, *New York Times Magazine*, June 4, 2000, 62–65, he wrote, "Her list read: Preservation, National Archives, Holocaust Museum, Smithsonian, Children and Families, NASA. It may be the least controversial list of political interests ever created."

287 **zillion projects:** Verbatim from Jan Schoonmaker interview.

288 **Madison's vice president:** Elbridge Gerry, 1813–14, who served in Madison's second term and died in office. Washington's secretary was Tobias Lear. Lincoln's valet was Charles Forbes. Also buried in Congressional Cemetery are Lincoln's landlady, Ann Sprigg, and David Herold, one of the conspirators hanged for his assassination.

288 **Pershing had lived there:** James Goode, *Best Addresses: A Century of Washington's Distinguished Apartment Houses* (Washington, D.C.: Smithsonian Institution Press, 1988), 148.

289 **"a manic monologue":** Harry Jaffe, "Conrad Cafritz," *Regardie's Magazine*, Vol. 10, No. 1, September 1989, 70.

289 **Conrad saw himself:** Peggy Cooper Cafritz interviews.

289 **Mother's Day gift:** Tully, "Story of Gwen," December 8, 1959.

289 **two detective novels:** Carter Cafritz interviews.

289 **skin diving and electronics:** A February 12, 1965, memorandum in Gwen Cafritz's FBI file No. 87-81099, Enclosure 5, 404.

290 **three buildings . . . along Connecticut:** At 4700 and 5410 Connecticut Avenue, as well as at 2029.

290 **"I'm bound and determined":** Donna Honeycutt, a schoolteacher, quoted in Carol Krucoff, "Hotels, Condos Displace Residents of Apartments in Foggy Bottom Area," *Post*, August 3, 1978, DC2.

290 **"Many people benefit":** "The Benefits of Going Condo," op-ed by Conrad Cafritz, identified as chairman of the board of the Investment Group Development Corporation, in the *Post*, May 19, 1979, A15.

290 **"and my dad always":** Peggy Cooper Cafritz interviews.

291 **"opening of an envelope":** Ibid.

291 **his core support:** Jaffe and Sherwood, *Dream City*, 113.

291 **"importance of being important":** An unidentified source quoted in Milton Coleman, "Paranoia Politics," *Washington Post Magazine*, August 27, 1978, 8.

291 **Conrad "will head the":** Diana McLellan, "The Ear," *Star*, November 10, 1978.

292 **almost doubled:** The commission's grants totaled $195,250 in 1979, $326,837 in 1980, and $590,120 in 1981.

292 **"field marshal brusqueness":** Dean, "The Meteoric Career," C-2: "At

first, Cooper's field marshal brusqueness in keeping the meetings on schedule bothered those used to the disarray that had characterized former commission meetings . . . But Cooper's business-like manner and occasional spurts of humor, coupled with the efficiency of the commission's executive secretary Mildred Bautiṣta and the commission's improved community and financial response, have won the respect and affection of newer commissioners anxious to make waves for the arts in D.C."

292   **"spur-of-the-moment thing":** Peggy Cooper Cafritz interviews.

292   **"Dark—YES!":** Letter to the editor, "Aside from All That, Are You Interested?" *Star,* August 27, 1977.

292   **first state dinner:** For Kenyan president Daniel arap Moi, February 20, 1980.

292   **as "Chocolate City":** Courtland Milloy, "WOL; New Image for Station," *Post,* December 2, 1979, C1.

292   **"Never!":** *Star,* March 24, 1980. Dean, "The Meteoric Career," C-2.

293   **"The new type of":** "Million-Dollar Baby," *Forbes,* October 15, 1976, 112.

293   **"holier-than-thou":** Thomas H. Boggs Jr. interviews.

293   **he could not remember:** Ibid.

293   **"The FTC as National Nanny":** *Post,* March 1, 1978, A22.

294   **"thou shalt not spend":** Thomas H. Boggs Jr. interviews.

294   **"started a trend":** Ibid.

294   **he wanted the best:** Robert B. Reich and John D. Donahue, *New Deals: The Chrysler Revival and the American System* (New York: Times Books, 1985), 96.

295   **supplied by Doug Fraser:** According to Howard Paster, who was then the UAW's in-house lobbyist, in an interview.

295   **"He conned them":** Tom Korologos, in an interview.

295   **on his own time:** Verbatim from Celra W. Dugger, "The Challenge and the Clout; Lobbying with Tommy Boggs," *Post,* September 25, 1979, C1.

295   **a subtle shift:** Reich and Donahue, *New Deals,* 106.

295   **"Can you walk?":** Thomas H. Boggs Jr. interviews.

Chapter Ten: REAGAN

297   **"Things are going to change":** According to a chronology of events prepared by the Post Office and Civil Service Committee, civil service subcommittee, U.S. House of Representatives, 97th Congress, 1st sess., published as an appendix in the transcript of its March 9, 1981, hearing, titled "Energy Department Violation of SES 120-Day Rule—the Tina Hobson Case," 63.

298   **"What is an operative?":** Ibid., p. 24, from Tina Hobson's testimony.

298   **"my own personal hearing":** Tina Hobson interviews.

298   **"violations of four laws":** "Tina Hobson Case" hearing transcript, 1.

299   **"own kind of radicalism"**: "A Goad for Change."

299   **"Carol, you've got to"**: Carol Joy (Hobson) Smith interviews.

299   **"became a best-seller"**: Ibid.

300   **"into a coma"**: Ibid.

300   **"I knew she wanted to"**: Barbara Boggs interview.

300   **$150,000 and $240,000**: James Goode, *Best Addresses: A Century of Washington's Distinguished Apartment Houses* (Washington, D.C.: Smithsonian Institution Press, 1988), 147.

300   **a dear friend**: Lewis, "Her Say at the See."

300   **calls for his presidential campaign**: George McGovern interview.

300   **"George, I wanted"**: Ibid.

300   **"couldn't say no"**: Ibid.

301   **Lindy never really liked**: Roberts and Roberts, *From This Day Forward*, 221.

301   **gift from Tommy Corcoran**: Cokie Roberts interviews.

301   **canny accordion-playing**: Robert Caro, *Master of the Senate: The Years of Lyndon Johnson, Vol.* 3 (New York: Alfred A. Knopf, 2002), 949.

301   **"stage-door Johnny"**: Jan Schoonmaker interview. His father dated Lindy Boggs in New Orleans.

301   **"Occasionally"**: Lindy Boggs interviews.

301   **"No, I'm not going"**: Jan Schoonmaker interview.

302   **"austere disapproval"**: George Will, "50 Years in Washington," *Post*, December 6, 1990, A23.

302   **"say 'no' to a nun"**: Jan Schoonmaker interview.

302   **"the best scam going"**: Boggs, *Purple Veil*, 360.

303   **"I think, frankly"**: From a videotape of the June 4, 1981, show, which the Library of Congress generously prepared and provided.

303   **almond-shaped eyes**: Verbatim from a poem, "Cokie in the Hospital," written by her dying sister, Barbara Sigmund, *An Unfinished Life* (Princeton, N.J.: The Arts Council of Princeton, 1990), 7.

303   **"always pretty horrible"**: Cokie Roberts interviews.

303   **"all that looks stuff"**: Ibid.

303   **Peggy Cooper objected**: Shirley, "D.C. Arts Divide."

304   **whose daughter she was**: Linda Winslow, producer and creator of *The Lawmakers*, in an interview.

304   **"people who can tell you"**: Cokie Roberts interviews.

304   **"I mean, Miss Baby"**: Ibid.

305   **"Congress—A Whale of"**: John J. O'Connor, "Congress—A Whale of a Show," *New York Times*, November 22, 1981, Sec. 2, 31.

305   **"It's an audience"**: Cokie Roberts interviews.

306   **"I did not go to Woodstock"**: Fisher, "Soul of a News Machine."

306   **"the Woodstock Network"**: Cokie Roberts interviews.

306   **a former senator**: Nina Totenberg's husband was Floyd Haskell, a Colorado Democrat, who was defeated in 1978 after a single term.

306   **Harvard sweatshirts:** Roberts and Roberts, *From This Day Forward*, 250.

306   **coauthored an article:** Cokie and Steven V. Roberts, "What's Got into the Voters This Year?" *New York Times Magazine*, June 15, 1980, 34ff.

306   **"Actually our bosses":** "Cokie and Steve Roberts: Washington's Power Couple," *Larry King Live*, CNN, July 21, 1998.

307   **Kennedy had telephoned Tommy Boggs:** Steven A. Holmes, *Ron Brown: An Uncommon Life* (New York: John Wiley & Sons, 2000), 118.

307   **"brought up in public":** "Ron Brown Remembered," *Washington Lawyer*, May/June 1996, 31.

307   **"copying each other":** Ibid.

307   **twelve or fourteen hours:** Tracey L. Brown, *The Life and Times of Ron Brown: A Memoir* (New York: William Morrow, 1998), 153.

308   **"You'd better not go":** Thomas H. Boggs interviews.

308   **"I've doubled the payment":** Ibid.

308   **"liked people who looked":** Timothy May interviews.

308   **a tax wizard:** Ernest S. Christian Jr. had been deputy assistant secretary for tax policy at the Treasury Department.

308   **"the quintessential case":** Frank Donatelli, in an interview.

308   **senator's chief tax aide:** David Raboy, the legislative director and adviser on taxes to Sen. William V. Roth Jr., Republican of Delaware, joined Patton Boggs as an economic consultant in 1986, after Congress passed the Kemp-Roth tax reform bill. The former senator Mark Andrews, Republican of North Dakota, affiliated his government relations firm, Andrews' Associates, in early 1987.

308   **dreary and decayed:** A D.C. planning study in April 1972 described the West End as an underused neighborhood of "dreariness and decay."

309   **forty thousand:** David F. Pike, "Washington's Lawyers; Rise of the Power Brokers," *U.S. News & World Report*, March 10, 1980, 52.

309   **"Hey, he pays the bills":** Holmes, *Ron Brown*, 135.

309   **see Tongsun Park:** Maxine Cheshire, "Tongsun Park and Friend," *Post*, July 27, 1980, H1.

309   **The major decisions:** Charles Verrill Jr. and Timothy May interviews.

310   **"to prevent Patton":** Timothy May interviews.

310   **Rolls Royces and a Bentley:** Stephanie Mansfield, "The Limousine Life," *Post*, January 13, 1981, B1.

310   **genteel and shabby:** Michael Kelly, in an interview.

310   **surpassed one million dollars:** W. John Moore, "The Gravy Train," *National Journal*, Vol. 24, No. 41, October 10, 1992, 2294–98.

310   **A survey of lawmakers:** Ann Cooper, "Lobbying in the '80s: High Tech Takes Hold," *National Journal*, September 14, 1985, 2030–325.

310   **a diet doctor:** Alan S. Murray and Jeffrey H. Birnbaum, *Showdown at Gucci Gulch* (New York: Random House, 1987), 178.

311   **"'Gentlemanly' is one word":** George Blow interview.

311   **"All interests are special"**: Op-ed of that title by Thomas Hale Boggs Jr., *New York Times*, February 16, 1993, 17.

311   **"dumbest thing"**: From the transcript of an interview conducted August 15, 1997, for Charles Lewis and the Center for Public Integrity, *The Buying of the Congress: How Special Interests Have Stolen Your Right to Life, Liberty, and the Pursuit of Happiness* (New York: Avon Books, 1998).

312   **"go out and hustle"**: Ibid.

312   **"*a* pioneer"**: Tom Korologos interview.

312   **junior partners:** Neil A. Lewis, "The Lawyer as Lobbyist," *New York Times*, December 29, 1989, A1.

312   **"But life happens"**: Peggy Cooper Cafritz interviews.

313   **"I was not sure"**: Ibid.

313   **"William Kunstler or whoever"**: Ibid.

313   **"Excuse me"**: Ibid.

313   **poetry, Hindu treatises:** Judith Valente, "Fresh Ideas on the D.C. School Board," *Post*, December 3, 1981, D.C. 1, 6.

314   **meeting place for radicals:** Harry S. Jaffe and Tom Sherwood, *Dream City: Race, Power, and the Decline of Washington* (New York: Simon & Schuster, 1994), 50.

314   **tiny woman:** Anne Pilsbury, a Maine-based lawyer for the American Civil Liberties Union.

315   **"Too bad he can't"**: Laura A. Kiernan, "Jury Awards $711,937.50 to Demonstrators," *Post*, December 24, 1981, A1, 9.

315   **"absolute amazement"**: Tina Hobson interviews.

315   **"wasn't a prejudiced man"**: Judith Valente, "Children Join in Dedicating School to Julius Hobson," *Post*, May 28, 1982, B3.

315   **"Hobson's granddaughter an F"**: Julius Hobson Jr. interviews.

316   **Fauntroy never acknowledged:** Walter Fauntroy interview.

316   **"A closing of the books"**: Julius Hobson Jr. interviews.

317   **"Walter, I've got"**: Ibid.

317   **"I'm not my father"**: Ibid.

317   **"no-saying son of a bitch"**: Ibid.

317   **"That was another benefit"**: Ibid.

318   **Fauntroy had himself in mind:** Ronald Smothers, "The Impact of Jesse Jackson," *New York Times Magazine*, March 4, 1984, 46.

318   **"And how long are"**: Tina Hobson interviews.

318   **"into a crusade"**: Julius Hobson Jr. interviews.

318   **"This is not working"**: Ibid.

319   **panoramic view:** LaBarbara Bowman, "Bids for SW Site Find Minorities Listed Up Front," *Post*, October 12, 1981, A1.

319   **"Emerging groups need"**: Carla Hall, "A Piece of the Portal; SW Development Plans Include Arts Element," *Post*, November 22, 1981, H1.

319   **"Handsome it might be"**: Benjamin Forgey, "Portal Combat; Off the Track at the 14th Street Gateway," *Post*, October 31, 1981, C1.

319   **Washington was booming:** Judith Miller, "The Capital Becomes a Boom Town," *New York Times Magazine*, May 3, 1981, 114.

320   **"an ego thing":** Carter Cafritz interviews.

320   **"simple and quiet":** David Childs, head of the Washington office of Skidmore, Owings and Merrill, quoted in Kenneth Bredemeier, "D.C. Portal Proposals Paraded," *Post*, June 28, 1985, C1.

320   **"I have lots of thoughts":** Kenneth Bredemeier, "Developer Designated for Portal Site at 14th Street Bridge," *Post*, September 13 1985, A1.

320   **"like a toddler":** Peggy Cooper Cafritz interviews.

320   **"he's probably better off":** Carter Cafritz interviews.

321   **"Yuppie clientele":** *The Alexandria Packet*, December 29, 1986.

321   **More than three thousand:** *Post*, June 11, 1986.

321   **"Snyder's appearance dramatized":** Ed Miller, "Redevelopment Evicts a Community," *Alexandria Packet*, December 29, 1986, A1.

322   **"bordering on chaos":** Roger K. Lewis, a University of Maryland architecture professor and practicing architect, in "Washington Harbour: Many-Splendored Thing," *Post*, July 26, 1986, F8, 9.

322   **"wonderfully wacky":** Peter Blake, a Catholic University architecture professor and practicing architect, in "Disney World? No, Washington World!" *Post* magazine, January 18, 1987, 38.

322   **"We believe it is":** David S. Hilzenrath, "Cafritz Buys Retail Office Parts of Washington Harbour," *Post*, 23 December 1988, D1.

323   **"Why not over here?":** Julius Hobson Jr. interviews. Dwight Cropp, who had been the secretary to the school board when Hobby was a member, had become the mayor's director of intergovernmental relations.

324   **"way of doing favors":** Ibid.

324   **"Everybody hated the District":** Ibid.

324   **"We've become the U.S.":** Eric Pianin, "Congressional Show of Muscle Leaves D.C. Officials Bruised," *Post*, October 2, 1988, B1.

324   **"when we fly alone":** Julius Hobson Jr. interviews.

324   **"The Hardest Lobbying":** Daniel Klaidman, in *Legal Times*, August 15, 1988, 6.

324   ***Washington Times* profiled him:** Chris Harvey, "Like Father, Not Like Son: Hobson Jr. Has Own Style," *Washington Times*, October 31, 1988, B1.

324   **"It's starting":** Julius Hobson Jr. interviews.

325   ***Post* got a tip:** Jaffe and Sharwood, *Dream City*, 232.

325   **"Such déjà vu":** Elizabeth Kastor, "A Glimpse of Grand Style," *Post*, June 11, 1986, B1. The guest was unidentified.

325   **"not her old self":** Carter Cafritz interviews.

325   **"This was the place":** Kastor, "Grand Style."

326   **"The Washington hostess is dead":** Quinn, "The Party's Over."

326   **She stopped drinking:** Liane Atlas interview.

326   **"Sorry to tell you":** Calvin Cafritz interviews.

327 **"the smartness of Gwen":** From a transcript of the memorial service, December 2, 1988, provided by the John Nicholas Brown Center for the Study of American Civilization, at Brown University in Providence, Rhode Island, courtesy of the estate of J. Carter Brown.

327 **"I don't want to":** Sheila Hines interview.

327 **Christian cemetery:** Parklawn Memorial Park.

327 **"rest in peace":** Conrad Cafritz, in an interview.

Chapter Eleven: BUSH

329 **"We said, 'Conrad:** Stephanie Mansfield, "Fetes and Lines in Texas Time," *Post*, 20 January 1989, B1.

330 **"a little more upscale":** Ibid.

330 **"That's the definition":** Ibid.

330 **"celebration of his candidacy":** Chuck Conconi, "Personalities," *Post*, April 21, 1988, C3.

330 **Peggy's family beach house:** Celia McGee, "Full House," *Town & Country Monthly*, Vol. 149, No. 5186, November 1995, 162–67.

330 **"When I become President":** Megan Rosenfeld, "The Whirl-Class Weekend," *Post*, April 25, 1988, B1.

330 **"I have this great house":** Peggy Cooper Cafritz interviews.

330– **"signaled the fading":** David Binder, "Ax-Grinding Era," *New York Times*,
331 "December 27, 1988, A18.

331 **"to serve civilization":** "This may sound pretentious, but my purpose in life is to serve civilization." Ruth Dean, "Gwen Was 'Fall Gal,'" *Star*, October 14, 1958.

331 **by her expressed wish:** Sarah Booth Conroy, "House Willed to State Dept.; Cafritz Estate Intended as Secretary's Home," *Post*, December 14, 1988, and Calvin Cafritz interviews. Her last will, written in 1981, technically left the Foxhall Road house to the Morris and Gwendolyn Cafritz Foundation.

331 **"her sons fight each other":** A six-page letter from Randall L. Rafler to Judge Emmet Sullivan of the Superior Court of D.C., found in the court files of *Conrad Cafritz, et al. v. The Riggs National Bank of Washington, D.C., et al.*, Admin. No. 3035-88, docketed in the probate division of D.C.'s Register of Wills on October 31, 1994.

332 **"to such person":** Morris Cafritz's last will and testament, signed on February 21, 1964, and filed the following June 17 with the clerk of the Probate Court, D.C. Register of Wills.

332 **"It has been patently clear":** A letter from Calvin Cafritz to the foundation board, dated May 26, 1992, about a proposed settlement in the lawsuit.

332 **"I thought my mother's":** Calvin Cafritz interviews.

333 **"If we had grown up":** Carter Cafritz interviews.

333 **"What is your definition":** *This Week with David Brinkley*, ABC-TV, February 26, 1989.

333 **"my brother's bookkeeper":** Cokie Roberts interviews.

334 **"you can't be too aggressive":** Ibid.

334 **"That treaty could":** *This Week*, December 6, 1987.

334 **"I did better":** Michaelson, "Liberated Look at PBS."

334 **"I can't express":** Cokie Roberts interviews.

334 **"It is hard to find":** On *Larry King Live*, CNN, December 3, 1991.

335 **"Throughout our lives":** Lindy Boggs, Barbara Sigmund, Cokie Roberts, Garry Clifford, "Lindy Boggs Quits Congress to Close Ranks with Her Two Remarkable Daughters, One Gravely Ill with Cancer," *People*, August 13, 1990, 57.

335 **"like Lindy Boggs's house":** Cokie Roberts and Linda Winslow interviews.

335 **the first woman . . . accepted:** Marc Gunther, *The House That Roone Built: The Inside Story of ABC News* (New York: Little, Brown and Co., 1994), 351.

335 **"repeating myself at NPR":** Cokie Roberts interviews.

335 **"ABC was nice":** Ben Kubasik, "TV Spots," *Newsday*, May 31, 1988, Nassau and Suffolk edition, Part 2, 11.

335 **hated the opera:** Victor Shargai, in an interview.

336 **a penetrating question:** Julia Sparkman Shepard, a longtime member of the foundation's advisory board, in an interview.

336 **"really a conscious decision":** Calvin Cafritz interviews.

337 **limousines rolled up:** Harry Jaffe, "Betrayal in the Boardroom: How Two Friends Sold Each Other Out in Their Attempts to Take Control of the Oldest Bank in Washington," *Regardie's Magazine*, Vol. 9, No. 4, December 1988, 46.

337 **Davy Crockett:** Jack Jonas, "Davy Crockett kept $40 in D.C. Bank Two Days," *Star*, April 24, 1955.

337 **"In those days":** Thomas H. Boggs Jr. interviews.

338 **"because it was *here*":** Ibid.

338 **and borrowed $980,000:** Harry Jaffe, "Bank job," *Regardie's Magazine*, Vol. 10, No. 12, August 1990, 32.

339 **Until 1988:** According to an article by Lynda Edwards, in *Washington Monthly*, Vol. 23, No. 5, May 1991, 17, titled "With Friends Like These, Who Needs Loan Officers? With a Little Greed and a Lot of Logrolling, D.C. Powerbrokers Like Brent Scowcroft and Thomas Boggs Destroyed the National Bank of Washington."

339 **"Remember, these directors":** Ibid. Kathleen Collins, a former general counsel for NBW.

339 **"They could be doing":** Deposition taken February 9, 1989, in *Washington Bancorporation and the National Bank of Washington v. Wafic Said, et al.,*

Civil Action No. 88-3111 U.S. District Court for the District of Columbia, 215, stored in the Federal Records Center in Suitland, Maryland.

339   **"figure of three million dollars":** Ibid., 99–100.

340   **"In banking, as in love":** Filed November 28, 1988, by Williams & Connolly, in *Washington Bancorporation et al., v. Wafic Said, et al.*, 1.

341   **"a big mess":** Rudolph A. Pyatt Jr., "Mired in the Mess Themselves, Regulators Point Fingers in Demise of NBW," *Post*, June 18, 1992, B12.

341   **"a surprisingly scrappy":** David R. Sands, "Government Case Sputters in NBW Lawsuit," *Washington Times,* November 29, 1992, A11.

341   **"FDIC does not allege":** In "Thomas Hale Boggs Jr.'s Motion to Dismiss or, Alternatively, for Summary Judgment," filed with the U.S. District for the District of Columbia on August 27, 1992, in *Washington Bancorporation, et al. v. Wafic Said, et al.* and *Federal Deposit Insurance Corp. v. Luther H. Hodges Jr., et al.*

341   **"prominent and identically situated":** In "Mr. Boggs' Reply to FDIC's Opposition to Defendants' Motions for Sanctions."

341   **"The failure of NBW":** Sharon Walsh and Michael York, "Most Charges in NBW Suit Dismissed," *Post*, February 18, 1993, A1.

342   **an estimated sixty million:** Daniel Isaac and Mark Pawlosky, "Cafritz Moves to Control Damage Brought On by Slump," *Washington Business Journal*, Vol. 8, No. 48, April 30, 1990.

342   **"When someone comes from":** Edwards, "With Friends Like These."

342   **considered to have a knack:** Isaac and Pawlosky, "Cafritz Moves."

342   **"Lots of people warned":** Peggy Cooper Cafritz interviews.

342   **"The people who get in trouble":** Rudolph A. Pyatt Jr., "Weep Not for the Dealmakers," *Post*, September 10, 1990, Washington Business, 3, 59. The executive was unidentified.

342   **"house of cards":** According to the unidentified head of a local bank quoted in David S. Hilzenrath, "Developer Cafritz Running Short of Cash," *Post*, April 26, 1990, A1, 10.

343   **"If Cafritz can't":** Isaac and Pawlosky, "Cafritz Moves."

343   **"just a microcosm":** Ibid., quoting Robert Pickeral, a former chief of commercial real estate for Riggs Bank who was a consultant to developers and banks.

343   **"Raising cash":** David S. Hilzenrath, "Cafritz Sells Washington Harbour Stake," *Post*, June 12, 1990, D1, 13.

343   **"Conrad Cafritz Owes":** David S. Hilzenrath, *Post*, September 5, 1990, A1.

343   **"Gee, Conrad":** Peggy Cooper Cafritz interviews.

343   **He was nervous:** Ibid.

343   **"Of course not":** Ibid.

344   **mainly to build warehouses:** Molly D. Rath, "Cafritz Puts 6 Properties in Bankruptcy," *Washington Business Journal*, September 24, 1990, 3.

344   **"smarts, luck, and cooperation":** Peggy Cooper Cafritz interviews.

345   **Jim Jones was closer:** Thomas H. Boggs Jr. interviews.

345   **Tommy had encouraged:** Holmes, *Ron Brown,* 150.

345   **"You should think":** Thomas H. Boggs Jr. interviews.

345   **He already had:** Holmes, *Ron Brown*, 150.

346   **a Louisianan's:** Senator John Breaux, Democrat of Louisiana.

346   **"I don't have time":** Tom Watson, "Firm Commitments; How Patton, Boggs Boosted Brown in DNC Race," *Legal Times,* February 6, 1989, 1, quoted by the other lawyer, who was not identified.

346   **"If we know somebody":** Judy Sarasohn, "Wright's Defense," *Legal Times,* May 22, 1989, 4.

346   **going to the rescue:** Tommy Boggs donated five thousand dollars to the legal defense fund for Representative Dan Rostenkowski, Democrat of Illinois, and one thousand dollars for Representative Joe McDade, Republican of Pennsylvania, after they were indicted. McDade was acquitted in 1996 of charges that he took bribes from defense contractors for steering Pentagon work their way.

347   **$1.6 million a year:** Stuart Taylor Jr., "Invading the Capitol," *American Lawyer,* May 1992, 56.

347   **a 1971 book:** Joseph C. Goulden, *The Superlawyers: The Small and Powerful World of the Great Washington Law Firms* (New York: Weybright & Talley, 1971).

347   **were nearing extinction:** W. John Moore, "Endangered Species?" *National Journal,* Vol. 23, No. 26, June 29, 1991, 1608.

347   **as BCCI's official counsel:** Peter H. Stone, "Patton, Boggs: In the BCCI Web; Firm's Work for Bank, Abu Dhabi Prompts Questions, Subpoenas," *Legal Times,* July 29, 1991, 1.

347   **lawyers as fungible:** Jim Patton and George Blow interviews.

347   **"Now what we do":** Lewis, "The Lawyer as Lobbyist."

347   **Tommy stood:** This story is recounted by William Fay, executive director of the Product Liability Coordinating Committee, which lobbied against Boggs's client, the Association of Trial Lawyers of America. Fay was quoted in Vicki Kemp, "Lawyers on Trial," *Common Cause Magazine,* Summer 1993. The cloture vote on the tort reform bill took place on September 10, 1992.

347   **To rival lobbyists he boasted:** Naftali Bendavid, "ATLA's Power of Quiet Persuasion," *Legal Times,* August 16, 1993, 1.

348   **"which always means":** Julius Hobson Jr. interviews.

348   **"If I didn't step out":** Ibid.

348   **"checkmark in every box":** Ibid.

348   **"Having a brand name":** Charles S. Robb, in an interview.

348   **"What I was trying":** Julius Hobson Jr. interviews.

348   **"Budget politics":** Francis X. Clines, "An Insider's View of Black Political Gains," *New York Times,* July 7, 1985, 26.

349   **"Lynda says I'm cheap":** Charles S. Robb interview.

349   **"mediocre pieces of shit":** Julius Hobson Jr. interviews.

349   **"was certainly a factor":** Charles S. Robb interview.

349   **also on personal ones:** Sheila Dwyer, who was Robb's scheduler, in an interview.

349   **"just by demonstrating":** Julius Hobson Jr. interviews.

349   **agitated or emotional:** Charles S. Robb interview.

349   **"a wonderful mother":** Susan Albert Carr, who was a legislative assistant, in an interview.

350   **"He didn't have the heart":** Julius Hobson Jr. interviews.

350   **"Six years can go":** Ibid.

350   **always loved his wife:** Ibid.

350   **"We are standing":** Lindy Boggs's July 19, 1990, statement, *Congressional Record*, 101st Congress, 2nd sess., July 31, 1990, 20660–61.

351   **That no major legislation:** According to Diana Pinckley, "Politics with Pearls," a profile of Lindy Boggs, *Tulanian*, Fall 1992, 10–17.

351   **"small role in opening":** Lindy Boggs statement. July 19, 1990.

351   **"Honey, I just can't":** Jan Schoonmaker interview.

351   **the hardest race:** Kim Mattingly, "Lindy Boggs Will Retire after This Term to Spend More Time with Her Daughter," *Roll Call*, July 23, 1990.

352   **Lindy felt uneasy:** Steven V. Roberts interviews.

352   **"family obligations":** Frances Frank Marcus, "Lindy Boggs to Quit House, Ending a Louisiana Dynasty," *New York Times*, July 21, 1990, A7.

352   **distaste for making people mad:** Paul Sigmund interview.

352   **"a little bit left out":** Quoted in Stephanie Mansfield, "A Boggs Political Dynasty," *Post*, May 21, 1982, B1.

352   **She wrote poems:** Barbara Sigmund, *An Unfinished Life* (Princeton, N.J.: The Arts Council of Princeton, 1990). Excerpted by permission.

353   **"private duty sister":** Ibid., "Cokie in the Hospital," November 9, 1989.

353   **"nightgown from Victoria's Secret?":** Lynda Robb interview.

353   **"on automatic pilot":** Boggs, *Purple Veil*, 365.

353   **"She feels strongly":** Lindy Boggs, Barbara Sigmund, C. Roberts, and Garry Clifford, "Lindy Boggs Quits Congress to Close Ranks with Her Two Remarkable Daughters, One Gravely Ill with Cancer," *People*, August 13, 1990, 57.

353   **Cokie never even saw:** Cokie Roberts interviews.

353   **missed being in Congress:** Lindy Boggs and Jan Schoonmaker interviews.

Chapter Twelve: CLINTON

355   **one of his law partners:** Lanny Davis, in an interview.

355   **"The most masterful":** Thomas H. Boggs interviews.

355   **respect was mutual:** Lanny Davis interview: "What Clinton said to me, he considers [Boggs] as almost a kind of political master."

355   **"world's great networkers":** Howard Paster, who had lobbied on the

Alaska pipeline alongside Tommy Boggs and who became the chief congressional lobbyist for President Clinton, in an interview.

355   **main fund-raiser in Washington:** Martin Walker, "How Bill Clinton Is Doing Fine with a Little Help from His Friends," *Guardian* (London), March 21, 1992, 10.

356   **"Ready to Cash In":** W. John Moore, "The Gravy Train," *National Journal*, Vol. 24, No. 41, October 10, 1992.

356   **Tommy urged him:** Holmes, *Ron Brown*, 245.

356   **"he can't service everyone":** Kim Eisler, "These Guns for Hire," *Washingtonian*, April 1993.

356   **society's A-list:** Chuck Conconi, *Washingtonian*, September 1993.

357   **When the Judiciary Committee met:** This account is drawn from Daniel Franklin, "Tommy Boggs and the Death of Health Care Reform," *Washington Monthly*, Vol. 27, No. 4, April 1995, 31.

357   **"cause some mischief":** Thomas H. Boggs interviews.

357   **calm, almost resigned:** Leon Panetta, in an interview.

358   **"What you said is":** Thomas H. Boggs interviews.

358   **"It's total bullshit":** Ibid.

358   **"Tommy Boggs doesn't waste":** Tony Blankley, quoted in Karen Hosler, "For Incoming Speaker, a Really Wonderful Life," *Sun* (Baltimore), November 27, 1994, 1F.

358   **"If you criticized the President":** Thomas H. Boggs interviews.

358   **only substantive political:** Ibid.

358   **"work for the AMA?":** Julius Hobson Jr. interviews.

359   **"still be in the game":** Ibid.

359   **"we hardly knew anybody":** Ibid.

359   **"I buy the houses":** Diane Lewis, in an interview.

360   **"another Crystal City":** Christopher Wright, "A Rare Chance to Shape the Future," *Star*, May 16, 1971.

360   **"ways you establish yourself":** Julius Hobson Jr. interviews.

360   **the doctors feared capitalism:** "The bulk of the AMA's lobbying on health care reform was directed at persuading the government to rein in managed care companies," Julie Kosterlitz wrote in "The Second Wave," *National Journal*, Vol. 26, No. 42, October 15, 1994, 2393–97.

361   **"I am never, never":** Julius Hobson Jr. interviews.

361   **held firm:** Ibid.

361   **"When he put out":** Ibid.

361   **phoned Lee Stillwell:** Mary Jacoby, "Paxon Scraps Lobby Lists," *Roll Call*, June 26, 1995, reported that Hobson "rubbed [DeLay] the wrong way." Hobson, in interviews, said, "I did not open my mouth in that meeting."

361   **"I should not be":** Julius Hobson Jr. interviews.

361   **"You could put up":** Ibid.

361   **"You can't typecast him":** Lee Stillwell, in an interview.

362   **"Process kills policy":** Julius Hobson Jr. interviews.

362   **George Washington University's:** The graduate school opened in September 1987 on the New York City campus of Baruch College and began a degree program on the George Washington University campus in September 1991. GWU acquired it in July 1995 and placed it within the School of Arts and Sciences.

362   **"If teaching paid":** Julius Hobson Jr. interviews.

362   **rooted for *Apollo 13*:** Margaret Carlson, "They Still Don't Get It," *Time*, April 8, 1996, 18.

363   **"It was great fun":** Peggy Cooper Cafritz interviews.

364   **"Most people in Washington":** Ibid.

364   **"I have asked Conrad":** Annie Groer and Ann Gerhart, "The Reliable Source," *Post*, May 5, 1997, D3.

365   **turned their inheritance into cash:** Verbatim from Maryann Hagerty, "At 1775 I St., the Cafritz Saga Ends with the Letter 'A,'" *Post,* October 20, 1997, F10.

365   **"it's the exact opposite":** Chet Dembeck, "Cafritz Starts Tech Firm," *Washington Business Journal*, September 18, 1998, 1.

366   **"I want you to hear":** Todd Purdum, "Jet Crash Casts a Sudden Shadow over Official Washington," *New York Times*, April 4, 1996, A1.

366   **choking back tears:** Kenneth R. Bazinet, "Clintons Visit Browns, Commerce Workers," United Press International, April 3, 1996.

366   **"was the only place":** Cokie Roberts interviews.

366   **and sat in his box:** Howard Paster interviews.

366   **$600,000 he had raised:** Carl Bernstein, "King of the Hill," *Vanity Fair*, March 1998, 184.

366   **"a loss leader":** Taylor, "'One-Stop Shopping.'"

366   **a Dickensian name:** George F. Will, ". . . Or Part of the Problem," *Post*, February 5, 1989, D7.

367   **Jews migrated back:** Andrew Silow Carroll, "Back to the Future," *Washington Jewish Week*, July 26, 1990, 15.

367   **two dozen sites:** Lee G. Rubenstein, who was cochairman of the building committee and first vice president of the JCC's executive committee, in interviews.

367   **Reconstructing a building:** Ibid.

367   **Vandals had stripped:** Eugene L. Meyer, "The Center of Their Lives," *Post*, January 20, 1992, B1.

368   **walk-in steam bath:** Erv Ornstein, a nephew of Morris Cafritz, in interviews.

368   **identical pledge:** A sum of $500,000, total, from the Washington Post Co., the Philip L. Graham Fund, and Katharine Graham, according to the booklet distributed at the dedication on January 12, 1997.

368   **"father had been instrumental":** Calvin Cafritz interviews.

369   **"preserve my father's legacy"**: "DCJCC Renovation Underway," *Washington Jewish Week*, March 23, 1995, 5.

369   **"to help 'Judaize'"**: Elaine Martin, the assistant executive director at the Jewish Community Center of Greater Washington, in Rockville, Maryland, quoted in "Monument to Jewish Culture Makes a Comeback," *New York Times*, June 14, 1992.

369   **"freshened up"**: Warren Berger, "The Master Skeptic Steps Aside," *New York Times*, November 3, 1996, Section 2, 37.

369   **the network's first woman:** Marc Gunther, *The House That Roone Built: The Inside Story of ABC News* (New York: Little, Brown and Co., 1994), 204.

370   **Tom Foley:** Larry J. Sabato, "The Smearing of Tom Foley," *Roll Call*, July 22, 1991, excerpted from his book *Feeding Frenzy* (New York: The Free Press, 1991).

370   **"took some shaking down"**: Mark Lorando, "It's Not the 'Week' That Was," *New Orleans Times-Picayune*, May 24, 1998, T10.

370   **at a bargain price:** "Goodnight, David: Hucksterism Taints Credibility," Maureen Dowd, *New York Times*, January 8, 1998, A9.

371   **two million dollars or so:** Ken Auletta, "Fee Speech," *New Yorker*, September 12, 1994, 40.

371   **"Fairly or unfairly"**: Howard Kurtz, "Money Talks," *Washington Post Magazine*, January 21, 1996, W11.

371   **typically $20,000:** James Warren, "Sunday Watch," *Chicago Tribune*, March 20, 1994, 5. In *Hot Air: All Talk, All the Time* (New York: Times Books, 1996), 209, Howard Kurtz reports that her fee was "at least" twenty thousand dollars.

371   **$300,000 in a year:** Kurtz, *Hot Air*, 209.

371   **$500,000 or more:** Between $500,000 and $600,000, according to an unidentified ABC official quoted in Auletta, "Fee Speech."

371   **Fort Lauderdale (for $35,000):** Alicia Shepard, "Take the Money and Talk," *American Journalism Review*, June 1995.

371   **for $45,000:** James Warren, "Sunday Watch," *Chicago Tribune*, October 2, 1994, 5, and Kurtz, *Hot Air*, 213.

371   **"a doyenne of"**: James Warren, "Sunday Watch," *Chicago Tribune*, February 6, 1994, 5.

371   **"the irrepressible moonlighting"**: Ibid., April 17, 1994, 5.

371   **"A reprehensible individual"**: Shepard, "Take the Money."

372   **"Cokie and Steve Inc."**: Kurtz, "Money Talks."

372   **"High Priestess of Insiders"**: Alicia Mundy, "Revolt of the Talking Heads," in *Mediaweek*, Vol. 6, No. 38, September 16, 1996, 18–24.

372   **"both stung by it"**: Steven V. Roberts interviews

372   **"looking for celebrity value"**: Kurtz, *Hot Air*, 213.

372   **"Are you Cokie Roberts?"**: Cokie Roberts interviews.

372   **"Even people who stop"**: Ibid.

372   **"depths of my stomach"**: Ibid.

372   **azaleas Hale had planted:** Lindy Boggs interviews.

372   **"I'm the most normal":** Howard Kurtz, "The Reporter Who Asked One Question Too Many," *Post*, September 5, 1994, B1.

373   **"the single worst idea":** Cokie Roberts and Steven Roberts, "Voters Show That Experience Counts," *Times-Picayune*, June 5, 1998.

373   **Lindy's memoir:** Lindy Boggs with Katherine Hatch, *Washington through a Purple Veil: Memoirs of a Southern Woman* (New York: Harcourt Brace & Co., 1994).

373   **"I'm fifty years old":** Cokie Roberts interviews.

373   *We Are Our Mothers' Daughters:* Published by William Morrow and Co. in 1998.

373   **"So much of the work":** Ibid.

373   *From This Day Forward:* Cokie Roberts and Steve Roberts, *From This Day Forward* (New York: William Morrow and Co., 2000).

374   **"Washington's power couple":** *Larry King Live,* CNN, July 21, 1998.

374   *Newsweek's* **political correspondent:** According to James Fallows, *Breaking the News: How the Media Undermine American Democracy* (New York: Pantheon Books, 1996), 79.

374   **"a very dear friend":** She said this as the emcee at a congressional dinner in Washington for Representative Bob Michel, Republican of Illinois, in February 1994, in which she called Tip O'Neill, the former Speaker, "our dear, dear love," according to James Warren, "Sunday Watch," *Chicago Tribune*, 6 February 1994, 5. She served as co-emcee with Charles Gibson for a tribute to Michel the following September that raised $1.3 million for Bradley University in Peoria, according to James Warren, "Sunday Watch," *Tribune*, September 25, 1994, 5.

374   **"a bias toward Congress":** Cokie Roberts interviews.

374   **"would be risky":** Roberts and Roberts, *From This Day Forward*, 262.

374   **recognized in airports:** Steven V. Roberts interviews.

374   **"hired me for that":** Ibid.

375   **"star-oriented":** Fallows, *Breaking the News*, 6.

375   **"Fallows has attacked":** Mundy, "Talking Heads."

375   **a regular on CNN's:** Fallows, *Breaking the News*, 101.

375   **Breaux, had prompted:** Thomas H. Boggs Jr. interviews.

375   **"She's taking the job":** Ibid.

375   **"fluent Catholic":** Gerard Perseghin, "New Ambassador to Vatican," *Catholic Standard*, October 30, 1997.

376   **"present Mother Teresa":** Joan McKinney, "Boggs' Confirmation Assured," *Advocate* (Baton Rouge, Louisianna), September 24, 1997, 1A.

376   **"There may be somewhere":** Transcript of the September 23, 1997, confirmation hearing for Boggs and three other ambassadorial nominees, by the Senate Foreign Relations Committee's subcommitteee on European affairs.

376   **Helms admired Cokie's skill:** James Broughton, press secretary to the then-senator Jesse Helms, Republican of North Carolina, in an interview.

376   **"And here we are"**: Steven V. Roberts interviews.

377   **"I have children"**: Gunther, *The House That Roone Built*, 351.

377   **"And Bill, where did"**: Seth Stevenson, "Invisible Ink," *Slate Magazine*, January 22, 1998.

377   **How bad was it?**: Lanny Davis interview.

377   **president's advisers believed**: Ibid.

378   **Usually, Tommy said**: Thomas Hale Boggs Jr. interviews.

378   **"Pretty good vote"**: Ibid.

378   **surprised at his optimism**: Ibid.

379   **"How did the conversation"**: President Clinton's Remarks at a Democratic National Committee Dinner in Chevy Chase, Maryland, April 27, 1999, in Weekly Compilation of *Presidential Documents, Administration of William J. Clinton, 1999*, Vol. 35, 650.

379   **his unconscious mannerisms**: Barbara Boggs interview.

379   **"make it to fifty-nine"**: Cokie Roberts interviews.

379   **"For what?"**: Julius Hobson Jr. interviews.

379   **personality and skills**: Lee Stillwell interview.

379   **"Hi, Julius"**: Julius Hobson Jr. interviews. The senator was John Warner, Republican of Virginia.

380   **"I'm the AMA"**: Ibid.

380   **"Let me tell you"**: Ibid.

380   **"testosterone problem"**: Ibid.

380   **"Also, I will only hire"**: Ibid.

380   **"a machine gunner"**: Ibid.

382   **"The vision for a garden"**: From the National Gallery of Art's videotape of the May 19, 1999, dedication ceremony.

382   **"copious water"**: Barbara Gamarekian, "Miró and Murrow, D.C.'s Latest Attractions," *New York Times*, February 13, 2000, Section 5, 21.

382   **"Both of my parents"**: Calvin Cafritz's prepared remarks, provided by the Morris and Gwendolyn Cafritz Foundation.

383   **"Boy toys?"**: Barbara Boggs interview.

383   **Chuck Colson's going-away party**: Ellen Gamerman, "The D.C. Dish," *Sun* (Baltimore), February 12, 1998, 1E.

383   **"Kind of like a 'Cheers'"**: Dawn Kopecki, "Friendly Service, Inside Information and a Hearty Menu Mark the Palm," *Washington Times*, June 23, 1997.

383   **an eating-in**: Michael Frome, *Washington: A Modern Guide to the Nation's Capital* (Garden City, N.Y.: Doubleday & Co., 1960), 125.

383   **The Kennedys had inspired**: According to Robert Shoffner, "First Came the Willard," *Washingtonian*, December 1998, 143. He reports that in May 1962 President Kennedy signed a bill that legalized standup bars in D.C. for the first time since 1917, making it feasible to open an upscale bar-restaurant such as Clyde's, on M Street in Georgetown, in 1963.

384   **"Duke Zeibert's at lunch"**: *Larry King Live*, CNN, December 3, 1991.

384   **"making his peace":** David Von Drehle, "Power Dinner: At Duke Zeibert's, the Meeting of the Bulls," *Post*, July 2, 1993.

384   **promoted to the press:** Ibid.

384   **"sort of a sweetheart deal":** John Jonas, quoted in Marian Burros, "Steak and Chips, and a Side of Politics," *New York Times*, August 30, 2000, A16.

384   **"a Washington-ambianced restaurant":** Ed Rogers, a partner of Haley Barbour's at Barbour Griffith & Rogers, in an interview.

385   **high-tech titans:** Sally Quinn, "Old Washington Meets Wired Washington," *Post*, April 5, 2000, C1.

385   **"We're not mean":** Brooks Jackson's interview of Tommy Boggs and Haley Barbour on CNN, *Inside Politics,* September 14, 2000.

386   **"Your father would turn":** Julius Hobson Jr. interviews.

386   **beds in hallways:** James Daniel, "Hospital Using Barracks Built During Civil War," *Daily News*, February 16, 1942.

386   **cockroaches in the kitchen:** James E. Chinn, "Mason, Ruhland Ouster Urged by Senators," *Star*, October 13, 1943, A-1, 16.

386   **tubercular nurses:** "Disgraceful Neglect," *Post* editorial, March 1, 1936.

386   **food stolen:** "Gallinger Scandal," *Post* editorial, September 29, 1943. Gallinger Municipal Hospital was the previous name for D.C. General.

387   **"a form of community service":** Julius Hobson Jr. interviews.

387   **"You've never been in":** Ibid.

387   **"not about intimidation":** Ibid.

388   **"rendered unto you!":** Avram Goldstein, "Hospital Slashing Services, 550 Jobs," *Post*, August 26, 2000, A1.

388   **virtually no option":** Ibid.

388   **"We'll be out of money":** Avram Goldstein, "Hospital's Fiscal Crisis Intensifies," *Post*, November 15, 2000, B2.

388   **"shame and embarrass":** Julius Hobson Jr. interviews.

389   **"citizens put it in place":** Dwight S. Cropp and Julius W. Hobson Jr., "It's Time to Suspend Home Rule; Congress Should Appoint a Receiver to Save the City, Then a Manager to Run It," *Post*, July 7, 1996, C1.

389   **"More draining than":** Julius Hobson Jr. interviews.

390   **"I decided that night":** Peggy Cooper Cafritz interviews.

390   **former city councilman:** Jonetta Rose Barras, "Why Not Bill Lightfoot?," *Washington Times*, August 25, 2000, A19.

390   **"I've run into so many":** Justin Blum, "D.C. Votes Revealing Old Divide," *Post*, October 30, 2000, B1.

390   **"All I ask you":** Justin Blum, "Two Hopefuls to Head School Board See Positive Steps," *Post*, October 5, 2000, J3.

391   **"a Marshall Plan":** "Election 2000 Voters Guide," *Post*, October 26, 2000, J24.

391 **she had spent $119,445:** As of October 25, 2000. The figure for the Reverend Robert Childs was as of October 30. Justin Blum, "Mayor's Motives Impugned by Childs," *Post*, November 10, 2000, B4.

391 **"People want reform":** Justin Blum, "First Lesson for D.C. Board: Cooperation," *Post*, November 9, 2000, B7.

392 **"the best thing possible":** Quoted by Rick Montgomery, "A Long History of Widows in Congress," *Kansas City Star*, October 27, 2000, A13.

392 **Jean Carnahan read:** Cokie Roberts interviews.

392 **inspired in part:** Neil A. Lewis, "In Missouri, Campaign Flourishes after the Death of the Candidate," *New York Times*, October 31, 2000, A1.

392 **"and it just seemed":** *This Week with Sam Donaldson and Cokie Roberts*, ABC-TV, November 5, 2000.

393 **Good Morning America instead:** Cokie Roberts interviews.

393 **"to poor John Ashcroft":** Ibid.

393 **$9.95 million:** Jo Ann Lewis, "House Gifts Deluxe," *Post*, December 5, 1996, T18.

393 **"Perfectly decent":** Calvin Cafritz interviews.

394 **"It seems to me":** Ibid.

394 **$9.3 million sale:** Elizabeth Ely, the founder and director of the Field School, in an interview.

394 **the crowning event:** Calvin Cafritz interviews.

Epilogue

395 **It was Phil Graham:** Ben Bradlee, *A Good Life: Newspapering and Other Adventures* (New York: Simon & Schuster, 1995), 249.

395 **"a transient metropolis":** Lindy Boggs interviews.

395 **"I guess it's peculiar":** Ibid.

396 **"a kind of grandomania":** "Wright's Lance Hurled at D.C." *Star*, October 26, 1938, A-7.

396 **Roughly half:** Timothy May interviews.

397 **"a microcosm of Washington":** Benjamin Ginsberg, in an interview.

397 **"My old man":** Thomas H. Boggs Jr. interviews.

397 **"always my question":** Cokie Roberts interviews.

397 **"I want a life":** Jennifer Harper, "*This Week* Hosts' Reported Ouster Rankles ABC," *The Washington Times*, March 6, 2002, A6.

397 **"I've redefined my standards":** Steven V. Roberts interviews.

398 **"then there's the cousins":** Cokie Roberts interviews.

398 **"This is home":** Ibid.

Acknowledgments

Washington is a far friendlier city than anyone outside the Beltway might imagine. In a quarter-century as a journalist in Washington, I have been amazed again and again at how people have gone out of their way to help me, usually with no realistic hope of having such favors returned. That this was true more than ever while I was writing this book I take as further evidence that metropolitan Washington is a nicer place to live and bring up children than its customary reputation would suggest.

It is hard to overstate how grateful I feel to the three families I've chronicled for letting me into their lives. They gave generously of their time and recollections, including painful ones. My deeply felt thanks to Lindy Boggs, Tommy and Barbara Boggs, Cokie and Steve Roberts, Paul Sigmund, Carol Joy Smith, Tina Hobson, Julius Hobson Jr., Diane Lewis, Jean Hobson-Richardson, Calvin Cafritz, Carter Cafritz, and Peggy Cooper Cafritz.

Telling the story of three families over a century's span takes learning much more than newspapers and books can offer. I can't thank enough the scores of people who shared their memories and insights in interviews, often of considerable length, including Gwen

Acsadi, Anita Allen, Liane Atlas, Jim Banks, Leon Billings, Byron Black, George Blow, John Brademas, Marvine Bradford, Sandy Brown, Vincent Burke, William Bryant, Jim Cafritz, Larry Cafritz, Susan Albert Carr, Charles Cassell, David Cohen, Lanny Davis, Frank Donatelli, H. G. Dulaney, Jim Eaton, Elizabeth Ely, Henry Fankhauser, Penny Farthing, Walter Fauntroy, John Fondersmith, Gerald R. Ford, Bill Foster, Carol Gelderman, Jim Gibson, Ben Ginsberg, Vic Gold, James Goode, Charles Goodrum, John Hechinger, Sheila Hines, Steny Hoyer, Gary Hymel, Jayne Ikard, Meredith Inderfurth, John Irelan, Jim Jones, Robert Kastenmeier, Sharon Pratt Kelly, Tom and Marguerite Kelly, Jack Kornmeier, Tom Korologos, Shirley Leva, Ken Levine, Chuck Lewis, Scott Lilly, Marilyn Lipnick, Linda Lipsen, Patrick Maney, Tim May, Eugene McCarthy, George McGovern, Barbara Meade, Arna Meyer Mickelson, Roscoe Nix, Gerson Nordlinger, David Obey, Erv Ornstein, Manny Ourisman, Leon Panetta, Scott Pannick, Joe Passonneau, Howard Paster, Jim Patton, Edward Peeks, Fred Pelzman, Michael Pertschuk, Roy Pfautch, Abe Pollin, Barbara Rathe, John Ray, Anne Reich, Frank Rich Sr., Chuck Robb, Lynda Johnson Robb, Ed Rogers, the Rev. Jefferson Rogers, Maurice Rosenblatt, Dan Rostenkowski, Elspeth Rostow, Lee Rubenstein, Pat Saltonstall, B. F. Saul II, Jan Schoonmaker, Pat Schroeder, Victor Shargai, Julia Shepard, Jerry Silverman, Sam Smith, Jacob Stein, Lee Stillwell, Jerry terHorst, Bardyl Tirana, Marty Tolchin, Jody Trapasso, Sterling Tucker, John Tydings, Jack Valenti, Chuck Verrill, Betty Warner, Walter Washington, Maggie Wimsatt, Linda Winslow, and Jim Wright.

For their kind help in arranging interviews or pursuing research or hunting up answers to my indiscriminate questions, I am indebted to Steve Allen, Cheryl Arvidson, Dick Baker, Sandra Bieri, Pat Bonds, Michele Bowling, Sam Brooks, Nancy Burris, Judy Capurso, Ellen Clark, Joan Cocker, Sheila Dwyer, Lois England, Pat Furguson, Manny Getachew, Cindy Janke, Kirstine Larsen, Bob Lyford, Helen Drury Macsherry, Bill Meneray, Barbara Piercy, Anne Ritchie, Leah Schroeder, Marian Smith, Karen Tecott, Rex Tomb, Wendy Turman, Serge Wauthier, Annie Whitworth, Peggy and Tad Wilson, Barbara Wolanin, and Beth Zacharias. Bill O'Brian, my good friend, helped in coming up with the title and in numerous other ways.

Librarians, as always, were a joy. The staff was unfailingly helpful in the Washingtoniana Room at D.C.'s Martin Luther King Memorial Library (thanks especially to Faye Haskins, Jerry McCoy, and Peggy Appleman) and at the U.S. Senate's excellent library. The same was true at Arlington's public library, where my dear sister-in-law, Lynn Sawyer, was particularly helpful.

My friends and colleagues at *National Journal* were an invaluable resource, including Rick Bloom, Jerry Hagstrom, Stuart Taylor, Bill Powers, Isobel Ellis, Kirk Victor, Jim Barnes, Keith White, Jake Welch, Alexis Simendinger, Julie Kosterlitz, Marilyn Werber Serafini, Dick Kirschten, Patrick Pexton, and—with unrelenting generosity—Rich Cohen, the dean of the staff, who painstakingly read the manuscript and constantly did whatever he could to help. Many thanks to John Fox Sullivan, Charlie Green, and the finest journalist I've ever known, the late Michael Kelly, for their support.

I am grateful to Henry Ferris, my editor at William Morrow, for his high standards and meticulous editing. Thanks also to his editorial assistant, Peter Hubbard, for saving me from myself. The grandest of hosannas go to my agent, Gail Ross, for suggesting the idea for this book and seeing it through.

The person who was, of course, indispensable in my surviving this entire experience was my wife, Nancy Tuholski. Besides offering her skill as a copy editor and a sensible reader, she never ceased being supportive and was wonderful at biting her tongue when she had every good reason not to.

Burt Solomon
Arlington, Virginia
April 2004

Index